DISABILITY AND MOTOR BEHAVIOR

SPECIAL EDUCATION LAW, POLICY, AND PRACTICE

Series Editors
Mitchell L. Yell, PhD, University of South Carolina
David F. Bateman, PhD, Shippensburg University of Pennsylvania

The *Special Education Law, Policy, and Practice* series highlights current trends and legal issues in the education of students with disabilities. The books in this series link legal requirements with evidence-based instruction and highlight practical applications for working with students with disabilities. The titles in the *Special Education Law, Policy, and Practice* series are designed not only to be required textbooks for general education and special education preservice teacher education programs but are also designed for practicing teachers, education administrators, principals, school counselors, school psychologists, parents, and others interested in improving the lives of students with disabilities. The *Special Education Law, Policy, and Practice* series is committed to research-based practices working to provide appropriate and meaningful educational programming for students with disabilities and their families.

Titles in Series:
The Essentials of Special Education Law by Andrew M. Markelz and David F. Bateman
Special Education Law Annual Review 2020 by David F. Bateman, Mitchell L. Yell, and Kevin P. Brady
Developing Educationally Meaningful and Legally Sound IEPs by Mitchell L. Yell, David F. Bateman, and James G. Shriner
Sexuality Education for Students with Disabilities edited by Thomas C. Gibbon, Elizabeth A. Harkins Monaco, and David F. Bateman
Creating Positive Elementary Classrooms: Preventing Behavior Challenges to Promote Learning by Stephen W. Smith and Mitchell L. Yell
Service Animals in Schools: Legal, Educational, Administrative, and Strategic Handling Aspects by Anne O. Papalia, Kathy B. Ewoldt, and David F. Bateman
Evidence-Based Practices for Supporting Individuals with Autism Spectrum Disorder edited by Laura C. Chezan, Katie Wolfe, and Erik Drasgow
Special Education Law Annual Review 2021 by David F. Bateman, Mitchell L. Yell, and Kevin P. Brady
Dispute Resolution Under the IDEA: Understanding, Avoiding, and Managing Special Education Disputes by David F. Bateman, Mitchell L. Yell, and Jonas Dorego
Advocating for the Common Good: People, Politics, Process, and Policy on Capitol Hill by Jane E. West
Related Services in Special Education: Working Together as a Team by Lisa Goran and David F. Bateman
The Essentials of Special Education Advocacy for Teachers by Andrew M. Markelz, Sarah A. Nagro, Kevin Monnin, and David F. Bateman
Disability and Motor Behavior: A Handbook of Research edited by Ali S. Brian and Pamela S. Beach

DISABILITY AND MOTOR BEHAVIOR

A Handbook of Research

EDITED BY

ALI S. BRIAN
University of South Carolina

PAMELA S. BEACH
State University of New York Brockport

ROWMAN & LITTLEFIELD
Lanham • Boulder • New York • London

Executive Editor: Mark Kerr
Assistant Acquisitions Editor: Sarah Rinehart
Sales and Marketing Inquiries: textbooks@rowman.com

Credits and acknowledgments for material borrowed from other sources, and reproduced with permission, appear on the appropriate pages within the text.

Published by Rowman & Littlefield
An imprint of The Rowman & Littlefield Publishing Group, Inc.
4501 Forbes Boulevard, Suite 200, Lanham, Maryland 20706
www.rowman.com

86-90 Paul Street, London EC2A 4NE

Copyright © 2024 by The Rowman & Littlefield Publishing Group, Inc.

All rights reserved. No part of this book may be reproduced in any form or by any electronic or mechanical means, including information storage and retrieval systems, without written permission from the publisher, except by a reviewer who may quote passages in a review.

British Library Cataloguing in Publication Information Available

Library of Congress Cataloging-in-Publication Data Available

ISBN 9781538168950 (cloth) | ISBN 9781538168967 (paperback) | ISBN 9781538168974 (epub)

Brief Contents

Acknowledgments	xiii
1 Motor Behavior and Visual Impairment *Adam Pennell and Alexandra Stribing*	1
2 Motor Behavior and Children Who Are Hard of Hearing, Deaf, or Deafblind *Pamela Beach, Melanie Perreault, and Lauren Lieberman*	15
3 Motor Behavior and Sensory Processing Disorder *Candice Howard-Smith*	27
4 Motor Behavior and Autism Spectrum Disorder *Ming-Chih Sung and Megan MacDonald*	37
5 Fundamental Motor Skill Interventions for Children with Autism Spectrum Disorder *Meghann Lloyd*	49
6 Motor Behavior and Emotional and Behavioral Disorders *Iva Obrusnikova and Albert R. Cavalier*	61
7 Motor Behavior and Specific Language Impairment *Matthias O. Wagner*	83
8 Motor Behavior and Cerebral Palsy *Melissa Pangelinan and Claire Bridges*	93
9 Motor Behavior and Neurodegenerative Disorders Associated with Aging *Nadja Schott*	105
10 Motor Behavior and Intellectual Disabilities *Alyssa LaForme Fiss and Julia Looper*	119
11 Developmental Delay, Developmental Coordination Disorder, and Motor Behavior *Daphne Golden and Nancy Getchell*	129
12 Motor Behavior and Traumatic Brain Injury *James Wilkes, Alexa Walter, and Sam Semyon Slobounov*	143

13	Motor Behavior and Rehabilitation after Spinal Cord Injury *Collin D. Bowersock and Jessica Lynn McDonnell*	157
14	Motor Behavior and Profound Intellectual and Multiple Disabilities *Bethany M. Sloane, Heather A. Feldner, Lisa K. Kenyon, and Samuel W. Logan*	171
15	Motor Competence and Health Impairments in Children *Emily Gilbert*	187

Index	197
About the Editors	207
About the Contributors	209

Contents

Acknowledgments	xiii
1 Motor Behavior and Visual Impairment	**1**
Adam Pennell and Alexandra Stribing	
Background	1
Guiding Frameworks and Assumptions	2
Gross Motor in Juvenescence	3
Fine Motor in Juvenescence	4
Gross Motor in Adulthood	4
Fine Motor in Adulthood	5
Honorable Mention: Postural Control and Balance	5
Systems Perspective: A Spotlight on Psychological Variables	5
Future Research	6
Practical Implications	7
Conclusion	7
References	8
2 Motor Behavior and Children Who Are Hard of Hearing, Deaf, or Deafblind	**15**
Pamela Beach, Melanie Perreault, and Lauren Lieberman	
Motor Milestones	16
Balance	17
Motor Competence	19
Practical Implications	22
Conclusion	22
References	23
3 Motor Behavior and Sensory Processing Disorder	**27**
Candice Howard-Smith	
Overview	27
Sensory Processing Disorders	27
Types of Sensory Processing Disorders	28

Sensory Processing Disorders and Motor Behavior	30
Sensory Processing Disorders, Disabilities, and Motor Behavior	30
Autism Spectrum Disorder	30
Down Syndrome	31
Attention-Deficit Hyperactivity Disorder	32
Future Research	32
Practical Implications	33
Conclusion	34
References	34

4 Motor Behavior and Autism Spectrum Disorder — 37
Ming-Chih Sung and Megan MacDonald

Overview	37
Young Children (Infants and Preschoolers) with Autism Spectrum Disorder	39
School-Aged Children with Autism Spectrum Disorder	40
Beyond School: Lifespan Motor Skills of Individuals with Autism Spectrum Disorder	41
Summary of Evidence	42
Future Research	43
Practical Implications	43
References	44

5 Fundamental Motor Skill Interventions for Children with Autism Spectrum Disorder — 49
Meghann Lloyd

Importance of Motor Skill Development	50
Fundamental Motor Skill Interventions	52
Future Research	54
Practical Implications	55
References	56

6 Motor Behavior and Emotional and Behavioral Disorders — 61
Iva Obrusnikova and Albert R. Cavalier

Definitions of Emotional and Behavioral Disorders	61
Prevalence of Emotional and Behavioral Disorders	62
Internalizing: Anxiety Disorders Defined	62
Prevalence of Anxiety Disorders	63
Conceptual Models of Anxiety Disorders	63
Motor Impairments and Anxiety Disorders	63
Externalizing: Attention-Deficit Hyperactivity Disorder Defined	66
Prevalence of Attention-Deficit Hyperactivity Disorder	66
Conceptual Models of Attention-Deficit Hyperactivity Disorder	67
Motor Impairments and Attention-Deficit Hyperactivity Disorder	68
Altered Cerebral Structures and Neurotransmitter Imbalance	70

Attention-Deficit Hyperactivity Disorder Comorbidities	70
Future Research and Practical Implications	71
References	72

7 Motor Behavior and Specific Language Impairment — 83
Matthias O. Wagner

Overview	83
Research Overview	84
Motor Control-Related Issues in Specific Language Impairment	84
Motor Learning-Related Issues in Specific Language Impairment	86
Motor Development-Related Issues in Specific Language Impairment	88
Future Research	89
Practical Implications	90
Conclusion	90
References	91

8 Motor Behavior and Cerebral Palsy — 93
Melissa Pangelinan and Claire Bridges

Definitions, Etiology, and Diagnosis	93
Overview	93
Risk Factor or Possible Causes of Cerebral Palsy	93
Symptoms	94
Types	94
Table 8.1 Motor Symptoms of Cerebral Palsy	94
Diagnosis and Classification	95
Empirical Research: Cerebral Palsy and Motor Behavior	96
Cerebral Palsy and Motor Behavior	96
Early Intervention	96
Interventions in Childhood and Beyond	98
Figure 8.1 Evidence alert system	99
Table 8.2 Brief Description of Effective ("Do It") Interventions for Motor Outcomes	100
Future Research	101
Practical Implications	102
Conclusion	102
References	103

9 Motor Behavior and Neurodegenerative Disorders Associated with Aging — 105
Nadja Schott

Overview	105
Table 9.1 Overview of Selected Neurodegenerative Diseases	106
Under the Magnifying Glass: Gait as an Important Predictor for Motor-Cognitive Performance in Alzheimer's and Parkinson's Disease	107

	Figure 9.1 Self-selected preferred gait speed (m/s) in patients with Alzheimer's and Parkinson's disease and healthy controls	108
	Motor Learning in Alzheimer's and Parkinson's Disease	109
	Alzheimer's Disease	110
	Parkinson's Disease	110
	Future Research	111
	Table 9.2 Challenges in Motor Behavior Research in Neurodegenerative Diseases	112
	Practical Implications	113
	Conclusion	114
	References	114
10	**Motor Behavior and Intellectual Disabilities**	**119**
	Alyssa LaForme Fiss and Julia Looper	
	Overview	119
	Table 10.1 Components of Adaptive Behavior	119
	Table 10.2 Potential Causes of Intellectual Disability	120
	Examples of Genetic Causes	120
	Research on Motor and Cognitive Development	120
	Motor Control and Motor Learning in Individuals with Intellectual Disabilities	121
	Table 10.3 Definitions of Key Principles of Motor Learning	123
	Future Research	123
	Practical Implications	124
	Conclusion	124
	References	125
11	**Developmental Delay, Developmental Coordination Disorder, and Motor Behavior**	**129**
	Daphne Golden and Nancy Getchell	
	Developmental Delay: An Early Sign of Developmental Coordination Disorder	129
	Developmental Coordination Disorder	131
	Identification and Diagnosis of Developmental Coordination Disorder	131
	The Developmental Conundrum in Developmental Coordination Disorder Identification and Diagnosis	132
	Motor Behavior Research Related to Developmental Coordination Disorder	132
	Future Research	135
	Practical Implications	135
	Conclusion	136
	References	136

12 Motor Behavior and Traumatic Brain Injury — 143
James Wilkes, Alexa Walter, and Sam Semyon Slobounov

- Overview — 143
  - Figure 12.1 TBI severity classified by Glasgow Coma Scale (GCS) score — 144
  - Table 12.1 Common Symptoms of Traumatic Brain Injury as Classified by the Centers for Disease Control and Prevention — 145
- Clinical Translation of Pathophysiology to Dysfunction — 146
- Motor Control Dysfunction after Traumatic Brain Injury — 146
  - Balance and Gait — 147
  - Reaction Time — 148
  - Oculomotor Function — 148
  - Kinesiophobia — 150
- Future Research — 150
- Practical Implications — 150
- Conclusion — 151
- Conflict of Interest — 151
- Acknowledgments — 151
- References — 151

13 Motor Behavior and Rehabilitation after Spinal Cord Injury — 157
Collin D. Bowersock and Jessica Lynn McDonnell

- Overview — 157
- Research Overview — 158
  - Figure 13.1 Illustration of a complete versus incomplete spinal cord injury — 159
  - Figure 13.2 Depiction of a lumbosacral implanted epidural stimulation electrode array — 162
  - Figure 13.3 EMG activity of left (L) lower limb muscles with and without epidural spinal cord stimulation in one individual with a complete spinal cord injury while standing overground with external assistance — 163
- Future Research — 164
- Practical Implications — 165
- Conclusion — 165
- References — 166

14 Motor Behavior and Profound Intellectual and Multiple Disabilities — 171
Bethany M. Sloane, Heather A. Feldner, Lisa K. Kenyon, and Samuel W. Logan

- Overview — 171
- Motor Behavior and Profound Intellectual and Multiple Disabilities Population Empirical Research Summary — 173
  - International Classification of Functioning, Disability and Health Model — 173
  - Table 14.1 Motor Behavior Topics Included in This Chapter Mapped onto the ICF Framework — 173

Body Functions and Structures	174
Motor Development	174
Challenging Behavior	175
Alertness Level	175
Summary	175
Activity and Participation	175
Motor Activity	176
Physical Activity	176
Environmental and Personal Factors	178
Assistive Technology	178
Figure 14.1 Photograph of child with a disability using a modified ride-on car	179
Supports and Relationships	180
Attitudes	180
Summary	181
Future Research	181
Practical Implications	181
Conclusion	182
References	182

15 Motor Competence and Health Impairments in Children — 187
Emily Gilbert

Overview	187
Pediatric Cancer	187
Obesity	188
Diabetes	188
Motor Competence Research in Youth with Health Impairments	189
Pediatric Cancer	189
Obesity	190
Diabetes	191
Future Research	191
Practical Implications	192
Table 15.1 Research to Practice: Next Steps to Action	192
Conclusion	193
References	193
Index	197
About the Editors	207
About the Contributors	209

Acknowledgments

We wish to thank the following reviewers whose thoughtful comments and expertise guided our writing and revisions for the development of this book. As always, any errors and omissions are our own:

Diane Anderson, *University of Minnesota*

Teresa Banks, *University of Memphis*

Jason Bishop, *Auburn University Montgomery*

Andrew Colombo-Dougovito, *University of North Texas*

Tim Davis, *SUNY Cortland*

Seth Eckler, *University of Louisville*

Jay Fischer, *California State University, Northridge*

Emily Gilbert, *SUNY Cortland*

Cathy Headley, *Rockford University*

Joann P. Judge, *The University of Southern Mississippi*

Lauren Lieberman, *SUNY Brockport*

1
Motor Behavior and Visual Impairment

Adam Pennell and Alexandra Stribing

■ ■ ■

In a 2014 nationwide survey of adults living within the United States, vision loss was identified as a preeminent, prospective fear (Scott et al., 2016). Immediate reflection of this outcome may lead readers to a general, if not obvious, conclusion: vision loss is an innate and universal trepidation of the human species given our propensity to heavily favor the sensory modality. Yet of most surprise was that a nationwide poll found that loss of sight was of greater concern than memory, limb, speech, and hearing loss, respectively (Scott et al., 2016). Insights into the profoundness of these outcomes may be grounded within the words of Director-General Dr. Tedros Adhanom Ghebreyesus who expertly stated:

> In a world built on the ability to see, vision, the most dominant of our senses, is vital at every turn of our lives. The newborn depends on vision to recognize and bond with its mother; the toddler, to master balance and learn to walk; the schoolboy, to walk to school, read and learn; the young woman to participate in the workforce; and the older woman, to maintain her independence. (World Health Organization [WHO], 2022, overview section, para. 1)

While we have reminded the reader that the importance of vision is self-evident, additional background speaking to the landscape and implications of visual impairment (VI) and loss are warranted.

BACKGROUND

From an epidemiologic perspective, 2.2 billion people have some form of VI (WHO, 2021). However, blindness and VI incidence are expected to increase into the future (Ackland et al., 2017). This is compounded by the fact that VI and blindness have significant economic impacts (Marques et al., 2021; WHO, 2021) and have been implicated in (for example) quality of life deficits (Chadha and Subramanian, 2011; Wang et al., 2014). Leading causes of VI and blindness include circumstances such as uncorrected refractive errors, cataracts, age-related macular degeneration, glaucoma, and diabetic retinopathy. The majority of individuals with VI and blindness are fifty years of age and older, although vision loss can affect individuals of all ages (WHO, 2021). VI and blindness etiologies vary widely. Yet such etiologies are defined by damage or dysfunction to structures within the visual, cerebral, or perceptual systems. It is important to note that VI is highly variable from person to person, both between and within diagnoses. Factors that have been known to interact with rates and presentations of vision loss include race or ethnicity, biological sex, family history of eye disease, socioeconomic position, and geographic location (National Academies of Sciences, Engineering, and Medicine, 2016).

Vision loss has been known to negatively impact a person's life in a multitude of domains such as health and physical activity (Caputo et al., 2022; Inoue et al., 2018; Leissner et al., 2014; Ong et al., 2018). However, movement-related outcomes such as increasing one's steps per day, initiating a new form of recreation, or mastering a functional motor skill would fall under the auspices of motor behavior which "includes every kind of movement from involuntary twitches to goal directed actions, in every part of the body from head to toe, in every physical and social context from solitary play to group interactions" (Adolph and Franchak, 2017, para. 1). Although human motor behavior encompasses the expanse of movement, such actions, by their very nature, "provide the raw material for perception, cognition, and social interaction" (Adolph and Franchak, 2017, para. 1). Thus, the empirical investigation of motor behavior and its resultant or purported biopsychosocial benefits are of enormous importance, especially in relation to individuals with VI and blindness who regularly present with impaired movement- and health-related outcomes (Augestad and Alsnes, 2021). However, various gaps remain.

Therefore, the purpose of this chapter will be to provide a concentrated review of empirical research pertaining to the motor behavior of individuals with VI and blindness. The following chapter is not meant to be exhaustive. Rather, broad brushstrokes of the extant literature will be introduced to the reader with what we hope will be a satisfactory level of depth and breadth. If a certain topic within this chapter piques one's curiosity or feels underwhelming (as literature on various subjects may be scant), we hope that the reader will feel inspired to complete their own, more targeted review, especially as new research is always being added to the literature base. Before examining the empirical milieu, the lens with which we curated this chapter must be acknowledged.

GUIDING FRAMEWORKS AND ASSUMPTIONS

Various concepts will permeate the ethos and scope of this chapter. First, while there are several strands within the field of motor behavior (e.g., motor learning or control), we have chosen to emphasize motor *development*, which refers to (a) dynamic, age-related, and sequential changes in motor behavior across the *lifespan*, as well as (b) factors underlying such changes (Haywood and Getchell, 2019). Implicit to the field of motor development is the focus on *functional* capacity (Haywood and Getchell, 2019), meaning that real-world, practical, applied, or translational forms of motor behavior (and/or their implications) have been favored over more basic perspectives of movement. As motor behavior does not exist in a vacuum, we have adopted a *systems- and constraints-based* viewpoint as it has been postulated that *interactions* between the individual, task, and environment foster emergent motor behaviors (Newell, 1986; Thelen, 1995). To this point, while action systems will be the focus of this chapter, brief attention will be given to (for example) the psychological system. Finally, there are many ways to classify motor behaviors. We have chosen to globally focus on the categories of fine (small musculature) and gross (large musculature) motor skills. Motor skills can be defined as goal-directed (i.e., problem solving), voluntary movements that enable independence and functional interaction with the world (Higgins, 1991). Gross motor skills constitute general human motor behaviors (e.g., locomotion, ballistic efforts) and therefore are prerequisites for mobility and countless sport, exercise, and physical activities. To this end, gross motor skills are the actions through which humans expend energy and foster large-scale physiological adaptations (e.g., metabolic, musculoskeletal). Likewise, fine motor skills are vital as limitless, small-scale, goal-directed tasks require neuromuscular manipulation and precision (e.g., self-care, eating, object-oriented play, tool use).

GROSS MOTOR IN JUVENESCENCE

The majority of the extant motor behavior research in individuals with VI has occurred in pediatric populations and focused on gross motor skills. This is unsurprising given that, in congenitally blind youngsters, motor-related concerns have been documented in infanthood (Celeste, 2002; Tröster and Brambring, 1993) and may, at the very least, track into early childhood (Tröster et al., 1994). Per Bakke and colleagues (2019), gross motor assessments (or subscales therein) have included versions of the Test of Gross Motor Development (Ulrich, 2000; Ulrich, 2019), the Bruininks-Oseretsky Test of Motor Proficiency (Bruininks and Bruininks, 2005), the Movement Assessment Battery for Children (Henderson and Sugden, 1992), and the Bailey Scales of Infant Motor Development (Visser et al., 2013), among others (Brambring, 2006; Pennell, 2021). In general, youngsters with VI tend to present with decreased levels of gross motor competence (Brian et al., 2021a; Brian et al., 2021c; Daneshmandi et al., 2021; Haegele et al., 2015; Pennell, 2021; Pennell et al., 2021; Tröster and Brambring, 1993; Wagner et al., 2013). Factors that may influence gross motor behavior may include, but not be limited to, etiology (e.g., cortical/cerebral versus ocular; Martín et al., 2016), degree of vision, biological sex, age, and multimorbidity, yet discrepancies remain (Brian et al., 2021a; Brian et al., 2021c; Haibach et al., 2014; Houwen et al., 2009; Pennell, 2021; Pennell et al., 2021). Much of the research in relation to motor skills (gross or otherwise) has been cross-sectional. However, Brian and colleagues (Brian et al., 2021a) provided landmark, longitudinal evidence that adolescents with VI did not improve their Test of Gross Motor Development-3 (Ulrich, 2019) locomotor scores across a three-year timespan (mean age at baseline = 11.75 ± 1.73 years). Even more concerning was that the average raw locomotor score at baseline for the sample was equivalent to the locomotor development of a 5.5-year-old. Not only are these results indicative of developmental delay (on average), but they also speak to the notion of long-term, arrested motor development. This highlights the importance of intervention as it has been shown that motor behavior is malleable in children and adolescents with VI (Brian et al., 2020a; da Cunha Furtado et al., 2015; Daneshmandi et al., 2021; Salar et al., 2022). However, limitations of rigor, bias, heterogeneity, and reporting are rife within the intervention-based literature (Elsman et al., 2019).

FINE MOTOR IN JUVENESCENCE

Knowledge surrounding fine motor skills in pediatric populations with VI is mixed and limited. Specific visual conditions may have a richer archive of fine motor research (e.g., amblyopia; Webber, 2018) compared to (a) other ocular conditions and (b) research study samples which tend to encompass a diverse array of visual diagnoses. Bakke and colleagues (2019) previously identified common fine motor assessments which have been used across children and adolescents with VI. Customary assessments have included variants (or subscales therein) of the Bruininks-Oseretsky Test of Motor Proficiency (Bruininks and Bruininks, 2005), the Movement Assessment Battery for Children (Bakke et al., 2017), the Jebsen-Taylor Hand Function Test (Jebsen et al., 1969), and the Test for Manual Dexterity in Visually Impaired Children (Reimer et al., 1999). However, other assessments and/or combinations of fine motor assessments have been used in children with VI (e.g., Brambring, 2007). In general, juveniles with VI present with decreased quantitative and qualitative fine motor skills when compared to sighted peers (Brambring, 2007; Reimer et al., 2015; Webber, 2018). The magnitude of differences seems to vary across individuals and assessments. For example, Brambring (2007) found that young children with VI were significantly delayed in manual skills involving tool use when compared to sighted peers (e.g., drinking from a cup, using a spoon). In older children, decrements in handwriting (Aki et al., 2008), aiming (Reimer et al., 2008), uni-manual speed (Houwen et al., 2008), as well as complex uni- and bi-manual tasks (Reimer et al., 2015) have been noted. Importantly, Reimer and colleagues (2015) noted that fine motor performance discrepancies between children with and without VI may fade, but not be fully attenuated, by early adolescence. Intervention research concerning fine motor skills in children and adolescents with VI is paltry and lacks robustness (Elsman et al., 2019). However, Reimer and associates (2011) found that various fine motor skills could be ameliorated in young children with VI following a six-week intervention. The investigators also concluded that fine motor progress during the intervention was age-related (Reimer et al., 2011). Likewise, Webber et al. (2016) found that a five-week binocular iPod dichoptic game-play intervention increased fine motor skills, and that such improvements persisted following a twelve-week retention period.

GROSS MOTOR IN ADULTHOOD

Knowledge surrounding motor behavior/development outcomes in adults with VI lacks comprehensiveness and synchrony. There is a large but unwieldy research base surrounding movement-related outcomes in adults of various ages with VI. Thus, a specific subset of studies will be emphasized herein. However, individuals interested in specific outcomes or populations may be best suited completing their own focalized review of the literature. In general, motor skills of adults with VI are believed to be inferior to sighted peers. Ray and collaborators (2007b) found that adults with vision loss were more conservative and cautious during walking and forward lunge tasks when compared to gender- and age-matched peers without vision loss (i.e., walk: decreased step length and speed; lunge: decreased lunge distance [percent of body height]; all results $p < 0.05$). Using an identical design, Ray and colleagues (2007a) found that adults with vision loss had impaired timed up-and-go (seconds;

$p = 0.02$) and thirty-second sit-to-stand (repetitions; $p = 0.018$) performance. Also, it has been suggested that adults with vision loss sacrifice efficiency for safety during postural control tasks (Horvat et al., 2003) and may employ suboptimal balance strategies (e.g., hip-dominant compensation during static balance conditions when somatosensory input is perturbed; Ray et al., 2008; p-values = 0.011 [Condition 6] and < 0.001 [Condition 4]). Concerning experimental studies, response variables, populations, results, and effects have been mixed, but interventions have been shown to positively impact gross motor outcomes (Blaylock and Vogtle, 2017; Hackney et al., 2015; Ray et al., 2005; Sweeting et al., 2020).

FINE MOTOR IN ADULTHOOD

Concerning fine motor skills, older adults with low vision have been found to have impaired performance across the right, left, and both hand Purdue Pegboard subtests (Wittich and Nadon, 2017). Likewise, Berger and Porell (2008) investigated self-reported basic (e.g., eating, dressing) and instrumental (e.g., preparing meals, using a phone) activities of daily living in older adults with vision loss. Many of these activities necessitate some level (or integration) of fine motor control. Berger and Porell (2008) found that poor near-vision was associated with self-reported instrumental and basic faculties of daily living using binary logistic regression (except for eating [basic activity], $p < 0.05$). Poor distance-vision was associated with instrumental ($p < 0.05$) but not basic activities of daily living. These findings should be viewed with concern as fine motor skills enable an infinite amount of precision-driven, functional, and goal-directed behaviors (Berger and Porell, 2008; Martiniello and Wittich, 2020; Wittich and Nadon, 2017). While targeted fine motor interventions are lacking, fields such as occupational therapy have a notable history of providing guidance toward the development of various fine motor skills and activities of daily living in adults with vision loss (Kaldenberg and Smallfield, 2020; Markowitz, 2006).

HONORABLE MENTION: POSTURAL CONTROL AND BALANCE

Postural control is a critical, multidimensional, and synergistic action system that should be considered in concert with mobility- and manipulative-based motor skills across the lifespan (Shumway-Cook and Woollacott, 2017). Due to space requirements, readers are directed to the works of Pennell (2021), Parreira and colleagues (2017), and Daneshmandi et al. (2021) for targeted commentaries on postural control in individuals with VI. Further, works by Sweeting et al. (2020), Salar and collaborators (2022), as well as Haibach-Beach and associates (2022) may be beneficial primers to the intervention-focused literature base surrounding postural control and balance in individuals with VI.

SYSTEMS PERSPECTIVE: A SPOTLIGHT ON PSYCHOLOGICAL VARIABLES

Motor behavior emerges as a result of interacting systems and constraints (Newell, 1986; Thelen, 1995). Thus, within an individual, mental systems (i.e., cognitive, psychological, emotional) should be viewed as synergists to actions systems (e.g., postural control, mobility, upper extremity function) (Shumway-Cook and Woollacott,

2017). For brevity, a narrow take on the psychological system will be presented here. In general, psychological constructs are categorized as individual constraints that are functional (as opposed to structural) in nature (Newell, 1986). Self-efficacy (Bandura, 1982) and related abstractions (Harter, 1999) are examples of latent constructs that have gained investigative traction within the field of motor behavior in individuals with VI. Examples have included perceived motor competence (Brian et al., 2018a; Brian et al., 2022), balance confidence (Pennell et al., 2022), self-perceptions (Stribing et al., 2022a), and metaperceptions (i.e., what an individual thinks, for example, their parents think about their motor competence; Stribing et al., 2022a). Such studies have directly elucidated or provided rationales which have spoken to the effect of psychological constructs on motor behavior outcomes in minors with VI. While additional psychogenic research is needed in various populations with VI, it is reasonable to conclude that endogenous constraints, such as psychological constructs, shape motoric behavior (Newell, 1986).

FUTURE RESEARCH

Empirical knowledge surrounding the motor behavior of individuals with VI has steadily increased over recent decades. However, gaps remain. Experimental investigations (ideally, with follow-up) and longitudinal studies (e.g., tracking, predictive validity) surrounding fine and gross motor skills are lacking across all populations with vision loss. Concerning issues of rigor and bias, there is a significant need for "gold standard" studies (i.e., randomized, double-blind, placebo-controlled; Misra, 2012). Likewise, lifespan discrepancies are pervasive within the literature base. Children, adolescents, and older adults are the most represented study samples. While additional insights across all ages would be helpful, early to middle-aged adults with VI appear most over-looked from a lifespan perspective. Concerning measurement, additional assessments scores (physical or otherwise) need to be vetted, adapted, and/or created specifically for individuals with VI. This is pivotal as measurement is everything (i.e., measurement defines reality [Manning et al., 2015], and subsequently, data). Cross-sectional (e.g., associational, normative, mediation, moderation) and longitudinal studies using latent (e.g., self-efficacy) and manifest variables or person-centered and variable-centered analyses are needed. Researchers should attempt to maximize sample sizes and, if possible, aim to capture extensive, medical-grade diagnostic information of participants (as performed by an optometrist or related vision care professional) to help address the heterogeneous nature of visual acuity across and within etiologies. Further, examinations delving into motor behavior determinants are needed. Variables such as age, sex, and degree of vision have been investigated to a greater extent; however, discrepancies remain. Factors such as being multimorbid deserve greater investigation (Pennell, 2021; Pennell et al., 2022), as does, for example, age of onset (e.g., congenital versus acquired). Last, inquiries involving significant others (e.g., parents, peers, teachers) and how their perceptions may be influencing the motor behavior of individuals with VI should be explored (Stribing et al., 2022a; Stribing et al., 2022b). While not exhaustive, it is hoped that this section has provided young and seasoned researchers with a guidepost for developing motor behavior and health-related investigations that will be novel and impactful.

PRACTICAL IMPLICATIONS

Various applications for practice could be gleaned for movement-related service providers and practitioners (e.g., physical or occupational therapists, [adapted] physical educators, health and fitness specialists). For example, professionals are safe to assume that individuals with vision loss may have inferior fine and gross motor skills when compared to sighted peers across the lifespan. This is a large generalization as exceptions will exist. Yet this outcome suggests that motor behavior should be assessed early and often, particularly in early life (Chen, 2014), as it has been posited that if children do not develop certain thresholds of motor competence by middle childhood (Brian et al., 2020b; Clark, 2007), such individuals may struggle to participate in complex, health-enhancing motor behaviors across the life course (Stodden et al., 2008; Wall, 2004). This point underscores the importance of having a solid foundation in assessment. Assessments should be (a) appropriate (e.g., have scores with stout measurement properties, assess functional and developmentally congruent tasks, designed with vision loss in mind [e.g., empirically vetted modifications]), (b) holistic, and (c) enable cogent score interpretation (e.g., Brian et al., 2018b; Brian et al., 2021c; Pennell et al., 2021; Wittich and Nadon, 2017). Such information could be used to ground and develop educational, therapeutic, or movement-related outcomes (e.g., Individualized Education Program, rehabilitative, or physical activity goals). Judicious goal development and assessment utilization should be aligned with evidence-based practices (Haegele and Lieberman, 2019; Ivy and Hatton, 2014; Lieberman and Haibach, 2016; Sugden and Wade, 2013) so that impactful interventions may be employed in individuals with vision loss across the lifespan. A final practical implication concerns the systems perspective (Thelen, 1995). Professionals should vigilantly consider interactions between individual, task, and environmental constraints when attempting to understand the nature of, and remediate, a person's motor behavior (Newell, 1986).

CONCLUSION

The purpose of this chapter was to provide a concentrated review of empirical research pertaining to the motor behavior of individuals with VI and blindness. Visual loss is a significant and global concern (Scott et al., 2016; WHO, 2022) that has considerable economic (Marques et al., 2021; WHO, 2021), quality of life (Chadha and Subramanian, 2011; Wang et al., 2014), and motor-related impacts (Augestad and Alsnes, 2021), among others. In general, when compared to sighted peers, individuals with VI appear to have lower fine and gross motor skills across the lifespan. Beyond movement-related outcomes, professionals should consider various systems and constraints (e.g., self-efficacy) when investigating the motor behavior of individuals with vision loss. A promising take-away is that the motor behavior of individuals with vision loss appears malleable with intervention. Regardless of a practitioner's or researcher's purview, caution is warranted as (a) there is a dearth of cross-sectional and longitudinal research and (b) concerns of rigor have been raised regarding the research found within the contemporary literature base (e.g., bias, heterogeneity, methodological issues; Elsman et al., 2019; Houwen et al., 2009; Pennell, 2021). It is hoped that professionals will view the current discrepancies as a clarion call to increase the knowledge base and to improve practice within the field of motor behavior in individuals with vision loss across the lifespan. Indeed, it is our duty to help champion their movement- and health-related vitality.

REFERENCES

Ackland, P., Resnikoff, S., and Bourne, R. (2017). World blindness and visual impairment: Despite many successes, the problem is growing. *Community Eye Health*, 30(100), 71–73.

Adolph, K., and Franchak, J. (2017). The development of motor behavior. *Wiley Interdisciplinary Reviews: Cognitive Science*, 8(1-2), e1430. https://doi.org/10.1002/wcs.1430

Aki, E., Atasavun, S., and Kayihan, H. (2008). Relationship between upper extremity kinesthetic sense and writing performance by students with low vision. *Perceptual and Motor Skills*, 106(3), 963–66. https://doi.org/10.2466/pms.106.3.963-966

Augestad, L., and Alsnes, I. (2021). Physical activity, fitness, body composition, and well-being among persons with visual impairments. In J. Haegele (Ed.), *Movement and visual impairment: Research across disciplines* (pp. 131–42). London: Routledge.

Bakke, H., Cavalcante, W., Oliveira, I., Sarinho, S., and Cattuzzo, M. (2019). Assessment of motor skills in children with visual impairment: A systematic and integrative review. *Clinical Medicine Insights: Pediatrics*, 13, 1–10. https://doi.org/10.1177/1179556519838287

Bakke, H., Sarinho, S., and Cattuzzo, M. (2017). Adaptation of the MABC-2 Test (Age Band 2) for children with low vision. *Research in Developmental Disabilities*, 71, 120–29. https://doi.org/10.1016/j.ridd.2017.10.003

Bandura, A. (1982). Self-efficacy mechanism in human agency. *American Psychologist*, 37(2), 122–47. https://doi.org/10.1037/0003-066X.37.2.122

Berger, S., and Porell, F. (2008). The association between low vision and function. *Journal of Aging and Health*, 20(5), 504–25. https://doi.org/10.1177/0898264308317534

Blaylock, S.E., and Vogtle, L.K. (2017). Falls prevention interventions for older adults with low vision: A scoping review. *Canadian Journal of Occupational Therapy*, 84(3), 139–47. https://doi.org/10.1177/0008417417711460

Brambring, M. (2006). Divergent development of gross motor skills in children who are blind or sighted. *Journal of Visual Impairment & Blindness*, 100(10), 620–34. https://doi.org/10.1177/0145482X0610001014

Brambring, M. (2007). Divergent development of manual skills in children who are blind or sighted. *Journal of Visual Impairment & Blindness*, 101(4), 212–25. https://doi.org/10.1177/0145482X0710100404

Brian, A., Bostick, L., Starrett, A., Klavina, A., Taunton Miedema, S., Pennell, A., Stribing, A., Gilbert, E., and Lieberman, L. (2020a). The effects of ecologically valid intervention strategies on the locomotor skills of children with visual impairments. *Adapted Physical Activity Quarterly*, 37(2), 177–92. https://doi.org/10.1123/apaq.2019-0019

Brian, A., Getchell, N., True, L., De Meester, A., and Stodden, D. (2020b). Reconceptualizing and operationalizing Seefeldt's proficiency barrier: Applications and future directions. *Sports Medicine*, 50(11), 1889–900. https://doi.org/10.1007/s40279-020-01332-6

Brian, A., Haegele, J., Bostick, L., Lieberman, L., and Nesbitt, D. (2018a). A pilot investigation of the perceived motor competence of children with visual impairments and those who are sighted. *Journal of Visual Impairment & Blindness*, 112(1), 118–24. https://doi.org/10.1177/0145482X1811200112

Brian, A., Starrett, A., Haibach-Beach, P., De Meester, A., Taunton Miedema, S., Pennell, A., and Lieberman, L. (2022). Perceived motor competence mediates the relationship between gross motor skills and physical activity in youth with visual impairments. *Research Quarterly for Exercise and Sport*, 93(2), 310–17. https://doi.org/10.1080/02701367.2020.1831688

Brian, A., Starrett, A., Pennell, A., Haibach-Beach, P., Gilbert, E., Stribing, A., Taunton Miedema, S., and Lieberman, L. (2021a). Longitudinal locomotor competence and body mass index across self-reported gender and vision level for youth with visual impairments: A 3-year investigation. *Adapted Physical Activity Quarterly, 38*(2), 268–85. https://doi.org/10.1123/apaq.2020-0082

Brian, A., Starrett, A., Pennell, A., Haibach-Beach, P., Taunton Miedema, S., Stribing, A., Gilbert, E., Patey, M., and Lieberman, L. (2021b). The brief form of the Test of Gross Motor Development-3 for individuals with visual impairments. *International Journal of Environmental Research and Public Health, 18*(15), 7962. https://doi.org/10.3390/ijerph18157962

Brian, A., Taunton Miedema, S., Johnson, J., and Chica, I. (2021c). A comparison of the fundamental motor skills of preschool-aged children with and without visual impairments. *Adapted Physical Activity Quarterly, 38*(3), 349–58. https://doi.org/10.1123/apaq.20190157

Brian, A., Taunton, S., Lieberman, L., Haibach-Beach, P., Foley, J., and Santarossa, S. (2018b). Psychometric properties of the Test of Gross Motor Development-3 for children with visual impairments. *Adapted Physical Activity Quarterly, 35*(2), 145–58. https://doi.org/10.1123/apaq.2017-0061

Bruininks, R., and Bruininks, B. (2005). *Bruininks-Oseretsky Test of Motor Proficiency* (second edition). Minneapolis, MN: Pearson.

Caputo, E., Porcellis da Silva, R., Leal da Cunha, L., Krüger, G., and Reichert, F. (2022). Physical activity and quality of life in people with visual impairments: A systematic review. *Journal of Visual Impairment & Blindness, 116*(1), 48–60. https://doi.org/10.1177/0145482X211072567

Celeste, M. (2002). A survey of motor development for infants and young children with visual impairments. *Journal of Visual Impairment & Blindness, 96*(3), 169–74.

Chadha, R., and Subramanian, A. (2011). The effect of visual impairment on quality of life of children aged 3-16 years. *British Journal of Ophthalmology, 95*(5), 642–45. https://doi.org/10.1136/bjo.2010.182386

Chen, D. (2014). *Essential elements in early intervention: Visual impairment and multiple disabilities* (second edition). New York: AFB Press.

Clark, J. (2007). On the problem of motor skill development. *Journal of Physical Education, Recreation & Dance, 78*(5), 39–44. https://doi.org/10.1080/07303084.2007.10598023

da Cunha Furtado, O., Allums-Featherston, K., Lieberman, L., and Gutierrez, G. (2015). Physical activity interventions for children and youth with visual impairments. *Adapted Physical Activity Quarterly, 32*(2), 156–76. https://doi.org/10.1123/APAQ.2014-0164

Daneshmandi, H., Norasteh, A., and Zarei, H. (2021). Balance in the blind: A systematic review. *Physical Treatments-Specific Physical Therapy Journal, 11*(1), 1–12. https://doi.org/10.32598/ptj.11.1.430.2

Elsman, E., Al Baaj, M., van Rens, G., Sijbrandi, W., van den Broek, E., van der Aa, H., Schakel, W., Heymans, M., de Vries, R., Vervloed, M., Steenbergen, B., and van Nispen, R. (2019). Interventions to improve functioning, participation, and quality of life in children with visual impairment: A systematic review. *Survey of Ophthalmology, 64*(4), 512–57. https://doi.org/10.1016/j.survophthal.2019.01.010

Hackney, M., Hall, C., Echt, K., and Wolf, S. (2015). Multimodal exercise benefits mobility in older adults with visual impairment: A preliminary study. *Journal of Aging and Physical Activity, 23*(4), 630–39. https://doi.org/10.1123/japa.2014-0008

Haegele, J., Brian, A., and Goodway, J. (2015). Fundamental motor skills and school-aged individuals with visual impairments: A review. *Review Journal of Autism and Developmental Disorders, 2*(3), 320–27. https://doi.org/10.1007/s40489-015-0055-8

Haegele, J., and Lieberman, L. (2019). Movement and visual impairment: Research and practice. In J. Ravenscroft (ed.), *The Routledge handbook of visual impairment* (pp. 189–201). London: Routledge.

Haibach-Beach, P., McNamera, S., and Lieberman, L. (2022). Home-based balance pilot intervention for adults with visual impairments. *British Journal of Visual Impairment*, 40(2), 145–59. https://doi.org/10.1177/0264619620935937

Haibach, P., Wagner, M., and Lieberman, L. (2014). Determinants of gross motor skill performance in children with visual impairments. *Research in Developmental Disabilities*, 35(10), 2577–84. https://doi.org/10.1016/j.ridd.2014.05.030

Harter, S. (1999). *The construction of the self: A developmental perspective.* New York: Guilford Press.

Haywood, K., and Getchell, N. (2019). Fundamental concepts. In K. Haywood and N. Getchell (eds.), *Life span motor development* (pp. 4–17). Champaign, IL: Human Kinetics.

Henderson, S., and Sugden, D. (1992). *Movement Assessment Battery for Children.* New York: The Psychological Corporation.

Higgins, S. (1991). Motor skill acquisition. *Physical Therapy*, 71(2), 123–39. https://doi.org/10.1093/ptj/71.2.123

Horvat, M., Ray, C., Ramsey, V., Miszko, T., Keeney, R., and Blasch, B. (2003). Compensatory analysis and strategies for balance in individuals with visual impairments. *Journal of Visual Impairment & Blindness*, 97(11), 695–703. https://doi.org/10.1177/0145482X0309701103

Houwen, S., Visscher, C., Lemmink, K., and Hartman, E. (2008). Motor skill performance of school-age children with visual impairments. *Developmental Medicine & Child Neurology*, 50(2), 139–45. https://doi.org/10.1111/j.1469-8749.2007.02016.x

Houwen, S., Visscher, C., Lemmink, K., and Hartman, E. (2009). Motor skill performance of children and adolescents with visual impairments: A review. *Exceptional Children*, 75(4), 464–92. https://doi.org/10.1177/001440290907500405

Inoue, S., Kawashima, M., Hiratsuka, Y., Nakano, T., Tamura, H., Ono, K., Murakami, A., Tsubota, K., and Yamada, M. (2018). Assessment of physical inactivity and locomotor dysfunction in adults with visual impairment. *Scientific Reports*, 8, 12032. https://doi.org/10.1038/s41598-018-30599-z

Ivy, S., and Hatton, D. (2014). Teaching skill acquisition to individuals with blindness: A systematic review of response-prompting procedures. *International Review of Research in Developmental Disabilities*, 46, 55–100. https://doi.org/10.1016/B978-0-12-420039-5.00005-8

Jebsen, R., Taylor, N., Trieschmann, R., Trotter, M., and Howard, L. (1969). An objective and standardized test of hand function. *Archives of Physical Medicine and Rehabilitation*, 50(6), 311–19.

Kaldenberg, J., and Smallfield, S. (2020). Occupational therapy practice guidelines for older adults with low vision. *The American Journal of Occupational Therapy*, 74(2), 7402397010p1–7402397010p23. https://doi.org/10.5014/ajot.2020.742003

Leissner, J., Coenen, M., Froehlich, S., Loyola, D., and Cieza, A. (2014). What explains health in persons with visual impairment? *Health and Quality of Life Outcomes*, 12, 65. https://doi.org/10.1186/1477-7525-12-65

Lieberman, L., and Haibach, P. (2016). *Gross motor development curriculum for children with visual impairments.* Louisville, KY: American Printing House for the Blind, Incorporated.

Manning, A., Khakimov, R., Dall, R., and Truscott, A. (2015). Wheeler's delayed-choice gedanken experiment with a single atom. *Nature Physics*, 11(7), 539–42. https://doi.org/10.1038/nphys3343

Markowitz, M. (2006). Occupational therapy interventions in low vision rehabilitation. *Canadian Journal of Ophthalmology*, 41(3), 340–47. https://doi.org/10.1139/I06-020

Marques, A.., Ramke, J., Cairns, J., Butt, T., Zhang, J., Muirhead, D., Jones, I., Tong, B., Swenor, B., Faal, H., Bourne, R., Frick, K., and Burton, M. (2021). Global economic productivity losses from VI and blindness. *eClinicalMedicine*, 35, 100852. https://doi.org/10.1016/j.eclinm.2021.100852

Martín, M., Santos-Lozano, A., Martín-Hernández, J., López-Miguel, A., Maldonado, M., Baladrón, C., Baur, C., and Merabet, L. (2016). Cerebral versus ocular visual impairment: The impact on developmental neuroplasticity. *Frontiers in Psychology, 7*, 1958. https://doi.org/10.3389/fpsyg.2016.01958

Martiniello, N., and Wittich, W. (2020). The association between tactile, motor and cognitive capacities and braille reading performance: A scoping review of primary evidence to advance research on braille and aging. *Disability and Rehabilitation, 44*(11), 2515–36. https://doi.org/10.1080/09638288.2020.1839972

Misra, S. (2012). Randomized double blind placebo control studies, the "gold standard" in intervention based studies. *Indian Journal of Sexually Transmitted Diseases and AIDS, 33*(2), 131–34. https://doi.org/10.4103/0253-7184.102130

National Academies of Sciences, Engineering, and Medicine. (2016). Understanding the epidemiology of vision loss and impairment in the United States. In S. Teutsch, M. McCoy, R. Woodbury, and A. Welp (eds.), *Making eye health a population health imperative: Vision for tomorrow* (pp. 55–134). Washington, DC: National Academies Press.

Newell, K. (1986). Constraints on the development of coordination. In M. Wade and H. Whiting (eds.), *Motor development in children: Aspects of coordination and control* (pp. 341–60). Boston, MA: Martinus Nijhoff Publishers.

Ong, S., Crowston, J., Loprinzi, P., and Ramulu, P. (2018). Physical activity, visual impairment, and eye disease. *Eye, 32*(8), 1296–303. https://doi.org/10.1038/s41433-018-0081-8

Parreira, R., Grecco, L., and Oliveira, C. (2017). Postural control in blind individuals: A systematic review. *Gait & Posture, 57*, 161–67. https://doi.org/10.1016/j.gaitpost.2017.06.008

Pennell, A. (2021). Postural control and balance. In J. Haegele (ed.), *Movement and visual impairment: Research across disciplines* (pp. 17–31). London: Routledge.

Pennell, A., Patey, M., Fisher, J., and Brian, A. (2022). The Activities-specific Balance Confidence (ABC) Scale in youth with visual impairments: Psychometrics and a population-specific short form. *Measurement in Physical Education and Exercise Science, 26*(2), 89–102. https://doi.org/10.1080/1091367X.2021.1949321

Pennell, A., Yee, N., Conforti, C., Yau, K., and Brian, A. (2021). Standing long jump performance in youth with visual impairments: A multidimensional examination. *International Journal of Environmental Research and Public Health, 18*(18), 9742. https://doi.org/10.3390/ijerph18189742

Ray, C., Horvat, M., Croce, R., Mason, R., and Wolf, S. (2008). The impact of vision loss on postural stability and balance strategies in individuals with profound vision loss. *Gait & Posture, 28*(1), 58–61. https://doi.org/10.1016/j.gaitpost.2007.09.010

Ray, C., Horvat, M., Keen, K., and Blasch, B. (2005). Using Tai Chi as an exercise intervention for improving balance in adults with visual impairments: Two case studies. *Review, 37*(1), 17–24.

Ray, C., Horvat, M., Williams, M., and Blasch, B. (2007a). Clinical assessment of functional movement in adults with visual impairments. *Journal of Visual Impairment & Blindness, 101*(2), 108–13. https://doi.org/10.1177/0145482X0710100205

Ray, C., Horvat, M., Williams, M., and Blasch, B. (2007b). Kinetic movement analysis in adults with vision loss. *Adapted Physical Activity Quarterly, 24*(3), 209–17. https://doi.org/10.1123/apaq.24.3.209

Reimer, A., Cox, R., Boonstra, F., and Nijhuis-van der Sanden, M. (2015). Measurement of fine-motor skills in young children with visual impairment. *Journal of Developmental and Physical Disabilities, 27*(5), 569–90. https://doi.org/10.1007/s10882-015-9433-5

Reimer, A., Cox, R., Boonstra, N., and Smits-Engelsman, B. (2008). Effect of visual impairment on goal-directed aiming movements in children. *Developmental Medicine & Child Neurology, 50*(10), 778–83. https://doi.org/10.1111/j.1469-8749.2008.03028.x

Reimer, A., Cox, R., Nijhuis-Van der Sanden, M., and Boonstra, F. (2011). Improvement of fine motor skills in children with visual impairment: An explorative study. *Research in Developmental Disabilities, 32*(5), 1924–33. https://doi.org/10.1016/j.ridd.2011.03.023

Reimer, A., Smits-Engelsman, B., and Siemonsma-Boom, M. (1999). Development of an instrument to measure manual dexterity in children with visual impairments aged 6–12. *Journal of Visual Impairment & Blindness, 93*(10), 643–58. https://doi.org/10.1177/0145482X9909301003

Salar, S., Karimizadeh Ardakani, M., Lieberman, L., Beach, P., and Perreault, M. (2022). The effects of balance and core stability training on postural control in people with visual impairment: A systematic review. *British Journal of Visual Impairment*. Advance online publication. https://doi.org/10.1177/02646196221077215

Scott, A., Bressler, N., Folkes, S., Wittenborn, J., and Jorkasky, J. (2016). Public attitudes about eye and vision health. *JAMA Ophthalmology, 134*(10), 1111–18. https://doi.org/10.1001/jamaophthalmol.2016.2627

Shumway-Cook, A., and Woollacott, M. (2017). Motor control: Issues and theories. In A. Shumway-Cook and M. Woollacott (eds.), *Motor control: Translating research into clinical practice* (pp. 3–20). Philadelphia, PA: Wolters Kluwer.

Stodden, D., Goodway, J., Langendorfer, S., Roberton, M., Rudisill, M., Garcia, C., and Garcia, L. (2008). A developmental perspective on the role of motor skill competence in physical activity: An emergent relationship. *Quest, 60*(2), 290–306. https://doi.org/10.1080/00336297.2008.10483582

Stribing, A., Pennell, A., Gilbert, E.N., Lieberman, L.J., and Brian. A. (2022a). Self-perceptions, parents' perceptions, metaperceptions, and locomotor skills in adolescents with visual impairments: A preliminary investigation. *Journal of Motor Learning and Development, 10*(1), 132–48. https://doi.org/10.1123/jmld.2021-0021

Stribing, A., Stodden, D., Monsma, E., Lieberman, L., and Brian, A. (2022b). Content/face validity of motor skill perception questionnaires for youth with visual impairments: A Delphi method. *British Journal of Visual Impairment, 40*(2), 369–77. https://doi.org/10.1177/0264619621990687

Sugden, D., and Wade, M. (2013). *Typical and atypical motor development*. London: Mac Keith Press.

Sweeting, J., Merom, D., Astuti, P., Antoun, M., Edwards, K., and Ding, D. (2020). Physical activity interventions for adults who are visually impaired: A systematic review and meta-analysis. *BMJ Open, 10*(2), e034036. https://doi.org/10.1136/bmjopen-2019-034036

Thelen, E. (1995). Motor development: A new synthesis. *American Psychologist, 50*(2), 79–95. https://doi.org/10.1037//0003-066x.50.2.79

Tröster, H., and Brambring, M. (1993). Early motor development in blind infants. *Journal of Applied Developmental Psychology, 14*(1), 83–106. https://doi.org/10.1016/01933973(93)90025-Q

Tröster, H., Hecker, W., and Brambring, M. (1994). Longitudinal study of gross-motor development in blind infants and preschoolers. *Early Child Development and Care, 104*(1), 61–78. https://doi.org/10.1080/0300443941040105

Ulrich, D. (2000). *Test of Gross Motor Development examiner's manual* (second edition). Austin, TX: PRO-ED.

Ulrich, D. (2019). *Test of Gross Motor Development examiner's manual* (third edition). Austin, TX: PRO-ED.

Visser, L., Ruiter, S., Van der Meulen, B., Ruijssenaars, W., and Timmerman, M. (2013). Validity and suitability of the Bayley-III Low Motor/Vision version: A comparative study among young children with and without motor and/or visual impairments. *Research in Developmental Disabilities, 34*(11), 3736–45. https://doi.org/10.1016/j.ridd.2013.07.027

Wagner, M., Haibach, P., and Lieberman, L. (2013). Gross motor skill performance in children with and without visual impairments—Research to practice. *Research in Developmental Disabilities*, *34*(10), 3246–52. https://doi.org/10.1016/j.ridd.2013.06.030

Wall, A. (2004). The developmental skill-learning gap hypothesis: Implications for children with movement difficulties. *Adapted Physical Activity Quarterly*, *21*(3), 197–218. https://doi.org/10.1123/apaq.21.3.197

Wang, C., Chan, C., and Chi, I. (2014). Overview of quality of life research in older people with visual impairment. *Advances in Aging Research*, *3*(2), 45495. https://doi.org/10.4236/aar.2014.32014

Webber, A. (2018). The functional impact of amblyopia. *Clinical and Experimental Optometry*, *101*(4), 443–50. https://doi.org/10.1111/cxo.12663

Webber, A., Wood, J., and Thompson, B. (2016). Fine motor skills of children with amblyopia improve following binocular treatment. *Investigative Ophthalmology & Visual Science*, *57*(11), 4713–20. https://doi.org/10.1167/iovs.16-19797

Wittich, W., and Nadon, C. (2017). The Purdue Pegboard test: Normative data for older adults with low vision. *Disability and Rehabilitation: Assistive Technology*, *12*(3), 272–79. https://doi.org/10.3109/17483107.2015.1129459

World Health Organization. (2021). Blindness and VI. https://www.who.int/news-room/fact-sheets/detail/blindness-and-visual-impairment

World Health Organization. (2022). Eye care, vision care, VI and blindness. https://www.who.int/health-topics/blindness-and-vision-loss#tab=tab_1

2
Motor Behavior and Children Who Are Hard of Hearing, Deaf, or Deafblind

Pamela Beach, Melanie Perreault, and Lauren Lieberman

■ ■ ■

In the United States, 13 percent of the population over the age of twelve years has hearing loss in both ears (National Institute on Deafness and Other Communication Disorders, 2021). Reported hearing loss among infants is 1.7 per one thousand, and for children ages three to seventeen years, it is roughly five per one thousand (Centers for Disease Control and Prevention, 2021). Deafness is congenital or present at birth, for most individuals (66 percent), with only one-third acquiring deafness sometime after birth. Causes of hearing loss vary greatly including injuries, genetic conditions, allergies to drugs, autoimmune conditions, recurring exposure to loud sounds, infections (e.g., herpes viruses), toxoplasmosis, and premature birth (Paludetti et al., 2012). Regardless of the cause, the major types of hearing loss include conductive, sensorineural, or a combination of conductive and sensorineural hearing loss. With conductive hearing loss, sound does not transmit well to the inner ear. A conductive loss is a mechanical problem where the nerves remain undamaged, so it can be corrected with the use of hearing aids that efficiently increase volume (Lieberman, 2022). Most children with a conductive hearing loss have intelligible speech. A sensorineural hearing loss occurs when damage is in the inner ear (cochlea) or the nerve pathways going from the inner ear (retrocochlear) to the brain (American Speech-Language-Hearing Association, n.d.). Sensorineural hearing loss is more severe than conductive hearing loss and more likely to be permanent. Children with sensorineural loss (with no cochlear implant) frequently have more difficulties with speech than those with a conductive loss and will most likely communicate with sign language (Lieberman, 2022). Hearing is most associated with communication; however, hearing loss and deafness not only affect speech, language, and communication, but also social development, academics, and motor competence (Rajendran and Roy, 2011).

Deafblindness is a low incidence disability impacting approximately ten thousand youth in the United States (National Center on Deaf-Blindness, 2022). Causes, severity, and type of vision and hearing loss vary greatly across individuals with deafblindness, with 90 percent having additional disabilities to their sensory disabilities. Understanding the cause to an individual's deafblindness may provide key information related to the age of onset and whether remaining vision and hearing are likely. This discussion on motor behavior in deafblindness will focus upon Usher syndrome and CHARGE syndrome, the two most common causes of deafblindness.

In adults, the leading cause of deafblindness is Usher syndrome. Usher syndrome is congenital and characterized by hearing loss at birth, or shortly thereafter, and the progressive deterioration of peripheral vision. There are three types of Usher syndrome with type I and II being the most common. Individuals with type I have congenital deafness and progressive retinitis pigmentosa, whereas those with type II have adventitious deafness and progressive retinitis pigmentosa. Individuals with type III have progressive hearing loss, progressive vision loss, and loss of vestibular function.

CHARGE syndrome is the leading cause of child onset deafblindness. Children with coloboma, heart defects, atresia choanae, restricted growth, genital hypoplasia, and ear abnormalities (CHARGE) syndrome are identified through the presence of a single gene (CHD7) and two major features (colobomas, choanal atresia, cranial nerve dysfunction, absent semicircular canals) and several minor features (genital hypoplasia, cardiovascular malformation, growth deficiency; Hartshorne et al., 2021). These children are recognized as having some of the most complex, multisensory impairments in the current educational environment (Pagon et al., 1981; Tegay and Yedowitz, 2009). Although rare, ranging between one per ten thousand and one per fifteen thousand live births (Deuce et al., 2012), it is still the leading cause of deafblindness (National Center on Deaf-Blindness, 2018).

The specific characteristics present in every child with CHARGE syndrome may vary, and there are wide variations in the level of severity of each characteristic. Most children with CHARGE syndrome are deaf and/or have various degrees of hearing loss. Colobomas in the eye are present in at least 70 to 90 percent of children with CHARGE syndrome (National Organization for Rare Disorders, Inc., 2019). The main etiology for most children with CHARGE syndrome includes a sensorineural hearing loss that damages the eighth cranial nerve, the inner sensory mechanism, the vestibule, and/or the cochlea/semicircular canals. Sensorineural hearing loss often causes the largest impact to balance and the kinesthetic control of one's body in space (Agrup et al., 2007). Additional research suggests that injured or missing vestibular organs that work in combination with vision can affect movement patterns and balance (Möller, 2011).

MOTOR MILESTONES

The effects of hearing loss upon the motor domain begins as early as infancy during the reflexive stage of development (Korver et al., 2010). Expectations for the emergence and disappearance of some reflexes will not be the same in infants with hearing loss in comparison with infants without hearing loss as some reflexes require auditory and vestibular stimuli (Veiskarami and Roozhahani, 2020). Currently, the literature on motor milestones in infants and young children with hearing loss is limited but findings indicate they often experience delays in developing head control and independent walking (Masuda and Kaga, 2014). The loss of auditory input can cause some individuals with low hearing or deafness to step with reduced velocity (Suarez et al., 2017) and shorter strides often resulting in shuffling or, conversely, stamping their feet (Jafarnezhadgero et al., 2017; Melo et al., 2017). Further research should examine the effects of deafness and hearing loss upon additional motor milestones including crawling, creeping, sitting, and standing unsupported.

Children with CHARGE syndrome often have significant delays in early motor milestones. Beach and colleagues (2021a) examined the achievement of nine gross motor milestones in children with and without CHARGE syndrome. These motor milestones included holding head, rolling over, sitting without support, crawling, creeping, standing with support, standing without support, cruising, and walking. The authors found that fewer children with CHARGE syndrome could crawl, creep, stand without support, and walk than their typically developing peers. Moreover, the children with CHARGE syndrome were significantly delayed at the age of onset for all nine motor milestones. These results suggest a need for early intervention.

Independent walking, which is typically achieved around twelve months of age, is considered the last motor milestone and serves as a gateway to the development of fundamental motor skills, such as running, jumping, and throwing. One of the most consistent findings in the literature is that children who are deafblind are significantly delayed in independent walking onset compared to their typically developing peers. Dammeyer (2012) found the average age of independent walking began at twenty-four months for children with Usher syndrome and thirty-eight months for children with CHARGE syndrome. Similarly, Foster et al. (2020) and Perreault et al. (2021) found children with CHARGE syndrome started independent walking at thirty-six months. However, other studies with children with CHARGE syndrome have found more varied results ranging from twenty-six months (Beach et al., 2021a) to more than forty-one months (Haibach and Lieberman, 2013; Perreault et al., 2020). Given the heterogenous nature of this population, the variability in these findings is not surprising.

Although many individual structural constraints could account for differences in motor milestones early in development, Beach and colleagues (2021a) examined the influence of the home environment on motor milestones in children with CHARGE syndrome using the Affordances in the Home Environment for Motor Development (AHEMD) assessment. They found that age of standing without support was positively associated with fine motor toys and the total AHEMD score, and age of walking was positively associated with outside space, fine motor toys, gross motor toys, and the total AHEMD score. Moreover, when parents were asked to identify affordances for independent walking in their children with CHARGE syndrome, they described several environmental and task constraints (Foster et al., 2020). These included furniture, open and flat areas, peer modeling, encouragement, practice, therapy support, assistive equipment, and fall safety. Thus, task and environmental influences provided early in life may have a positive influence on the achievement of certain motor milestones.

BALANCE

Young children with hearing loss and deafness, particularly when their hearing loss includes damage to the semicircular canals, such as sensorineural hearing loss, often have impaired balance in comparison to their peers without sensory losses, during walking or dynamic balance tasks (Jafarnezhadgero et al., 2017; Melo et al., 2017). These balance issues typically result from the vestibular damage rather than from deafness (Fellinger et al., 2015; McPhillips, 2015). One of the main roles of the vestibular system is to assist in the maintenance of balance and antigravity postures including both static and dynamic balance. As such, the vestibular system is integral in all movement.

Individuals with cochlear dysfunction or sensorineural hearing loss often experience vestibular dysfunction due to the similarities of the cochlear and vestibular systems. Children with profound sensorineural hearing loss may regain auditory sensation through cochlear implantation (CI). While CI improves audition in these children, there is also secondary damage to vestibular organs and resulting vestibular dysfunction (Motasaddi et al., 2010). Children with cochlear dysfunction often have balance problems and require increased visual information to maintain balance (Veiskarami and Roozhahani, 2020). Balance challenges are also found in children with profound sensorineural hearing loss without CI in comparison those with CI (De Kegel et al., 2015; Leigh et al., 2015; Suarez et al., 2017). The timing of CI can also impact the severity of the effects upon balance and motor development, such that children with CI prior to age three years have significantly slower gait (Suarez et al., 2017).

Deaf children's balance challenges are due to a variety of causes and may or may not be caused by vestibular damage. To improve balance, deaf children should participate in more physical activities that incorporate balance activities. For example, deaf children significantly improved their balance following a rhythmic gymnastics intervention (Fotiadou et al., 2010). This improvement in balance may be due to its emphasis on static and dynamic balance when used in children with low hearing and deafness aged seven to nine years over a period of sixteen weeks. Further research should examine benefits for younger children with hearing loss and deafness to increase the benefits of balance and lead to higher motor competence.

In children with CHARGE syndrome, Imel and colleagues (2020) found that balance was the most frequently cited individual barrier to participation in recreation activities. Vision is often the primary sense used by children without sensory impairments to aid in balance and postural adjustments when developing motor skills, such as standing with support (Delorme et al., 1989); thus, individuals who are deafblind often struggle with their balance due to the absence of this sensory information.

Haibach and Lieberman (2013) examined balance in young children with and without CHARGE syndrome using the Pediatric Balance Scale. They found that the children with CHARGE syndrome scored lower on all balance tasks compared to their typically developing peers and had a 57 percent greater risk of falling compared to the controls. The children with CHARGE syndrome performed best on the sitting with back unsupported, standing to sitting, transferring, turning, and picking up an object tasks, whereas they performed worst on the tandem stance and one-footed stance tasks. The authors also measured the participants self-efficacy of balance with a modified version of the Activities-Specific Balance Confidence Scale and found that the children with CHARGE syndrome scored lower than the children without disabilities and were most comfortable in familiar settings, such as walking around home and picking up a pencil.

In a similar study, Haibach-Beach and colleagues (2022) examined differences in balance between children with and without CHARGE syndrome using the Mini-BEST test, which assesses four areas of balance: anticipatory control, reactive postural control, sensory orientation, and dynamic gait. They found that the children with CHARGE syndrome had lower scores on all balance measures when compared to their typically developing peers. Moreover, the authors found a negative relationship between the balance measures and age of walking onset in the children with CHARGE syndrome. Balance has also been shown to play a role in the development of fundamental motor skills in children who are deafblind. Perreault and colleagues (2020) examined the relationship between balance measures on the Mini-BEST test and five fundamental motor skills (run, jump, slide, kick, throw) from the Test of Gross Motor Development-2 (TGMD-2) in children with CHARGE syndrome. They found that anticipatory control was positively associated with all five motor skills; reactive postural control was positively associated with the slide and kick; sensory orientation was positively associated with the run, slide, and kick; and dynamic gait was positively associated with the run and kick. Taken together, these findings suggest that early balance interventions may help decrease the delay in independent walking and fundamental motor skills for children who are deafblind.

MOTOR COMPETENCE

The learning of fundamental motor skills is essential to an individual's ability to lead an active lifestyle. In Seefeldt's (1980) model, children need to gain a threshold of motor proficiency in a variety of fundamental motor skills to pass a proficiency barrier, which will allow them to learn more complex motor skills. Brian and colleagues (2020) expanded Seefeldt's (1980) hypothetical barrier to include a transition from stability to mobility through the practice of a variety of skills and contexts. Children do not naturally develop these skills and progress to more complex mobility strategies without practicing specific skills (Brian et al., 2020). Without these skills, children may enter a negative spiral of disengagement that can lead to decreased physical activity and physical fitness as well as an increased chance of obesity (Stodden et al., 2008; Barnett et al., 2022).

Stability skills, including static or dynamic balance tasks, are essential for competently performing locomotor (i.e., running, jumping, skipping) or object control skills (i.e., throwing, kicking, catching). A child who cannot maintain balance in a static position will not be able to jump, a skill which requires the coordination and strength to leave the ground on both feet and the dynamic balance to be able to land. As such, it is not surprising that children without hearing loss perform better than deaf children on motor skills (Dummer et al., 1996; Hartman et al., 2011). Hartman and colleagues (2011) conducted a study at special schools for deaf children aged six through twelve years. They found that most of the children performed with lower scores in manual dexterity (61.9 percent) and ball skills (52.4 percent) and many (45.3 percent) also struggled with balance skills. A key factor in ball skill level was experience in sports, indicating that motor skill interventions may be beneficial for deaf children. Dummer and colleagues (1996) found similar results wherein children without hearing loss had higher performances for all locomotor skills and five out of six ball skills in comparison to deaf children. Of particular interest was that this differentiation was only found in children older than age five years, indicating the potential differences in physical education curriculum for deaf children in comparison to their peers who are not deaf. Other studies have revealed mixed results in motor competence between children with and without hearing loss (Jenice and Nonis, 2017; Zwierzchowska et al., 2008). Surprisingly, Jenice and Nonis (2017) found significantly lower balance scores in adolescent deaf participants in comparison to controls, but no significant differences in fine or gross motor skills were found between the groups.

Lower motor competence often leads to reduced fitness and health indices (Denysschen, et al., 2021). According to Ellis (2001), hearing loss or deafness without additional disabilities should not equate to reduced fitness levels. Deaf children can benefit from early exposure to all types of balance activities, motor skills, and sports skills (Lieberman, 2022). Parental influence and physical activity participation can greatly benefit fitness and health indices in youth with hearing loss and deafness (Dair et al., 2006; Ellis et al., 2014). Deaf children with deaf parents are encouraged more to participate in physical activity and have higher participation levels than deaf children of parents without hearing loss (Ellis, 2001; Ellis et al., 2014). Appropriate communication is also essential when teaching motor skills to deaf children. Radomir and colleagues (2012) found similar fitness scores in deaf children compared to children without hearing loss when modified communication and tests were administered.

In addition to coordination delays, other motor deficits have been reported in deaf children including visual-motor skills, slower reaction times, and movement execution speed (Hartman et al., 2011; Savelsbergh et al., 1991). Improvements in the visual domain due to sensory reorganization from the loss of auditory input are not always found in deaf and hard of hearing individuals with some exhibiting poorer visual skills than individuals without sensory impairments. Bavelier and colleagues (2006) propose a decline in visual skills is possible due to the attentionally demanding components of vision that typically assists with auditory-visual convergence. Delays in sequence processing have been found in deaf adults in comparison to adults without hearing loss (Levesque et al., 2014). Sequence processing is a critical component in learning complex motor skills with delays in such processing reducing the efficiency and possible quality of the acquisition and performance of new motor skills. Conway and colleagues (2009) proposed that sound exposure provides essential experience to learning sequential patterns due to the temporal aspects of a sound, such that a lack of this experience inhibits processing sequential patterns.

Children who are deafblind are often behind their peers without disabilities in motor competence of fundamental motor skills. Haibach-Beach and colleagues (2019) assessed children with and without CHARGE syndrome on five motor skills (run, jump, slide, kick, overhand throw) from the TGMD-2 and found that the children with CHARGE syndrome performed with significantly lower proficiency on all five skills compared to the controls. When they examined the individual components of each skill, the authors discovered that the children with CHARGE syndrome struggled most with two components of the run (narrow foot placement and nonsupport leg bent ninety degrees), one component of the kick (an elongated stride or leap before the kick), and all components of the throw. Perreault and colleagues (2021) expanded on this research by assessing children with and without CHARGE syndrome on all thirteen motor skills from the Test of Gross Motor Development-3 (TGMD-3). They found that the children with CHARGE syndrome scored significantly lower compared to their peers without disabilities on all motor skills, with the largest effects found in the hop, underhand roll, and skip. Age of walking onset was also negatively associated with all motor skills, with the underhand roll, one-hand strike, two-hand strike, run, and skip having the strongest relationship. These findings further indicate the need for early interventions in this population to improve the development of motor milestones and fundamental motor skills.

Although deficits in fundamental motor skill competence in this population can be attributed to individual structural constraints, other constraints have also been examined. Lane and colleagues (2021) found that many parents of children with CHARGE syndrome valued adapted physical education experiences for their child but were dissatisfied with the knowledge of their child's physical education teacher about CHARGE syndrome and how to modify lessons appropriately. Beach and colleagues (2021b) examined differences in parental perceptions and support of their child with and without CHARGE syndrome's motor competence. In their study, parents of children with and without CHARGE syndrome completed a Parent Perceptions Questionnaire wherein they rated their child's competence on twelve fundamental motor skills and indicated their value and support for their child's motor competence. The results revealed that parents of children with CHARGE syndrome rated their child lower on all motor skills compared to parents of children without disabilities; however, they participated with their child in movements skills and tracked their child's motor skill practice more often than parents of children without disabilities.

Haibach-Beach and colleagues (2021) extended these findings by examining the influence of parent perceptions and support on their child's actual motor competence. In addition to parents completing the Parent Perceptions Questionnaire, their children with CHARGE syndrome were assessed on all skills from the TGMD-3. The results revealed significant positive relationships between parental ratings of locomotor, ball skills, and total skill scores and their child with CHARGE syndrome's locomotor, ball skill, and total skill scores on the TGMD-3, respectively. Moreover, parental ratings of locomotor skills and how often parents participated with their child in motor skills significantly predicted their child with CHARGE syndrome's locomotor, ball skill, and total skill score, with the variance explained ranging from 54.9 percent to 58.2 percent. These findings suggest that parents play an integral role in the development of fundamental motor skills for children who are deafblind and should be included in motor skill interventions.

The need for motor skill interventions is clear for children who are deafblind; however, very little research has been conducted to date. Lieberman and colleagues (2021) took a first step at developing a motor skill intervention by examining the feasibility of a six-week home-based intervention for children with CHARGE syndrome. Prior to the intervention, six children with CHARGE syndrome were assessed on the TGMD-3 while their parents were provided with equipment and instructional materials. Parents were instructed to have their child practice any motor skills from the TGMD-3 at least twice a week for thirty minutes during the six-week period. Following the intervention, the children and parents were interviewed, and the children were reassessed on the four motor skills from the TGMD-3 they practiced most often during the intervention. The findings indicated that the children and parents adhered to the intervention protocol and accepted the intervention by setting personal goals to improve motor skills as well as stamina and balance. Although several of the participants encountered barriers, such as attention span and balance issues, many parents were able to use strategies to overcome these challenges. Intervention efficacy was also evident by the improvement in motor skill scores from pre- to post-intervention. This study provides preliminary support for the use of motor skill interventions; thus, future research should focus on the development and implementation of larger-scale interventions for children who are deafblind.

PRACTICAL IMPLICATIONS

In particular, deaf and deafblind youth benefit from a variety of teaching strategies, such as visual demonstrations and the use of videos, posters, and iPads (Lieberman, 2022). Deaf sports are a large part of deaf culture that can facilitate deaf children's involvement with hearing peers as well as with deaf friends. Deaf sports organizations today are one of the small number of places where deaf people exercise near total control over their own lives. They develop their own procedures and rules to determine eligibility and competition requirements (Mckee et al., 2019). Moreover, deaf sport and the Deaflympics serve as a powerful cultural and social event for deaf people internationally. It is important to keep in mind that every deaf child should learn the American Sign Language signs for each sport and terminology within each sport as well as the printed word, so they comprehend written words associated with the sign for complete understanding.

For children who are deafblind, it is extremely important to ensure they get early intervention as soon as possible. Early intervention should include all members of the child's multidisciplinary team and should incorporate goals in motor skills at home and in preschool. Focusing on development in all areas of the psychomotor domain can aid in improving the age of onset of walking, as well as building stamina and balance skills. Balance and stamina will help in developing early motor milestones as well as advancing to fundamental motor skills, such as running, jumping, kicking, and throwing (Foster et al., 2019; Foster et al., 2021). Motivation is needed to increase circumstances and opportunities for a child to explore new movement patterns (Foster et al., 2019). Using the right type of motivator is key, and parents usually know their child's preferences (e.g., iPad, slide, vibrating ball). Modifying the task constraints, such as the equipment, the goal of the task, or the rules, can be beneficial. Utilizing bright or auditory equipment as well as changing the texture and weight can be motivational for many children. The use of assistive equipment, such as a chair, walker, pushcart, or a gait trainer, can be used to increase balance and muscle tone while also performing motor skills. In addition, using visual cues such as picture cards, video modeling, or demonstrations can clarify the understanding of the task (Foster et al., 2019; Foster et al., 2021; Lieberman, 2022). Most importantly, children who are deaf, hard of hearing, or deafblind should be taught the same physical education units as their same age peers in order to be self-determined adults (Lieberman et al., 2018).

CONCLUSION

There are a variety of causes of hearing loss and deafblindness. Every child will experience the sensory loss differently depending upon the age of onset and environmental factors (e.g., family, education). As such, expectations in motor milestones, balance, and motor competence will vary greatly. It should also be stressed that much of the differences in motor development in individuals with hearing loss, deafness, and deafblindness are due to lack of opportunity. Youth with these sensory impairments are rarely given the same opportunities as their peers without sensory deficits. Parents and practitioners must accommodate children with deafness and deafblindness with their preferred form of communication, which may be verbal, American Sign Language, or a combination of both. Currently, there is a lack of research on effective interventions for deaf and deafblind populations for all ages. Young hard of hearing, deaf, and deafblind children who are exposed to more opportunities to be physically active and given appropriate communication and modifications are much more likely to become motor competent adolescents and adults who lead more physically active lifestyles.

REFERENCES

Agrup, C., Gleeson, M., and Rudge, P. (2007). The inner ear and the neurologist. *Journal of Neurology, Neurosurgery, and Psychiatry*, 78(2), 114–22. https://doi.org/10.1136/jnnp.2006.092064

American Speech-Language-Hearing Association. (n.d.). Causes of hearing loss in children. www.asha.org/public/hearing/disorders/causes.htm

Barnett, L.M., Webster, E.K., Hulteen, R.M., De Meester, A., Valentini, N.C., Lenoir, M., Pesce, C., Getchell, N., Lopes, V.P., Robinson, L.E., Brian, A., and Rodrigues, L.P. (2022). Through the looking glass: A systematic review of longitudinal evidence, providing new insight for motor competence and health. *Sports Medicine*, 52, 875–920. https://doi.org/10.1007/s40279-021-01516-8

Bavelier, D., Dye, M.W., and Hauser, P.C. (2006). Do deaf individuals see better? *Trends in Cognitive Science*, 10, 512–18. https://doi.10.1016/j.tics.2006.09006

Beach, P., Perreault, M., and Lieberman, L. (2021a). Affordances for motor development in the home environment for young children with and without CHARGE syndrome. *International Journal of Environmental Research and Public Health*, 18, 11936. https://doi.org/10.3390/ijerph182211936

Beach, P., Stribing, A., Perreault, M., and Lieberman, L. (2021b). Parent perceptions of movement skills in children with and without CHARGE syndrome. *European Journal of Adapted Physical Activity*, 14, 13. https://doi.org/10.5507/euj.2021.005

Brian, A., Getchell, N., True, L., De Meester, A., and Stodden, D. (2020). Reconceptualizing and operationalizing Seefeldt's proficiency barrier: Applications and future directions. *Sports Medicine*, 50, 1889–900. https://doi.org/10.1007/s40279-020-01332-6

Centers for Disease Control and Prevention. (2022, July 21). Data & statistics. Hearing loss in children. https://www.cdc.gov/ncbddd/hearingloss/data.html

National Organization for Rare Disorders, Inc. (2019). CHARGE syndrome. https://rarediseases.org/rare-diseases/charge-syndrome/

Conway, C.M., Pisoni, D.B., and Kronenberger, W.G. (2009). The importance of sound for cognitive sequencing abilities: the auditory scaffolding hypothesis. *Current Directions in Psychological Science*, 18, 275–79. https://10.1111/j.1467-8721.2009.01651.x

Dair, J., Ellis, M.K., and Lieberman, L.J. (2006). Prevalence of overweight among deaf children. *American Annals of the Deaf*, 151(3), 318–26.

Dammeyer, J. (2012). Development and characteristics of children with Usher syndrome and CHARGE syndrome. *International Journal of Pediatric Otorhinolaryngology*, 76, 1292–96. http://dx.doi.org/10.1016/j.ijporl.2012.05.021

De Kegel, A., Maes, L., Van Waelvelde, H., and Dhooge, I. (2015). Examining the impact of cochlear implantation on the early gross motor development of children with a hearing loss. *Ear Hear*, 36(3), e113–121. https://doi:10.1097/AUD0000000000000133

Delorme, A., Frigon, J.Y., and Lagace, C. (1989). Infants' reactions to visual movement of the environment. *Perception*, 18(5), 667–73. https://doi.org/10.1068/p180667

Denysschen, M., Coetzee, D., and Smits-Engelsman, B.C.M. (2021). Children with poor motor skills have lower health-related fitness compared to typically developing children. *Children*, 8(10), 867. http://dx.doi.org/10.3390/children8100867

Deuce, G., Howard, S., Rose, S., and Fuggle, C. (2012). A study of CHARGE syndrome in the UK. *British Journal of Visual Impairment*, 30(2), 91–100. https://doi.org/10.1177/0264619612443883

Dummer, G.M., Haubenstricker, J.L., and Stewart, D.A. (1996). Motor skill performances of children who are deaf. *Adapted Physical Activity Quarterly*, 13, 400–14.

Ellis, M.K. (2001). Influences of parents and school on sports participation and fitness levels of deaf children. *Palaestra*, 17(1), 44–49.

Ellis, M.K., Lieberman, L.J., Fittipauldi-Wert, J., and Dummer, G. (2005). Passing rates of deaf children on health-related fitness: How do they measure up? *Palaestra*, 21(3), 36–43.

Ellis, M.L., Lieberman, L.J., and Dummer, G.M. (2014). Parent influences on physical activity participation and physical fitness of deaf children. *The Journal of Deaf Studies and Deaf Education*, 19(2), 270–81. https://doi.org/10.1093/deafed/ent033

Fellinger, M.J., Holzinger, D., Aigner, M., Beitel, C., and Fellinger J. (2015). Motor performance and correlates of mental health in children who are Deaf or hard of hearing. *Dev. Med. Child. Neurol.*, 57, 942–47.

Foster, E.A., Silliman-French, L., and Grenier, M. (2020). Parents' perceptions of constraints impacting the development of walking in children with CHARGE syndrome. *Research and Practice for Persons with Severe Disabilities*, 45(3), 196–211. https://doi.org/10.1177/1540796920927656

Foster, E.A., Haibach-Beach, P., Lieberman, L.J., and Perreault, M.E. (2021). Strategies and activities to increase balance in children with CHARGE syndrome. *Journal of Visual Impairment & Blindness*, 115(1), 63–70. https://doi.org/10.1177/0145482X20987321

Foster, E., Lieberman, L., Perreault, M., and Haibach-Beach, P. (2019). Constraints model for improving motor skills in children with CHARGE Syndrome. *Palaestra*, 33(2), 39–44.

Fotiadou, E., Giagazoglou, P., Kokaridas, D., Angelopoulou, N., Tsimaras, V., and Tsorbatzoudis, C. (2010). Effect of rhythmic gymnastics on the dynamic balance of children with deafness, *European Journal of Special Needs Education*, 17(3), 301–09. https://doi.org/10.1080/08856250210162211

Haibach, P.S., and Lieberman, L.J. (2013). Balance and self-efficacy of balance in children with CHARGE syndrome. *Journal of Visual Impairment & Blindness*, 107(4), 297–309. https://doi.org/10.1177/0145482X1310700406

Haibach-Beach, P., Perreault, M., Foster, E., and Lieberman, L. (2019). Gross motor skill performance in children with and without CHARGE syndrome: Research to practice. *Research in Developmental Disabilities*, 91, 103423. https://doi.org/10.1016/j.ridd.2019.05.002

Haibach-Beach, P., Perreault, M., and Lieberman, L. (2022). Independent walking and balance in children with CHARGE syndrome. *British Journal of Visual Impairment*, 40(1), 94–103. https://doi.org/10.1177/0264619620946068

Haibach-Beach, P., Perreault, M., Lieberman, L.J., and Stribing, A. (2021). Associations between parent perspectives and motor competence in children with CHARGE syndrome. *Journal of Motor Learning and Development*, 9(2), 313–26. https://doi.org/10.1123/jmld.2020-0057

Hartman, E., Houwen, S., and Visscher, C. (2011). Motor skill performance and sports participation in deaf elementary school children. *Adapted Physical Activity Quarterly*, 28, 132–45.

Hartshorne, S., Hefner, M.A., Davenport, S.L.H., and Thelin, J.W. (2021). *CHARGE syndrome*. San Diego, CA: Plural Publishing.

Imel, G.E., Slavin, L.J., Hartshorne, T.S., and Kanouse, S.K. (2020). Participation in and barriers to recreation participation in CHARGE syndrome. *Palaestra*, 34(1), 38–43.

Jafarnezhadgero, A.A., Shad, M.M., Majliesi, M., and Granacher, U. (2017). A comparison of running kinetics in children with and without genu varus: A cross sectional study. *PLoS One*, 12(9), e0185057. https://doi.org/10.1371/journal.pone.0185057

Jenice, T.S.Y., and Nonis, K. (2017). The motor skills of adolescents with hearing impairment in a regular physical education environment. *International Journal of Special Education*, 32(3), 596–607.

Korver, A.M., Konings, S., Dekker, F.W., Beers, M., Wever, C.C., Frijns, J.H., Oudesluys-Murphy, A.M., and DECIBEL Collaborative Study Group. (2010). Newborn hearing screening vs later hearing screening and developmental outcomes in children with permanent childhood hearing impairment. *JAMA*, 304(15), 1701–08.

Lane, K., Lieberman, L.J., Haibach-Beach, P., Perreault, M., and Columna, L. (2021). Parental perspectives on physical education services for children with CHARGE syndrome. *Journal of Special Education*, 55(2), 90–100. https://doi.org/10.1177/0022466920942769

Leigh, G., Ching, T.Y., Crowe, K., Cupples, L., Marnane, V., and Seeto, M. (2015). Factors affecting psychosocial and motor development in 3-year old children who are deaf or hard of hearing. *Journal of Deaf Students & Deaf Education*, 20(4), 331–42. https://doi:10.1093/deafed/env028

Levesque, J., Theoret, H., and Champoux, F. (2014). Reduced procedural motor learning in deaf individuals. *Frontiers in Human Neuroscience*, 8, 1–6.

Lieberman, L.J. (2022). Hard of hearing and deafness. In D. Porretta and J.P. Winnick (eds.), *Adapted Physical Education & Sport*. Champaign, IL: Human Kinetics.

Lieberman, L.J., Beach, P., Perreault, M., Brian, A., and Bebrisa-Fedotova, L. (2021). Feasibility of a home motor skill intervention for children with CHARGE syndrome. *Research, Advocacy, and Practice for Complex and Chronic Conditions*, 40(1), 4–23. https://doi.org/10.14434/rapcc.v40i1.31710

Lieberman, L.J., Kirk, T.N., and Haegele, J.A. (2018). Physical education and transition planning experiences relating to recreation among adults who are deafblind: A recall analysis. *Journal of Visual Impairment and Blindness*, 112, 73–86.

Lieberman, L.J., Volding, L., and Winnick, J.P. (2004). A comparison of the motor development of deaf children of deaf parents and hearing parents. *American Annals for the Deaf*, 149(3), 281–89.

Masuda, T., and Kaga, K. (2014). Relationship between acquisition of motor function and vestibular function in children with bilateral severe hearing loss. *Acta Otolaryngology*, 134(7), 672–78. https://doi:10.3109/00016489.2014.890290

Mckee, R.L., Iseli, J., and Murray, A. (2019) Sign language interpreting in the Pacific: A snapshot of progress in raising the participation of deaf people. *Journal of New Zealand & Pacific Studies*, 7(2), 185–96.

McPhillips, M. (2015). Motor difficulties and mental health in children who are Deaf. *Dev. Med. Child. Neurol.*, 57, 893–94. https://doi:10.1111/dmcn.12831

Melo, R.S., Marinho, S.E.D.S., Freire, M.E.A., Souza, R.A., Damasceno, H.A.M., and Raposo, M.C.F. (2017). Static & dynamic balance of children & adolescents with sensorineural hearing loss. *Einstein*, 15(3), 262–68. https://doi:10.1590/S1679-45082017AO3976

Möller, C. (2011). Overview of balance and the vestibular system. In T.S. Hartshorne, M.A. Hefner, S.L.H. Davenport, and J.W. Thelin (eds.), *CHARGE Syndrome*. San Diego, CA: Plural Publishing.

Motasaddi Zarandy, M., Khorsandi, M.T., Rezazadeh, N., Yazdani, N., Mokhtarinejad, F., Bayat, A., et al. (2010). Vestibular dysfunctions in cochlear implant patients; A vestibular evoked myogenic potential study. Persian. *Audiology*, 19(2), 18–24.

National Center on Deaf-Blindness. (2022). About the National Center on Deaf-Blindness. https://www.nationaldb.org/about/#:~:text=There%20are%20approximately%2010%2C000%20children,of%20hearing%20and%20vision%20loss

National Institute on Deafness and Other Communication Disorders. (2021). *Quick statistics about hearing.* https://www.nidcd.nih.gov/health/statistics/quick-statistics-hearing

Paludetti, G., Conti, G., Di Nardo, W., De Corso, E., Rolesi, R., Picciotti, P.M., and Fetoni, A.R. (2012). Infant hearing loss: From diagnosis to therapy Official Report of XXI conference of Italian Society of Pediatric Otorhinolaryngology, *Acta Otorhinolaryngol Italy*, 32(6), 347–70.

Pagon, R.A., Graham Jr., J.M., and Zonana, J.Y.S.L. (1981). Coloboma, congenital heart disease, and choanal atresia with multiple anomalies: CHARGE association. *Journal of Pediatrics*, 99(2), 223–27.

Perreault, M., Haibach-Beach, P., Lieberman, L., and Foster, E. (2020). Relationship between motor skills, balance, and physical activity in children with CHARGE syndrome. *Journal of Visual Impairment & Blindness*, 114(4), 315–24. https://doi.org/10.1177/0145482X20939469

Perreault, M., Haibach-Beach, P., Lieberman, L., and Foster, E. (2021). Motor competence in children with CHARGE syndrome. *Research and Practice for Persons with Severe Disabilities*, 46(2), 67–76. https://doi.org/10.1177/1540796921998011

Radomir, A., Slavnic, S., and Kovacevic, J. (2012). Sports activities as a factor in socialization of deaf students. *Journal of Physical Education and Sport*, 12(1), 3–8.

Rajendran, V., and Roy, F. G. (2011). An overview of motor skill performance and balance in hearing impaired children. *Italian Journal of Pediatrics*, 37(1), 1–5.

Savelsbergh, G.J., Netelenbos, J.B., and Whiting, H.T. (1991). Auditory perception and the control of spatially coordinated action of deaf and hearing children. *Journal of Child Psychology & Psychiatry*, 32, 489–500. https://doi.10.1111/j.1469-7610.1991.tb00326.x

Seefeldt, V. (1980). Developmental motor patterns: Implications for elementary school physical education. In C. Nadeau, W. Holliwell, and G. Roberts (eds.), *Psychology of motor behavior and sport* (pp. 314–23). Champaign, IL: Human Kinetics.

Stodden, D.F., Goodway, J.D., Langendorfer, S.J., Roberton, M.A., Rudisill, M.E., Garcia, C., and Garcia, L.E. (2008). A developmental perspective on the role of motor skill competence in physical activity: An emergent relationship. *Quest*, 60, 290–306. https://doi.org/10.1080/00336297.2008.10483582

Suarez, H., Alonso, R., Arocena, S., Ferreira, E., Roman, C.S., Suarez, A., et al. (2017). Sensorimotor interaction in deaf children. Relationship between gait performance and hearing input during childhood assessed in pre-lingual cochlear implant users. *Acta Otolaryngology*, 137(4), 346–51. https://doi:10.1080/00016489.2016.1247496

Tegay, D., and Yedowitz, J. (2009). CHARGE syndrome. https://emedicine.medscape.com/article/942350-overview

Veiskarami, P., and Roozbahani, M. (2020). Motor development in deaf children based on Gallahue's model: A review study. *Audition & Vestibular Research*, 29(1), 10–25. https://doi.10.18502/avr.v29i1.2364

Zwierzchowska, A., Gawlik, K., and Grabara, M. (2008). Deafness & motor abilities level. *Biology of Sport*, 25(3), 263–74.

3

Motor Behavior and Sensory Processing Disorder

Candice Howard-Smith

■ ■ ■

OVERVIEW

This chapter provides an overview of sensory processing disorders and motor behavior. The chapter is divided into three sections with the first part focusing on sensory processing disorders, the second part focusing on the effects of sensory processing disorders on motor behavior, and the third part focusing on sensory processing disorders in children with disabilities and effects on motor behavior.

SENSORY PROCESSING DISORDERS

Sensory processing (sometimes called "sensory integration" [SI]) refers to the way the brain receives messages from the sensory receptors and elicits an appropriate motor and behavioral response. Most individuals are born with the ability to receive sensory information and unconsciously organize it into an appropriate motor and behavioral response. For example, if we touch a hot stove with our hand, we are able to retract our hand to prevent being burned. Simultaneously, our body produces a physiological response: increased respiration, increased heart rate, rise in blood pressure, etc. (Miller, 2006). SI was first studied and defined by Dr. Jean Ayres, an occupational therapist, in 1972 when she developed the theory and framework of SI. The Ayres Sensory Integration theory proposes that SI is a neurobiologic process that organizes and discriminates sensations received from one's body through sensory systems and makes it possible to use the body purposefully and appropriately to respond to the environment (Ayres, 1972). Since her work, researchers and practitioners have widely debated components of Ayres' theory and more recently use the term "sensory processing disorder" (SPD). SPD was first published by Dr. Lucy Miller in 2006 and is based on Ayres' original SI theory. SPD is when an individual's body does not have the ability to process sensory information from one or more of the senses, and does not have the ability to generate an appropriate motor and behavioral response. This leads to a decreased ability to respond to sensory information in a meaningful way and can lead to difficulty in applying sensory information. Because an individual cannot plan and organize body movements that properly interpret the environment from sensory information, their ability to learn is affected (Miller, 2006).

SPD can affect one's ability to function in all environments, adversely affecting a child's social skills, attention and focus, academic performance, and motor development. A person's level of responsivity (over-responsivity, under-responsivity, or sensory seeking) is closely related to their ability to interpret sensory stimuli and generate adaptive responses. Over-responsivity (sensory hypersensitivity) is when a response to stimuli is faster, longer, or more intense than what is expected. Under-responsivity (sensory hyposensitivity) is when an individual is slow to respond to sensory input, and the last type of responsivity is sensory seeking where individuals crave sensory experiences (Ghanizadeh, 2011). It is estimated that SPD affects 5 to 16 percent of school-aged children and can result in long-term intellectual and social development deficits (Owen et al., 2013). Children with SPD often do not demonstrate skills at the expected age level for motor and cognitive learning (Cermak, 1985). Some children exhibit difficulties playing with others and show signs of being less playful when compared to same-aged peers (Bar-Shalita et al., 2008). Research observing and evaluating play sessions indicates the use of developmental scales is useful in early identification of children with SPD. A study comparing children with SPD to those without found SPD to often be related to other pathologies such as autism, Down syndrome (DS), cerebral palsy, attention deficit disorders, developmental coordination disorder, and regulatory disorders (Bolanos et al., 2016).

Types of Sensory Processing Disorders
There are three main types of SPD, including sensory modulation disorder (SMD), sensory discrimination disorder (SDD), and sensory-based motor disorder (SBMD). "Sensory modulation" describes the ability to organize behavioral responses and reactions to sensory input, filter unnecessary input, and respond to relevant input. This capacity of human function affects the regulation of one's interactions with others and the environment (Bar-Shalita et al., 2005). SMD is characterized by extreme avoidant and defensive behaviors to sensory input that do not match the intensity of the sensory information. It has been estimated that 5 to 10 percent of the non-disabled population and 30 percent of children with disabilities experience unusual responses to sensory stimuli that interrupts participation in daily living activities at home, at school, and in the community (Baranek, 1998). Approximately 5 percent of the pediatric population in the United States has SMD. These children can over-react (sensory over-responsivity), under-react (sensory under-responsivity), or can crave sensory experiences (sensory seeking), all of which interfere with daily life functioning and learning (Bar-Shalita et al., 2008). Further using the example provided earlier of touching a hot stove, an individual with SMD may have a delayed response to touching a hot stove (under-respond). Some children over-respond, some do neither, and yet others seek additional sensory stimuli. Children with SMD seem to dislike light touch and do not like the feeling of certain textures such as food textures and clothing (i.e., do not like tags, certain fabrics, etc.). They find certain tactile stimuli to be irritating, unpleasant, and even painful. Some children with SMD exhibit delayed motor skill development due to the dislike of tactile stimuli. For example, an infant may not enjoy crawling or creeping on the floor because they do not like tactile stimulation of certain floor textures. Infants may have problems eating, sleeping, or playing. They may be considered "fussy" and do not like to be held or cuddled.

Toddlers may or may not engage in play with certain toys, and as the child decides not to touch and move due to their dislike of tactile stimuli, motor skill development is affected. While preschoolers tend to exhibit symptoms to include over-sensitivity to touch (i.e., crying when hair is brushed), noises (covers ears in class), and smells (does not like smells such as cleaning products), school-age children may have trouble paying attention, socializing, and learning (Critz et al., 2015). Research indicates it is imperative caregivers and practitioners provide support for children with SMD and facilitate participation in play and determine ways in which to engage children with SMD in behaviors and responses that are appropriate to stimuli (Critz et al., 2015).

Children with SDD cannot determine a response due to confusion of sensory stimuli. For example, a child who cannot tell by touch whether a coin is a nickel or a quarter has SDD as a tactile discrimination disorder. A child struggling to determine whether a food is lightly sweet or too sweet has SDD as a gustatory discrimination disorder. Commons signs of SDD are descriptive to the sense in which it is linked. For example, common signs of vestibular discrimination that may affect motor skill development include difficulty determining head or body position (kinesthetic awareness), poor perception of elevation, clumsiness, and constant falling and being unable to stop the self (Miller et al., 2009).

While SMD and SDD may contribute to motor development delays, SBMD is the SPD that is highly linked to motor development delays because of motor deficits in controlling, planning, and supporting balanced, coordinated actions such as opening a drawer and retrieving an item from the drawer (Miller, 2006). Dyspraxia and postural disorder are the two types of SBMD.

Children diagnosed with dyspraxia have difficulty creating physical, sequenced movements from sensory information such as planning how to walk across a room by walking around obstacles such as furniture to take an item to the garbage can. Dyspraxia affects large (gross motor) and small (fine motor) body movements. A child with dyspraxia not only has difficulty with planning, organizing, and executing motor actions (praxis), but memory and the speed of processing information can also be affected (Bodison, 2015). Symptoms may include poor balance and posture, fatigue, clumsiness, perception problems, speech problems, and poor hand-eye coordination. Children with dyspraxia may prefer to be sedentary; have trouble concentrating and processing thoughts (behavior); may exhibit clumsiness in the form of bumping into things, falling over, and dropping items (gross motor); and may have difficulty getting dressed, tying shoes, using a zipper, or buttoning a button (fine motor). Children with dyspraxia may be less playful than typically developing children, thereby limiting participation in age-related play and leisure activities (Bodison, 2015).

Postural disorder is the second type of SBMD. Children with postural disorder cannot maintain control of their bodies to initiate motor tasks. They may have poor muscle tone and seem weak when compared to peers. A child with postural disorder may appear lazy and unmotivated (behavior), may have difficulty using both hands at the same time (gross motor), and possibly has messy handwriting (fine motor). Postural disorder is often seen in combination with other subtypes of SPD. Studies show when dysfunction in the generation of ideas and participation in age-appropriate play and leisure activities occur, other areas of development to include motor development and behavior coincide.

SENSORY PROCESSING DISORDERS AND MOTOR BEHAVIOR

It is important to keep in mind the sensorimotor system seems to have been evolutionarily designed to reflexively respond to signals from the environment via various sensory receptors without the need for conscious activity as a survival mechanism. Research indicates children with SPD often have organization difficulties. They are distracted by their body's need for sensory integration and are challenged to focus on tasks at hand (i.e., motor response). SPD can impact self-organizing behavior influencing daily life activities, learning, and motor development (Galiana-Simal et al., 2020). The association of SPDs with specific neurodevelopmental disorders is frequent, particularly the sensory processing dysfunction related to social communicative deficits in autism spectrum disorder (ASD).

SENSORY PROCESSING DISORDERS, DISABILITIES, AND MOTOR BEHAVIOR

SPD is often linked with other disorders such as ASD (80 to 90 percent of cases) (Baranek et al., 2006), DS (49 percent), attention-deficit hyperactivity disorder (ADHD) (60 percent), and some diseases such as asthma (25.7 percent) and epilepsy (49 percent) (Bruni et al., 2010). SPD is also linked to anxiety and aggressive behavior in children. Although there is no identified origin, SPD development can be related to prenatal or birth complications, low birth weight (less than 2.2 kg/4.5–5 lbs), premature birth (less than thirty-two weeks of gestation), parental stress, alcohol and drug abuse during pregnancy, and genetic and environmental factors (Galiana-Simal et al., 2020).

Autism Spectrum Disorder

According to the *Diagnostic and Statistical Manual of Mental Disorders* (fifth edition), individuals with ASD demonstrate characteristics of hindered social communication, limited interests, and repetitive behaviors, to include sensory problems (American Psychiatric Association, 2013). SPD and ASD commonly overlap with over 90 percent of children with ASD also having sensory issues to include the most common of hypersensitivity to loud noise, touch, and light (Mulligan et al., 2019). Children with ASD that exhibit characteristics of sensory dysfunction have problems responding to sensations and specific stimuli (overstimulated or understimulated). These atypical sensory responses indicate poor sensory integration in the central nervous system. A study using diffusion tensor imaging (DTI) has been used to identify microstructure changes or differences in neuropathology. DTI detects how water travels along the white matter tracts in the brain. White matter is linked with sensory functioning, especially in the back of the brain where tracts are responsible for relaying sensory information. When children with and without SPD were compared using DTI, the DTI identified white matter tracts in the SPD subjects that serve as connections for auditory, visual, and tactile systems used in sensory processing, including both halves of the brain. The abnormality of the microstructure of the sensory white matter tracts identified likely alters the timing of sensory transmission. This causes processing of sensory stimuli and the integration of information of multiple senses to become difficult or impossible (Leigh, 2016). Further research is needed but this neurologic testing seems promising in identifying sensory challenges to better customize treatment for a child. Sensory-based programs and therapy are used to engage children in activities that provide vestibular, proprioceptive, auditory, and tactile inputs. Some studies have shown that the action and sensory integration in children with ASD show difficulty in visual space, kinesthetic sense, and activities that require multisensory integration and show stereotyped movements or SMs (Li et al., 2012). SMs are motor responses that occur frequently and at an excessive rate and are repetitious (American Psychiatric Association, 2013). SMs are a common part of appropriate motor development. The persistence of SMs beyond early childhood is considered to be linked to the child's diagnosed disorder, such as the inability to understand context or impaired functioning, which is the case with autism (Gal et al., 2010).

A study conducted with four hundred children with ASD that showed patterns of sensory processing issues reported six factors they found to be consistent: low energy/weak muscle strength, tactile and movement sensitivity, taste/smell sensitivity, auditory and visual sensitivity, sensory seeking, and hypo-responsivity. By using the Short Sensory Profile (a thirty-eight-item caregiver-report measure) in an ASD diagnosed population (average age five years, one month), Tomchek and colleagues (2014) found there are noted differences between ASD and non-ASD participants and support the notion there are qualitative differences in sensory processing in ASD when compared to that of non-ASD peers. Of the six factors studied, low energy/weak muscle strength and tactile and movement sensitivity were the highest indicators. Low energy and weak muscle strength were common along with tactile and movement sensitivity. Such indicators on Short Sensory Profile were items such as "becomes anxious or distressed when feet leave the ground" and "has difficulty standing in line or close to other people." Some items indicated could potentially impact learning and the child's ability to engage in activities to include daily functioning activities (Tomchek et al., 2014). Developments of this study provide direction for future sensory processing research with individuals with ASD to encourage early diagnosis, intervention, and practical implications. Karim and Mohammed (2015) investigated the effectiveness of sensory integration programs in children with ASD. Their work concluded sensory integration therapy increased motor skills in children with ASD. It assisted children with ASD to become more independent and participate in daily activities.

Down Syndrome
Although little is known about sensory processing difficulties with DS, several researchers have explored sensory processing difficulties within DS and behavior. In a study conducted by Wuang and Su (2011) in two hundred school-aged children with DS, approximately 41 percent of the children with DS were reported having "low registration," 40 percent low endurance/muscle tone (similar to findings by Tomchek et al., 2014, when studying children with ASD), and 39 percent sensory sensitivity. Bruni et al. (2010) studied children with DS and found the factor of low energy/weak muscle strength to be the highest indicator which makes a functional impact on motor behavior, while Will et al. (2019) found participants in their study to also have difficulties in the areas of low energy/weak muscle strength (65 percent) and under-responsivity/seeks sensation (35 percent). Both contributed to maladaptive behavior (i.e., behavior that interferes with daily living activities or ability to adjust and participate in a certain setting) which interrupts learning and impacts fine

and gross motor behavior. Will et al. (2019) found low energy/weak muscle strength along with decreased sensory regulation to be high factors consistent with sensory processing impairments and motor behavior.

Attention-Deficit Hyperactivity Disorder
Studies comparing children with ADHD with children without ADHD have researched the relationship between sensory processing difficulties and behavioral symptoms in children. In one such study, thirty-seven children with ADHD were compared with thirty-seven children without ADHD using the "Sensory Profile" answered by parents/caregivers, Child Behavior Check List, and the Behavioral Teaching Rating Scale. Shimizu and colleagues (2014) found children with ADHD showed significant impairments in sensory processing behaviors and behavioral and emotional responses when compared to the control group (without ADHD). Their study concluded children with ADHD present sensory processing impairments (that may be diagnosed as SPD) that account for behavioral and learning difficulties shown in children with ADHD. Ghanizadeh (2011) found sensory motor abilities of ADHD children are less than those of a control group (children without ADHD) and that sensory functioning highly correlates with academic achievement and cognitive processing in ADHD. The number of studies about SPD in children with ADHD are increasing but the underlying structure and pathophysiology is not well known in ADHD or other disabilities.

FUTURE RESEARCH

While mounds of information exist for SPDs, there is limited research of SPDs and disabilities, both of which can include motor behavior issues and/or limitations in motor development. In the area of SPDs, current studies indicate early motor and sensory processing skills should be monitored in high-risk infants to facilitate early identification and intervention. However, future research to include longitudinal studies to characterize the early signs of SPD could assist in identifying high-risk infants and improve results of intervention and school-based programs (Flanagan et al., 2019). Studies indicate low energy/weak muscle strength and endurance are factors common to children with ASD and DS. These factors are associated with under-responsivity and sensation seeking (sensory) that are associated with maladaptive behavior which interrupts learning and daily functioning (Gal et al., 2010; Ghanizadeh, 2011; Shimizu et al., 2014; Tomchek et al., 2014; Will et al., 2019). Researchers agree there is limited knowledge about sensory processing in children with ASD and DS and their relation to motor behavior. Most published articles regarding sensory problems rely on parental/caregiver reports. Currently, there is no research to identify underlying mental health disorders or other causes of non-reliant reporting by parents/caregivers for their children's sensory processing problems. It is not studied if parental psychiatric disorders such as anxiety and depression impact their report for their children's sensory processing issues. Another important step for future research is the development of psychometrically sound, performance-based instruments for diagnosing SPD, its types, and its subtypes. Research focused on studying the brain and its involvement in sensory processing and comparing it with that of children with neurodevelopmental conditions is needed (Mulligan et al., 2021). Research supports various sensory integration intervention, therapy, and educational programs (i.e., adapted physical education) to be effective in the treatment of those with ASD to become more independent and participate in everyday activities (Karim and Mohammed, 2015). However, there is limited research connecting research evidence to practical implementation regarding children with SPD and the effects on motor behavior. There are considerable differences between sensory systems, which may reflect the different types of information each system contributes to motor performance. As studies are conducted, there is a need for the information to be shared among clinical practitioners, educators, and families for intervention and program implementation (Sugiyama et al., 2017).

The same disconnect of research is found between sensory processing and children with ADHD. SPD in children with ADHD can impact behavior and education. Therefore, more developed, valid, and reliable measurements are needed to investigate different sensory systems. From research, educators and practitioners can determine how to properly address these issues for early and proper intervention and program implementation (Ghanizadeh, 2010). Future studies are needed to understand sensory processing difficulties for a child with ADHD to possibly contribute to identifying and diagnosing ADHD and preventing motor delays or limitations (Shimizu et al., 2014).

PRACTICAL IMPLICATIONS

Children with SPD benefit from fun, engaging activities that take place in a controlled yet stimulating environment. The purpose is to provide appropriate sensory stimuli without overwhelming the child, so always provide an out. Let the child know that if the environment becomes too overwhelming, they can let the teacher know and take a break. For a child with SPD, it is appropriate to seek out a multidisciplinary evaluation that includes occupational therapists, educators, and counselors (if necessary). Knowing the child's needs is imperative as if the child is over-responsive to noise, the child may need to wear noise-reducing headphones during class. Activities that utilize fine and gross motor skills addressing sensory and motor needs that assist a child in daily functioning activities are beneficial. The multidisciplinary team should derive goals in sensory and motor abilities to implement at home and the school setting. Activities that use gross motor skills, object control skills, functional skills, fine motor skills, and perceptual motor skills are taught in adapted physical education and general physical education and can be applied to everyday living activities. Skills may be taught in a different format or with modified equipment. It is important to teach one skill at a time and provide multiple modes of instruction. For example, visual perception and integration is used when catching and kicking a ball (both are object control skills). For a child with poor visual discrimination, judging the distance between their body and the object being caught or kicked is problematic. By using modified equipment (such as a lightweight beachball or a brightly colored ball), the student may be able to identify the ball in order to make contact (whether catching or kicking the ball). Another example is a child with SPD in the vestibular domain. The student may have poor body awareness and get disoriented easily. In physical education, this is "kinesthetic awareness." There are many activities that practice body awareness in physical education such as placing students in their own hula hoop and having them perform various skills such as hopping, jumping, or running in place, all while in their own hula hoop. This prevents them from running into a peer and allows them their own space for participation. Modifications to equipment, games, and exercises may be needed. Other teaching strategies to employ are starting and ending times for tasks, visual schedules, specific directions, and clear class rules and expectations. Use visual cues to demonstrate and indicate directions for games and activities. Emphasize a positive environment to all students and avoid bringing attention to a difficulty the child may be having in front of peers. By being educated and recognizing not all students with SPD have the same strengths and weaknesses, you as the educator can work with the multidisciplinary team to create an innovative, beneficial, and fun environment for the student.

CONCLUSION

Children with SPD are not born with the ability to receive sensory information and unconsciously organize it into an appropriate motor and behavioral response. Due to maladaptive behavior, children with SPD are often misinterpreted by peers. Children with SPD exhibit issues when eliciting motor responses whether they are sensory over-responsivity, sensory under-responsivity, or sensory seeking. Often, SPDs are associated with disabilities, with ASD, DS, and ADHD as the most common. Parents and practitioners must be aware of the child's particular needs to best accommodate the child in the school setting. Children with SPD and associated motor inabilities and/or a neurodevelopmental disorder can participate in physical activities and become physically active adults. A key component is early identification, proper early intervention, and consistent multidisciplinary strategies to provide opportunities for successful participation in adapted physical education or general physical education.

REFERENCES

American Psychiatric Association. (2013). *Diagnostic and statistical manual of mental disorders* (fifth edition). Washington, DC: American Psychiatric Association.

Ayres, A.J. (1972). Improving academic scores through sensory integration. *Journal of Learning Disabilities*, 5(6), 23–28.

Baranek, G.T. (1998). Sensory processing in persons with autism and developmental disabilities: considerations for research and clinical practice. *Sensory Integration Special Interest Quarterly*, 21, 1–3.

Baranek, G.T., David, F.J., Poe, M.D., Stone, W.L., and Watson, L.R. (2006). Sensory experiences questionnaire: Discriminating sensory features in young children with autism, developmental delays, and typical development. *Journal of Child Psychology and Psychiatry*, 47(6), 591–601.

Bar-Shalita, T., Goldstand, S., Hahn-Markowitz, J., and Parush, S. (2005). Typical children's responsivity patterns of the tactile and vestibular systems. *American Journal of Occupational Therapy*, 59, 148–56.

Bar-Shalita, T., Vatine, J.J., and Parush, S. (2008). Sensory modulation disorder: a risk factor for participation in daily life activities. *Developmental Medicine & Child Neurology*, 50, 932–37. https://doi:10.1111/j.1469-8749.2008.03095

Bodison, S. (2015). Developmental dyspraxia and the play skills of children with autism. *The American Journal of Occupational Therapy*, 69(5), 1–6.

Bolanos, C., Gomez, M.M., Ramos, G., and Rios J. (2016). Developmental risk signals as a screening tool for early identification of sensory processing disorders. *Journal of Occupational Therapy*, 23, 154–64. https://doi: 10.1002/oti.1420

Bruni, M., Cameron, D., Dua, S., and Noy, S. (2010). Reported sensory processing of children with down syndrome. *Physical & Occupational Therapy in Pediatrics, 30*(4), 280–93.

Cermak, S. (1985). *Neuropsychological studies of apraxia and related disorders*. Amsterdam: Elsevier Science.

Critz, C., Blake, K., and Nogueira, E. (2015). Sensory processing challenges in children. *The Journal for Nurse Practitioners, 11*(7), 710–16.

Flanagan, J.E., Schoen, S., and Miller, L.J. (2019). Early identification of sensory processing difficulties in high-risk infants. *The American Journal of Occupational Therapy, 73*(2).

Gal, E., Dyck, M.J., and Passmore, A. (2010). Relationships between stereotyped movements and sensory processing disorders in children with and without developmental or sensory disorders. *The American Journal of Occupational Therapy, 64*(3), 453–61.

Galiana-Simal, A., Vela-Romero, M., Romero-Vela, V.M., Oliver-Tercero, N., Garcia-Olmo, V., Benito-Castellanos, P.J., Munoz-Martinez, V., and Beato-Fernandez, L. (2020). Sensory processing disorder: Key points of a frequent alteration in neurodevelopmental disorders, *Cogent Medicine, 7*(1). https://doi.org/10.1080/2331205X.2020.1736829

Ghanizadeh, A. (2010). Targeting neurotensin as a potential novel approach for the treatment of autism. *Journal of Neuroinflammation, 7*(1), 58–60.

Ghanizadeh, A. (2011). Sensory processing problems in children with ADHD, a systematic review. *Psychiatric Investigation, 8*, 89–94.

Karim, A.E.A., and Mohammed, A.H. (2015). Effectiveness of sensory integration program in motor skills in children with autism. *The Egyptian Journal of Medical Human Genetics, 16*, 375–80. http://dx.doi.org/10.1016/j.ejmhg.2014.12.008

Leigh, S. (2016). Brain's wiring connected to sensory processing disorders. *Research*, 1–3.

Li, K., Lou, S., Tsai, H., and Shih, R. (2012). The effects of applying game-based learning to webcam motion sensory games for autistic students' sensory integration training. *Turkish Journal of Educational Technology, 11*(4), 451–59.

Miller, L.J. (2006). *Sensational kids*. New York: G.P. Putnam's Sons.

Miller, L.J., Nielsen, D.M., Schoen, S.A., and Brett-Green, B.A. (2009). Perspectives on sensory processing disorder: a call for translational research. *Frontiers in Integrative Neuroscience, 3*(22), 1–12. https://www.frontiersin.org/articles/10.3389/neuro.07.022.2009/full

Mulligan, S., Douglas, S., and Armstrong, C. (2021). Characteristics of idiopathic sensory processing disorder in young children. *Frontiers in Integrative Neuroscience, 15*, 1–10.

Mulligan, S., Schoen, S., Miller, L., Valdez, A., Wiggins, A., Hartford, B., and Rixon, A. (2019). Initial studies of validity of the sensory processing 3-dimenstions scale. *Physical & Occupational Therapy in Pediatrics, 39*, 94–106.

Owen, J.P., Marco, E.J., Desai, S., Fourie, E., Harris, J., Hill, S.S., Arnett, A.B., and Mukherjee, P. (2013). Abnormal white matter microstructure in children with sensory processing disorders. *NeuroImage: Clinical, 2*, 844–53. http://dx.doi.org/10.1016/j.nicl.2013.06.009

Shimizu, V.T., Bueno, O.F.A., and Miranda, M.C. (2014). Sensory processing abilities of children with ADHD. *Brazilian Journal of Physical Therapy, 18*(4), 343–52.

Sugiyama, T., Liew, S.L., and Chan, T.H. (2017). The effects of sensory manipulations on motor behavior: From basic science to clinical rehabilitation. *Journal of Motor Behavior, 49*(1), 67–77.

Tomchek, S.D., Huebner, R.A., and Dunn, W. (2014). Patterns of sensory processing in children with an autism spectrum disorder. *Research in Autism Spectrum Disorders, 8*, 1214–24.

Will, E.A., Daunhauer, L.A., Fidler, D.J., Lee, N.R., Rosenberg, C.R., and Hepburn, S.L. (2019). Sensory processing and maladaptive behavior: Profiles within the down syndrome phenotype. *Physical & Occupational Therapy in Pediatrics, 39*(5), 461–76.

Wuang, Y., and Su, C. (2011). Correlations of sensory processing and visual organization ability with participation in school-aged children with down syndrome. *Research in Developmental Disabilities, 32*(6), 2398–407.

4

Motor Behavior and Autism Spectrum Disorder

Ming-Chih Sung and Megan MacDonald

■ ■ ■

OVERVIEW

Autism spectrum disorder (ASD) is a pervasive developmental disorder affecting people all over the world. In the United States, ASD affects about one in forty-four people and is commonly diagnosed during childhood (Centers for Disease Control and Prevention, 2020). The characteristics associated with ASD primarily affect a person's social communicative skills and repetitive behaviors or restricted interests. While there is much research focused on the etiology of ASD, the evidence suggests genetic underpinnings. In recent years it has gained much public attention, notably because its prevalence has risen substantially over the past two decades (Maenner, 2020). In 2007, the American Academy of Pediatrics recommended that every child was screened for ASD twice before their second birthday, a profound public health measure to ensure early screening for ASD, a pervasive developmental disability. In the United States, pediatricians and other healthcare workers have conducted screenings diligently during young children's well child visits.

Since early in the 2000s, diagnostic tools have improved with substantial changes from 2000 to 2010, including the creation of gold standard behavioral assessments (e.g., Autism Diagnostic Observation Schedule™, second edition; Autism Diagnostic Interview—Revised) and algorithms more accurately depicting the "severity of ASD" (Gotham et al., 2006; Gotham et al., 2009; Lord et al., 2012; also review ADI-R updates combined for better practice). The great news is that better and more accurate diagnostic tools have helped to identify ASD earlier, ultimately resulting in earlier service access to children with or at risk for ASD early in life. These tools have also likely contributed to the misdiagnosis of ASD as something else (e.g., intellectual or developmental disability). Their specific focus on ASD characteristics has been critical with respect to holistic diagnostic practices, which also include more traditional cognition and language assessments (Risi et al., 2006). Of interest, one of the earliest diagnostic markers that have been indicated in young children with ASD is motor behavior related: head lag. Landa's group found that one of the earliest indicators of risk for ASD in infant siblings (infants with high risk of ASD based on having a biological older sibling diagnosed with ASD) who were later diagnosed with ASD had early delays in head lag (Flanagan et al., 2012).

To that end, motor behaviors are essential early in life; they provide foundational means for children to interact with their surroundings (Robinson et al., 2015). For example, fine motor skills involve small muscles of hands, fingers, and forearms and provide movement needed for reaching, grasping, manipulating objects, and handwriting, which are essential for performing activities of daily living such as eating, playing, dressing, and engaging in academic activities (Grissmer et al., 2010). Gross motor skills, on the other hand, involve movement and coordination of larger muscles in the legs and torso for walking, running, and jumping, which help children navigate their surroundings and participate in physical activities and sports (Lin et al., 2017). The positive trajectory of motor skills could also impact various fundamental aspects of child development, including school readiness (Cameron et al., 2015), academic performance (Greenburg et al., 2020; Macdonald et al., 2018), social interaction (Leonard and Hill, 2014), and physical well-being (Barnett et al., 2016). The evidence highlights the need to foster motor skills development in early childhood.

While social and communication impairments are the defining feature of individuals with ASD including older children, motor behavior deficits and delays are often observed (West, 2019). Empirical research has revealed that people with ASD have a moderate to high prevalence of motor difficulty as they age, ranging from atypical gait patterns to handwriting difficulties. Dewey et al. (2007) reported that 59 percent of children with ASD were classified as motor functioning impaired, Liu and Breslin (2013) stated that 77 percent of children with ASD experienced significant motor delays, Green et al. (2009) identified 79 percent of children with ASD had motor problems, Hilton et al. (2012) found that 83 percent of children with ASD demonstrated motor impairments, and Bhat (2020) revealed that 87 percent of school-aged children with ASD were at risk for motor impairment. While the prevalence of motor impairments in people with ASD varies, reflecting different sample sizes, age ranges, and methods of evaluation used in different studies, the evidence showcases that motor impairment constitutes a core characteristic of ASD. The early delays and high prevalence of motor impairment pose opportunities for intervention. The good news is that motor skill development is malleable (see chapter 5), with the right interventions and supports.

The motor impairments exhibited in people with ASD could be explained by the differences in neural connectivity between brain areas among individuals with ASD (Hanaie et al., 2013; Mostofsky et al., 2009). For example, evidence has shown that increased asynchrony between visual and motor regions was observed in children with ASD, with less synchronization showing more severe autistic traits (Nebel et al., 2016). In addition, the motor deficits observed in this population might be a result of reduced connectivity within frontal and parietal cortices and cerebellum; all of these areas involve the function of motor planning and control. Further, atypical sensory and motor connections were implicated in empirical research on individuals with ASD (Thompson et al., 2017). These neuroanatomical studies provided the initial evidence of motor impairments in individuals with ASD.

The mastery of motor skills has been purported to contribute to individuals' physical, cognitive, and social development and is further recognized to lay the foundation for an active lifestyle. However, the motor deficits and delays might impact a variety of developmental and functional aspects of people with ASD. For instance, deficiencies in manual dexterity can affect a person's activities of daily living, writing, and object control. Gross motor deficits can hinder a person's willingness to participate in physical activities or sports, which will have a cascading effect on other health aspects. Without knowing the evidence of motor behaviors and development in the autism population, service providers, interventionists, educators, and other professionals can only guess at appropriate educational techniques and strategies for facilitating motor behavior development. Thus, the following content is focused on summarizing the extant empirical research examining motor behavior and development in people with ASD at different developmental stages.

YOUNG CHILDREN (INFANTS AND PRESCHOOLERS) WITH AUTISM SPECTRUM DISORDER

In the mid-twentieth century, Kanner (1943) reported a group of *young* children with ASD as being "somewhat clumsy in their gait and gross motor performances" while they performed well in fine motor skills. After that, there has been a dramatic proliferation of research concerned with motor behaviors among young children with ASD. Although evidence has indicated the delays or deficits of motor behaviors started early in the development of children with ASD, including delays in motor milestones (Harris, 2017; Liu, 2012), abnormal muscle tone and reflexes (Serdarevic et al., 2017; Shetreat-Klein et al., 2014), motor stereotypies (Melo et al., 2020), fine and gross motor skills (Landa et al., 2013; Lloyd et al., 2013), and postural instability (Travers et al., 2013), motor symptomatology is not *currently* included in the diagnostic criteria for ASD.

Recent years have seen a burgeoning of using motor assessments as early detection markers in infants and toddlers who have a higher probability of developing ASD than the general population. For instance, a hallmark prospective study conducted by Landa and Garrett-Mayer (2006) utilized a longitudinal research design to examine eighty-seven infants at high risk (siblings of children with ASD) and low risk (no family history of ASD) at the ages of six, fourteen, and twenty-four months using the Mullen Scales of Early Learning. They further categorized these participants into three groups: ASD (n = 24), language delayed (n = 11), and unaffected group (n = 52) based on language test, Autism Diagnostic Observation Schedule, and clinical judgment at twenty-four months of their age. Their results indicated that motor skills deficits were evident in children with ASD at fourteen and twenty-four months of age compared to children with language delays and typical development, especially in gross and fine motor skills.

Similar findings were revealed by Lloyd and colleagues (2013). Their study involved a large sample of 162 children with ASD aged twelve to thirty-six months for cross-sectional comparison, in which fifty-eight of them were followed longitudinally. The Mullen Scales of Early Learning was used to objectively measure their fine and gross motor skill. Results indicated that the differences in fine and gross motor skills among children with ASD became progressively more delayed with each six-month period of chronological age, and these developmental gaps for gross and fine motor skills became more pronounced in young children with ASD at an older age. Notably, in the same study the cross-sectional result was confirmed with a longitudinal subsample from the group. In the same vein, Provost et al. (2007) evaluated the motor skills of three groups of young children aged twenty-one to forty-one months (n = 56): children with ASD, children with developmental delay, and children with developmental concerns without motor delay. Results showed that children with ASD had delays in fine and gross motor skills and more than 60 percent of children with ASD qualified for early intervention. Together, these studies underscored the importance of measuring motor skills early on with a large sample size and longitudinal design study. Further, the existence of motor delays or deficits could be the earliest indicator in the diagnosis of autism. Thus, the possibility that motor impairments might substantially contribute to the clinical profile of young children with ASD should not be over-looked.

SCHOOL-AGED CHILDREN WITH AUTISM SPECTRUM DISORDER

Proficient motor skills are not only essential for foundational skills but also for complex exercise and sport-specific skills needed to participate in various physical activities and sports. For instance, object control skills and balance are required in participating in school playground games (e.g., hopscotch and four-square) during recess or after school; locomotor skills and coordination are crucial for engaging in sports (e.g., soccer and basketball). However, empirical evidence revealed motor impairments in school-aged children with ASD in multiple areas, including manual dexterity (Liu et al., 2021), gross motor coordination (Fournier et al., 2010; Hilton et al., 2007), ball skills (Berkeley et al., 2001), and static and dynamic balance (Fournier, et al., 2010).

Jansiewicz and colleagues (2006) evaluated motor control between forty children with ASD and fifty-five typically developing children aged six to seventeen years. Motor control was measured using the Physical and Neurological Exam for Subtle Signs, an assessment for subtle neurological signs and motor skills in children. Their results indicated that children with ASD demonstrated impairments in balance and gait, slower speed and more dysrhythmia with timed movements of the hands and feet, and greater overflow during movement performance compared to their typically developing peers. Similarly, Pan (2014) examined the motor proficiency of sixty-two children with (n = 31) and without (n = 31) ASD aged ten to seventeen years using Bruininks–Oseretsky Test of Motor Proficiency, second edition (BOT-2). Findings indicated that children with ASD performed significantly poorer on all domains of BOT-2, including fine motor control, manual coordination, body coordination, and strength and agility than children without ASD. A study by Liu et al. (2021) also suggested that children with ASD aged seven to fourteen years demonstrated significantly delayed in all subtests of BOT-2 mentioned earlier.

A seminal paper by Staple and Reid (2010) measured the motor skills of twenty-five school-aged children with ASD compared with three typically developing comparison groups, each individually matched according to (a) chronological age, (b) movement skill performance, and (c) mental age. The Test of Gross Motor Development was utilized to measure participants' motor skills. Results indicated that (a) children with ASD exhibited significantly poorer locomotor and object control scores compared with their typically developing peers matched in the chronological group, (b) children with ASD performed similarly to the group matched on movement skills approximately half their age, and (c) children with ASD demonstrated more impaired motor skills than the typically developing group matched on mental age equivalence, reflecting both deficits and delays in locomotor and object control skills among children with ASD. This study painted a visual picture—imagining school-aged children with ASD performing motor skills similarly to children about half their age (e.g., a ten-year-old performing like a five-year-old) really hones in on other related implications, for example peer play, age-related sport and physical activity interests, and to a degree independence (e.g., two-wheeled bicycle riding related to active transportation).

Motor skill proficiency lays the foundation for being physically active, participating in a variety of sports, and contributing to other developmental aspects and beyond (Stodden et al., 2008). The evidence mentioned earlier, however, suggests that school-aged children with ASD demonstrated less proficiency in motor skills than their typically developing peers. Thus, improving various domains of motor skills, including fundamental motor skills and sports-related motor skills, should be recognized as a priority as it helps achieve sufficient physical activity levels and maintain aspects of health-related fitness. To ensure that children with ASD can continue to participate in sports and recreational activities as they age, it is critical to address the needs for motor skill development in children with ASD as early as possible.

A debated area within the field of motor development is whether motor skills relate to intellectual/cognitive abilities in children with ASD (Ramos-Sánchez et al., 2022; Yu et al., 2018). Some research has indicated that motor function is significantly associated with IQ in children with ASD. For example, Green et al. (2009) conducted a study including a large population-derived group of school-aged children with ASD demonstrating a wide range of IQ. The fine and gross motor skills of 101 children with ASD aged ten to fourteen years (eighty-nine males, twelve females) were examined using Movement Assessment Battery for Children. The study found that 79.2 percent of children with ASD had motor problems, and the motor impairments was more common and more severe in children with ASD with lower-level IQ (IQ < 70) compared to those with higher IQ (IQ ≥ 70). Other studies, however, have suggested that motor impairments are universal in people with ASD, regardless of their IQ levels (Kaur et al., 2018). A study by Kaur and colleagues (2018) utilized a comprehensive profile of motor function assessments to evaluate three groups of children aged five to twelve years: children with ASD with high IQ (IQ > 70), children with ASD with low IQ (IQ ≤ 70), and typically developing children. Results indicated that motor impairment was pervasive in both ASD groups, including fine and gross motor performance, praxis/imitation, and bilateral coordination. In addition, both high and low IQ children with ASD were equally impaired in most motor functions. Overall, the lack of consensus regarding whether motor skills pertain to IQ/cognitive skills in ASD warrants further investigation.

BEYOND SCHOOL: LIFESPAN MOTOR SKILLS OF INDIVIDUALS WITH AUTISM SPECTRUM DISORDER

While considerable attention has been given to the motor delays and deficits in children with ASD, to date, there has been far less research within the field of motor development on motor behaviors of adults with ASD across the lifespan.

Munoz Orozco et al. (2021) examined skipping performance and kinematics in twenty college students with and without ASD. A combination of Everyone Can! and the Halverson Developmental Sequences for Skipping was used to measure skipping performance. Kinematic data was captured using a three-dimensional, twelve-camera motion capture system that was placed on the upper and lower extremities of participants. Their results revealed that young adults with ASD demonstrated less proficiency in skipping performance than young adults without ASD; however, these findings were not reflected in the biomechanical kinematics analysis, with the exception of the increased medial-lateral center of mass excursion in individuals with ASD. The increased center of mass excursion suggests that people with ASD might have difficulty coordinating and might lack the sufficient strength and stability to move themselves forward, therefore compensating by moving in a side-to-side motion. This evidence suggests that motor skill deficits, especially skipping, may persist into adulthood.

More recently, Todd et al. (2020) evaluated the kinematics and developmental level of overhand throws among twenty college students with and without ASD. Roberton's developmental sequence of throwing and a twelve-camera, three-dimensional motion capture system with two force plates were used to measure overhand throw performance. The findings revealed that young adults with ASD were less proficient at the overarm throw than young adults without ASD. Specifically, the kinematic analysis revealed a statistically significant difference in ball velocity and a difference approaching significance in the duration of the acceleration phase of the throw. Such results suggested that motor deficits, especially overhand throws, are more likely to persist into adulthood in this population.

The evidence of motor performance found in adults with ASD is concerning, given that skipping and overhand throws are used in various leisure activities and sports. These findings may partially explain the lower levels of physical activity and less motivation for sports participation among individuals with ASD. Without the ability to perform these motor skills proficiently, people with ASD might be reluctant to participate in sports and other recreational activities to the same extent as their typically developing peers. Although the aforementioned studies showed initial evidence regarding motor skills in adults with ASD, this is an imperative avenue for future studies to further investigate, given the importance of motor skills needed to promote a healthy, active lifestyle through engaging in physical and recreational activities and sports among individuals with ASD.

SUMMARY OF EVIDENCE

The good news is that the motor behavior of people with ASD has been more readily studied in recent years, and motor behavior and its related impacts on participation and daily life for people with ASD have been growing. Of note, the pervasiveness of motor skill delays and deficits in people with ASD starts early and persists. When Lloyd et al. (2013) examined the motor skills of a group of young children with ASD, the results indicated a nine-month to one-year delay in both fine and gross motor skills at thirty-six months (three years old). Staples and Reid (2010) found that school-aged children with ASD were qualitatively performing motor skills similar to children about half their age (e.g., a ten-year-old performing motor skills similar to a five-year-old). And while there has been a paucity of empirical research focused specifically on lifetime motor development in adults with ASD, the evidence indicates proficiency deficits. Given known links between better motor skills and other aspects of development (e.g., MacDonald et al., 2013), and the widespread impacts of motor skill development on daily living, it is surprising that there has not been more focus on motor skills.

While motor skill development is gaining attention, the global nature of the deficits (e.g., development, coordination, and chaining various movements together) leaves space for specific mechanistic questions (e.g., is development generally delayed or does it regress?). Furthermore, as indicated in chapter 5, motor skill development is malleable, and time on task, as well as adapted equipment and individualized instruction, can be key with respect to learning. How motor skill development is prioritized in intervention, education, and an individual's personal goals matters. The primary focus of early intervention, education, and adult learning on core characteristics of ASD for people with ASD is laudable. Yet it is time to break down some of the silos; the evidence encourages it—motor skill development does impact aspects of social communication skills and restricted and repetitive interests. In fact, many interventions include aspects of physically active behavior, but what is limiting is the assumption that the prerequisite motor skills exist, and the intentionality of how motor skill development is taught and adapted for people with ASD.

There is work to do and opportunity to examine and build upon the empirical work that has been conducted to date.

FUTURE RESEARCH

Future directions are abundant; most notably, developing and testing effective interventions aimed at improving motor skill development for people with ASD at all ages is a high priority. Careful, intentional, and science-driven studies need to be conducted in order to holistically create programs that are feasible to be implanted by practitioners (educators) and the general population.

Notably, more empirical work has focused on mechanisms associated with core characteristics of ASD, yet the specific relationship of various aspects of motor skills and the inclusion of motor skills in related interventions needs to be studied. Working together with peers within and beyond and field will be critical toward providing the access and opportunity to all people.

PRACTICAL IMPLICATIONS

Based on the information mentioned, this chapter proposes several practical implications. First, motor impairments should be an integral part of the core difficulties faced by people with ASD. Comprehensive motor measurements are warranted for individuals with ASD, regardless of age, and for infants at risk for ASDs. A variety of motor impairments in individuals with ASD are a critical focus of assessments. Thus, clinicians and practitioners should evaluate all aspects of motor behaviors in ASD using a comprehensive battery of standardized tests as well as behavioral tasks. Second, understanding early motor skill status among children with ASD is vital for facilitating other developmental domains. Educators and practitioners can help facilitate physical activity participation and development of physical fitness in children with ASD through teaching their motor skills. Thus, children with ASD can reap the benefits from other developmental domains by improving their motor skills. Lastly, when interventions are recommended for people with ASD, the multisystem nature of autism necessitates an interdisciplinary team approach in which physical educators, camp directors, physical therapists, occupational therapists, and physical activity promotion specialists should collaborate with families to evaluate, intervene, and prevent further progression of motor impairments in this population. In sum, service providers play a significant role in understanding and assessing motor behavior among individuals with ASD, which could lay a foundation for further interventions to facilitate their motor development.

REFERENCES

Barbeau, E.B., Meilleur, A.A. S., Zeffiro, T.A., and Mottron, L. (2015). Comparing motor skills in autism spectrum individuals with and without speech delay. *Autism Research*, 8(6), 682–93. https://doi.org/10.1002/aur.1483

Barnett, L.M., Lai, S.K., Veldman, S.L.C., Hardy, L.L., Cliff, D.P., Morgan, P.J., Zask, A., Lubans, D.R., Shultz, S.P., Ridgers, N.D., Rush, E., Brown, H.L., and Okely, A.D. (2016). Correlates of gross motor competence in children and adolescents: A systematic review and meta-analysis. *Sports Medicine*, 46(11), 1663–88. https://doi.org/10.1007/s40279-016-0495-z

Berkeley, S.L., Zittel, L.L., Pitney, L.V., and Nichols, S.E. (2001). Locomotor and object control skills of children diagnosed with autism. *Adapted Physical Activity Quarterly*, 18(4), 405–16. https://doi.org/10.1123/apaq.18.4.405

Bhat, A.N. (2020). Is motor impairment in autism spectrum disorder distinct from developmental coordination disorder? A report from the SPARK Study. *Physical Therapy*, 100(4), 633–44. https://doi.org/10.1093/ptj/pzz190

Cameron, C.E., Brock, L.L., Hatfield, B.E., Cottone, E.A., Rubinstein, E., LoCasale-Crouch, J., and Grissmer, D.W. (2015). Visuomotor integration and inhibitory control compensate for each other in school readiness. *Developmental Psychology*, 51(11), 1529–43. https://doi.org/10.1037/a0039740

Cameron, C.E., Cottone, E.A., Murrah, W.M., and Grissmer, D.W. (2016). How are motor skills linked to children's school performance and academic achievement? *Child Development Perspectives*, 10(2), 93–98. https://doi.org/10.1111/cdep.12168

Centers for Disease Control and Prevention. (2020, March 25). Data and statistics on autism spectrum disorder. https://www.cdc.gov/ncbddd/autism/data.html

Dewey, D., Cantell, M., and Crawford, S.G. (2007). Motor and gestural performance in children with autism spectrum disorders, developmental coordination disorder, and/or attention deficit hyperactivity disorder. *Journal of the International Neuropsychological Society*, 13(02). https://doi.org/10.1017/S1355617707070270

Fernandes, V.R., Ribeiro, M.L.S., Melo, T., de Tarso Maciel-Pinheiro, P., Guimarães, T.T., Araújo, N.B., Ribeiro, S., and Deslandes, A.C. (2016). Motor coordination correlates with academic achievement and cognitive function in children. *Frontiers in Psychology*, 7. https://doi.org/10.3389/fpsyg.2016.00318

Flanagan, J.E., Landa, R., Bhat, A., and Bauman, M. (2012). Head lag in infants at risk for autism: A preliminary study. *The American Journal of Occupational Therapy*, 66(5), 577–85. https://doi.org/10.5014/ajot.2012.004192

Fournier, K.A., Hass, C.J., Naik, S.K., Lodha, N., and Cauraugh, J.H. (2010). Motor coordination in autism spectrum disorders: A synthesis and meta-analysis. *Journal of Autism and Developmental Disorders*, 40(10), 1227–40.

Fournier, K.A., Kimberg, C.I., Radonovich, K.J., Tillman, M.D., Chow, J.W., Lewis, M.H., Bodfish, J.W., and Hass, C.J. (2010). Decreased static and dynamic postural control in children with autism spectrum disorders. *Gait & Posture*, 32(1), 6–9. https://doi.org/10.1016/j.gaitpost.2010.02.007

Gotham, K., Pickles, A., and Lord, C. (2009). Standardizing ADOS scores for a measure of severity in autism spectrum disorders. *Journal of Autism and Developmental Disorders*, 39(5), 693–705. https://doi.org/10.1007/s10803-008-0674-3

Gotham, K., Risi, S., Pickles, A., and Lord, C. (2006). The Autism Diagnostic Observation Schedule: Revised algorithms for improved diagnostic validity. *Journal of Autism and Developmental Disorders*, 37(4), 613. https://doi.org/10.1007/s10803-006-0280-1

Green, D., Charman, T., Pickles, A., Chandler, S., Loucas, T., Simonoff, E., and Baird, G. (2009). Impairment in movement skills of children with autistic spectrum disorders. *Developmental Medicine & Child Neurology*, 51(4), 311–16. https://doi.org/10.1111/j.1469-8749.2008.03242.x

Greenburg, J.E., Carlson, A.G., Kim, H., Curby, T.W., and Winsler, A. (2020). Early visual-spatial integration skills predict elementary school achievement among low-income, ethnically diverse children. *Early Education and Development*, 31(2), 234–52. https://doi.org/10.1080/10409289.2019.1636353

Grissmer, D., Grimm, K.J., Aiyer, S.M., Murrah, W.M., and Steele, J.S. (2010). Fine motor skills and early comprehension of the world: Two new school readiness indicators. *Developmental Psychology*, 46(5), 1008–17. https://doi.org/10.1037/a0020104

Hanaie, R., Mohri, I., Kagitani-Shimono, K., Tachibana, M., Azuma, J., Matsuzaki, J., Watanabe, Y., Fujita, N., and Taniike, M. (2013). Altered microstructural connectivity of the superior cerebellar peduncle is related to motor dysfunction in children with autistic spectrum disorders. *The Cerebellum*, 12(5), 645–56. https://doi.org/10.1007/s12311-013-0475-x

Harris, S.R. (2017). Early motor delays as diagnostic clues in autism spectrum disorder. *European Journal of Pediatrics*, 176(9), 1259–62. https://doi.org/10.1007/s00431-017-2951-7

Hilton, C., Wente, L., LaVesser, P., Ito, M., Reed, C., and Herzberg, G. (2007). Relationship between motor skill impairment and severity in children with Asperger syndrome. *Research in Autism Spectrum Disorders*, 1(4), 339–49. https://doi.org/10.1016/j.rasd.2006.12.003

Hilton, C.L., Zhang, Y., Whilte, M.R., Klohr, C.L. and Constantino, J. (2012). Motor impairment in sibling pairs concordant and discordant for autism spectrum disorders. *Autism*, 16(4), 430–41.

Jansiewicz, E.M., Goldberg, M.C., Newschaffer, C.J., Denckla, M.B., Landa, R., and Mostofsky, S.H. (2006). Motor signs distinguish children with high functioning autism and Asperger's syndrome from controls. *Journal of Autism and Developmental Disorders*, 36(5), 613–21. https://doi.org/10.1007/s10803-006-0109-y

Kanner, L. (1943). Autistic disturbances of affective contact. *Nervous Child*, 2(3), 217–50.

Kaur, M., M. Srinivasan, S., and N. Bhat, A. (2018). Comparing motor performance, praxis, coordination, and interpersonal synchrony between children with and without autism spectrum disorder (ASD). *Research in Developmental Disabilities*, 72, 79–95. https://doi.org/10.1016/j.ridd.2017.10.025

Landa, R., and Garrett-Mayer, E. (2006). Development in infants with autism spectrum disorders: a prospective study. *Journal of Child Psychology and Psychiatry*, 47(6), 629–38.

Landa, R.J., Gross, A.L., Stuart, E.A., and Faherty, A. (2013). Developmental trajectories in children with and without autism spectrum disorders: The first 3 years. *Child Development*, 84(2), 429–42. https://doi.org/10.1111/j.1467-8624.2012.01870.x

Leonard, H.C., and Hill, E.L. (2014). Review: The impact of motor development on typical and atypical social cognition and language: a systematic review. *Child and Adolescent Mental Health*, 19(3), 163–70. https://doi.org/10.1111/camh.12055

Lin, L.-Y., Cherng, R.-J., and Chen, Y.-J. (2017). Relationship between time use in physical activity and gross motor performance of preschool children. *Australian Occupational Therapy Journal*, 64(1), 49–57. https://doi.org/10.1111/1440-1630.12318

Liu, T. (2012). Motor milestone development in young children with autism spectrum disorders: An exploratory study. *Educational Psychology in Practice*, 28(3), 315–26. https://doi.org/10.1080/02667363.2012.684340

Liu, T., and Breslin, C.M. (2013). Fine and gross motor performance of the MABC-2 by children with autism spectrum disorder and typically developing children. *Research in Autism Spectrum Disorders*, 7(10), 1244–49. https://doi.org/10.1016/j.rasd.2013.07.002

Liu, T., Capistran, J., and ElGarhy, S. (2021). Fine and gross motor competence in children with autism spectrum disorder. *The Physical Educator*, 78(3). https://doi.org/10.18666/TPE-2021-V78-I3-9644

Lloyd, M., MacDonald, M., and Lord, C. (2013). Motor skills of toddlers with autism spectrum disorders. *Autism*, 17(2), 133–46. https://doi.org/10.1177/1362361311402230

Lord, C., Rutter, M., DiLavore, P.C., Risi, S., Gotham, K., and Bishop, S. (2012). *Autism diagnostic observation schedule–2nd edition (ADOS-2)*. Torrance, CA: Western Psychological Corporation.

Macdonald, K., Milne, N., Orr, R., and Pope, R. (2018). Relationships between motor proficiency and academic performance in mathematics and reading in school-aged children and adolescents: A systematic review. *International Journal of Environmental Research and Public Health*, 15(8), 1603. https://doi.org/10.3390/ijerph15081603

MacDonald, M., Lord, C., and Ulrich, D.A. (2013). The relationship of motor skills and social communicative skills in school-aged children with autism spectrum disorder. *Adapted Physical Activity Quarterly*, 30(3), 271–82. https://doi.org/10.1123/apaq.30.3.271

Maenner, M.J. (2020). Prevalence of autism spectrum disorder among children aged 8 years—Autism and Developmental Disabilities Monitoring Network, 11 Sites, United States, 2016. *MMWR. Surveillance Summaries*, 69. https://doi.org/10.15585/mmwr.ss6904a1

Melo, C., Ruano, L., Jorge, J., Pinto Ribeiro, T., Oliveira, G., Azevedo, L., and Temudo, T. (2020). Prevalence and determinants of motor stereotypies in autism spectrum disorder: A systematic review and meta-analysis. *Autism*, 24(3), 569–90. https://doi.org/10.1177/1362361319869118

Mostofsky, S.H., Powell, S.K., Simmonds, D.J., Goldberg, M.C., Caffo, B., and Pekar, J.J. (2009). Decreased connectivity and cerebellar activity in autism during motor task performance. *Brain*, 132(9), 2413–25. https://doi.org/10.1093/brain/awp088

Munoz Orozco, I., Hernandez, K., Mata, J., Todd, T., Mache, M., and Jarvis, D. (2021). Evaluation of skipping in college students with and without autism spectrum disorder. *International Journal of Exercise Science: Conference Proceedings*, 14(1). https://digitalcommons.wku.edu/ijesab/vol14/iss1/5

Nebel, M.B., Eloyan, A., Nettles, C.A., Sweeney, K.L., Ament, K., Ward, R.E., Choe, A.S., Barber, A.D., Pekar, J.J., and Mostofsky, S.H. (2016). Intrinsic visual-motor synchrony correlates with social deficits in autism. *Biological Psychiatry*, 79(8), 633–41. https://doi.org/10.1016/j.biopsych.2015.08.029

Pan, C.-Y. (2014). Motor proficiency and physical fitness in adolescent males with and without autism spectrum disorders. *Autism*, 18(2), 156–65. https://doi.org/10.1177/1362361312458597

Provost, B., Lopez, B.R., and Heimerl, S. (2007). A comparison of motor delays in young children: Autism spectrum disorder, developmental delay, and developmental concerns. *Journal of Autism and Developmental Disorders*, 37(2), 321–28. https://doi.org/10.1007/s10803-006-0170-6

Ramos-Sánchez, C.P., Kortekaas, D., Van Biesen, D., Vancampfort, D., and Van Damme, T. (2022). The relationship between motor skills and intelligence in children with autism spectrum disorder. *Journal of Autism and Developmental Disorders*, 52(3), 1189–99. https://doi.org/10.1007/s10803-021-05022-8

Risi, S., Lord, C., Gotham, K., Corsello, C., Chrysler, C., Szatmari, P., Cook, E.H., Leventhal, B.L., and Pickles, A. (2006). Combining information from multiple sources in the diagnosis of autism spectrum disorders. *Journal of the American Academy of Child & Adolescent Psychiatry*, 45(9), 1094–103. https://doi.org/10.1097/01.chi.0000227880.42780.0e

Robinson, L., Stodden, D.F., Barnett, L.M., Lopes, V.P., Logan, S.W., Rodrigues, L.P., and D'Hondt, E. (2015). Motor competence and its effect on positive developmental trajectories of health. *Sports Medicine*, 45(9), 1273–84. https://doi.org/10.1007/s40279-015-0351-6

Serdarevic, F., Ghassabian, A., van Batenburg-Eddes, T., White, T., Blanken, L.M.E., Jaddoe, V.W.V., Verhulst, F.C., and Tiemeier, H. (2017). Infant muscle tone and childhood autistic traits: A longitudinal study in the general population. *Autism Research, 10*(5), 757–68. https://doi.org/10.1002/aur.1739

Shetreat-Klein, M., Shinnar, S., and Rapin, I. (2014). Abnormalities of joint mobility and gait in children with autism spectrum disorders. *Brain and Development, 36*(2), 91–96. https://doi.org/10.1016/j.braindev.2012.02.005

Staples, K.L., and Reid, G. (2010). Fundamental movement skills and autism spectrum disorders. *Journal of Autism and Developmental Disorders, 40*(2), 209–17. https://doi.org/10.1007/s10803-009-0854-9

Stodden, D.F., Goodway, J.D., Langendorfer, S.J., Roberton, M.A., Rudisill, M.E., Garcia, C., and Garcia, L.E. (2008). A developmental perspective on the role of motor skill competence in physical activity: An emergent relationship. *Quest, 60*(2), 290–306. https://doi.org/10.1080/00336297.2008.10483582

Tepfer, A.T.S. (2015). *Predicting school readiness using motor skill proficiency of at-risk preschoolers*. Corvallis, OR: Oregon State University.

Thompson, A., Murphy, D., Dell'Acqua, F., Ecker, C., McAlonan, G., Howells, H., Baron-Cohen, S., Lai, M.-C., Lombardo, M.V., MRC AIMS Consortium, and Marco Catani. (2017). Impaired communication between the motor and somatosensory homunculus is associated with poor manual dexterity in autism spectrum disorder. *Biological Psychiatry, 81*(3), 211–19. https://doi.org/10.1016/j.biopsych.2016.06.020

Todd, T.A., Ahrold, K., Jarvis, D.N., and Mache, M.A. (2020). Evaluation of overhand throwing among college students with and without autism spectrum disorder. *Adapted Physical Activity Quarterly, 38*(1), 43–61. https://doi.org/10.1123/apaq.2019-0178

Travers, B.G., Powell, P.S., Klinger, L.G., and Klinger, M.R. (2013). Motor difficulties in autism spectrum disorder: Linking symptom severity and postural stability. *Journal of Autism and Developmental Disorders, 43*(7), 1568–83. https://doi.org/10.1007/s10803-012-1702-x

West, K.L. (2019). Infant motor development in autism spectrum disorder: A synthesis and meta-analysis. *Child Development, 90*(6), 2053–70. https://doi.org/10.1111/cdev.13086

Yu, T.-Y., Chou, W., Chow, J. C., Lin, C.-H., Tung, L.-C., and Chen, K.-L. (2018). IQ discrepancy differentiates levels of fine motor skills and their relationship in children with autism spectrum disorders. *Neuropsychiatric Disease and Treatment, 14*, 597–605. https://doi.org/10.2147/NDT.S153102

5

Fundamental Motor Skill Interventions for Children with Autism Spectrum Disorder

Meghann Lloyd

■ ■ ■

Hans Asperger (translated in Frith) and Leo Kanner, both credited with the early descriptions of what is now called autism spectrum disorder (ASD), identified motor clumsiness in their early descriptions of the disorder (Frith, 1991; Kanner, 1943). However, for a long time research and clinical practice ignored, over-looked, or de-emphasized the fact that children with ASD experience motor delays and/or motor difficulties, paying more attention to challenges related to the core domains of social interactions, communication, and behavior (Lloyd et al., 2013; Zampella et al., 2021). Research in the last twenty years has led to a substantial body of evidence describing the motor differences and delays experienced by these children as outlined in the previous chapter (Berkeley et al., 2001; Bhat, 2021; Gandotra et al., 2020; Ghaziuddin and Butler, 1998; Green et al., 2002; Lloyd et al., 2013; Ozonoff et al., 2008; Vernazza-Martin et al., 2005; Zampella et al., 2021). The delays and/or difficulties are real and have consequences for activities of daily living, school-based learning, social interactions, interventional therapies, sport participation, as well as playing with friends. It is interesting that even though this evidence base is now quite robust, less is known about intervention strategies to promote motor proficiency in children with ASD and why it is important that we intervene (Healy et al., 2021; Zampella et al., 2021). Traditionally, early intervention services for children with ASD are delivered in a clinical setting or by rehabilitation specialists (e.g., occupational therapists, speech and language pathologists, physiotherapists, and behavior analysts) at varying intensities targeted at the core characteristics of ASD (Copeland and Buch, 2013). Adding to the complexity of this issue is the relationship between motor impairments and ASD severity (Bhat, 2021), meaning that those who would qualify for significant early intervention services are also likely to have significant motor impairments. Additionally, the relationship between IQ and motor proficiency in children with ASD, especially in those with a co-occurring diagnosis of an intellectual disability adds to the complexity of the issues (Ramos-Sánchez et al., 2022). While the motor delays and differences are well established, what is often missing in the context of early intervention for children with ASD is the development and promotion of fundamental motor skills. These are the skills that are critical to active play, engagement with peers, formal and informal games, and free play at recess or on the playground that provide essential opportunities for inclusion, skill development, and social interactions (Byers and Walker, 1995; Jobling and Virji-Babul, 2004; Leonard and Hill, 2014; Ridgers et al., 2006).

IMPORTANCE OF MOTOR SKILL DEVELOPMENT

The development of motor skills in babies and young children is almost universally celebrated by parents, grandparents, and health professionals alike (e.g., when a child takes their first steps or sits independently for the first time). Motor milestones are often part of the child's baby book kept by parents but also as part of the clinical developmental record kept by pediatricians. In fact, delays in early motor development are often the first red flags related to developmental concerns for both parents and/or health professionals (Wilson et al., 2018). While Piaget (1954) attributed great importance to the interaction of movement and learning in children, historically, motor development has been over-looked and/or underappreciated in the field of child development or developmental psychology, leading Rosenbaum (2005) to label motor behavior the "Cinderella" of psychology. More recently, Adolph and Hoch (2019) argued that motor development is "enabling," that it prompts new opportunities for learning and doing, that can bring about cascades of development in related domains (Adolph and Hoch, 2019; Campos et al., 2000; Leonard and Hill, 2014). Therefore, the development of motor skills is critical to the overall development of children.

The causal links between motor skill acquisition and the development of perceptual, cognitive, and social abilities are not always obvious, but movement skills are believed to facilitate and/or enable perception, cognition, connections, exploration, and social interactions (Adolph and Hoch, 2019; Leonard and Hill, 2014; Rosenbaum, 2005). All of these cascading effects of movement behaviors occur within the environment, and how this environment is configured can either promote or inhibit motor behavior; to complete the circle, new motor abilities can make different aspects of the environment available to the developing child (Adolph and Hoch, 2019; Gibson, 1988). For example, once a child has the motor skills necessary to use an object (e.g., sitting upright or walking independently, the arms are now free to be able to manipulate a ball or a racquet), that object now takes on a whole new meaning and new opportunities are afforded to the child. Similarly, the ability to move with competence and confidence in early childhood allows for opportunities to both explore one's body capabilities and the environment, but also to engage in developmentally appropriate social exchanges with peers and family members, for example hide and seek or a game of tag (Leonard and Hill, 2014). This is relevant to children with ASD who experience both gross and fine motor delays, and/or atypical motor patterns, in addition to their challenges in the social, behavioral, and communication domains of development (Berkeley et al., 2001; Ghaziuddin and Butler, 1998; Green et al., 2002; Leary and Hill, 1996; Leonard and Hill, 2014; Lloyd et al., 2013; Ozonoff et al., 2008; Vernazza-Martin et al., 2005; Wilson et al., 2018). Children with ASD experience a double burden; they have significant challenges with social interactions as part of the core characteristics of ASD, and this is exacerbated by their poor motor skills which limit participation on the playground, at the park, school, and/or on a sports team (Ohara et al., 2020; Watkinson and Muloin, 1988).

One of the reasons that motor proficiency is of such interest is because active play is a critically important childhood activity that facilitates the development of social skills, motor skills, creativity, communication skills, and an understanding of the world (Byers and Walker, 1995; Jobling and Virji-Babul, 2004; Leonard and Hill, 2014; Ridgers et al., 2006). Motor skills in young children are important mediators to the development of social and behavioral skills, and have a significant influence on the ability of a child to participate in active play and activities of daily living (Larkin and Summers, 2004; Leonard and Hill, 2014; Menear, 2007; Pellegrini and Smith, 1998; Watkinson and Muloin, 1988). For children with disabilities, movement proficiency is even more important for participation because school, sport, recreation, and play are critical venues for inclusion (Bailey, 2005; Townsend and Hassall, 2007).

Fundamental motor skills are the foundation movements, or precursor patterns, to more specialized, complex skills in games, sports, dance, gymnastics, and recreational physical activities (Burton and Miller, 1998; Cattuzzo et al., 2016; Gandotra et al., 2020; Payne and Isaacs, 2002). Fundamental motor skills, compared to earlier motor milestones, also have a social aspect to them. For example, playing a game of catch with another person, being able to run proficiently in a game of tag, playing on the playground at recess, engaging with sibling, cousins, or friends in the backyard—these are all examples of developmentally appropriate physical activities that are limited if a child with ASD does not have the motor proficiency to engage (Leonard and Hill, 2014). A recent systematic review by Gandotra and colleagues (2020) on the fundamental motor skills of children with ASD found that impairments in fundamental movement skills are prevalent and that the children with ASD exhibited greater impairments when compared to children with typical development as well as those with other developmental disorders. Importantly, this systematic review also concluded that the impairments persist into childhood (Gandotra et al., 2020). Another systematic review by Liang and colleagues (2020) found that only 42 percent of children with ASD meet physical activity guidelines when physical activity is measured by accelerometry. There is substantial research that indicates that children with more proficient motor skills are more likely to engage in physical activity for longer durations and at higher intensities; children with less proficient motor skills are less likely to engage in sport, recreation, physical education class, play on the playground, or engage in active play at home (Cattuzzo et al., 2016; Lubans et al., 2010; Rodrigues et al., 2013; Stodden et al., 2012; Stodden et al., 2013). Some might question the emphasis on fundamental motor skills and physical activity for children with ASD when parents are sincerely focused on managing behavior, promoting communication, and improving social skills. However, there is evidence that children with ASD who engage in physical activity and exercise, for which fundamental motor skills are prerequisites, have more positive behavioral outcomes (e.g., reductions in self-stimulatory behaviors) (Bremer et al., 2016). Therefore, the motor delays and/or difficulties experienced by children with ASD have consequences for many different areas of their lives. The purpose of this chapter is to address two questions related to these motor skill delays in children with ASD: (a) are fundamental motor skill interventions effective for this population, and (b) are there developmental benefits outside of gains in motor skills themselves?

FUNDAMENTAL MOTOR SKILL INTERVENTIONS

As a natural consequence of the overwhelming evidence on the motor skill delays in children with ASD, there has been a proliferation of motor skill *intervention* research over the past fifteen years. The types of interventions, the durations, the measures used, the sample sizes, and the ages of the participants all vary. To make sense of all this new data, in the past three years alone, three high-quality reviews have been published on the topic: a meta-analysis by Case and Yun (2019), a systematic review by Ruggeri and colleagues (2020), and another systematic review by Healy and colleagues (2021). All three of these reviews concluded that children with ASD demonstrate improvements in motor skills after intervention.

Ruggeri and colleagues' (2020) systematic review included forty-one studies comprised of 1,173 children with ASD between the ages of three and nineteen years. While they found that overall the interventions improved the motor skills of the children with ASD, they also found that the overall quality of the evidence to be low. The majority of the low-quality ratings were attributed to lack of a control group and inadequate power/small sample size. The types of interventions included in this review were very heterogenous; for example, they included hippotherapy interventions along with motor skill interventions, exergaming, and physical education interventions. The heterogeneity of the interventions is a tribute to the creative ways researchers have tried to support this population; however, it makes broad conclusions on effective interventions more challenging. Also of note, the outcome measures used by the forty-one studies were extremely variable, further complicating the interpretation of the results in a consistent manner. The consequence of the heterogeneity of the research is that practical recommendations are difficult to communicate. What is a community leader to do when there is little to no agreement within the literature on what type of intervention, for what age group, and how to measure change? Ruggeri and colleagues (2020) conclude that it is critical for standardized assessment methods, with strong psychometrics, that are aligned with the goals and intentions of the intervention itself be utilized—for example, if the intervention is targeting fundamental movement skills, then the assessment should measure fundamental movement skills. They also suggest that the dose response relationship of motor skill interventions be investigated since the data suggests that a longer time period with an increased intensity might result in better outcomes. Despite the challenges, the evidence in this review is clear that motor skill interventions for children and youth with ASD do result in improvements in motor skills.

Healy and colleagues' (2021) systematic review focused primarily on methodological issues related to fundamental motor skill interventions for children with ASD. Their review included twenty-two studies comprised of only 314 participants between the ages of three and nineteen years of age. They found that only two of the studies used a true experimental design with random assignment of participants; the majority of the studies were quasi-experimental designs where participants were not randomly assigned. In addition to study design variability (intervention intensity, duration, setting, measurement, etc.), the high variability in the sample sizes of the studies and the high variability in the types of interventions make concrete conclusions difficult. Healy and colleagues (2021) highlight the challenges related to the measurement of fundamental motor skills among children with ASD; they state that regardless of research design, measurement of fundamental motor skills is a "constant threat to internal validity" (p. 15). While Healy and colleagues did find that the fundamental motor skills of children with ASD improve with intervention, they conclude the quality of the evidence is low. It is clear that researchers experience challenges in recruitment and retention of participants, the ethical dilemma of a true control group in their study designs (some address this using waitlist control studies), in addition to using intervention modalities that are both feasible to run and of interest to the participants and their families (e.g., martial arts versus horseback riding). However, despite these well-documented challenges and limitations of the research, the results indicate that fundamental motor skill interventions for children and youth with ASD are effective.

Case and Yun's study (2019) on gross motor outcomes for children with ASD is different from the previous two systematic reviews because it also included a meta-analysis as part of the results. With eighteen studies included in the analysis, there were twenty interventions included and participants were between three and twelve years of age for a total sample of 597 participants. Case and Yun (2019) found that children with ASD demonstrate significant improvements in gross motor performance following intervention (with a large overall effect size). Interestingly, their results did not indicate whether one type of intervention was more effective than another; however, the intervention time and setting were found to be important moderators of the effects. Interventions with sixteen or more hours of intervention time within a research or experimental setting elicited significantly higher effect sizes than those with less than sixteen hours and in clinical or service settings. It is not a surprise that intensity of intervention has an impact on the outcomes; however, it is important to note that lower intensity interventions *also* had positive outcomes. Much more research is needed on how to translate research/experimental designs into effective community-based, accessible options for families. Similar to Healy and colleagues (2021), the authors also emphasized the importance of choosing the "right" assessment tool (Case and Yun, 2019). The importance of this point cannot be overstated; if an intervention is targeting fundamental movement skills, the assessment tool used to measure change should measure fundamental movement skills. However, one cannot ignore the possibility that even the best assessment tool might not be well suited for children with ASD due to the fact that all assessment tools require the individual to understand complex tasks (e.g., understand verbal instructions) leading to the tool not accurately capturing the child's actual motor ability (Wilson et al., 2018). Finally, Case and Yun (2019) emphasized that children with ASD may need motor skill interventions across their lifespan and they point out how little is known about the movement abilities of older children, adolescents, and young adults with ASD.

Despite the methodological challenges found in all three reviews, the evidence indicates that motor skill interventions do improve the motor skills of children with ASD (Case and Yun, 2019; Healy et al., 2021; Ruggeri et al., 2020). It is important to spend a moment to address some inherent biases within this research base. Research with a small sample and/or small statistical effect is harder to publish (Ferguson and Brannick, 2012), community-based intervention programs have been running for years if not decades (e.g., local recreation centers, Special Olympics, therapeutic recreation, adapted physical education classes), but these settings are less likely to be studied due in part to the perceived inability to control for confounding variables (Israel et al., 1998), and children with ASD are by definition a heterogenous population and these families have significant demands on their time, focus, and energy, especially while waiting for traditional intervention services (Jones et al., 2017). Research, but also society in general, is preoccupied with "statistical significance" or a "statistically significant improvement," and often ignores the clinical or practical significance of new skills for children with ASD. For children with disabilities, learning a new skill can open doors, both literally and figuratively. Being able to engage with family or friends may have benefits that are not adequately captured in a standardized test or statistical model, and very probably lead to a cascade of future opportunities at school, at home, and within the community (Adolph and Hoch, 2019). In fact, there is also evidence that improvements in motor skills after a motor skill intervention also lead to improvements in social skills and adaptive behavior as well (Bremer et al., 2015; Bremer and Lloyd, 2016; Ketcheson et al., 2017; Wilson et al., 2018), supporting Adolph and Hoch's hypothesis of cascading effects with motor competence. Therefore, despite the limitations of the three reviews, it is critical that educators, policymakers, and rehabilitation specialists begin to think outside of the traditional early intervention modalities to offer more diverse opportunities that could benefit the children and their families (Bhat, 2021). Community-based recreation centers (e.g., municipal parks and recreation centers, YMCAs) often provide early motor skill programs for young children under the umbrella of "kinder-skills" or "active start programs" or the like. These programs are traditionally designed for children without disabilities, who also would benefit from motor skill intervention programs, but these programs exist today and children with ASD would benefit from inclusion in them. To successfully execute this recommendation, it is critical that organizations hire qualified individuals *and* train their staff to work with children with ASD. The best program/curriculum in the world is not going to be successful without adequate behavioral management to both promote skill development and ensure the safety of all participants. To actually make a difference in the lives of the millions of children with ASD, we cannot rely on the small-scale research studies to provide these types of programs; this research must be implemented at the community level.

FUTURE RESEARCH

The fact that there is a growing body of scientific evidence about the effectiveness of motor skill interventions is extremely encouraging. However, while all these recent reviews indicate that children with ASD demonstrate improvements in motor skills with intervention (Case and Yun, 2019; Healy et al., 2021; Ruggeri et al., 2020), none of the intervention studies reviewed were longitudinal in design (i.e., had a follow-up period longer than six months). The persistent question remains: what impact do these motor skill interventions have on the lives of children with ASD once the intervention is complete? Are skill gains maintained five years post intervention? Do children with ASD who participate in a motor skill intervention early in their life engage in physical activity, recreation, and/or sport later in childhood? There is a critical need for the long-term benefits of a motor skill intervention to be studied. This is particularly relevant because motor skill proficiency enables opportunities for learning and meaningful participation within one's environment (Adolph and Hoch, 2019).

It is also critical that intervention research study the effect on more than just motor skills. In other words, if motor skills improve, do other relevant developmental domains also improve? Bremer and colleagues (2015) found that in addition to motor skill improvements there were also improvements in adaptive behavior and social skills. A second study by Bremer and Lloyd (2016) also provides preliminary evidence that with a motor skill intervention the children with ASD improved their motor skills but also their social skills in a school setting. In a study by Elliott and colleagues (2021), the secondary effects of a motor skill intervention were investigated by interviewing parents after their children with ASD had participated in the intervention. They found that parents reported improvements in motor skills, social skills, listening skills, turn-taking skills, and transition skills, all of which were meaningful developmental gains to the parents. These three small studies indicate that Adolph and Hoch's (2019) hypothesis regarding the cascading effect of motor proficiency warrants further study in a systematic way.

Finally, an area that needs further research is the individualization of motor skill interventions: or, more broadly, ensuring that the interventions are designed and implemented to achieve maximum results. Age, overall developmental level, social skills, and adaptive behavior are factors that can impact on the appropriateness of any intervention. For example, Bremer and Lloyd (2021) looked at baseline characteristics to determine whether they predicted outcomes of a motor skill intervention for three- to five-year-olds with ASD. They found that children with ASD who had higher levels of adapted behavior and lower levels of emotional and behavioral challenges at the start of the intervention were more likely to have greater improvements in their motor skills. This indicates that it is possible to identify and tailor interventions to the skill-sets of the participants, thereby increasing the likelihood of meaningful outcomes. Even small developmental gains are important for both the children and their parents, and if an intervention is at a mismatched level (either too high or too low) for the children, the desired outcomes are not likely to be achieved; conversely, a well-matched intervention has the potential to result in very meaningful results for the child and their families. Researchers and clinicians need to think about the factors that could contribute to the success of the intervention such as developmental level (i.e., IQ), adaptive behavior skills, social skills, and communication skills when designing their intervention and recruitment strategies. On a cautionary note, I am not suggesting that we only intervene on the groups that are easy to work with; what I am advocating for is designing our interventions to best suit the skills and challenges of the children receiving the intervention.

PRACTICAL IMPLICATIONS

Once a child has been diagnosed with ASD, the next step for parents is often figuring out what interventions they are eligible for, navigating the private and publicly funded systems that provide services, and deciding what is best for their child in the context of their family. Considering the importance, and potentially important cascade of benefits, fundamental motor skill interventions should be part of the intervention "buffet" for parents to choose from, even if it is just to introduce the parents to options regarding therapeutic recreation, inclusive community-based programs, etc. Parents need to be informed that the development of these skills is important. Parents of children with ASD in Jones and colleagues' study (2017) identified community-based recreation as an important part of their overall family quality of life. While the new diagnosis is often overwhelming, meaningful play and participation experiences for children with ASD need to be available in addition to traditional therapeutic options. Elliott and colleagues (2021) found that parents often develop "tunnel vision" in the early years after their child is diagnosed with ASD. That the parents are often so focused on other aspects of development that are deemed to be a very high priority for their child with ASD (i.e., behavior, communication, social skills) that other aspects of their child's development such a developing motor skill proficiency fell into the background. It was only once their child participated in the motor skill intervention that they recognized the importance and relevance of something so seemingly simple as learning to catch a ball.

From a practical, programmatic point of view, it is important the community-based programs have adequate staff-to-child ratios for both pedagogical purposes, but also safety. Parents are more likely to engage with a program if they feel their child's needs are going to be met and their child will be kept safe at all times (e.g., preventing elopement, behavior management, overall assistance with skills). But having numbers of staff is not enough; staff need to be adequately trained and supported while working with children with ASD in a physical activity setting. Many community centers hire adolescents still in high school and young adults in college or university to staff their programs (e.g., afterschool programs, summer camps, etc.). While this is common practice and entirely appropriate, what is not appropriate is to assume these young people have the training and experience to serve the needs of children with ASD. Community centers need to budget for extensive training with scaffolded support from more experienced leaders to ensure the success of all involved. These types of experiences are critical to the development and coaching of young people who may be inclined to pursue a career working with individuals with disabilities in rehabilitation sciences, education, or social services. The evidence is clear that children with ASD who receive a motor skill intervention improve their motor skills. More research is needed to study this in more detail; however, in the meantime, there is a need to develop accessible, affordable, and effective community-based programs where children with ASD can learn alongside their peers.

REFERENCES

Adolph, K.E., and Hoch, J.E. (2019). Motor development: Embodied, embedded, enculturated, and enabling. *Annual Review of Psychology, 70*, 141–64.

Bailey, R. (2005). Evaluating the relationship between physical education, sport and social inclusion. *Educational Review, 57*(1), 71–90.

Berkeley, S.L., Zittel, L.L., Pitney, L.V., and Nichols, S. E. (2001). Locomotor and object control skills of children diagnosed with autism. *Adapted Physical Activity Quarterly, 18*, 405–16.

Bhat, A.N. (2021). Motor impairment increases in children with autism spectrum disorder as a function of social communication, cognitive and functional impairment, repetitive behavior severity, and comorbid diagnoses: a SPARK study report. *Autism Research, 14*(1), 202–19.

Bremer, E., Balogh, R.S., and Lloyd, M. (2015). Effectiveness of a fundamental motor skill intervention for 4-year-old children with autism spectrum disorder: A pilot study. *Autism, 19*(8), 980–91.

Bremer, E., Crozier, M., and Lloyd, M. (2016). A systematic review of the behavioural outcomes following exercise interventions for children and youth with autism spectrum disorder. *Autism*, 20(8), 899–915.

Bremer, E., and Lloyd, M. (2016). School-based fundamental motor skill intervention for children with autism-like characteristics: A preliminary case study. *Adapted Physical Activity Quarterly*, 33(1), 66–88.

Bremer, E., and Lloyd, M. (2021). Baseline behaviour moderates movement skill intervention outcomes among young children with autism spectrum disorder. *Autism*, 25(7), 2025–33.

Burton, A.W., and Miller, D.E. (1998). *Movement skill assessment*. Champaign, IL: Human Kinetics.

Byers, J.A., and Walker, C. (1995). Refining the motor training hypothesis for the evolution of play. *The American Naturalist*, 146(1), 25–40.

Campos, J.J., Anderson, D.I., Barbu-Roth, M.A., Hubbard, E.M., Hertenstein, M.J., and Witherington, D. (2000). Travel broadens the mind. *Infancy*, 1(2), 149–219.

Case, L., and Yun, J. (2019). The effect of different intervention approaches on gross motor outcomes of children with autism spectrum disorder: A meta-analysis. *Adapt Phys Activ Q*, 36(4), 501–26.

Cattuzzo, M.T., Dos Santos Henrique, R., Nicolai Ré, A.H., Santos de Oliveira, I., Melo, B.M., de Sousa Moura, M., de Araújo, R.C., and Stodden, D. (2016). Motor competence and health related physical fitness in youth: A systematic review. *Journal of Science and Medicine in Sport*, 19, 123–29.

Copeland, L., and Buch, G. (2013). Early intervention issues in autism spectrum disorders. *Autism*, 3(109), 2–7.

Elliott, L.K., Weiss, J.A., and Lloyd, M. (2021). Beyond the motor domain: Exploring the secondary effects of a fundamental motor skill intervention for children with autism spectrum disorder. *Adapted Physical Activity Quarterly*, 38(2), 195–214.

Ferguson, C.J., and Brannick, M.T. (2012). Publication bias in psychological science: prevalence, methods for identifying and controlling, and implications for the use of meta-analyses. *Psychological Methods*, 17(1), 120.

Frith, U. (1991). *Autism and Asperger's syndrome*. Cambridge: Cambridge University Press.

Gandotra, A., Kotyuk, E., Szekely, A., Kasos, K., Csirmaz, L., and Cserjesi, R. (2020). Fundamental movement skills in children with autism spectrum disorder: A systematic review. *Research in Autism Spectrum Disorders*, 78, 101632.

Ghaziuddin, M., and Butler, E. (1998). Clumsiness in autism and Asperger syndrome: A further report. *J Intellect Disabil Res*, 42(Pt 1), 43–48. http://www.ncbi.nlm.nih.gov/entrez/query.fcgi?cmd=Retrieve&db=PubMed&dopt=Citation&list_uids=9534114

Gibson, E.J. (1988). Exploratory behavior in the development of perceiving, acting, and the acquiring of knowledge. *Annual Reviews of Psychology*, 39, 1–41.

Green, D., Baird, G., Barnett, A.L., Henderson, L., Huber, J., and Henderson, S.E. (2002). The severity and nature of motor impairment in Asperger's syndrome: a comparison with specific developmental disorder of motor function. *J Child Psychol Psychiatry*, 43(5), 655–68. http://www.ncbi.nlm.nih.gov/entrez/query.fcgi?cmd=Retrieve&db=PubMed&dopt=Citation&list_uids=12120861

Healy, S., Obrusnikova, I., and Getchell, N. (2021). Fundamental motor skill interventions in children with autism spectrum disorder: A systematic review of the literature including a methodological quality assessment. *Research in Autism Spectrum Disorders*, 81, 101717.

Israel, B.A., Schulz, A.J., Parker, E.A., and Becker, A.B. (1998). Review of community-based research: assessing partnership approaches to improve public health. *Annual Review of Public Health*, 19(1), 173–202.

Jobling, A., and Virji-Babul, N. (2004). *Down syndrome: Play, move and grow*. Burnaby, Canada: Down Syndrome Research Foundation.

Jones, S., Bremer, E., and Lloyd, M. (2017). Autism spectrum disorder: family quality of life while waiting for intervention services. *Qual Life Res*, 26(2), 331–42.

Kanner, L. (1943). Autistic disturbances of affective contact. *Nervous Child*, 2, 217–50.

Ketcheson, L., Hauck, J., and Ulrich, D.A. (2017). The effects of an early motor skill intervention on motor skills, levels of physical activity, and socialization in young children with autism spectrum disorder: A pilot study. *Autism*, 21(4), 481–92.

Larkin, D., and Summers, J. (2004). Implications of movement difficulties for social interaction, physical activity, play and sports. In D. Dewey and D.E. Tupper (Eds.), *Developmental motor disorders: A neuropsychological perspective* (pp. 443–60). New York: The Guilford Press.

Leary, M.R., and Hill, D.A. (1996). Moving on: Autism and movement disturbance. *Ment Retard*, 34(1), 39–53. http://www.ncbi.nlm.nih.gov/entrez/query.fcgi?cmd=Retrieve&db=PubMed&dopt=Citation&list_uids=8822025

Leonard, H.C., and Hill, E.L. (2014). The impact of motor development on typical and atypical social cognition and language: A systematic review. *Child and Adolescent Mental Health*, 19(3), 163–70.

Liang, X., Li, R., Wong, S.H., Sum, R.K., and Sit, C.H. (2020). Accelerometer-measured physical activity levels in children and adolescents with autism spectrum disorder: A systematic review. *Preventive Medicine Reports*, 19, 101147.

Lloyd, M., MacDonald, M., and Lord, C. (2013). Motor skills of toddlers with autism spectrum disorders. *Autism*, 17(2), 133–46.

Lubans, D.R., Morgan, P.J., Cliff, D.P., Barnett, L.M., and Okely, A.D. (2010). Fundamental movement skills in children and adolescents: review of associated health benefits. *Sports Medicine*, 40(12), 1019–35.

Menear, K. (2007). Parents' perceptions of health and physical activity needs of children with Down syndrome. *Downs Syndr Res Pract*, 12(1), 60–68. http://www.ncbi.nlm.nih.gov/entrez/query.fcgi?cmd=Retrieve&db=PubMed&dopt=Citation&list_uids=17692190

Ohara, R., Kanejima, Y., Kitamura, M., and Kazuhiro, P.I. (2020). Association between social skills and motor skills in individuals with autism spectrum disorder: A systematic review. *European Journal of Investigation in Health, Psychology and Education*, 10(1), 276–96.

Ozonoff, S., Young, G.S., Goldring, S., Greiss-Hess, L., Herrera, A.M., Steele, J., Macari, S., Hepburn, S., and Rogers, S. J. (2008). Gross motor development, movement abnormalities, and early identification of autism. *J Autism Dev Disord*, 38(4), 644–56. http://www.ncbi.nlm.nih.gov/entrez/query.fcgi?cmd=Retrieve&db=PubMed&dopt=Citation&list_uids=17805956

Payne, V.G., and Isaacs, L.D. (2002). *Human motor development: A lifespan approach* (fifth edition). Boston: McGraw Hill.

Pellegrini, A.D., and Smith, P.K. (1998). Physical activity play: the nature and function of a neglected aspect of playing. *Child Development*, 69(3), 577–98. http://www.ncbi.nlm.nih.gov/entrez/query.fcgi?cmd=Retrieve&db=PubMed&dopt=Citation&list_uids=9680672

Piaget, J. (1954). *The construction of reality in the child*. New York: Basic Books.

Ramos-Sánchez, C.P., Kortekaas, D., Van Biesen, D., Vancampfort, D., and Van Damme, T. (2022). The relationship between motor skills and intelligence in children with autism spectrum disorder. *Journal of Autism and Developmental Disorders*, 52(3), 1189–99.

Ridgers, N.D., Stratton, G., and Fairclough, S.J. (2006). Physical activity levels of children during school playtime. *Sports Med*, 36(4), 359–71. http://www.ncbi.nlm.nih.gov/entrez/query.fcgi?cmd=Retrieve&db=PubMed&dopt=Citation&list_uids=16573359

Rodrigues, L.P., Stodden, D.F., and Lopes, V.P. (2013). Developmental pathways of change in health-related fitness and motor competence are related to obesity development in childhood. *Journal of Sport and Exercise Psychology*, 35, S71–S71.

Rosenbaum, D.A. (2005). The Cinderella of psychology: the neglect of motor control in the science of mental life and behavior. *Am Psychol*, 60(4), 308–17. http://www.ncbi.nlm.nih.gov/entrez/query.fcgi?cmd=Retrieve&db=PubMed&dopt=Citation&list_uids=15943523

Ruggeri, A., Dancel, A., Johnson, R., and Sargent, B. (2020). The effect of motor and physical activity intervention on motor outcomes of children with autism spectrum disorder: A systematic review. *Autism*, 24(3), 544–68.

Stodden, D.F., Goodway, J.D., Stephen, J., Roberton, M.A., Rudisill, M.E., Garcia, C., and Garcia, L.E. (2012). A developmental perspective on the role of motor skill competence in physical activity: An emergent relationship. *Motor Competence and Physical Activity*, 6297, 37–41.

Stodden, D.F., True, L.K., Langendorfer, S.J., and Gao, Z. (2013). Associations among selected motor skills and health-related fitness: indirect evidence for Seefeldt's proficiency barrier in young adults? *Research Quarterly for Exercise and Sport*, 84(3), 397–403.

Townsend, M., and Hassall, J. (2007). Mainstream students' attitudes to possible inclusion in unified sports with students who have an intellectual disability. *Journal of Applied Research in Intellectual Disabilities*, 20, 265–73.

Vernazza-Martin, S., Martin, N., Vernazza, A., Lepellec-Muller, A., Rufo, M., Massion, J., and Assaiante, C. (2005). Goal directed locomotion and balance control in autistic children. *J Autism Dev Disord*, 35(1), 91–102. http://www.ncbi.nlm.nih.gov/entrez/query.fcgi?cmd=Retrieve&db=PubMed&dopt=Citation&list_uids=15796125

Watkinson, E.J., and Muloin, S. (1988). Playground skills of moderately mentally handicapped youngsters in integrated elementary schools. *The Mental Retardation and Learning Disability Bulletin*, 16(2), 3–13.

Wilson, R.B., Enticott, P.G., and Rinehart, N.J. (2018). Motor development and delay: advances in assessment of motor skills in autism spectrum disorders. *Current Opinion in Neurology*, 31(2), 134.

Zampella, C.J., Wang, L.A., Haley, M., Hutchinson, A.G., and de Marchena, A. (2021). Motor skill differences in autism spectrum disorder: A clinically focused review. *Current Psychiatry Reports*, 23(10), 1–11.

6

Motor Behavior and Emotional and Behavioral Disorders

Iva Obrusnikova and Albert R. Cavalier

■ ■ ■

This chapter provides (a) definitions of the general umbrella category of emotional and behavioral disorders (EBDs) and two specific subcategories—anxiety disorders (AnxDs) and attention-deficit hyperactivity disorder (ADHD)—(b) overviews of the major causal factors of the characteristics subsumed under those subcategories, (c) descriptions of the major behavioral and motor characteristics of children and adults diagnosed with those disorders, (d) a summary of current trends and issues in relevant motor-behavior research, and (e) implications for research and practice.

DEFINITIONS OF EMOTIONAL AND BEHAVIORAL DISORDERS

The landmark Individuals with Disabilities Education Act (IDEA, 2004) defines "emotional disturbance" as:

> a condition exhibiting one or more of the following characteristics over a long period of time and to a marked degree that adversely affects a child's educational performance:
> (a) an inability to learn that cannot be explained by intellectual, sensory, or health factors;
> (b) an inability to build or maintain satisfactory interpersonal relationships with peers and teachers;
> (c) inappropriate types of behavior or feelings under normal circumstances;
> (d) a general pervasive mood of unhappiness or depression; and
> (e) a tendency to develop physical symptoms or fears associated with personal or school problems. (45 C. F. R. 121a5[b][8][1978])

This is one of the most widely used definitions to classify children with manifestations in the EBD area. However, it is important to note that, despite the label, this definition includes disorders characterized not just by aberrant emotions but also by thoughts and behaviors. In practical terms, these disorders can manifest as severe physical or verbal aggression, impulsiveness, distractibility, hallucinations, social withdrawal, unusual motor acts, heightened fears, and phobias. In addition, the definition emphasizes "over a long period of time and to a marked degree." Many children and adolescents engage in one or more of these characteristics at some point in their development. A person would not qualify for such a clinical condition until those characteristics are excessive and extend over time.

According to the American Psychiatric Association (APA; 2013), individuals with EBD display a wide range of behavior patterns classified into two broad categories—internalizing and externalizing. The *internalizing* category represents emotional disorders with prominent anxiety, depressive, and somatic symptoms (e.g., AnxDs, bipolar and depressive disorders, somatic complaints). The *externalizing* category represents behavioral disorders with prominent impulsive, disruptive conduct, and substance-use symptoms (e.g., ADHD, conduct disorders [CD], oppositional-defiant disorder [ODD], antisocial disorders, impulse-control disorders, substance use disorders). Some individuals exhibit patterns of thoughts, feelings, and behaviors in both categories (Papachristou and Flouri, 2020).

PREVALENCE OF EMOTIONAL AND BEHAVIORAL DISORDERS

The National Center for Education Statistics (2021) reported that in 2019, approximately 5 percent (365,000) of children, aged six to twenty-one years, served in public schools under IDEA were diagnosed with emotional disturbance. These children comprised about 0.7 percent of the total school enrollment in the United States. However, due to the challenges that the IDEA definition entails (e.g., in many cases, the definition can be stigmatizing and ambiguous; Gresham, 2007), many authorities believe the diagnosis is greatly underreported across the United States (Scardamalia et al., 2019; Smith et al., 2015). Consistent with this belief, the National Health Interview Survey data (Simpson et al., 2008) showed that in 2005 to 2006, parents of over eight million children (approximately 14.5 percent), aged four to seventeen years, have consulted with school or private clinicians about their child's emotional or behavioral problems. The COVID-19 lockdowns further contributed to significant declines in mental and behavioral health for parents and their children (Patrick et al., 2020). This makes emotional and behavioral difficulties of children among the leading health concerns among US parents.

INTERNALIZING: ANXIETY DISORDERS DEFINED

Anxiety disorders are characterized by excessive fear and anxiety and related behavioral disturbances lasting beyond developmentally appropriate lengths of time (i.e., typically lasting six months or more) (APA, 2013). *Fear* is the emotional response to a real or perceived imminent threat and is associated with surges of autonomic arousal, thoughts of immediate danger, and escape behaviors (Janelle, 2002). *Anxiety* is the anticipation of future threats and is associated with muscle tension and vigilance in preparation for future danger and cautious or avoidant behaviors. When such fear and anxiety are repetitive, excessive, and/or seemingly uncontrollable, an AnxD may be present. There are several types of AnxDs, including generalized AnxD, panic disorders, social AnxD, and various phobia-related disorders (National Institute of Mental Health, 2021).

PREVALENCE OF ANXIETY DISORDERS

Most AnxDs develop in childhood and persist if not treated (APA, 2013). The National Comorbidity Survey revealed that AnxDs are the most common mental illness in the United States; they affect 31.9 percent of youth between ages thirteen and eighteen years and 19.1 percent (forty million) of individuals eighteen years and older (Harvard Medical School, 2017). However, although available treatments can improve these disorders, according to the Anxiety and Depression Association of America (2023), 63.1 percent of affected adults do not receive treatment. Likewise, according to the Child Mind Institute (2015), 80 percent of children with diagnosable AnxDs do not receive treatment. Even though AnxDs tend to be highly comorbid with each other, they can be differentiated by close examination of the types of situations that are feared or avoided and the content of the associated thoughts or beliefs (APA, 2013).

CONCEPTUAL MODELS OF ANXIETY DISORDERS

Two opposing theoretical models have been used to explain how anxiety affects perceptual-motor performance. Based on the attentional control theory (Eysenck et al., 2007), individuals with anxiety have too little attention available to calibrate and adjust movements in relation to task-relevant information (Wilson, 2008). As a result, their task-relevant focus decreases and task-irrelevant fixations in the environment increase, which together cause a decrease in performance (Nieuwenhuys and Oudejans, 2012). In the alternate view—the execution focus model—rather than reducing on-task attention, anxiety draws attention inward, leading to explicit attempts to monitor or control movements. As a result, the automatic execution of a task is disrupted, causing movement behavior to be less efficient and performance to be reduced (e.g., Beilock and Carr, 2001). Both theories imply motor performance can be influenced by the way individuals perceive the environment or the task (Stern et al., 2013). For example, individuals with increased anxiety levels may overestimate distance or height (Stefanucci and Proffitt, 2009; Teachman et al., 2008) or perceive performance goals to appear more extreme (Stern et al., 2013). If perceptions of the environment are distorted, individuals may perform worse because they calibrate movements erroneously. They may also subjectively feel that the task is more difficult, which could, in turn, enhance their anxiety and lead to distracting thoughts and, consequently, less efficient task performance.

MOTOR IMPAIRMENTS AND ANXIETY DISORDERS

The relationship between AnxDs and motor impairments has not been studied extensively. The limited research provides evidence of the relationship between elevated anxiety levels and poor balance and/or experiences of dizziness (e.g., Erez et al., 2004; Kroenke et al., 1993; Yardley and Redfern, 2001). For example, a small clinical study by Erez et al. (2004) found that children with AnxDs made more balance mistakes and/or were slower at completing static or dynamic balance tasks either when (a) walking on unsteady surfaces (i.e., two-leg balancing on an unsteady cylinder and one-leg balancing on an unsteady trampoline) or (b) having a narrow-lateral foot base (i.e., stepping on a rope stretched on the floor) than age-matched controls without AnxDs. In addition, only children with an AnxD were predisposed to recurrent episodes of dizziness, motion sickness, and nausea due to changes in posture or head position, certain movements, and darkness. However, the findings of this study are difficult to interpret with confidence because thirteen of the twenty children with AnxDs had a comorbid diagnosis of ADHD, which could have confounded the authors' data interpretation (Skirbekk et al., 2012).

Skirbekk et al. (2012) attempted to address these limitations by comparing balance assessed via the Movement Assessment Battery for Children (M-ABC; Henderson and Sugden, 1992) among four groups of children (forty-one with AnxDs, thirty-nine with ADHD, twenty-five with comorbid AnxDs and ADHD, and thirty-six controls), aged seven to thirteen years. Even though the clinical groups did not significantly differ in their motor profiles (i.e., there were no fundamental differences in their patterns of motor impairment), children with an AnxD had significantly worse total M-ABC and manual dexterity-subtest scores ($p < 0.001$). In addition, the AnxD group had the worst balance score, but the group differences were not statistically significant ($p < 0.05$). This conflicting evidence calls for more research to explain the causal direction between AnxDs and balance problems, if any. On the one hand, balance dysfunction can be considered a psychosomatic manifestation of anxiety and fear (Yardley and Redfern, 2001), with the neurologic basis for this relationship being the shared central neural circuits for control of vestibular processing, autonomic function, emotional responses, and anxiety (for details, see Balaban et al., 2011; Balaban and Thayer, 2001). Erez et al. (2004) concluded this reasoning might explain why participants with an AnxD abandoned attempts to maintain balance in challenging situations. On the other hand, if "equipped with poor balance-restoring movements" (p. 353) or other cerebellar dysfunctions, frequent exposure to balance-challenging situations may lead to repeated fear responses that may eventually trigger the development of a chronic AnxD (Yardley and Redfern, 2001).

A growing body of evidence also suggests a strong relationship between anxiety levels and motor coordination difficulties or clumsiness (e.g., Kristensen and Torgersen, 2007; Schoemaker and Kalverboer, 1994; Skinner and Piek, 2001; Skirbekk et al., 2012). For example, Schoemaker and Kalverboer (1994) found that six- to seven-year-old children who met the criteria for clumsiness as measured by the Test of Motor Impairment (Stott et al., 1984; an earlier version of the M-ABC) had significantly higher levels of state and trait anxiety ($p < 0.05$) and introversion ($p < 0.01$) and significantly lower levels of perceived physical ($p < 0.01$) and social ($p = 0.05$) competence than age-matched controls. About 33 percent of the clumsiness group (n = 18) exhibited an increase on the state anxiety scale before the assessment of motor skills (i.e., feeling uncomfortable, unsure about themselves, or terrified and troubled). Likewise, 22 percent of the clumsiness group reported more trait anxiety (i.e., feeling unhappy or shy, having trouble making up their minds and deciding what to do, worrying about school and what others think of them, and having a faster heartbeat). Furthermore, parents of 50 percent of the participants in the clumsiness group reported their children to have difficulties making contact with peers (versus none in the control group). According to their teachers, children who were clumsy differed from controls in their introversion (i.e., being more seriously insecure and isolated). These findings reveal a clinically important area of concern because children as young as three and four years of age may be developing internalizing behaviors (e.g., anxiety and depression) associated with motor impairments (Piek et al.,

2008). Avoiding social situations and motor activities at this age due to the fear of failure and peer criticism or concealing physical awkwardness can have long-term consequences for a person's motor performance, abilities, and overall health (Bouffard et al., 1996; Kirkcaldy et al., 2002).

Similar findings were obtained in a study by Skinner and Piek (2001). Children (aged eight to ten years, n = 58) and adolescents (aged twelve to fourteen years, n = 51) who scored poorly on the M-ABC had significantly higher levels of state and trait anxiety and low levels of perceived competence in four domains (i.e., scholastic, athletic, physical appearance, and global self-worth) compared to age-matched controls ($p < 0.001$; Harter, 1985). Feeling competent is important for children to participate in activities and attempt further mastery (Harter, 1985). The significantly higher anxiety scores and less favorable perceptions of social support in the adolescent group compared to their younger counterparts ($p < 0.001$) suggest the cumulative effect of failed mastery attempts and the increasing accuracy of self-judgments as children get older (Skinner and Piek, 2001). Social support and acceptance from peers and close friends become more important with age (Harter, 1987; Losse et al., 1991). Thus, it is plausible that adolescents in this study might have avoided certain social situations to conceal their motor performance difficulties (Nicholls, 1984). Kristensen and Torgersen (2007) found similar avoidant behaviors in children with motor impairments and social anxiety or impulsive personality traits, aged eleven to twelve years. Because M-ABC scores did not correlate with state anxiety scores but with other personality disorder scores, the researchers concluded anxiety alone does not explain a person's motor impairments. Future research needs to account for other psychological factors in this relationship.

In summary, the existing research findings raise an important question about the mechanism underlying the relationship between motor impairments and anxiety or other social-emotional characteristics. Although many researchers have tried to determine the causal relationship between the two, the precursor has yet to be determined. However, it has been shown poor motor performance and failed attempts at mastery in childhood and adolescence are antecedents of avoidant behaviors and social isolation that can lead to the development of an AnxD over time (Piek et al., 2010; Rettew et al., 2003). Being exposed to possible scrutiny by others when doing something one is not particularly good at may provoke fear or anxiety in anyone, and even more so in individuals predisposed to certain personality traits, such as being impulsive, avoidant, dependent, or depressive (Bernstein et al., 1996; Kristensen and Torgersen, 2007; Piek et al., 2008; Skinner and Piek, 2001). Regardless of whether motor impairments cause AnxDs or vice versa, strong evidence suggests that fear and anxiety associated with poor motor performance can develop as early as three years (Piek et al., 2008), with self-concept and perceived competence declining in adolescence (Skinner and Piek, 2001). If not addressed, the negative emotions associated with poor motor performance in childhood can lead to chronic anxiety states and negatively influence gross motor development and possibly even personality functioning and academic performance, particularly in more vulnerable or less resilient adolescents or adults (Balaban and Porter, 1998; Bernstein et al., 1996; Skinner and Piek, 2001). Future research is needed to examine the interplay of factors contributing to negative experiences associated with poor motor performance in this population.

EXTERNALIZING: ATTENTION-DEFICIT HYPERACTIVITY DISORDER DEFINED

ADHD is a neurodevelopmental disorder characterized by a pattern of inattention and/or hyperactivity-impulsivity (APA, 2013). *Inattention* refers to persistent attention deficits that are not due to defiance or lack of comprehension (e.g., failing to stay on task for a sustained length of time, losing focus easily because of distracting stimuli, being disorganized, and losing materials necessary for tasks). *Hyperactivity* refers to excessive motor activity when it is inappropriate to the situation (e.g., running out of the classroom, excessive fidgeting, tapping an object, and talking excessively). *Impulsivity* refers to actions that occur quickly without forethought and have a high potential for harm to the person (e.g., climbing on dangerous equipment, interrupting someone talking, and acting before it is their turn). To be diagnosed with ADHD, a person must manifest several symptoms before twelve years of age and at levels that impair their functioning in two or more settings (e.g., home, school, workplace, community) (APA, 2013). The APA (2013) recognizes three different presentations of the symptoms of ADHD: (a) predominantly inattentive presentation, (b) predominantly hyperactive-impulsive presentation, and (c) combined presentation.

PREVALENCE OF ATTENTION-DEFICIT HYPERACTIVITY DISORDER

National parent-survey data from 2016 revealed that an estimated 6.1 million US children and youth between the ages of two and seventeen years (9.4 percent) had received an ADHD diagnosis at some point in their lives (Danielson et al., 2018). Of those, 5.4 million (8.4 percent) currently had ADHD. Among children with current ADHD, 14.5 percent were reported to have severe ADHD, 43.7 percent moderate ADHD, and 41.8 percent mild ADHD. Additionally, nearly two-thirds (63.8 percent) of children with current ADHD had at least one comorbidity, with behavioral or conduct problems being the most common (51.5 percent), followed by AnxDs (32.7 percent), depression (16.8 percent), autism spectrum disorders (13.7 percent), and Tourette syndrome (1.2 percent) (Danielson et al., 2018). Over half of the children and youth with ADHD also have been reported to have developmental coordination disorder (DCD) symptomology (Dahan et al., 2018). In adults with ADHD, the most common psychiatric comorbidities were depression, AnxDs, bipolar disorder, substance use disorder, and personality disorder (Katzman et al., 2017).

It is probably no surprise that many children's diagnoses of ADHD occur during elementary school (National Institute of Mental Health, 2021). With their entry into formal schooling, the typical expectations and demands on a child dramatically change—they must be silent for extended periods, complete assignments on time, wait their turn to participate, listen to an adult for long stretches, do tasks in a particular order, find the right materials quickly, and walk in an orderly way with their hands to themselves, in addition to many other tasks requiring self-control. As they advance through the grade levels, academic tasks become lengthier and more complicated, and their need for special education services becomes more evident (Hinshaw, 2018). ADHD is also a co-diagnosis for a large percentage of students who are eligible for services under different IDEA disability categories, including other health impairments (65.8 percent), emotional disturbance (57.9 percent), intellectual disability (20.6 percent), specific learning disability (20.2 percent), and speech/language impairment (4.5 percent) (Schnoes et al., 2006). As stated in the 2004 authorization of IDEA, a child will qualify for special education in the category of other health impairment *if* the child has,

> limited strength, vitality, or alertness, including a heightened alertness to environmental stimuli, that results in limited alertness with respect to the educational environment, that (i) Is due to chronic or acute health problems such as . . . attention deficit hyperactivity disorder . . . ; and (ii) Adversely affects a child's educational performance. (34 C. F. R. § 300.8[c][9])

If a child with ADHD is determined to be eligible for services under IDEA, a school-based team that includes a student's parents develops an *individualized education program* with goals to address the student's academic, social-emotional, and behavioral needs. Conversely, if a child with ADHD is not determined to be eligible under IDEA, that child's accommodations and learning supports could be determined under Section 504 of the Rehabilitation Act (34 C.F.R. Part 104).

CONCEPTUAL MODELS OF ATTENTION-DEFICIT HYPERACTIVITY DISORDER

Three opposing conceptual models of ADHD have been heavily cited in research and clinical literature to help explain and predict the diverse symptomology in children with ADHD, including the behavioral disinhibition model, the working memory (WM) model, and the emotion dysregulation model.

The centerpiece of the *behavioral disinhibition model* is a person's abnormality in behavioral inhibition (Alderson et al., 2017; Barkley, 1997; Castellanos et al., 2002; Dahan et al., 2018; Durston, 2003; Rapport et al., 2001). According to Barkley (1997, p. 67), *behavioral inhibition* refers to "three interrelated processes: (a) inhibition of the initial prepotent response to an event; (b) stopping of an ongoing response, which thereby permits a delay in the decision to respond, and (c) the protection of this period of delay and the self-directed response that occur within it from disruption by competing events and responses." Behavioral inhibition has been postulated to be vital to the preparation and selection of motor responses and the normal performance of many behavioral and cognitive tasks (Mostofsky et al., 2003). Meta-analytic reviews (Alderson et al., 2017; Alderson et al., 2007; Lijffijt et al., 2005; Oosterlaan et al., 1998) indicate individuals with ADHD have significantly slower and more variable reaction times on measures of behavioral inhibition compared to the controls. The model suggests that a person's inability to inhibit responses interferes with their development and execution of other functions, including WM, goal-directed behavior, and emotional regulation (Barkley, 1997; Durston, 2003; Rapport et al., 2001). Although the behavioral disinhibition model of ADHD has been studied extensively, perhaps due to the intuitive sense of a relationship between behavioral inhibition and core features of the disorder, Rapport et al. (2001) have argued that the disinhibition model itself "cannot easily account for the actual control of inhibition or lack thereof" (p. 57).

The *WM model* hypothesizes that WM plays a central role in the behavioral manifestations of ADHD (Baddeley, 2003; Rapport et al., 2008; Rapport et al., 2001). WM is a limited-capacity executive function that involves "the temporary storage, maintenance, and manipulation of information used to guide behavior" (Alderson et al., 2017, p. 257). This model suggests WM deficits underlie the core ADHD symptoms of inattention (Kofler et al., 2019), impulsivity (Patros et al., 2015), and hyperactivity (Rapport et al., 2009) because the internal representation of information to guide a child's decisions and control their behavior (e.g., instructions, rules, warnings, prohibitions) during an activity is either degraded or lost, leaving the behavior at the mercy of the sensory stimuli currently impinging on the child (Martinussen et al., 2005). When a person performs a task that involves goal-directed behavior, their WM system must have the capacity to both harbor the goal and allow the executive system to determine the most suitable strategy. Research suggests approximately 62 percent to 85 percent of children and youth with ADHD have WM deficits and score significantly worse on WM tasks than those without ADHD (Kasper et al., 2012; Kofler et al., 2019). Furthermore, meta-analytic reviews revealed children and youth with ADHD typically perform significantly worse on phenological and visuospatial tasks than those without ADHD, with visuospatial tasks having more significant effects on between-group differences compared to phenological tasks (Kasper et al., 2012; Martinussen et al., 2005; Willcutt et al., 2005). Even though research suggests WM deficits are causally linked with ADHD-related symptomology (Kofler et al., 2019; Rapport et al., 2009), the direction of the pathways and the role of emotion regulation (Schmeichel et al., 2008) or response inhibition in this process is still poorly understood and needs further investigation.

The role of emotion regulation—a possible significant contributor to the functional impairment experienced by individuals with ADHD (Bunford et al., 2015)—has been studied under the *emotion dysregulation model* of ADHD (Beheshti et al., 2020; Bunford et al., 2015; Graziano and Garcia, 2016; Shaw et al., 2014). Bunford et al. (2015, p. 188) defined emotion dysregulation as "an individual's inability to exercise any or all aspects of the modulatory processes involved in emotion regulation, to such a degree that the inability results in the individual functioning meaningfully below his or her baseline." These processes regulate the speed and degree of escalation and de-escalation and the intensity of "the physiological, experiential, and behavioral expression of an emotion" (Bunford et al., 2015, p. 188). Cross-sectional studies of psychopathology have affirmed that a high prevalence of children, adolescents, and adults with ADHD have a comorbid emotional disturbance diagnosis (for reviews, see Beheshti et al., 2020; Graziano and Garcia, 2016). Typical manifestations of emotional disturbance in individuals with ADHD are quick irritability, low tolerance for frustration, triggering negative emotions by mild stimuli, experiencing emotions at more intense levels, and emotional lability (Hirsch et al., 2018; Retz et al., 2012).

MOTOR IMPAIRMENTS AND ATTENTION-DEFICIT HYPERACTIVITY DISORDER

Systematic reviews indicate that reduced motor control and function are common traits of ADHD (Dahan et al., 2018; Demers et al., 2013; Gillberg, 2003; Goulardins et al., 2017; Harvey and Reid, 2003; Kaiser et al., 2015). In addition, research has shown children with ADHD are more likely to experience impairments in fine and gross motor skills than those without ADHD (Carte et al., 1996; Fliers et al., 2008; Harvey et al., 2009; Piek et al., 1999). Using the Test of Gross Motor Development-2 descriptors (Ulrich, 2000), Harvey et al. (2009) classified the fundamental motor skill performance of six boys with ADHD and six without ADHD, aged nine to twelve years, as average to poor and as above-average to average, respectively. Furthermore, interviews revealed the ADHD group rarely initiated and organized opportunities to play or be active with other children and seemed to enjoy being involved in isolated, individual sports or leisure activities. Furthermore, the boys with ADHD reported that they "devote little time to acquire the specific details of physical activities, whereas their peers without ADHD would purposely learn about their activity of interest" (Harvey et al., 2009, p. 145). The authors speculated the lack of attention to detail, poor problem-solving skills, and minimal time deliberately spent learning and practicing basic motor skills or movements by the boys with ADHD could have contributed to their delayed motor development (Harvey et al., 2009). These experiences need our attention because motor impairments at a younger age have been shown to strongly predict ADHD (Kooistra et al., 2005; Kroes et al., 2002; Livesey et al., 2006; Van Damme et al., 2015). For example, in a prospective study of precursors of ADHD, Kroes et al. (2002) found that the Maastricht Motor Test's qualitative aspects of motor performance (Vles et al., 2004) of five- to six-year-olds (n = 401) predicted their ADHD diagnosis eighteen months later.

The critical role of attention in motor control and function of children with ADHD has received attention in research (Fliers et al., 2008; Piek et al., 1999; Pitcher et al., 2003). Pitcher et al. (2003) demonstrated children with either the predominantly inattentive or combined presentations of ADHD, aged seven to twelve years, had significantly more severe gross motor skill impairments as measured by M-ABC and fine motor skill impairments as measured by the Purdue Pegboard test (Tiffin, 1968), compared with children with the hyperactive/impulsive presentation or a comparison group without ADHD. Furthermore, the findings revealed that a high percentage of participants with ADHD displayed movement impairments consistent with DCD. The APA (2013) characterizes DCD as deficits in motor coordination, motor control, and motor planning that significantly interferes with academic achievement or activities of daily living. The group with the predominantly inattentive ADHD presentation in Pitcher et al. (2003) had the largest percentage of participants with DCD symptomology (42 percent), followed by the hyperactive/impulsive (31 percent) and the combined (29 percent) presentations. Considerable DCD prevalence was also found in Watemberg et al. (2007) and Piek et al. (1999). Watemberg et al. (2007) found that 55 percent of children with ADHD scored in the DCD range on the M-ABC, with significantly higher prevalence ($p < 0.05$) of the predominantly inattentive (64 percent) and combined (59 percent) presentations than the predominantly hyperactive-impulsive presentation (11 percent). In a smaller sample of boys with ADHD, Piek et al. (1999) found a greater prevalence of motor impairments: 69 percent with the predominantly inattentive and 56 percent in the combined presentations. The high prevalence was further confirmed by parents and teachers in Fliers et al. (2008), who reported that 29 percent of girls and 34 percent of boys with ADHD, aged five to nineteen years, experienced DCD symptomatology.

These coordination difficulties may lead to substandard performance in sports activities, which also may affect the quality and quantity of social interaction with peers (Demers et al., 2013).

The most cited hypotheses to explain motor impairments in individuals with ADHD include (a) altered cerebral structures and neurotransmitter imbalance (Dahan et al., 2018; Demers et al., 2013; Gillberg, 2003; Kaiser et al., 2015; Sharma and Couture, 2014) and (b) ADHD comorbidities (Gillberg, 2003; Goulardins et al., 2017; Kaiser et al., 2015).

Altered Cerebral Structures and Neurotransmitter Imbalance

Imaging studies have provided substantial evidence of structural and functional alterations in the cerebral structure (i.e., frontal lobes, basal ganglia, corpus callosum, and parietal lobes) of individuals with ADHD compared to age-matched controls that may influence their motor performance (Biederman, 2005; Castellanos et al., 2002; Demers et al., 2013; Depue et al., 2010; Makris et al., 2009; Swanson et al., 1998). These structural areas (particularly the prefrontal cortex) play a key role in attention and organization of thoughts, inhibition of motor responses, and motor planning (Cortese, 2012; Depue et al., 2010). Other hypotheses contend that motor impairments result from neurotransmitter imbalances (i.e., dopamine and norepinephrine) in the prefrontal cortex area (Sharma and Couture, 2014). An appropriate level of these neurotransmitters is required for optimal functioning of the cortex area. For example, transcranial magnetic stimulation in the motor cortex revealed children and youth with ADHD showed significantly lower short-interval intracortical inhibition than those without ADHD (e.g., Gilbert et al., 2011; Mostofsky et al., 2003). The short-interval intracortical inhibition plays a critical role in modulating neural function during skill acquisition (Ljubisavljevic, 2006). A child with abnormal dopaminergic input to the basal ganglia may have impaired development of the cortical mechanisms necessary for efficient response selection and control (Casey et al., 2001). Medication (e.g., methylphenidate, amphetamines) can enhance the dopamine levels in individuals with ADHD, which can improve their inhibition control and their executive functions of sustained attention, inhibitory control, WM, self-regulation, and cognitive flexibility (Casey et al., 2001; Kaiser et al., 2015; Pedersen et al., 2004; Rubia et al., 2003). Although medication has proved to be beneficial to motor skill performance in children with ADHD, its long-term effects and whether the medication influences motor skill performance directly or indirectly remains unknown (Kaiser et al., 2015; Klimkeit et al., 2005).

ATTENTION-DEFICIT HYPERACTIVITY DISORDER COMORBIDITIES

Comorbidity of ADHD with other developmental disorders has consistently been reported in epidemiological studies (Danielson et al., 2018; Jarrett and Ollendick, 2008; Jensen et al., 2001; Katzman et al., 2017). Research has demonstrated children with ADHD experience significant motor impairments when diagnosed with other EBDs, such as CD and ODD (Kooistra et al., 2005; Kroes et al., 2002; Pitcher et al., 2003; Van Damme et al., 2015), AnxDs (Bloemsma et al., 2013; Danielson et al., 2018; Jarrett and Ollendick, 2008; Oosterlaan and Sergeant, 1998; Pliszka, 1992; Reale et al., 2017; Schatz and Rostain, 2006), and autism spectrum disorders

(Dewey et al., 2007; Kopp et al., 2010; Pan et al., 2009; Papadopoulos et al., 2013; Reiersen et al., 2008).

Of a substantial interest to ADHD researchers and clinicians has been the ADHD comorbidity with CD or ODD due to the high rates of delinquent and aggressive behaviors in the ADHD population (Connor and Doerfler, 2008; Jensen et al., 2001; Kuhne et al., 1997; Oosterlaan and Sergeant, 1998). For example, a cross-sectional study by Connor and Doerfler (2008) compared ADHD symptom severity among three groups of male children and youth diagnosed with ADHD only (n = 65), ADHD+ODD (n = 85), and ADHD+CD (n = 50). Although ODD and CD typically have similar symptomology (Loeber et al., 2000), parent reports revealed significant differences in ADHD severity among the three groups, with the ADHD+CD group having more severe ADHD symptoms than the ADHD+ODD or ADHD-only groups (Connor and Doerfler, 2008). In addition, Kuhne et al. (1997) found that ADHD+CD comorbidity altered ADHD correlates across other areas, including greater social dysfunction; higher aggression, anxiety, and maternal pathology; and decreased self-esteem. This line of research suggests that motor impairments in individuals with ADHD heavily depend on co-occurring EBDs (Emck et al., 2011; Kooistra et al., 2005; Pitcher et al., 2003; Van Damme et al., 2015). The overlap of symptoms has caused researchers to question the notion of discrete diagnostic categories (Kaplan et al., 2001). Some researchers even have suggested conceptualizing ADHD as a spectrum using a dimensional rather than a categorical approach to diagnosis and treatment (Heidbreder, 2015; Katzman et al., 2017). Under this model, motor skill impairments associated with ADHD would be part of this spectrum of co-occurring symptoms rather than a result of comorbid developmental disorders (Kaiser et al., 2015; Kaplan et al., 2001). Therefore, researchers are encouraged to recruit sufficiently large and well-defined samples of participants to examine the contribution of co-occurring disorders to ADHD symptomatology within the same analytic model.

In summary, motor impairments are highly prevalent in children, youth, and adults with ADHD. Despite this strong evidence of motor impairment, ADHD research literature continues to lack a conceptual model that integrates seemingly fragmented findings according to the different stages of motor control to help us understand the causal relationships that underlie motor impairments in this population. The two most cited hypotheses to explain these motor impairments include (a) altered cerebral structures and neurotransmitter imbalances and (b) the presence of comorbidities. Although behavioral disinhibition was identified as a core deficit in ADHD for decades, other researchers argue that the disinhibition model itself does not explain the causality of the disorder and that the WM model and the emotion dysregulation model better explain the core features of ADHD. In addition, because the motor profiles of individuals with ADHD differ dramatically from those of individuals without ADHD, it is still debated whether ADHD and another motor disorder, such as DCD, are comorbidities, overlap in the diagnostic criteria, cause symptoms of the other, or are a separate disorder with an independent nosology.

FUTURE RESEARCH AND PRACTICAL IMPLICATIONS

The detrimental effects of motor impairment on a child's overall development and health call for the assessment of both fine and gross motor performance and self-perception of motor competence through the use of psychometrically sound instruments at either an early age or the first sign of an EBD (Dunlap et al., 2006; Emck et al., 2009). It is also important to identify comorbidities because comorbidity profiles can have important implications for the etiology, assessment, and intervention plans of children with EBDs. In addition, early identification of signs of motor impairments that are associated with a particular EBD will lead to more successful intervention efforts (Landrum, 2017).

Effective interventions to address EBD symptoms may include pharmacologic treatments, neurofeedback, cognitive training, cognitive behavioral therapy, behavior intervention, psychotherapy, or their combination (Bandelow et al., 2018; Bruhn et al., 2015; Garwood et al., 2021; Knouse and Safren, 2010; Patel et al., 2018; Sharma and Couture, 2014; Stonerock et al., 2015). An up-and-coming framework that employs a comprehensive, systemic approach to EBDs in school-aged children is labeled Multi-Tiered Systems of Support, and it is supported by an evidence base that has been increasing over the past decade (Berger, 2019; Bohnenkamp et al., 2021; Collins et al., 2019; Fabiano and Pyle, 2019; Jones et al., 2019; Kern et al., 2021; Lyon and Bruns, 2019). A growing body of evidence also points to the beneficial effects of physical exercise or physical activity as non-invasive and supplemental (to medication) interventions to reduce symptoms of AnxDs (Bartley et al., 2013; Dunn et al., 2001; Herring et al., 2014; Jayakody et al., 2014; Stonerock et al., 2015) and ADHD (Cerrillo-Urbina et al., 2015; Den Heijer et al., 2017; Hoza et al., 2016; Kamp et al., 2014; Neudecker et al., 2019; Vysniauske et al., 2020). However, the wide variety of exercise modalities, prescriptions, and assessment tools utilized in the exercise studies involving individuals with AnxD and ADHD symptomology makes comparing the effects and formulation of clinical recommendations challenging. In addition, studies of the effects of these interventions on the motor performance or motor control of individuals with AnxDs or ADHD are sparse (Chang et al., 2014; Kamp et al., 2014; Kosari et al., 2013; Pan et al., 2017; Smith et al., 2013; Tantillo et al., 2002; Verret et al., 2012). Future well-designed intervention studies that examine the effects of different exercise modalities on motor performance or motor control of individuals with different EBDs are greatly needed. Future studies also should address the interaction of physical exercise and other interventions (e.g., stimulant medication, cognitive behavior therapy) in controlled designs, examining possible complementary or differing effects.

REFERENCES

Alderson, R.M., Patros, C.H.G., Tarle, S.J., Hudec, K.L., Kasper, L.J., and Lea, S.E. (2017). Working memory and behavioral inhibition in boys with ADHD: An experimental examination of competing models. *Child Neuropsychology*, 23(3), 255–72. https://doi.org/10.1080/09297049.2015.1105207

Alderson, R.M., Rapport, M.D., and Kofler, M.J. (2007). Attention-deficit/hyperactivity disorder and behavioral inhibition: A meta-analytic review of the stop-signal paradigm. *Journal of Abnormal Child Psychology*, 35(5), 745–58. https://doi.org/10.1007/s10802-007-9131-6

American Psychiatric Association. (2013). *Diagnostic and statistical manual of mental disorders* (fifth edition). Washington, DC: American Psychiatric Association.

Anxiety and Depression Association of America, Facts & Statistics. https://adaa.org/about-adaa/press-room/facts-statistics. Accessed September 5, 2023.

Baddeley, A. (2003). Working memory: Looking back and looking forward. *Nature Reviews Neuroscience, 4*(10), 829–39. https://doi.org/10.1038/nrn1201

Balaban, C.D., Jacob, R.G., and Furman, J.M. (2011). Neurologic bases for comorbidity of balance disorders, anxiety disorders and migraine: Neurotherapeutic implications. *Expert Review of Neurotherapeutics, 11*(3), 379–94. https://doi.org/10.1586/ern.11.19

Balaban, C.D., and Porter, J.D. (1998). Neuroanatomic substrates for vestibulo-autonomic interactions. *Journal of Vestibular Research, 8*, 7–16. https://doi.org/10.3233/VES-1998-8102

Balaban, C.D., and Thayer, J.F. (2001). Neurological bases for balance–anxiety links. *Journal of Anxiety Disorders, 15*(1), 53–79. https://doi.org/https://doi.org/10.1016/S0887-6185(00)00042-6

Bandelow, B., Sagebiel, A., Belz, M., Görlich, Y., Michaelis, S., and Wedekind, D. (2018). Enduring effects of psychological treatments for anxiety disorders: Meta-analysis of follow-up studies. *The British Journal of Psychiatry, 212*(6), 333–38. https://doi.org/10.1192/bjp.2018.49

Barkley, R.A. (1997). Behavioral inhibition, sustained attention, and executive functions: Constructing a unifying theory of ADHD. *Psychological Bulletin, 121*(1), 65.

Bartley, C.A., Hay, M., and Bloch, M.H. (2013). Meta-analysis: Aerobic exercise for the treatment of anxiety disorders. *Progress in Neuro-Psychopharmacology and Biological Psychiatry, 45*, 34–39. https://doi.org/https://doi.org/10.1016/j.pnpbp.2013.04.016

Beheshti, A., Chavanon, M.-L., and Christiansen, H. (2020). Emotion dysregulation in adults with attention deficit hyperactivity disorder: A meta-analysis. *BMC Psychiatry, 20*(1), 120. https://doi.org/10.1186/s12888-020-2442-7

Beilock, S.L., and Carr, T.H. (2001). On the fragility of skilled performance: What governs choking under pressure? *Journal of Experimental Psychology: General, 130*(4), 701–25. https://doi.org/10.1037/0096-3445.130.4.701

Berger, E. (2019). Multi-tiered approaches to trauma-informed care in schools: A systematic review. *School Mental Health, 11*(4), 650–64. https://doi.org/10.1007/s12310-019-09326-0

Bernstein, D.P., Cohen, P., Skodol, A., Bezirganian, S., and Brook, J.S. (1996). Childhood antecedents of adolescent personality disorders. *The American Journal of Psychiatry, 153*(7), 907–13. https://doi.org/10.1176/ajp.153.7.907

Biederman, J. (2005). Attention-deficit/hyperactivity disorder: A selective overview. *Biological Psychiatry, 57*(11), 1215–20. https://doi.org/10.1016/j.biopsych.2004.10.020

Bloemsma, J.M., Boer, F., Arnold, R., Banaschewski, T., Faraone, S.V., Buitelaar, J.K., Sergeant, J.A., Rommelse, N., and Oosterlaan, J. (2013). Comorbid anxiety and neurocognitive dysfunctions in children with ADHD. *European Child & Adolescent Psychiatry, 22*(4), 225–34. https://doi.org/10.1007/s00787-012-0339-9

Bohnenkamp, J.H., Schaeffer, C.M., Siegal, R., Beason, T., Smith-Millman, M., and Hoover, S. (2021). Impact of a school-based, multi-tiered emotional and behavioral health crisis intervention on school safety and discipline. *Prevention Science, 22*(4), 492–503. https://doi.org/10.1007/s11121-020-01195-3

Bouffard, M., Watkinson, E.J., Thompson, L.P., Causgrove Dunn, J.L., and Romanow, S.K.E. (1996). A test of the activity deficit hypothesis with children with movement difficulties. *Adapted Physical Activity Quarterly, 13*(1), 61–73. https://doi.org/10.1123/apaq.13.1.61

Bruhn, A., Mcdaniel, S., and Kreigh, C. (2015). Self-monitoring interventions for students with behavior problems: A systematic review of current research. *Behavioral Disorders, 40*(2), 102–21. https://doi.org/10.17988/bd-13-45.1

Bunford, N., Evans, S.W., and Wymbs, F. (2015). ADHD and emotion dysregulation among children and adolescents. *Clinical Child and Family Psychology Review, 18*(3), 185–217. https://doi.org/10.1007/s10567-015-0187-5

Carte, E.T., Nigg, J.T., and Hinshaw, S.P. (1996). Neuropsychological functioning, motor speed, and language processing in boys with and without ADHD. *Journal of Abnormal Child Psychology*, 24(4), 481–98. https://doi.org/10.1007/BF01441570

Casey, B.J., Durston, S., and Fossella, J.A. (2001). Evidence for a mechanistic model of cognitive control. *Clinical Neuroscience Research*, 1(4), 267–82. https://doi.org/https://doi.org/10.1016/S1566-2772(01)00013-5

Castellanos, F.X., Lee, P.P., Sharp, W., Jeffries, N.O., Greenstein, D.K., Clasen, L.S., Blumenthal, J.D., James, R.S., Ebens, C.L., Walter, J.M., Zijdenbos, A., Evans, A.C., Giedd, J.N., and Rapoport, J.L. (2002). Developmental trajectories of brain volume abnormalities in children and adolescents with attention-deficit/hyperactivity disorder. *The Journal of the American Medical Association*, 288(14), 1740–48. https://doi.org/10.1001/jama.288.14.1740

Cerrillo-Urbina, A.J., García-Hermoso, A., Sánchez-López, M., Pardo-Guijarro, M.J., Santos Gómez, J.L., and Martínez-Vizcaíno, V. (2015). The effects of physical exercise in children with attention deficit hyperactivity disorder: A systematic review and meta-analysis of randomized control trials. *Child: Care, Health and Development*, 41(6), 779–88. https://doi.org/https://doi.org/10.1111/cch.12255

Chang, Y.-K., Hung, C.-L., Huang, C.-J., Hatfield, B.D., and Hung, T.-M. (2014). Effects of an aquatic exercise program on inhibitory control in children with ADHD: A preliminary study. *Archives of Clinical Neuropsychology*, 29(3), 217–23. https://doi.org/10.1093/arclin/acu003

Child Mind Institute. (2015). *Children's mental health report*. New York: Child Mind Institute. https://childmind.org/awareness-campaigns/childrens-mental-health-report/2015-childrens-mental-health-report/

Collins, T.A., Dart, E.H., and Arora, P.G. (2019). Addressing the internalizing behavior of students in schools: Applications of the MTSS model. *School Mental Health*, 11(2), 191–93. https://doi.org/10.1007/s12310-018-09307-9

Connor, D.F., and Doerfler, L.A. (2008). ADHD with comorbid oppositional defiant disorder or conduct disorder: Discrete or nondistinct disruptive behavior disorders? *Journal of Attention Disorders*, 12(2), 126–34. https://doi.org/10.1177/1087054707308486

Cortese, S. (2012). The neurobiology and genetics of attention-deficit/hyperactivity disorder (ADHD): What every clinician should know. *European Journal of Paediatric Neurology*, 16(5), 422–33. https://doi.org/https://doi.org/10.1016/j.ejpn.2012.01.009

Dahan, A., Ryder, C.H., and Reiner, M. (2018). Components of motor deficiencies in ADHD and possible interventions. *Neuroscience*, 378, 34–53. https://doi.org/https://doi.org/10.1016/j.neuroscience.2016.05.040

Danielson, M.L., Bitsko, R.H., Ghandour, R.M., Holbrook, J.R., Kogan, M.D., and Blumberg, S.J. (2018). Prevalence of parent-reported ADHD diagnosis and associated treatment among U.S. children and adolescents, 2016. *Journal of Clinical Child & Adolescent Psychology*, 47(2), 199–212. https://doi.org/10.1080/15374416.2017.1417860

Demers, M.M., McNevin, N., and Azar, N.R. (2013). ADHD and motor control: A review of the motor control deficiencies associated with attention deficit/hyperactivity disorder and current treatment options. *Critical Reviews in Physical and Rehabilitation Medicine*, 25(3-4), 231–39. https://doi.org/10.1615/CritRevPhysRehabilMed.2013009763

Den Heijer, A.E., Groen, Y., Tucha, L., Fuermaier, A.B.M., Koerts, J., Lange, K.W., Thome, J., and Tucha, O. (2017). Sweat it out? The effects of physical exercise on cognition and behavior in children and adults with ADHD: A systematic literature review. *Journal of Neural Transmission*, 124(1), 3–26. https://doi.org/10.1007/s00702-016-1593-7

Depue, B.E., Burgess, G.C., Bidwell, L.C., Willcutt, E.G., and Banich, M.T. (2010). Behavioral performance predicts grey matter reductions in the right inferior frontal gyrus in young adults with combined type ADHD. *Psychiatry Research: Neuroimaging*, 182(3), 231–37. https://doi.org/https://doi.org/10.1016/j.pscychresns.2010.01.012

Dewey, D., Cantell, M., and Crawford, S. G. (2007). Motor and gestural performance in children with autism spectrum disorders, developmental coordination disorder, and/or attention deficit hyperactivity disorder. *Journal of the International Neuropsychological Society*, 13(2), 246–56. https://doi.org/10.1017/S1355617707070270

Dunlap, G., Strain, P.S., Fox, L., Carta, J.J., Conroy, M., Smith, B.J., Kern, L., Hemmeter, M.L., Timm, M.A., Mccart, A., Sailor, W., Markey, U., Markey, D.J., Lardieri, S., and Sowell, C. (2006). Prevention and intervention with young children's challenging behavior: Perspectives regarding current knowledge. *Behavioral Disorders*, 32(1), 29–45. https://doi.org/10.1177/019874290603200103

Dunn, A.L., Trivedi, M.H., and O'Neal, H.A. (2001). Physical activity dose-response effects on outcomes of depression and anxiety. *Medicine & Science in Sports & Exercise*, (6), S587–S597.

Durston, S. (2003). A review of the biological bases of ADHD: What have we learned from imaging studies? *Mental Retardation and Developmental Disabilities Research Reviews*, 9(3), 184–95. https://doi.org/https://doi.org/10.1002/mrdd.10079

Emck, C., Bosscher, R., Beek, P., and Doreleijers, T. (2009). Gross motor performance and self-perceived motor competence in children with emotional, behavioural, and pervasive developmental disorders: A review. *Developmental Medicine & Child Neurology*, 51(7), 501–17. https://doi.org/https://doi.org/10.1111/j.1469-8749.2009.03337.x

Emck, C., Bosscher, R.J., Van Wieringen, P.C.W., Doreleiers, T., and Beek, P.J. (2011). Gross motor performance and physical fitness in children with psychiatric disorders. *Developmental Medicine & Child Neurology*, 53(2), 150–55. https://doi.org/https://doi.org/10.1111/j.1469-8749.2010.03806.x

Erez, O., Gordon, C.R., Sever, J., Sadeh, A., and Mintz, M. (2004). Balance dysfunction in childhood anxiety: Findings and theoretical approach. *Journal of Anxiety Disorders*, 18(3), 341–56. https://doi.org/10.1016/S0887-6185(02)00291-8

Eysenck, M.W., Derakshan, N., Santos, R., and Calvo, M.G. (2007). Anxiety and cognitive performance: Attentional control theory. *Emotion*, 7(2), 336–53. https://doi.org/10.1037/1528-3542.7.2.336

Fabiano, G.A., and Pyle, K. (2019). Best practices in school mental health for attention-deficit/hyperactivity disorder: A framework for intervention. *School Mental Health*, 11(1), 72–91. https://doi.org/10.1007/s12310-018-9267-2

Fliers, E., Rommelse, N., Vermeulen, S.H.H.M., Altink, M., Buschgens, C.J.M., Faraone, S.V., Sergeant, J.A., Franke, B., and Buitelaar, J.K. (2008). Motor coordination problems in children and adolescents with ADHD rated by parents and teachers: Effects of age and gender. *Journal of Neural Transmission*, 115(2), 211–20. https://doi.org/10.1007/s00702-007-0827-0

Garwood, J.D., Peltier, C., Sinclair, T., Eisel, H., McKenna, J.W., and Vannest, K.J. (2021). A quantitative synthesis of intervention research published in flagship EBD journals: 2010 to 2019. *Behavioral Disorders*, 47(1), 14–27. https://doi.org/10.1177/0198742920961341

Gilbert, D.L., Isaacs, K.M., Augusta, M., Macneil, L.K., and Mostofsky, S.H. (2011). Motor cortex inhibition: A marker of ADHD behavior and motor development in children. *Neurology*, 76(7), 615–21. https://doi.org/10.1212/WNL.0b013e31820c2ebd

Gillberg, C. (2003). Deficits in attention, motor control, and perception: A brief review. *Archives of Disease in Childhood*, 88(10), 904. https://doi.org/10.1136/adc.88.10.904

Goulardins, J.B., Marques, J.C.B., and De Oliveira, J.A. (2017). Attention deficit hyperactivity disorder and motor impairment: A critical review. *Perceptual and Motor Skills*, 124(2), 425–40. https://doi.org/10.1177/0031512517690607

Graziano, P.A., and Garcia, A. (2016). Attention-deficit hyperactivity disorder and children's emotion dysregulation: A meta-analysis. *Clinical Psychology Review*, 46, 106–23. https://doi.org/https://doi.org/10.1016/j.cpr.2016.04.011

Gresham, F.M. (2007). Response to intervention and emotional and behavioral disorders: Best practices in assessment for intervention. *Assessment for Effective Intervention*, 32(4), 214–22. https://doi.org/10.1177/15345084070320040301

Harter, S. (1985). *Manual for the self-perception profile for children*. Denver: University of Denver.

Harter, S. (1987). The determinants and mediational role of global self-worth in children. In N. Eisenberg (Ed.), *Contemporary topics in developmental psychology* (pp. 219–42). Hoboken, NJ: Wiley.

Harvard Medical School. (2007). National Comorbidity Survey (NCS). (2017, August 21). Retrieved from https://www.hcp.med.harvard.edu/ncs/index.php. Data Table 2: 12-month prevalence DSM-IV/WMH-CIDI disorders by sex and cohort.

Harvey, W., and Reid, G. (2003). Attention-deficit/hyperactivity disorder: A review of research on movement skill performance and physical fitness. *Adapted Physical Activity Quarterly*, 20, 1–25. https://doi.org/10.1123/apaq.20.1.1

Harvey, W.J., Reid, G., Bloom, G.A., Staples, K., Grizenko, N., Mbekou, V., Ter-Stepanian, M., and Joober, R. (2009). Physical activity experiences of boys with and without ADHD. *Adapted Physical Activity Quarterly*, 26(2), 131–50. https://doi.org/10.1123/apaq.26.2.131

Heidbreder, R. (2015). ADHD symptomatology is best conceptualized as a spectrum: A dimensional versus unitary approach to diagnosis. *ADHD Attention Deficit and Hyperactivity Disorders*, 7(4), 249–69. https://doi.org/10.1007/s12402-015-0171-4

Henderson, S.E., and Sugden, D.A. (1992). *Movement assessment battery for children*. San Antonion, TX: The Psychological Corporation.

Herring, M.P., Lindheimer, J.B., and O'Connor, P.J. (2014). The effects of exercise training on anxiety. *Am J Lifestyle Med*, 8(6), 388–403. https://doi.org/10.1177/1559827613508542

Hinshaw, S. P. (2018). Attention Deficit Hyperactivity Disorder (ADHD): Controversy, developmental mechanisms, and multiple levels of analysis. *Annual Review of Clinical Psychology*, 14(1), 291-316. https://doi.org/10.1146/annurev-clinpsy-050817-084917

Hirsch, O., Chavanon, M., Riechmann, E., & Christiansen, H. (2018). Emotional dysregulation is a primary symptom in adult Attention-Deficit/Hyperactivity Disorder (ADHD). *Journal of Affective Disorders*, 232, 41–47. https://doi.org/https://doi.org/10.1016/j.jad.2018.02.007

Hoza, B., Martin, C.P., Pirog, A., and Shoulberg, E.K. (2016). Using physical activity to manage ADHD symptoms: The state of the evidence. *Current Psychiatry Reports*, 18(12), 113. https://doi.org/10.1007/s11920-016-0749-3

Janelle, C.M. (2002). Anxiety, arousal and visual attention: A mechanistic account of performance variability. *Journal of Sports Sciences*, 20(3), 237–51. https://doi.org/10.1080/026404102317284790

Jarrett, M.A., and Ollendick, T.H. (2008). A conceptual review of the comorbidity of attention-deficit/hyperactivity disorder and anxiety: Implications for future research and practice. *Clinical psychology review*, 28(7), 1266–80. https://doi.org/https://doi.org/10.1016/j.cpr.2008.05.004

Jayakody, K., Gunadasa, S., and Hosker, C. (2014). Exercise for anxiety disorders: Systematic review. *British Journal of Sports Medicine*, 48(3), 187–96. https://doi.org/10.1136/bjsports-2012-091287

Jensen, P.S., Hinshaw, S.P., Kraemer, H.C., Lenora, N., Newcorn, J.H., Abikoff, H.B., March, J.S., Arnold, L.E., Cantwell, D.P., Conners, C.K., Elliott, G.R., Greenhill, L.L., Hechtman, L., Hoza, B., Pelham, W.E., Severe, J.B., Swanson, J.M., Wells, K.C., Wigal, T., and Vitiello, B. (2001). ADHD comorbidity findings from the MTA study: Comparing comorbid subgroups. *Journal of the American Academy of Child & Adolescent Psychiatry*, 40(2), 147–58. https://doi.org/https://doi.org/10.1097/00004583-200102000-00009

Jones, A.M., West, K.B., and Suveg, C. (2019). Anxiety in the school setting: A framework for evidence-based practice. *School Mental Health*, *11*(1), 4–14. https://doi.org/10.1007/s12310-017-9235-2

Kaiser, M.L., Schoemaker, M.M., Albaret, J.M., and Geuze, R.H. (2015). What is the evidence of impaired motor skills and motor control among children with attention deficit hyperactivity disorder (ADHD)? Systematic review of the literature. *Research in Developmental Disabilities*, *36*, 338–57. https://doi.org/https://doi.org/10.1016/j.ridd.2014.09.023

Kamp, C.F., Sperlich, B., and Holmberg, H.C. (2014). Exercise reduces the symptoms of attention-deficit/hyperactivity disorder and improves social behaviour, motor skills, strength and neuropsychological parameters. *Acta Paediatrica*, *103*(7), 709–14. https://doi.org/https://doi.org/10.1111/apa.12628

Kaplan, B.J., Dewey, D.M., Crawford, S.G., and Wilson, B.N. (2001). The term comorbidity is of questionable value in reference to developmental disorders: Data and theory. *Journal of Learning Disabilities*, *34*(6), 555–65. https://doi.org/10.1177/002221940103400608

Kasper, L.J., Alderson, R.M., and Hudec, K.L. (2012). Moderators of working memory deficits in children with attention-deficit/hyperactivity disorder (ADHD): A meta-analytic review. *Clinical Psychology Review*, *32*(7), 605–17. https://doi.org/https://doi.org/10.1016/j.cpr.2012.07.001

Katzman, M.A., Bilkey, T.S., Chokka, P.R., Fallu, A., and Klassen, L.J. (2017). Adult ADHD and comorbid disorders: Clinical implications of a dimensional approach. *BMC Psychiatry*, *17*(1), 302. https://doi.org/10.1186/s12888-017-1463-3

Kern, L., Weist, M.D., Mathur, S.R., and Barber, B.R. (2021). Empowering school staff to implement effective school mental health services. *Behavioral Disorders*, *47*(3), 207–19. https://doi.org/10.1177/01987429211030860

Kirkcaldy, B.D., Shephard, R.J., and Siefen, R.G. (2002). The relationship between physical activity and self-image and problem behaviour among adolescents. *Social Psychiatry and Psychiatric Epidemiology*, *37*(11), 544–50. https://doi.org/10.1007/s00127-002-0554-7

Klimkeit, E.I., Mattingley, J.B., Sheppard, D.M., Lee, P., and Bradshaw, J.L. (2005). Motor preparation, motor execution, attention, and executive functions in attention deficit/hyperactivity disorder (ADHD). *Child Neuropsychology*, *11*(2), 153–73. https://doi.org/10.1080/092970490911298

Knouse, L.E., and Safren, S.A. (2010). Current status of cognitive behavioral therapy for adult attention-deficit hyperactivity disorder. *The Psychiatric Clinics of North America*, *33*(3), 497–509. https://doi.org/10.1016/j.psc.2010.04.001

Kofler, M.J., Irwin, L.N., Soto, E.F., Groves, N.B., Harmon, S.L., and Sarver, D.E. (2019). Executive functioning heterogeneity in pediatric ADHD. *Journal of Abnormal Child Psychology*, *47*(2), 273–86. https://doi.org/10.1007/s10802-018-0438-2

Kooistra, L., Crawford, S., Dewey, D., Cantell, M., and Kaplan, B.J. (2005). Motor correlates of ADHD: Contribution of reading disability and oppositional defiant disorder. *Journal of Learning Disabilities*, *38*(3), 195–206. https://doi.org/10.1177/00222194050380030201

Kopp, S., Beckung, E., and Gillberg, C. (2010). Developmental coordination disorder and other motor control problems in girls with autism spectrum disorder and/or attention-deficit/hyperactivity disorder. *Research in Developmental Disabilities*, *31*(2), 350–61. https://doi.org/https://doi.org/10.1016/j.ridd.2009.09.017

Kosari, S., Hemayat-Talab, R., Arab-Ameri, E., and Keyhani, F. (2013). The effect of physical exercise on the development of gross motor skills in children with attention deficit/hyperactivity disorder [Research Article]. *Zahedan Journal of Research in Medical Sciences*, *15*(2), 74–78. https://brieflands.com/articles/zjrms-93113.html

Kristensen, H., and Torgersen, S. (2007). The association between avoidant personality traits and motor impairment in a population-based sample of 11–12-year-old children. *Journal of Personality Disorders*, *21*(1), 87–97. https://doi.org/10.1521/pedi.2007.21.1.87

Kroenke, K., Lucas, C.A., Rosenberg, M.L., and Scherokman, B.J. (1993). Psychiatric disorders and functional impairment in patients with persistent dizziness. *Journal of General Internal Medicine*, 8(10), 530–35. https://doi.org/10.1007/BF02599633

Kroes, M., Kessels, A.G.H., Kalff, A.C., Feron, F.J.M., Vissers, Y.L.J., Jolles, J., and Vles, J.S.H. (2002). Quality of movement as predictor of ADHD: Results from a prospective population study in 5- and 6-year-old children. *Developmental Medicine & Child Neurology*, 44(11), 753–60. https://doi.org/10.1017/S0012162201002882

Kuhne, M., Schachar, R., and Tannock, R. (1997). Impact of comorbid oppositional or conduct problems on attention-deficit hyperactivity disorder. *Journal of the American Academy of Child & Adolescent Psychiatry*, 36(12), 1715–25. https://doi.org/https://doi.org/10.1097/00004583-199712000-00020

Landrum, T.J. (2017). Emotional and behavioral disorders. In J. M. Kauffman and D. P. Hallahan (Eds.), *Handbook of special education* (pp. 312–24). London: Routledge.

Lijffijt, M., Kenemans, J.L., Verbaten, M.N., and van Engeland, H. (2005). A meta-analytic review of stopping performance in attention-deficit/hyperactivity disorder: Deficient inhibitory motor control? *Journal of Abnormal Psychology*, 114(2), 216.

Livesey, D., Keen, J., Rouse, J., and White, F. (2006). The relationship between measures of executive function, motor performance and externalising behaviour in 5- and 6-year-old children. *Human Movement Science*, 25(1), 50–64. https://doi.org/https://doi.org/10.1016/j.humov.2005.10.008

Ljubisavljevic, M. (2006). Transcranial magnetic stimulation and the motor learning-associated cortical plasticity. *Experimental Brain Research*, 173(2), 215–22. https://doi.org/10.1007/s00221-006-0538-z

Loeber, R., Burke, J.D., Lahey, B.B., Winters, A., and Zera, M. (2000). Oppositional defiant and conduct disorder: A review of the past 10 years, Part I. *Journal of the American Academy of Child & Adolescent Psychiatry*, 39(12), 1468–84. https://doi.org/https://doi.org/10.1097/00004583-200012000-00007

Losse, A., Henderson, S.E., Elliman, D., Hall, D., Knight, E., and Jongmans, M. (1991). Clumsiness in children-do they grow out of it? A 10-year follow-up study. *Developmental Medicine & Child Neurology*, 33(1), 55–68. https://doi.org/https://doi.org/10.1111/j.1469-8749.1991.tb14785.x

Lyon, A.R., and Bruns, E.J. (2019). From evidence to impact: Joining our best school mental health practices with our best implementation strategies. *School Mental Health*, 11(1), 106–14. https://doi.org/10.1007/s12310-018-09306-w

Makris, N., Biederman, J., Monuteaux, M.C., and Seidman, L.J. (2009). Towards conceptualizing a neural systems-based anatomy of attention-deficit/hyperactivity disorder. *Developmental Neuroscience*, 31(1-2), 36–49. https://doi.org/10.1159/000207492

Martinussen, R., Hayden, J., Hogg-Johnson, S., and Tannock, R. (2005). A meta-analysis of working memory impairments in children with attention-deficit/hyperactivity disorder. *Journal of the American Academy of Child & Adolescent Psychiatry*, 44(4), 377–84. https://doi.org/https://doi.org/10.1097/01.chi.0000153228.72591.73

Mostofsky, S.H., Schafer, J.G.B., Abrams, M.T., Goldberg, M.C., Flower, A.A., Boyce, A., Courtney, S.M., Calhoun, V.D., Kraut, M.A., Denckla, M.B., and Pekar, J.J. (2003). fMRI evidence that the neural basis of response inhibition is task-dependent. *Cognitive Brain Research*, 17(2), 419–30. https://doi.org/https://doi.org/10.1016/S0926-6410(03)00144-7

National Center for Education Statistics. (2021). *Students with disabilities. Condition of education*. Washington, DC: US Department of Education, Institute of Education Sciences. https://nces.ed.gov/programs/coe/indicator/cgg

National Institute of Mental Health. (2021). *Anxiety disorders*. https://www.nimh.nih.gov/health/topics/anxiety-disorders?rf=32471

Neudecker, C., Mewes, N., Reimers, A.K., and Woll, A. (2019). Exercise interventions in children and adolescents with ADHD: A systematic review. *Journal of Attention Disorders*, 23(4), 307–24. https://doi.org/10.1177/1087054715584053

Nicholls, J. (1984). Conceptions of ability and achievement motivation. In R. Ames and C. Ames (Eds.), *Research on motivation in education: Student motivation* (volume 1, pp. 39–77). Cambridge, MA: Academic Press.

Nieuwenhuys, A., and Oudejans, R.R.D. (2012). Anxiety and perceptual-motor performance: Toward an integrated model of concepts, mechanisms, and processes. *Psychological Research*, 76(6), 747–59. https://doi.org/10.1007/s00426-011-0384-x

Oosterlaan, J., Logan, G.D., and Sergeant, J.A. (1998). Response inhibition in AD/HD, CD, comorbid AD/HD+CD, anxious, and control children: A meta-analysis of studies with the Stop Task. *The Journal of Child Psychology and Psychiatry and Allied Disciplines*, 39(3), 411–25. https://doi.org/10.1017/S0021963097002072

Oosterlaan, J., and Sergeant, J.A. (1998). Response inhibition and response re-engagement in attention-deficit/hyperactivity disorder, disruptive, anxious and normal children. *Behavioural Brain Research*, 94(1), 33–43. https://doi.org/https://doi.org/10.1016/S0166-4328(97)00167-8

Pan, C.-Y., Chang, Y.-K., Tsai, C.-L., Chu, C.-H., Cheng, Y.-W., and Sung, M.-C. (2017). Effects of physical activity intervention on motor proficiency and physical fitness in children with ADHD: An exploratory study. *Journal of Attention Disorders*, 21(9), 783–95. https://doi.org/10.1177/1087054714533192

Pan, C.-Y., Tsai, C.-L., and Chu, C.-H. (2009). Fundamental movement skills in children diagnosed with autism spectrum disorders and attention deficit hyperactivity disorder. *J Autism Dev Disord*, 39(12), 1694. https://doi.org/10.1007/s10803-009-0813-5

Papachristou, E., and Flouri, E. (2020). The codevelopment of internalizing symptoms, externalizing symptoms, and cognitive ability across childhood and adolescence. *Development and Psychopathology*, 32(4), 1375–89.

Papadopoulos, N., Rinehart, N., Bradshaw, J.L., and McGinley, J.L. (2013). Brief report: Children with ADHD without co-morbid autism do not have impaired motor proficiency on the movement assessment battery for children. *J Autism Dev Disord*, 43(6), 1477–82. https://doi.org/10.1007/s10803-012-1687-5

Patel, D.R., Feucht, C., Brown, K., and Ramsay, J. (2018). Pharmacological treatment of anxiety disorders in children and adolescents: A review for practitioners. *Translational Pediatrics*, 7(1), 23–35. https://doi.org/10.21037/tp.2017.08.05

Patrick, S.W., Henkhaus, L.E., Zickafoose, J.S., Lovell, K., Halvorson, A., Loch, S., Letterie, M., and Davis, M.M. (2020). Well-being of parents and children during the COVID-19 pandemic: A National Survey. *Pediatrics*, 146(4). https://doi.org/10.1542/peds.2020-016824

Patros, C.H.G., Alderson, R.M., Lea, S.E., Tarle, S.J., Kasper, L.J., and Hudec, K.L. (2015). Visuospatial working memory underlies choice-impulsivity in boys with attention-deficit/hyperactivity disorder. *Research in Developmental Disabilities*, 38, 134–44. https://doi.org/https://doi.org/10.1016/j.ridd.2014.12.016

Pedersen, S.J., Surburg, P.R., Heath, M., and Koceja, D.M. (2004). Fractionated lower extremity response time performance in boys with and without ADHD. *Adapted Physical Activity Quarterly*, 21(4), 315–29. https://doi.org/10.1123/apaq.21.4.315

Piek, J.P., Barrett, N.C., Smith, L.M., Rigoli, D., and Gasson, N. (2010). Do motor skills in infancy and early childhood predict anxious and depressive symptomatology at school age? *Human Movement Science*, 29(5), 777–86. https://doi.org/https://doi.org/10.1016/j.humov.2010.03.006

Piek, J.P., Bradbury, G.S., Elsley, S.C., and Tate, L. (2008). Motor coordination and social–emotional behaviour in preschool-aged children. *International Journal of Disability, Development and Education*, 55(2), 143–51. https://doi.org/10.1080/10349120802033592

Piek, J.P., Pitcher, T.M., and Hay, D.A. (1999). Motor coordination and kinaesthesis in boys with attention deficit–hyperactivity disorder. *Developmental Medicine & Child Neurology*, *41*(3), 159–65. https://doi.org/10.1017/S0012162299000341

Pitcher, T.M., Piek, J.P., and Hay, D.A. (2003). Fine and gross motor ability in males with ADHD. *Developmental Medicine & Child Neurology*, *45*(8), 525–35. https://doi.org/10.1017/S0012162203000975

Pliszka, S.R. (1992). Comorbidity of attention-deficit hyperactivity disorder and overanxious disorder. *Journal of the American Academy of Child & Adolescent Psychiatry*, *31*(2), 197–203. https://doi.org/10.1097/00004583-199203000-00003

Rapport, M.D., Alderson, R.M., Kofler, M.J., Sarver, D.E., Bolden, J., and Sims, V. (2008). Working memory deficits in boys with attention-deficit/hyperactivity disorder (ADHD): The contribution of central executive and subsystem processes. *Journal of Abnormal Child Psychology*, *36*(6), 825–37. https://doi.org/10.1007/s10802-008-9215-y

Rapport, M.D., Bolden, J., Kofler, M.J., Sarver, D.E., Raiker, J.S., and Alderson, R.M. (2009). Hyperactivity in boys with attention-deficit/hyperactivity disorder (ADHD): A ubiquitous core symptom or manifestation of working memory deficits? *Journal of Abnormal Child Psychology*, *37*(4), 521–34. https://doi.org/10.1007/s10802-008-9287-8

Rapport, M.D., Chung, K.-M., Shore, G., and Isaacs, P. (2001). A conceptual model of child psychopathology: Implications for understanding attention deficit hyperactivity disorder and treatment efficacy. *Journal of Clinical Child & Adolescent Psychology*, *30*(1), 48–58. https://doi.org/10.1207/S15374424JCCP3001_6

Reale, L., Bartoli, B., Cartabia, M., Zanetti, M., Costantino, M.A., Canevini, M.P., Termine, C., Bonati, M., and Lombardy ADHD Group. (2017). Comorbidity prevalence and treatment outcome in children and adolescents with ADHD. *European Child & Adolescent Psychiatry*, *26*(12), 1443–57. https://doi.org/10.1007/s00787-017-1005-z

Reiersen, A.M., Constantino, J.N., and Todd, R.D. (2008). Co-occurrence of motor problems and autistic symptoms in attention-deficit/hyperactivity disorder. *Journal of the American Academy of Child & Adolescent Psychiatry*, *47*(6), 662–72. https://doi.org/https://doi.org/10.1097/CHI.0b013e31816bff88

Rettew, D.C., Zanarini, M.C., Yen, S., Grilo, C.M., Skodol, A.E., Shea, M.T., McGlashan, T.H., Morey, L.C., Culhane, M.A., and Gunderson, J.G. (2003). Childhood antecedents of avoidant personality disorder: A retrospective study. *Journal of the American Academy of Child & Adolescent Psychiatry*, *42*(9), 1122–30. https://doi.org/https://doi.org/10.1097/01.CHI.0000070250.24125.5F

Retz, W., Stieglitz, R.-D., Corbisiero, S., Retz-Junginger, P., & Rosler, M. (2012). Emotional dysregulation in adult ADHD: What is the empirical evidence? [Report]. *Expert Review of Neurotherapeutics*, *12*, 1241+. https://link.gale.com/apps/doc/A305720666/HRCA?u=udel_main&sid=googleScholar&xid=15a37788

Rubia, K., Noorloos, J., Smith, A., Gunning, B., and Sergeant, J. (2003). Motor timing deficits in community and clinical boys with hyperactive behavior: The effect of methylphenidate on motor timing. *Journal of Abnormal Child Psychology*, *31*(3), 301–13. https://doi.org/10.1023/A:1023233630774

Scardamalia, K., Bentley-Edwards, K.L., and Grasty, K. (2019). Consistently inconsistent: An examination of the variability in the identification of emotional disturbance. *Psychology in the Schools*, *56*(4), 569–81. https://doi.org/https://doi.org/10.1002/pits.22213

Schatz, D.B., and Rostain, A.L. (2006). ADHD with comorbid anxiety: A review of the current literature. *Journal of Attention Disorders*, *10*(2), 141–49. https://doi.org/10.1177/1087054706286698

Schmeichel, B.J., Volokhov, R.N., and Demaree, H.A. (2008). Working memory capacity and the self-regulation of emotional expression and experience. *Journal of Personality and Social Psychology*, *95*(6), 1526.

Schnoes, C., Reid, R., Wagner, M., and Marder, C. (2006). ADHD among students receiving special education services: A National Survey. *Exceptional Children*, 72(4), 483–96. https://doi.org/10.1177/001440290607200406

Schoemaker, M.M., and Kalverboer, A.F. (1994). Social and affective problems of children who are clumsy: How early do they begin? *Adapted Physical Activity Quarterly*, 11(2), 130–40. https://doi.org/10.1123/apaq.11.2.130

Sharma, A., and Couture, J. (2014). A review of the pathophysiology, etiology, and treatment of attention-deficit hyperactivity disorder (ADHD). *Annals of Pharmacotherapy*, 48(2), 209–25. https://doi.org/10.1177/1060028013510699

Shaw, P., Stringaris, A., Nigg, J., and Leibenluft, E. (2014). Emotion dysregulation in attention deficit hyperactivity disorder. *American Journal of Psychiatry*, 171(3), 276–93. https://doi.org/10.1176/appi.ajp.2013.13070966

Simpson, G., Cohen, R.A., Pastor, P.N., and Reuben, C.A. (2008). *Use of mental health services in the past 12 months by children aged 4-17 years; United States, 2005-2006*. Hyattsville, MD: National Center for Health Statistics.

Skinner, R.A., and Piek, J.P. (2001). Psychosocial implications of poor motor coordination in children and adolescents. *Human Movement Science*, 20, 73. https://doi.org/http://dx.doi.org.udel.idm.oclc.org/10.1016/S0167-9457(01)00029-X

Skirbekk, B., Hansen, B.H., Oerbeck, B., Wentzel-Larsen, T., and Kristensen, H. (2012). Motor impairment in children with anxiety disorders. *Psychiatry Research*, 198(1), 135–39. https://doi.org/https://doi.org/10.1016/j.psychres.2011.12.008

Smith, A.L., Hoza, B., Linnea, K., McQuade, J.D., Tomb, M., Vaughn, A.J., Shoulberg, E.K., and Hook, H. (2013). Pilot physical activity intervention reduces severity of ADHD symptoms in young children. *Journal of Attention Disorders*, 17(1), 70–82. https://doi.org/10.1177/1087054711417395

Smith, C.R., Katsiyannis, A., Losinski, M., and Ryan, J.B. (2015). Eligibility for students with emotional or behavioral disorders: The social maladjustment dilemma continues. *Journal of Disability Policy Studies*, 25(4), 252–59. https://doi.org/10.1177/1044207313513641

Stefanucci, J.K., and Proffitt, D.R. (2009). The roles of altitude and fear in the perception of height. *Journal of Experimental Psychology: Human Perception and Performance*, 35(2), 424.

Stern, C., Cole, S., Gollwitzer, P.M., Oettingen, G., and Balcetis, E. (2013). Effects of implementation intentions on anxiety, perceived proximity, and motor performance. *Personality and Social Psychology Bulletin*, 39(5), 623–35. https://doi.org/10.1177/0146167213479612

Stonerock, G.L., Hoffman, B.M., Smith, P.J., and Blumenthal, J.A. (2015). Exercise as treatment for anxiety: Systematic review and analysis. *Annals of Behavioral Medicine*, 49(4), 542–56. https://doi.org/10.1007/s12160-014-9685-9

Stott, D.H., Moyes, F.A., and Henderson, S.E. (1984). *The Henderson revision of the test of motor impairment*. San Antonio, TX: Psychological Corporation.

Swanson, J.M., Sergeant, J.A., Taylor, E., Sonuga-Barke, E.J.S., Jensen, P.S., and Cantwell, D.P. (1998). Attention-deficit hyperactivity disorder and hyperkinetic disorder. *The Lancet*, 351(9100), 429–33. https://doi.org/10.1016/S0140-6736(97)11450-7

Tantillo, M., Kesick, C.M., Hynd, G.W., and Dishman, R.K. (2002). The effects of exercise on children with attention-deficit hyperactivity disorder. *Medicine & Science in Sports & Exercise*, 311, 114509.

Teachman, B.A., Stefanucci, J.K., Clerkin, E.M., Cody, M.W., and Proffitt, D.R. (2008). A new mode of fear expression: Perceptual bias in height fear. *Emotion*, 8(2), 296–301. https://doi.org/10.1037/1528-3542.8.2.296

Tiffin, J. (1968). *Purdue pegboard examiner manual*. Chicago, IL: Science Research Associates.

Ulrich, D.A. (Ed.). (2000). *Test of gross motor development* (second edition). Austin, TX: Pro-Ed.

Van Damme, T., Sabbe, B., van West, D., and Simons, J. (2015). Motor abilities of adolescents with a disruptive behavior disorder: The role of comorbidity with ADHD. *Research in Developmental Disabilities*, 40, 1–10. https://doi.org/https://doi.org/10.1016/j.ridd.2015.01.004

Verret, C., Guay, M.-C., Berthiaume, C., Gardiner, P., and Béliveau, L. (2012). A physical activity program improves behavior and cognitive functions in children with ADHD: An exploratory study. *Journal of Attention Disorders*, 16(1), 71–80. https://doi.org/10.1177/1087054710379735

Vles, J.S.H., Kroes, M., and Feron, F.J.M. (2004). *Maastricht motoriek test*. Tilburg, The Netherlands: Pits BV.

Vysniauske, R., Verburgh, L., Oosterlaan, J., and Molendijk, M.L. (2020). The effects of physical exercise on functional outcomes in the treatment of ADHD: A meta-analysis. *Journal of Attention Disorders*, 24(5), 644–54. https://doi.org/10.1177/1087054715627489

Watemberg, N., Waiserberg, N., Zuk, L., and Lerman-Sagie, T. (2007). Developmental coordination disorder in children with attention-deficit–hyperactivity disorder and physical therapy intervention. *Developmental Medicine & Child Neurology*, 49(12), 920–25. https://doi.org/https://doi.org/10.1111/j.1469-8749.2007.00920.x

Willcutt, E.G., Pennington, B.F., Olson, R.K., Chhabildas, N., and Hulslander, J. (2005). Neuropsychological analyses of comorbidity between reading disability and attention deficit hyperactivity disorder: In search of the common deficit. *Developmental Neuropsychology*, 27(1), 35–78. https://doi.org/10.1207/s15326942dn2701_3

Wilson, M. (2008). From processing efficiency to attentional control: A mechanistic account of the anxiety–performance relationship. *International Review of Sport and Exercise Psychology*, 1(2), 184–201. https://doi.org/10.1080/17509840802400787

Yardley, L., and Redfern, M.S. (2001). Psychological factors influencing recovery from balance disorders. *Journal of Anxiety Disorders*, 15(1), 107–19. https://doi.org/https://doi.org/10.1016/S0887-6185(00)00045-1

7

Motor Behavior and Specific Language Impairment

Matthias O. Wagner

■ ■ ■

OVERVIEW

Following common meta-theoretical frameworks such as Bronfenbrenner's ecological systems theory (1977) or respective extensions, such as the bioecological model (Bronfenbrenner and Ceci, 1994), human development throughout the lifespan presupposes continuous interaction between the growing individual and the changing social settings and contexts in which it is embedded. Social interaction in turn implies behavior, which Ekman (1957) in his early work distinguished in a verbal, vocal, as well as a nonverbal component. Following Ekman's distinction, verbal behavior "can be defined as the content of an organism's spoken statement and vocal behavior the timbre, pitch, and intensity of a spoken statement" (Ekman, 1957, p. 141). Contrariwise, nonverbal behavior may be simply viewed as "any movement or position of the face and/or the body" (Ekman and Friesen, 1969, p. 49). Hereby, the term movement basically describes the process "when an individual changes from one position to another" and thus, "Positions [e. g. facial expression, gesture, posture] can be conceived as any prescribed discrete aspect of motor behavior" (Ekman, 1957, p. 143).

From the perspective of human movement research, motor behavior represents a collective term under which three concepts can be subsumed: these are motor control, motor learning, and motor development. While "Motor control refers to the nervous system's control of the muscles to permit skilled and coordinated movements" (Haywood and Getchel, 2009, p. 5), motor learning basically describes "a relatively permanent change in the ability to execute a motor skill as a result of practice or experience" (Haibach-Beach et al., 2018, p. 8). Close to the chronological dimension of the meta-theoretical framework set earlier, motor development "refers to the continuous, age-related process of change in movement, as well as the interacting constraints (or factors) in the individual, environment, and task that drive these changes" (Haywood and Getchell, 2009, p. 5).

Motor issues—such as developmental coordination disorder (DCD; see chapter 7)—are often discussed in light of a broad spectrum of potential comorbidities including disorders related to verbal and vocal behavior (e.g., Wisdom et al., 2007). Despite the critism of terminological arbitrariness (Reilly et al., 2014) and with reference to recent studies published in journals of undeniable relevance for the field such as the *Journal of Speech, Language, and Hearing Research* (e.g., Selin et al., 2022), respective disorders will be grouped under the collective term specific language impairment (SLI) within this chapter. SLI is indicated when:

> (i) Language is significantly below level expected from age and IQ, usually interpreted as scoring in the lowest 10% on a standardized test of expressive and/or receptive language, (ii) Nonverbal IQ and nonlinguistic aspects of development (self-help skills, social skills) fall within broadly normal limits, (iii) Language difficulties cannot be accounted for by hearing loss, physical abnormality of the speech apparatus, or environmental deprivation and (iv) Language difficulties are not caused by brain damage. (Bishop, 2006, p. 218)

With respect to reported prevalences, SLI (5 to 7 percent; Conti-Ramsden and Bottig, 2006) as well as motor issues (e.g., DCD: 5 to 6 percent; Blank et al., 2012) should both be considered in terms of a comprehensive depiction of human development. In order to foster a better understanding of social interaction from a developmental disability perspective, the aim of this chapter is to elaborate on the nature, origin, and impact of motor issues in individuals with SLI. For this purpose, the essence of significant reviews and meta-analysis on motor control–, motor learning–, and motor development–related issues in SLI will be highlighted within a comprehensive research overview; selected recent original works are also discussed within the research overview section to expand and update the identified body of knowledge. The chapter closes with implications for researchers and practitioners as well as a brief conclusion.

RESEARCH OVERVIEW

Motor Control–Related Issues in Specific Language Impairment

In her groundbreaking work for the field, Hill (2001) reviewed twenty-eight original works assessing limb coordination difficulties in children with SLI published between 1964 and 1998. Hill (2001) summarized her findings in three subsections on the nature of the motor deficits as well as on fine/gross motor ability and the (limb) praxis ability.

Regarding the nature of motor deficits, five respective studies indicate the DCD prevalence in children with SLI to be significantly higher (40 to 90 percent) than what would be expected in the normal population (see overview section). In the author's reading, these findings indicate "that children with SLI [apparently] do have very significant movement difficulties" (Hill, 2001, p. 155).

When considering motor performance of children with SLI in detail, these children were reported to be impaired relative to same age normally developing controls in the gross motor area of balance as well as in time-related (with the exception of certain repetitive finger tapping tasks) but not in accuracy-related fine motor tasks. Cross-study comparison-based observations led Hill (2001) to the assumption that motor issues in children with SLI display similar to those seen in children with DCD; this assumption was substantiated in a single original study by the author herself, indicating that children with SLI basically resemble those with DCD (and younger normally developing children) in the number of sequences completed and errors made within a twenty-second finger opposition task.

When focusing on the ability to produce purposeful skilled movements (limb praxis ability) in children with SLI, Hill (2001) identified nine respective studies addressing either representational (familiar) transitive (involving the use of an object, e.g., toothbrush) or intransitive (no object involved, e.g., salute) gestures investigated under two output conditions (pantomime to verbal command, imitation of the experimenter pantomiming the action) or non-symbolic (unfamiliar) single hand postures/sequences (via direct imitation or immediate recall). In sum, Hill (2001) considers "the production of representational gestures . . . [apparently] to be impaired in children with SLI relative to normally developing controls, while results on the production of non-symbolic gestures is less clear" (p. 162).

Taking together the findings on the performance of children with SLI on gross/fine motor tasks as well as on tasks addressing limb praxis ability, Hill (2001) sees supporting evidence for the assumption of substantial comorbidity between SLI and poor motor skills.

Rechetnikov and Maitra continued Hill's work in 2009, aiming to empirically substantiate the relationship between motor impairment and SLI based on a meta-analytic review. The authors (2009) hypothesized, that "Children with speech-language impairments, compared with children with normal development, would exhibit motor difficulties, specifically in three composite measures of motor error, motor score, and motor time" (pp. 256–57). For hypothesis testing, they analyzed sixteen original studies covering 621 children with speech-language impairment, 446 typically developing control children, and 110 effect sizes. Across all selected studies, I-squared values reflected a medium (motor score) to high (motor error; motor time) extent of heterogeneity indicating random effects model as an appropriate analytic approach. Identified group differences pointed in the expected direction with corresponding effect sizes ranging between medium (motor score; motor time) and high (motor error). Taken together, results clearly supported Rechetnikov and Maitra's hypothesis that children with SLI also show impairments concerning different aspects of motor control–related performances (see Rechetnikov and Maitra, 2009).

More recently, Sanjeevan et al. (2015) narratively reviewed motor issues in SLI, particularly in the area of fine and gross motor abilities, speech-motor ability, and manual gestures. While Sanjeevan's et al. (2015) subsection on fine and gross motor abilities was basically set in order to add new research to Hill's (2001) respective remarks as well as on her remarks on the nature of motor deficits in SLI, their subsection on manual gestures aimed to expand the body of knowledge in what Hill (2001) called (limb) praxis ability. The authors' remarks on speech-motor ability refer to the motor control aspect of the speech apparatus in producing language, a field that has received comparatively little to no attention within the aforementioned reviews.

In the area of fine and gross motor abilities, Sanjeevan et al. (2015) discussed seven studies published between 2002 and 2010. While selected studies support Hill's initial conclusion concerning the general severity of motor impairment in SLI, the authors themselves conclude that "The range of motor deficits seen in children with SLI is wider then was picked up at the time of Hill's review" (Sanjeevan et al., 2015, p. 230). Sanjeevan et al. (2015) hereby particularly refer to "new insights" on motor coordination of legs and arms and imitation of simple and complex movements; noticeably, and in accordance with Hill's (2001) earlier conclusion, the authors state that motoric timing might be unaffected in SLI when performing certain rather simple (drawing and) tapping tasks.

Manual gestures have been addressed by two studies published in 2010 and 2011, respectively; one paper was under review at the time when the authors were screening the field. Respective conclusions drawn by Sanjeevan et al. (2015) differ from Hill's (2001) to the effect that manual communicative gesturing appears to be essentially unimpaired in SLI.

Finally, the authors identified five studies published between 1999 and 2014 on speech-motor ability indicating that children with SLI exhibited greater variability and a lower stability in their articulatory movements in comparison to age-matched typically developed children as well as a non-persisting slower speech rate at the ages of three and four years. In the authors' reading and "despite the absence of basic oral-motor dysfunction in children with SLI, these children do have some problems with speech rate and articulatory control, especially when producing sequences of sounds and words with increased complexity" (Sanjeevan et al., 2015, p. 231).

Since Sanjeevan et al. (2015) published their comprehensive literature review in 2015, selected studies further addressed motor control–related issues in SLI, three of which turn out to particularly fit within the previous discussion and can be summarized as follows.

Consistent with the main conclusions drawn by Sanjeevan et al. (2015), Sanjeevan and Mainela-Arnold (2019) found significant lower performances on gross, fine, and speech motor tasks in children with SLI relative to children without disabilities (here: typical development), whereby in the latter task, only focal oromotor control (i.e., movements of the jaw, lips, and tongue) as well as sequencing but not general motor control were particularly affected.

Vuolo et al. (2017) particularly addressed motor timing in SLI. The authors' findings indicate that timing problems are only detectable in tasks requiring bi-manual but not uni-manual coordination and thus—in accordance with the conclusion drawn by Sanjeevan et al. (2015) as well as Hill (2001)—that the presence of timing problems is depending on the complexity of the motor request.

Within the context of the previous remarks on limb (praxis) ability (Hill, 2001) and manual gestures (Sanjeevan et al., 2015), Wray et al. (2016) showed that children with SLI achieved significantly lower scores on measures of gesture production and gesture comprehension relative to typically developing children.

When considering the findings reviewed within this subsection from the perspective of cognitive science research, motor control–related issues in balance, speed, timing, and sequencing "appear to be of a type that would be expected from impairments of procedural memory or from a dysfunction of frontal/basal-ganglia circuits or the cerebellum" (Ullman and Pierpont, 2005, pp. 420–21). Empirical evidence substantiating a respective cognitive explanatory approach was initially reviewed by Lum et al. (2014); the authors' work serves as starting point for the following subsection.

Motor Learning–Related Issues in Specific Language Impairment

Lum et al. (2014) directed their scope on Ullman and Pierpont's (2005) procedural deficit hypothesis, which basically "predicts that individuals with SLI should generally perform worse than typically-developing individuals on tasks assessing the learning and memory functions of the procedural memory system" (p. 2). For the evaluation of existing empirical evidence on the procedural deficit hypothesis, the authors focused their search on original works based on the serial reaction time task, a paradigm set to examine visuo-motor sequence learning. Within the serial reaction time task, a visual stimulus appears in one of four predefined locations on screen in sequenced and random blocks, and participants are asked to locate the stimulus on a topographically matched four-button response box. Under the assumption of the procedural deficit hypothesis, one would expect reaction times in individuals without procedural memory impairments to become faster across sequenced and then slow down in random blocks indicating that information about the sequences have been learned; on the flipside, procedural memory impairments—likely caused by neural abnormalities within the basal ganglia and the frontal cortex which underlie the procedural memory system, as suspected in individuals with SLI—would result in absent or smaller changes between sequenced and random blocks (see Lum et al., 2014), indicating that those individuals at best take longer to learn such sequences. In terms of methodological precision, it should be noted that the authors conducted their meta-analysis of studies based on serial reaction time task performances according to the respective Nissen and Bullemer (1987) task proposal, which were therefore accepted or published as original works later than 1986. Selected studies (n = 8) included 186 participants with SLI and 203 typically developing peers. Results displayed a small to medium effect size, indicating that the difference in reaction times between sequenced and random blocks was larger in typically developed controls than in participants with SLI as assumed. Based on their analysis, Lum et al. (2014) see supporting evidence for the assumption of SLI being associated with impairments of procedural learning as measured by the serial reaction time task. In-depth meta-regression analyses of effect-size variability revealed both age and number of exposures as significant predicting variables with older participants and increased exposures to the sequences resulting in comparably smaller effect sizes.

Within the same year as Lum et al. (2014), Hsu and Bishop (2014) tested the procedural deficit hypothesis in SLI on the basis of two motor procedural learning tasks (serial reaction time task, non-sequential pursuit rotor learning task) and a task addressing implicit learning of word sequences (verbal memory task; Hepp effect). Following their results, children with SLI only performed poorer than typically developing children when the task addressed learning motor and word sequences. In accordance with Lum et al. (2014), Hsu and Bishop (2014) interpret their results in terms of SLI being characterized by deficits in learning sequence-specific information, rather than generally (including non-sequential) weak procedural learning.

Further evidence for impairments in implicit sequence learning in terms of the procedural deficit hypothesis affecting both nonverbal (i.e., motor) as well as verbal (i.e., language) information processing was subsequently provided by Desmottes and colleagues (2016). The authors focused their work on implicit spoken words sequences learning and visuo-motor sequences learning using the (verbal and motor) serial search task. In accordance with Hsu and Bishop (2014), their results displayed deficits in both types of learning in children with SLI compared to typically developing children suggesting the presence of a domain general implicit sequence learning impairment in those children.

Narrowing results to the assumption of motor sequence learning deficits were provided by Sanjeevan and Mainela-Arnold (2017). The authors aimed to test the procedural deficit hypothesis by examining the procedural motor learning abilities of children with and without SLI using a knot-tying task as a measure of motor sequencing and a mirror-drawing task as a measure of visual-motor adaptation. Their results indicate that children with SLI generally perform comparable to typically developing children in motor sequencing (with the exception of certain "more difficult" knot-tying tasks) as well as in visual-motor adaptation and thus that the general assumption of a deficient procedural memory causing the motor difficulties in SLI requires certain specifications.

By transferring the latter findings on the linkage between cognition and action in the chronological dimension of our meta-theoretical framework, the developmental impact of nonverbal (i.e., motor) on verbal (i.e., language) behavior in SLI finally remains to be addressed.

Motor Development–Related Issues in Specific Language Impairment

Leonard and Hill (2014) reviewed the developmental relationship between poor motor skills and social cognitive difficulties (in particular: atypical development of language) in children with SLI. The authors identified forty-three studies; seventeen of these studies were investigating (typical) development in infancy and the early years, and twenty-five studies were investigating atypical development including five studies addressing children with SLI. Results of identified cross-sectional studies mostly displayed significant correlations between locomotion or gross motor scores, respectively, and auditory comprehension, verbal ability, communication scores as well as articulation in children with SLI. Fine motor scores were significantly correlated with expressive language composite, articulation, and communication, whereas no significant correlations were found between fine motor scores and auditory comprehension as well as verbal ability. Within the five identified studies in children with SLI, only one study included longitudinal data; based on a seven-year follow-up starting with children between the ages of twenty to thirty-four months diagnosed with SLI, these data indicate parent-reported gross motor skills during early childhood to be a significant predictor for expressive language by means of developmental sentence scoring. When linking back their results to those referring to typically developing infants, Leonard and Hill (2014) cautiously conclude that "reduced or delayed locomotion could . . . be a contributing factor in the development of language difficulties in children with SLI" (p. 8).

Following Leonard and Hill's (2014) suggestion to focus on early motor differences, Diepeveen et al. (2018) retrospectively compared the state of motor development of children with SLI between the ages of four to eleven years with an age- and gender-matched control group. Results make clear that between the ages of fifteen to thirty-six months, proportion of failure was significantly higher in SLI in five out of six fine motor milestones, indicating delayed motor development in those individuals.

Corresponding prospective longitudinal research was recently provided by Sack et al. (2022). The authors aimed to assess the extent to which language, speech, and fine/gross motor skills in preschoolers with SLI (here: developmental language disorder) predicted language outcome two years later. Therefore, Sack et al. (2022) assessed corresponding measures annually on three consecutive timepoints in a group of developmental language disorder and a typical developed group starting at the ages between four to five years. Their results indicate that year three language scores were predicted by year one fine and gross motor scores in the developmental language disorder group or year one language scores in the typical developed group, respectively; noticeably, language, speech-sound, and speech-motor scores did not predict language scores in children with developmental language disorder, pointing out the predictive relevance of the motor component.

FUTURE RESEARCH

The aim of this chapter was to elaborate on the nature, origin, and impact of motor issues in individuals with SLI in order to foster a better understanding of social interaction from a developmental disability perspective. A corresponding research overview was divided into three consecutive subsections on motor control–, motor learning–, and motor development–related issues in SLI.

With reference to our socioecological meta-theoretical framework, we can basically state that suspected social interaction problems in individuals with SLI likely refer to both verbal (i.e., language) as well as nonverbal (i.e., motor) behavior. While supposedly obvious evidence for speech-motor ability-related articulatory issues in SLI could be identified in selected works, the majority of studies addressed and proved evidence for respective issues in gross and fine motor skills as well as in (manual) gesturing. Thus, presented findings on motor control–related issues clearly support Ullman and Pierpont (2005) who stated that "Motor deficits in SLI are not . . . restricted to face and mouth movements" (p. 421). Conflicting results, particularly in the area of manual communicative gesturing and motor timing, are supposed to be due to measures (e.g., cognitive simple finger-tapping) that "may not draw on the higher-level sequencing faculty that may be disrupted in SLI" (Sanjeevan et al., 2015, p. 232). The latter explanation is substantiated by conflicting results to the assumption of (motor) sequence learning deficits in SLI presented by Sanjeevan and Mainela-Arnold (2017); their research indicates that the validity of the procedural deficit hypothesis might be restricted to more difficult tasks requiring the production of rather complex sequences. In designing appropriate studies to test this pending hypothesis within replicative learning experiments, researchers need to be aware of the challenge of measuring sequential learning especially in childhood (see Krishnan and Watkins, 2019).

When researchers manage to reliably measure sequential learning and further proceed in evidencing validity of the procedural deficit hypothesis in SLI, subsequent questions on how to transfer the respective body of knowledge into treatments to strengthen procedural skills arise. What we have learned from Lum et al. (2014) so far is that older individuals with SLI obviously show fewer difficulties in learning motor sequences in comparison to younger individuals in this population; however, in face of existing evidence on the persistence of (untreated) DCD from childhood to adolescence (e.g., Cantell et al., 1994) into adulthood (Kirby et al., 2013), the author would not overweight this finding in terms of an outgrowing hypothesis. What Lum et al. (2014) also showed is that children with SLI can match typically developed children in motor sequence performance under the condition of an increased exposure. In addition, Desmottes et al. (2016) provided initial evidence for the relative superiority of distributed over massed training conditions on a serial reaction time task. When aiming to replicate and transfer corresponding effects in terms of our socioecological meta-theoretical framework, we should be aware of the importance of an ecologically valid and meaningful task selection as evidenced in the context of

DCD-specific top-down approaches (e.g., neuromotor task training; Niemeijer et al., 2007).

What we can further derive from contextual aligned DCD-related research such as on the environmental stress hypothesis (Mancini et al., 2016) is that an isolated treatment of motor skill–related issues tends to be insufficient in counteracting developmental pathways leading to internalizing problems such as anxiety and depression. Consequently, corresponding middle-range theories also need to be applied in SLI in order to identify potential secondary (interpersonal) stressors as well as corresponding mediating and moderating social and personal resources. The elaboration of such stress-process models would enable researchers in the field of SLI to proceed with a holistic perspective on the impact of impaired verbal (i.e., language) and concomitantly impaired nonverbal (i.e., motor) behaviors on the individual's development within its social settings and contexts and thus foster the understanding of social interaction from a developmental disability perspective.

PRACTICAL IMPLICATIONS

From a practical point of view, the decisive question is, which therapeutic approach should be favored in case of concomitant motor impairment in SLI? Unfortunately, this question can currently not be answered satisfactorily on the basis of the empirical findings discussed within this chapter. Thus, practical recommendations must be limited to a few fundamental aspects. Practitioners delivering clinical service in SLI should be aware of the fact that impairments in communicative skills in those individuals are not exclusively verbal or vocal in nature and that concomitant early movement difficulties apparently do have an impact on the development of domains within their own specialty. This knowledge in turn gives rise for the necessity to expand one's own clinical assessment repertoire by measures addressing early movement milestones as well as fundamental movement skills. Following such assessments and in awareness of existing research displaying rather mixed evidence, therapists could try to foster (motor) sequence learning in SLI. In any case, they are called upon to use every resource to foster active participation and involvement in the individual's social settings and contexts. These measures in turn are supposed to positively impact nonverbal (i.e., motor) as well as verbal (i.e., language) behaviors and thus presumably enable an overall improved social interaction and development.

CONCLUSION

The findings on motor issues reviewed within this chapter confirm that comorbidity represents the rule rather than the exception also in case of SLI. Following this observation, motor and inherent language impairments in SLI are assumed to share a common etiology grounded in the procedural memory system. However, leading approaches in the field—namely the procedural deficit hypothesis—need to be further challenged in respective replication studies before we can answer the question whether and how a strengthening of procedural skills should be addressed. In any case, the current body of knowledge justifies an increased awareness for the developmental impact of concomitant motor impairments on language difficulties in clinical SLI practice.

REFERENCES

Bishop, D.V. (2006). What causes specific language impairment in children? *Current Directions in Psychological Science*, 15(5), 217–21. https://doi.org/10.1111/j.1467-8721.2006.00439.x

Blank, R., Smits-Engelsman, B., Polatajko, H., and Wilson, P. (2012). European Academy for Childhood Disability (EACD): Recommendations on the definition, diagnosis and intervention of developmental coordination disorder (long version). *Developmental Medicine & Child Neurology*, 54(1), 54–93. https://doi.org/10.1111/j.1469-8749.2011.04171.x

Bronfenbrenner, U. (1977). Toward an experimental ecology of human development. *American Psychologist*, 32(7), 513–31. https://doi.org/10.1037/0003-066x.32.7.513

Bronfenbrenner, U., and Ceci, S. (1994). Nature-nurture reconceptualized in developmental perspective: A bioecological model. *Psychological Review*, 101(4), 568–86. https://doi.org/10.1037/0033-295X.101.4.568

Cantell, M., Smyth, M.M., and Ahonen, T.P. (1994). Clumsiness in adolescence: Educational, motor, and social outcomes of motor delay detected at 5 years. *Adapted Physical Activity Quarterly*, 11, 115–29.

Conti-Ramsden, G., and Botting, N. (2006). Specific language impairment. *Encyclopedia of Language & Linguistics*, 629–32. https://doi.org/10.1016/b0-08-044854-2/00844-0

Desmottes, L., Meulemans, T., and Maillart, C. (2016). Implicit spoken words and motor sequences learning are impaired in children with specific language impairment. *Journal of the International Neuropsychological Society*, 22(5), 520–29. https://doi.org/10.1017/s135561771600028x

Diepeveen, F.B., van Dommelen, P., Oudesluys-Murphy, A.M., and Verkerk, P.H. (2018). Children with specific language impairment are more likely to reach motor milestones late. *Child: Care, Health and Development*, 44(6), 857–62. https://doi.org/10.1111/cch.12614

Ekman, P. (1957). A methodological discussion of nonverbal behavior. *The Journal of Psychology*, 43(1), 141–49. https://doi.org/10.1080/00223980.1957.9713059

Ekman, P., and Friesen, W.V. (1969). The repertoire of nonverbal behavior: Categories, origins, usage, and coding. *Semiotica*, 1(1), 49–98. https://doi.org/10.1515/semi.1969.1.1.49

Haywood, K.M., and Getchell, N., (2009). *Life span motor development* (fifth edition). Champaign, IL: Human Kinetics.

Hill, E.L. (2001). Non-specific nature of specific language impairment: a review of the literature with regard to concomitant motor impairments. *International Journal of Language & Communication Disorders*, 36(2), 149–71. https://doi.org/10.1080/13682820010019874

Hsu, H.J., and Bishop, D.V. (2014). Sequence-specific procedural learning deficits in children with specific language impairment. *Developmental Science*, 17(3), 352–65. https://doi.org/10.1111/desc.12125

Haibach-Beach, P., Reid, G., and Collier, D. (2018). *Motor learning and development* (second edition). Champaign, IL: Human Kinetics.

Kirby, A., Williams, N., Thomas, M., and Hill, E.L. (2013). Self-reported mood, general health, wellbeing and employment status in adults with suspected DCD. *Research in Developmental Disabilities*, 34, 1357–64. https://doi.org/10.1016/j.ridd.2013.01.003

Krishnan, S., and Watkins, K.E. (2019). A challenge for the procedural deficit hypothesis: How should we measure sequential learning in childhood? *Developmental Science*, 22 (2019), e12815. https://doi.org/10.1111/desc.12815

Leonard, H.C., and Hill, E.L. (2014). Review: The impact of motor development on typical and atypical social cognition and language: a systematic review. *Child and Adolescent Mental Health*. https://doi.org/10.1111/camh.12055

Lum, J.A., Conti-Ramsden, G., Morgan, A.T., and Ullman, M.T. (2014). Procedural learning deficits in specific language impairment (SLI): A meta-analysis of serial reaction time task performance. *Cortex*, 51, 1–10. https://doi.org/10.1016/j.cortex.2013.10.011

Mancini, V.O., Rigoli, D., Cairney, J., Roberts, L.D., and Piek, J.P. (2016). The elaborated environmental stress hypothesis as a framework for understanding the association between motor skills and internalizing problems: A mini-review. *Frontiers in Psychology*, 7. https://doi.org/10.3389/fpsyg.2016.00239

Niemeijer, A.S., Smits-Engelsman, B.C.M., and Schoemaker, M.M. (2007). Neuromotor task training for children with developmental coordination disorder: a controlled trial. *Developmental Medicine & Child Neurology*, 49(6), 406–11. https://doi.org/10.1111/j.1469-8749.2007.00406.x

Nissen, M.J., and Bullemer, P. (1987). Attentional requirements of learning: Evidence from performance measures. *Cognitive Psychology*, 19(1), 1–32. https://doi.org/10.1016/0010-0285(87)90002-8

Rechetnikov, R.P., and Maitra, K. (2009). Motor impairments in children associated with impairments of speech or language: A meta-analytic review of research literature. *The American Journal of Occupational Therapy*, 63(3), 255–63. https://doi.org/10.5014/ajot.63.3.255

Reilly, S., Tomblin, B., Law, J., McKean, C., Mensah, F.K., Morgan, A., Goldfeld, S., Nicholson, J.M., and Wake, M. (2014). Specific language impairment: a convenient label for whom? *International Journal of Language & Communication Disorders*, 49(4), 416–51. https://doi.org/10.1111/1460-6984.12102

Sack, L., Dollaghan, C., and Goffman, L. (2022). Contributions of early motor deficits in predicting language outcomes among preschoolers with developmental language disorder. *International Journal of Speech-Language Pathology*, 24(4), 362–74. https://doi.org/10.1080/17549507.2021.1998629

Sanjeevan, T., and Mainela-Arnold, E. (2017). Procedural motor learning in children with specific language impairment. *Journal of Speech, Language, and Hearing Research*, 60(11), 3259–69. https://doi.org/10.1044/2017_jslhr-l-16-0457

Sanjeevan, T., and Mainela-Arnold, E. (2019). Characterizing the motor skills in children with specific language impairment. *Folia Phoniatrica et Logopaedica*, 71(1), 42–55. https://doi.org/10.1159/000493262

Sanjeevan, T., Rosenbaum, D.A., Miller, C., van Hell, J.G., Weiss, D.J., and Mainela-Arnold, E. (2015). Motor issues in specific language impairment: A window into the underlying impairment. *Current Developmental Disorders Reports*, 2(3), 228–36. https://doi.org/10.1007/s40474-015-0051-9

Selin, C., Rice, M.L., and Jackson, Y. (2022). Adversity exposure, syntax, and specific language impairment: An exploratory study. *Journal of Speech, Language, and Hearing Research*, 65(9), 3471–90.

Ullman, M.T., and Pierpont, E.I. (2005). Specific language impairment is not specific to language: The procedural deficit hypothesis. *Cortex*, 41(3), 399–433. https://doi.org/10.1016/s0010-9452(08)70276-4

Vuolo, J., Goffman, L., and Zelaznik, H.N. (2017). Deficits in coordinative bimanual timing precision in children with specific language impairment. *Journal of Speech, Language, and Hearing Research*, 60(2), 393–405. https://doi.org/10.1044/2016_jslhr-l-15-0100

Wisdom, S.N., Dyck, M.J., Piek, J.P., Hay, D., and Hallmayer, J. (2007). Can autism, language and coordination disorders be differentiated based on ability profiles? *European Child & Adolescent Psychiatry*, 16(3), 178–86. https://doi.org/10.1007/s00787-006-0586-8

Wray, C., Norbury, C.F., and Alcock, K. (2016). Gestural abilities of children with specific language impairment. *International Journal of Language & Communication Disorders*, 51(2), 174–82. https://doi.org/10.1111/1460-6984.12196

8

Motor Behavior and Cerebral Palsy

Melissa Pangelinan and Claire Bridges

■ ■ ■

DEFINITIONS, ETIOLOGY, AND DIAGNOSIS

Overview
Cerebral palsy (CP) refers to a group of neurodevelopmental conditions that affect movement and coordination. It is the most common childhood motor disability and affects roughly three children per one thousand live births in the United States (Durkin et al., 2016). CP is considered non-progressive (i.e., it does not get worse over time) and permanent (i.e., there is no "cure"). CP is caused by damage or abnormal brain development before, during, or after birth in areas of the brain needed for motor control, muscle tone, coordination, balance, and posture. "Cerebral" refers to the brain, and "palsy" refers to motor or muscle function problems.

Risk Factor or Possible Causes of Cerebral Palsy
The etiology of CP is complex with many different prenatal, perinatal, and postnatal risk factors (Korzeniewski et al., 2018). CP is split into *congenital CP* (born with CP; 85 to 95 percent of children) or *acquired* CP (begins more than twenty-eight days after birth). The most common risk factor for congenital CP is preterm birth (born before thirty-six weeks of pregnancy; Graham et al., 2016), accounting for up to half of the CP diagnoses. Other risk factors for congenital CP include:

- Low birth weight (<5.5 pounds at birth)
- Multiple births (twins, triplets, etc.)
- Assistive reproductive technology for infertility
- Jaundice or kernicterus (buildup of bilirubin)
- Maternal infection during pregnancy
- Maternal medical conditions (e.g., thyroid problems, seizures, intellectual disability, obesity, clotting disorders)
- Birth complications (e.g., detachment of the placenta, uterine rupture, umbilical cord problems, breech presentation)

Many prenatal factors are associated with an elevated risk of preterm birth. Additional risk factors for acquired CP include hypoxia (loss or reduced oxygen to the brain), neonatal seizures, meningitis, infection, and traumatic brain injury.

Symptoms

Table 8.1 presents different motor symptoms of CP. Non-motor symptoms may also include intellectual disability, seizures, and sensory dysfunction. The presence and severity of motor and non-motor symptoms depend on the extent of brain injury or abnormal brain development.

Types

CP classification is based on the type of movement problems present and body parts involved. *Spastic CP*, the most common form of CP (80 percent of children), is characterized by muscle stiffness or increased muscle tone and awkward movements (Rosenbaum et al., 2007). It is primarily due to damage or atypical development of the motor cortex. There are three types of spastic CP:

- *Spastic hemiplegia/hemiparesis* affects one side of the body, with the arm more affected than the leg. It is due to damage to one side of the motor cortex and leads to problems controlling the muscles on one side of the body.
- *Spastic diplegia/diparesis* mainly affects the legs. Babies born prematurely or with low birth weight are at increased risk of this type of CP. It is due to damage to the parts of the motor cortex that control the lower body.
- *Spastic quadriplegia/quadriparesis* affects all four limbs, the trunk, and the face. This type of CP is due to extensive damage to both sides of the motor cortex.

Dyskinetic CP is characterized by slow and uncontrollable movements of the hands, arms, feet, legs, trunk, or face. The movements can be writhing or jerky. Muscle tone can vary from "floppy" to "stiff" over a day. The child may have difficulty sitting, walking, talking, and performing other daily activities. This type of CP is due to damage to the basal ganglia (Rosenbaum et al., 2007).

Ataxic CP is characterized by difficulties in balance, coordination, and gait. The child may have difficulties balancing when walking, controlling fast or precise

Table 8.1 Motor Symptoms of Cerebral Palsy

Symptom	Description
Ataxia	Lack of muscle coordination during voluntary movements
Atypical gait	"Scissored" gait, toe-walking, crouched gait
Delayed achievement of motor milestones	Delayed onset of independent sitting, rolling over, crawling, standing, walking, etc.
Low or high muscle tone	Muscles that are "floppy" or "stiff"
Poor fine motor control	Difficulty controlling the small muscles of the hands (e.g., buttoning clothes, using utensils, writing, using scissors, etc.)
Poor oral-motor control	Difficulty swallowing, difficulty speaking, drooling
Spasticity	Muscle stiffness and exaggerated reflexes
Tremor or involuntary movements	Rhythmic or random and uncontrolled movements of one or more limbs or the trunk
Weakness	Difficulty producing and maintaining sufficient muscle force with one or more limbs or the trunk

movements, or controlling their arms/hands when reaching or interacting with objects. This type of CP is due to damage to the cerebellum (Rosenbaum et al., 2007).

Mixed CP includes a combination of symptoms or types of CP. For example, a child with spastic-dyskinetic CP may have some muscles that are stiff and exhibit uncontrollable movements. This type of CP may be due to hypoxia or birth asphyxia affecting different regions of the brain (Graham et al., 2016)

Diagnosis and Classification

Most children with CP are diagnosed by age two years, but those with mild symptoms may not be diagnosed until age four or five. Early diagnosis of CP, diagnosis of CP subtypes, and long-term prognosis is difficult before two (Novak et al., 2017). Diagnosis is based on an evaluation by a pediatrician, neurologist, or health practitioner with training in physical medicine or rehabilitation using standardized infant motor assessments (e.g., general movement assessment, the Alberta Infant Motor Scale, Test of Infant Motor Performance) or other clinical evaluations (e.g., muscle tone, reflexes, posture/gait, motor milestones). Magnetic resonance imaging, computerized tomography, ultrasound, and electroencephalography may be used to identify brain damage and the presence of seizures. Novak and colleagues (2017) provide details regarding accurate early diagnosis of CP and which diagnostic tests are most appropriate by age.

Delayed achievement of motor milestones can be used as an early sign of CP. For babies younger than six months, early signs include difficulty controlling the head, stiff or floppy limbs, overextension of the back and neck when carried, and legs that scissor or cross when the baby is lifted. For babies older than six months, early signs include difficulty rolling over, bringing the hands together, bringing the hands to the mouth, or keeping one hand fisted. For babies older than ten months, early signs include abnormal crawling (e.g., asymmetrical, dragging the arm or leg), scooting, or knee hopping.

The Gross Motor Function Classification System (GMFCS; Palisano et al., 1997; Rosenbaum et al., 2008) is a standard tool to describe a child's level of self-initiated movement emphasizing sitting, transfers, and mobility. For each level, descriptions are provided based on age. These descriptors consider environmental and personal factors that influence movement.

There are five GMFCS levels. Children in level I can walk without physical assistance in different settings, climb stairs without using a railing, and perform locomotor gross motor skills (e.g., running, jumping) but may have difficulties with speed, balance, or coordination. Children in level II can walk in most settings but may have difficulty with long distances, balancing on uneven or inclined surfaces, or moving in confined or crowded spaces. They may walk with physical assistance, hand-held mobility device, or use wheeled mobility over long distances. They may hold onto a railing while climbing stairs. They have greater difficulty performing locomotor gross motor skills. Children in level III walk using a hand-held mobility device in indoor settings. They may self-propel a wheeled mobility device over short distances. They may hold onto a railing with assistance while climbing stairs. Children in level IV require physical assistance or powered mobility in most settings. At home, they may walk for short distances with physical assistance, body supported walker, or powered mobility device. At school or outdoors, they may use a manual or powered wheelchair. Children in level V are transported in a wheeled mobility device in all settings. They have a limited ability to maintain their head or trunk in antigravity positions or limb movements.

EMPIRICAL RESEARCH: CEREBRAL PALSY AND MOTOR BEHAVIOR

Cerebral Palsy and Motor Behavior

Given that CP is a childhood movement disorder identified based on delayed acquisition of motor milestones and impaired motor function, research investigating the trajectory of motor function based on CP classification provides insights to the acquisition and development of motor skills in children with CP. Several large longitudinal studies have evaluated the trajectory and stability of motor behavior in children with CP (Beckung et al., 2007; Hanna et al., 2009; Rosenbaum et al., 2002). Rosenbaum et al. (2002) examined longitudinal performance of children ages one to thirteen years on the Gross Motor Function Measure-66, which measures common gross motor skills (e.g., lying, rolling, crawling, kneeling, standing, walking, running, jumping). Although different gross motor performance trajectories/curves were found by GMFCS level, motor performance plateaued by around age seven for all GMFCS levels. Based on these different motor development curves, the average age of acquisition for specific motor tasks could be predicted. For example, the ability of a child to sit on a mat unsupported by their arms for three seconds may be achieved by children in levels I to III between the ages of six months to 1.5 years, while children in level IV may not achieve this skill until about three years. Children in level V are unlikely to achieve this skill at any age. The ability to walk forward ten steps unsupported may be achieved by children in level I by age two and level II by age three. Those in levels III and IV are unlikely to achieve this skill at any age. Beckung et al. (2007) examined children ages one to fifteen years and created gross motor developmental trajectories for subtypes of CP. On average, gross motor development did not differ between children with spastic hemiplegia compared to those with spastic diplegia. However, there was more variability in scores for those with hemiplegia. Hanna et al. (2009) longitudinally examined children ages sixteen months to twenty-one years to determine if individuals with CP experience a loss of gross motor function during adolescence and adulthood. On average, those in levels III to V showed clinically significant declines in gross motor function that began around age eight. Although there was considerable variability in the degree of decline observed, any change in gross motor function may represent a loss of functional independence and greater reliance on caregivers to accomplish daily motor tasks.

Early Intervention

Early diagnosis and intervention for children with CP are critical for many reasons. First, the early years of life represent a crucial period of brain development. Early interventions can capitalize on the ability of the developing brain to create new neural pathways to facilitate the development of new motor skills (Sterling et al., 2013; Sutcliffe et al., 2007). Second, early interventions promote muscle, ligament, and bone development (Novak et al., 2017); impairments like hip displacement (Hägglund et al., 2007) and scoliosis (Persson-Bunke et al., 2012) can interfere with treatment outcomes. Third, motor skill acquisition is greatest from birth to age five (Beckung et al., 2007; Hanna et al., 2009; Rosenbaum et al., 2002). After age seven, gross motor performance plateaus (Hanna et al., 2009; Rosenbaum et al., 2002) and may decline into adolescence and adulthood (Beckung et al., 2007). Thus, early intervention may increase the quality and quantity of motor behaviors achieved, delay or prevent plateau, and attenuate decline later in development.

A recent systematic review examined early intervention outcomes in infants with or at risk for CP (Damiano and Longo, 2021). Only a small number of high-quality research studies (i.e., randomized controlled trials [RCTs]) have been conducted to measure the efficacy of early intervention in infants. Notwithstanding, the most effective early interventions include constraint-induced movement therapy (CIMT) and early, intense, and task-specific interventions (Damiano and Longo, 2021; Novak et al., 2020).

CIMT is a common therapy in children with spastic hemiplegic CP and involves casting the less affected limb. The children undergo intensive physical or occupational therapy (e.g., six or more hours/day for twenty or more consecutive days) to increase the functional abilities of the more affected limb. Activities include reaching, grasping, holding, and manipulating objects of different sizes and weights. Taub and colleagues (2004) conducted an RCT of CIMT in young children with spastic hemiplegia ages seven to ninety-six months. Children who received CIMT (six hours/day for twenty-one days; ~126 hours total) acquired more motor skills and demonstrated better movement quality with the more affected arm during home- and laboratory-based assessments. Improvements were maintained for at least six months. Eliasson et al. (2005) replicated these results using a modified CIMT in children with spastic hemiplegia ages eighteen to forty-eight months using a splinted glove to constrain movement of the less affected hand. The therapy dose was two hours daily for two months (~120 hours total). Significant improvements in hand function were observed immediately after the intervention and maintained for six months.

More recently, the effects of CIMT in younger infants have been shown (Deluca et al., 2016; Eliasson et al., 2018). Infants ages seven to twenty-four months with hemiplegia that underwent CIMT (six hours/day for twenty days) significantly increased the number of upper extremity skills, increased the frequency and quality of hand use during everyday tasks, and showed a 75 percent improvement in gross motor functional skills (Deluca et al., 2016). Eliasson et al. (2018) used a modified baby-CIMT with infants ages three to eight months using a mitten to constrain the less affected limb. Two six-week training periods (thirty minutes/day; thirty-six hours total) were separated by six weeks with no therapy. Training was delivered at home by parents and supervised by an occupational therapist. Compared to controls, baby-CIMT resulted in a greater improvement in hand score of the affected hand.

These results support the use of CIMT as an effective early intervention. The program can be administered with a lower dose by parents with significant improvements in functional outcomes. However, many factors need to be examined for future application of CIMT in infants and young children. Indeed, the CIMT outcomes can be affected by child characteristics (e.g., child's age, severity, lesion characteristics), constraint used (e.g., sling, mitt, splint, glove, cast), training characteristics (e.g., dose, environment, provider), and which outcomes are measured (Eliasson et al., 2014).

One example of an early, intense, and task-specific intervention is the Goals-Activity-Motor Enrichment (GAME) intervention (Morgan et al., 2014). This intervention incorporates principles of motor learning, neurorehabilitation, and early intervention strategies such as family-centered practice and environmental enrichment. GAME consists of three key components: goal-oriented intensive motor training, parent education, and enrichment of the child's motor learning environment. Therapists evaluate weakness, selective motor control, and tone to determine their impact on goal achievement and how to scaffold motor tasks. The motor performance environment or task is adjusted to promote problem-solving and practice variability. Therapists work with parents to set goals and expectations, develop timelines/practice schedules, and create individualized home programs with pictures, goals, strategies, and environmental enrichment. Parents are coached to identify the infant's voluntary movement attempts, the trajectory of motor skills, and how to promote the development of these skills through simple task analysis and by providing specific feedback. Parents and siblings promote learning opportunities through structured home practice and independent play. Environmental enrichments are tailored to the physical home environment, and home affordances are used to increase specific motor task practice, play, self-generated movement, and exploration. A single-blind RCT of GAME was conducted with infants ages three to five months (Morgan et al., 2014). Improvements in motor performance were observed immediately following sixteen weeks of therapy (m = 47.40 minutes/day; 21.91 hours total) and maintained through twelve months of age, compared to standard care. Although these results are promising, additional research is needed to determine if age, brain injury characteristics, and intervention dose affect the immediate and long-term effects of GAME.

Interventions in Childhood and Beyond

A recent systematic review categorized and summarized the efficacy of a broad range of interventions for children with CP (Novak et al., 2020). Figure 8.1 shows the different types of interventions color-coded by effectiveness. Each circle represents the number of RCTs for each intervention. Interventions were categorized into allied health interventions (59%), pharmacological interventions (18%), surgical interventions (13%), regenerative medicine interventions (3%), and complementary and alternative medicine interventions (7%). Table 8.2 provides a brief description of each of the "Do-It" interventions shown to improve motor outcomes (e.g., activity and participation, balance, hand function, goal achievement, gross motor, muscle strength, walking endurance, walking speed). Given the heterogeneity of symptoms and characteristics of CP, a combination of therapies may be needed to address specific outcomes.

Interventions aimed at improving muscle tone (e.g., spasticity or dystonia), reducing contractures, and improving joint alignment may also improve the quality of motor performance and reduce pain (Novak et al., 2020) (see Figure 8.1). The effective pharmacologic and neurosurgical treatments targeting muscle tone include botulinum toxin, intrathecal baclofen, diazepam, and selective dorsal rhizotomy. The effective treatments to reduce contracture and improve joint alignment include monitoring hip displacement, lower limb serial casting with or without botulinum toxin, and orthopedic surgery (e.g., soft tissue or bone surgery).

The interventions described earlier were limited to RCTs involving medical and allied health professionals (i.e., clinical interventions). Some of these "Do It" interventions may be implemented in adapted physical education or recreation therapy settings (e.g., strength training, task-specific training). Moreover, some of the "Probably Do It" interventions described by Novak et al. (2020) could be implemented in

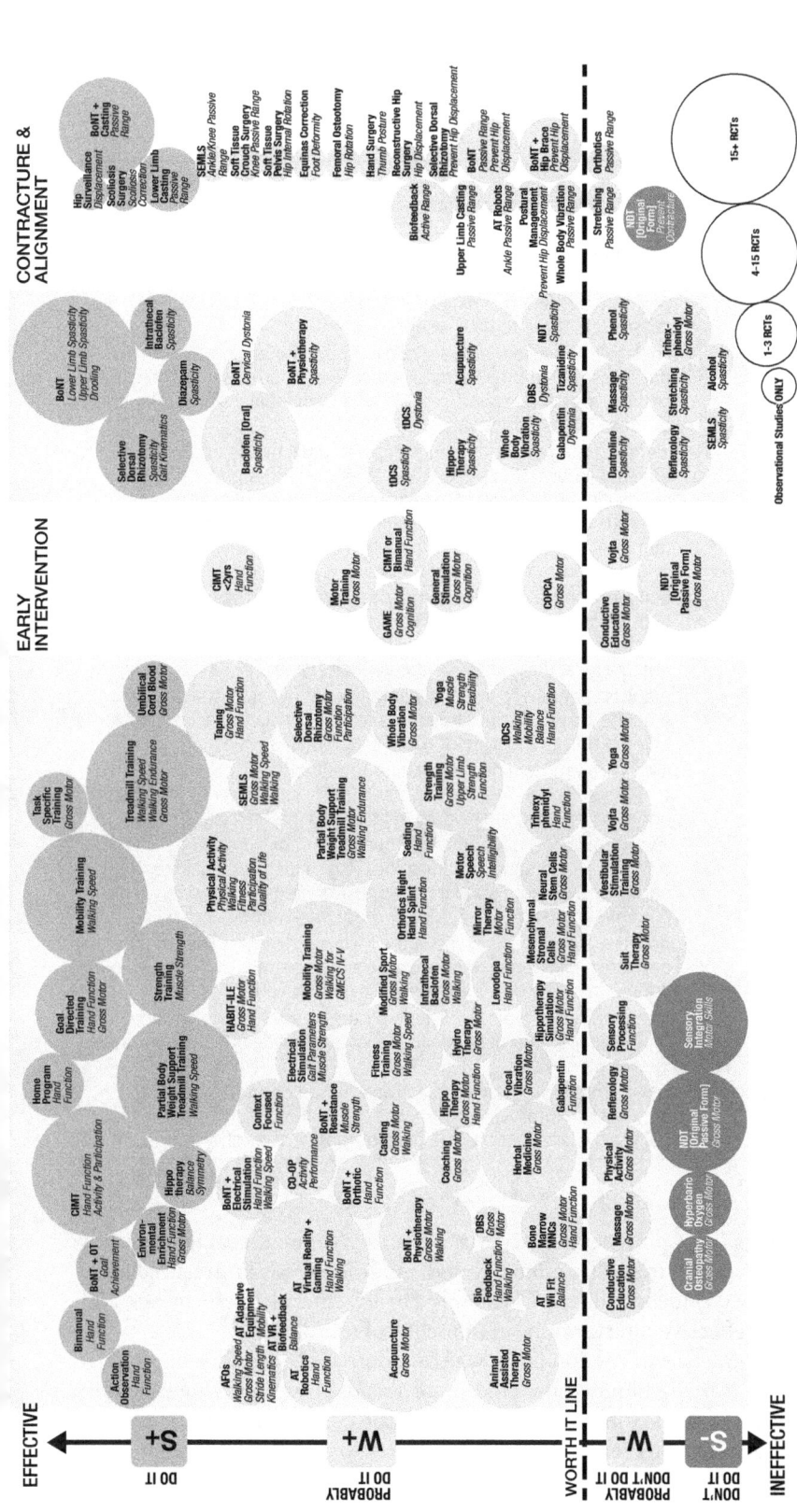

Figure 8.1 Evidence alert system

Legend: AFOs = ankle foot orthoses; AT = assistive technology; BoNT = botulinum toxin; CIMT = constraint-induced movement therapy; CO-OP = cognitive orientation to occupational performance; COPCA = coping with and caring for infants with special needs - a family-centered program; DBS = deep brain stimulation; GAME = goals activity motor enrichment; NDT = neurodevelopmental therapy; OT = occupational therapy; RCTs = randomized controlled studies; SEMLS = single-event multi-level surgery; tDCS = transcranial direct current stimulation

Source: Novak et al., 2020, CC BY 4.0

Table 8.2 Brief Description of Effective ("Do It") Interventions for Motor Outcomes

Intervention	Description
Action observation	Watch videos of daily activities of the hands/arms and execute each activity (approximately fifteen hours: one hour/day, five days/week, three weeks).
Bi-manual training	Practice bi-manual tasks such as reaching, grasping, releasing, in-hand manipulation, and using the more-affected hand to assist in task performance (approximately ninety hours: two to six hours/day, five days/week, three to nine weeks).
Botulinum toxin and occupational therapy (BoNT + OT)	Complete adjunctive therapies following BoNT injection. Adjunctive therapies that improved motor outcomes included serial and fixed casting, resistance training, CIMT, and bi-manual training. The dose of these interventions varies.
Constraint-induced movement therapy (CIMT)	Undergo casting or use of a mitt/glove to prevent use of the less-affected limb. Complete intensive therapy with a physical or occupational therapist to increase functional abilities of the more affected limb. The dose of these interventions varies, but the total number of hours is typically large (e.g., approximately 120 hours: six or more hours/day, twenty or more consecutive days).
Environmental enrichment	Parents receive training or coaching to learn strategies to interact with their infant, modify the physical environment for motor task practice, and provide frequent opportunities for infant-initiated practice. The dose of these interventions varies.
Hippotherapy	Therapists set goals to improve coordination, dynamic stability, mobility, postural strength/endurance, and reduce spasticity while riding a horse. The dose of these interventions varies.
Home program	Parents received training or coaching to deliver task- or goal-oriented training at home. The dose of these interventions varies, but ideally, home-based programs would enable a "higher dose."
Mobility training	Gait or mobility training practiced overground or on a treadmill with or without additional modifications (e.g., auditory/visual feedback, partial body weight support, progressive intensity, transcranial direct current stimulation). The dose of these interventions varies.
Partial body weight supported treadmill training	Supports are provided to reduce the load on the lower body during gait or mobility training to enable upright posture and improve gait parameters. The dose of these interventions varies.
Strength training	Programs vary but typically include progressive resistance training, cycle training, and general muscle strengthening. The dose of these interventions varies.
Task-specific training	Practice gross motor skills and activities based on motor learning principles to improve performance, gross motor function, functional skills, and participation. The dose of these interventions varies.

Source: Novak et al. (2020)

non-clinical settings (e.g., physical activity, virtual reality/gaming, coaching, fitness training, modified sport, strength training, yoga). Additional RCTs are needed to provide confirmatory evidence for the "Probably Do It" clinical interventions and implementation of effective interventions in non-clinical settings.

To this end, one recent randomized, waitlist-controlled, assessor-blind trial (Clutterbuck et al., 2022) examined the efficacy of an adaptive sports intervention in children with CP (GMFCS levels I and II) on motor competence, participation, and quality of life. The intervention was administered by a physical therapist at community parks. The intervention consisted of eight weeks (one hour/week) of sport-specific skill training, sport education, teamwork, and confidence for soccer, netball, T-ball, and cricket. Clinically and statistically significant improvements were observed for the Canadian Occupational Performance Measure (performance and satisfaction) and Test of Gross Motor Development (total, locomotor, and ball skills) immediately following and twelve weeks post-intervention for program participants compared to controls. However, no improvements in other motor outcomes (i.e., GMFM-challenge module, timed up and go, sprint tests, vertical and standing broad jump, or seated throw) were observed. These results suggest that even a small dose intervention (eight hours) may improve perceptions and satisfaction in achieving motor performance goals and fundamental gross motor skills but may not be sufficient to improve other functional movement and fitness skills.

Overall, there is a growing body of evidence from well-powered RCTs that the therapeutic interventions described here improve motor control and development in children with CP. Across these different interventions, there are common characteristics that facilitate motor performance, motor control, and long-term skill learning in children with CP (Novak et al., 2020):

1. Training involves real-life activities and daily tasks (including sports, recreation, and play).
2. The child and parents select the activities/tasks to increase motivation, goal orientation, and enjoyment.
3. Training promotes independent and self-generated actions.
4. Training has a high practice intensity or dose.

FUTURE RESEARCH

The National Institutes of Health developed a strategic plan for CP research based on recommendations from a broad community of constituents including people living with CP and caregivers, clinicians, researchers, and advocates (https://www.ninds.nih.gov/about-ninds/strategic-plans-evaluations/strategic-plans/ninds-nichd-strategic-plan-cerebral-palsy-research). Those related to motor behavior research can be categorized into:

1. Exercise and strength training: identify evidence-based programs to improve stamina, endurance, flexibility, activity, participation, independence, and health
2. Differences across the lifespan and GMFCS level: how do symptoms, treatment efficacy, and co-occurring conditions differ as a function of age (children, adolescents, adults, older adults) and GMFCS level
3. Neuroplasticity and neuroscience tools: determine how to measure and leverage neuroplasticity to improve motor function
4. Complementary and alternative therapies: evaluate the efficacy and costs associated with these therapies (e.g., hippotherapy, swimming/aquatic, yoga, tai chi, recreation, etc.)
5. Combination and comparative therapies: evaluate the efficacy of different treatment modalities used in conjunction (e.g., functional electrical stimulation *and* CIMT) and in comparison (functional electrical stimulation *or* CIMT) for different types of participants/patients (e.g., age, GMFCS, with co-occurring conditions)

The Cerebral Palsy Research Network (https://cprn.org/) was developed to address these research priorities. The Cerebral Palsy Research Network includes a registry of clinical trials as well as patient-reported and clinical outcomes from a network of hospitals and clinics. The goal is to recruit large and more diverse samples (e.g., age, GMFCS, and other demographics), address the priority research areas identified by the community, and monitor the long-term outcomes from treatments/interventions using common data elements. The common data elements help ensure the use of standard tools for greater consistency in characterizing participant characteristics, clinical assessments, standard practices for common treatments, and outcomes (https://www.commondataelements.ninds.nih.gov/cerebral%20palsy).

PRACTICAL IMPLICATIONS

Novak et al. (2020) provided recommendations for selecting treatments for individuals with CP in the clinic or lab. First, the child and parents should work collaboratively with the clinician/researcher to determine intervention goals. Second, the clinician/researcher will identify the most effective treatment to achieve that goal. Third, the clinician/researcher should be clear with families that *on average* the treatment is effective but that individual differences may affect the treatment efficacy. The clinician/researcher administers the treatment using standardized procedures and monitors outcomes using common data elements. If the most effective treatment is not available or the family does not want that treatment, other effective treatments may be implemented, and the expected and actual treatment outcomes discussed with parents. These recommendations ensure that treatments align with child/parent goals and transparency throughout the treatment.

In addition to individual factors that affect treatment efficacy (e.g., CP subtype, child's age, GMFCS level), Rosenbaum and Gorter (2012) describe six other factors ("F-words") that interact and contribute to clinical outcomes for children with CP. Family, friends, and fun are three of these "F-words" particularly useful for motor intervention. Parents can contribute to the development of treatment goals and, for some interventions (e.g., GAME), parents play an active role in providing opportunities for children to practice tasks at home. Also, siblings can support task practice as models and partners. Friends and opportunities to develop friendships can also enhance task practice and improve motor skill outcomes. Incorporating parents, siblings, and friends into games and other activities can make skill practice more fun. Indeed, children with CP should help identify tasks/activities that they enjoy and the people they want to include in the practice. Making tasks fun can increase a child's motivation during practice leading to goal achievement, greater confidence, and satisfaction.

CONCLUSION

CP is the most common childhood motor disability. Damage or atypical development of different brain regions underlie differences in CP subtype and symptom presentation. Early intervention and ongoing therapeutic interventions throughout childhood are needed to improve the quantity and quality of motor behaviors and facilitate the independent performance of daily tasks. Additional studies are needed to understand the impact of individual (e.g., CP subtype, age, GMFCS level) and environmental factors (e.g., intervention, family, friends, therapy setting) on motor outcomes across the lifespan.

REFERENCES

Beckung, E., Carlsson, G., Carsldotter, S., and Uvebrant, P. (2007). The natural history of gross motor development in children with cerebral palsy aged 1 to 15 years. *Developmental Medicine & Child Neurology, 49*, 751–56. https://doi.org/10.1111/j.1469-8749.2007.00751.x

Clutterbuck, G.L., Auld, M.L., and Johnston, L.M. (2022). SPORTS STARS: a practitioner-led, peer-group sports intervention for ambulant children with cerebral palsy. Activity and participation outcomes of a randomised controlled trial. *Disability and Rehabilitation, 44*(6), 948–56. https://doi.org/10.1080/09638288.2020.1783376

Damiano, D.L., and Longo, E. (2021). Early intervention evidence for infants with or at risk for cerebral palsy: an overview of systematic reviews. *Developmental Medicine & Child Neurology, 63*(7), 771–84. https://doi.org/10.1111/dmcn.14855

Deluca, S., Ramey, S., Trucks, M., and Wallace, D. (2016). Constraint-induced movement therapy (CIMT) for infants and toddlers. *Developmental Medicine & Child Neurology, 58*, 15. https://doi.org/https://doi.org/10.1111/dmcn.13_13224

Durkin, M.S., Benedict, R.E., Christensen, D., Dubois, L.A., Fitzgerald, R.T., Kirby, R.S., Maenner, M.J., van Naarden Braun, K., Wingate, M.S., and Yeargin-Allsopp, M. (2016). Prevalence of cerebral palsy among 8-year-old children in 2010 and preliminary evidence of trends in its relationship to low birthweight. *Paediatric and Perinatal Epidemiology, 30*(5), 496–510. https://doi.org/10.1111/ppe.12299

Eliasson, A.C., Krumlinde-Sundholm, L., Gordon, A.M., Feys, H., Klingels, K., Aarts, P.B.M., Rameckers, E., Autti-Rämö, I., and Hoare, B. (2014). Guidelines for future research in constraint-induced movement therapy for children with unilateral cerebral palsy: An expert consensus. *Developmental Medicine & Child Neurology, 56*(2), 125–37. https://doi.org/10.1111/dmcn.12273

Eliasson, A.C., Nordstrand, L., Ek, L., Lennartsson, F., Sjöstrand, L., Tedroff, K., and Krumlinde-Sundholm, L. (2018). The effectiveness of Baby-CIMT in infants younger than 12 months with clinical signs of unilateral-cerebral palsy; an explorative study with randomized design. *Research in Developmental Disabilities, 72*, 191–201. https://doi.org/10.1016/j.ridd.2017.11.006

Eliasson, A.-C., Krumlinde-Sundholm, L., Shaw, K., and Wang, C. (2005). Effects of constraint-induced movement therapy in young children with hemiplegic cerebral palsy: An adapted model. *Developmental Medicine & Child Neurology, 47*(4), 266–75. https://doi.org/10.1017/s0012162205000502

Graham, H.K., Rosenbaum, P., Paneth, N., Dan, B., Lin, J.P., Damiano, D.L., Becher, J.G., Gaebler-Spira, D., Colver, A., Reddihough, D.S., Crompton, K.E., and Lieber, R.L. (2016). Cerebral palsy. *Nature Reviews Disease Primers, 2*, 15082. https://doi.org/10.1038/nrdp.2015.82

Hägglund, G., Lauge-Pedersen, H., and Wagner, P. (2007). Characteristics of children with hip displacement in cerebral palsy. *BMC Musculoskeletal Disorders, 8*, 101. https://doi.org/10.1186/1471-2474-8-101

Hanna, S.E., Rosenbaum, P.L., Bartlett, D.J., Palisano, R.J., Walter, S.D., Avery, L., and Russell, D.J. (2009). Stability and decline in gross motor function among children and youth with cerebral palsy aged 2 to 21 years. *Developmental Medicine & Child Neurology, 51*(4), 295–302. https://doi.org/10.1111/j.1469-8749.2008.03196.x

Korzeniewski, S.J., Slaughter, J., Lenski, M., Haak, P., and Paneth, N. (2018). The complex aetiology of cerebral palsy. *Nature Reviews Neurology, 14*(9), 528–43. https://doi.org/10.1038/s41582-018-0043-6

Morgan, C., Novak, I., Dale, R.C., Guzzetta, A., and Badawi, N. (2014). GAME (Goals–Activity–Motor Enrichment): Protocol of a single blind randomised controlled trial of motor training, parent education and environmental enrichment for infants at high risk of cerebral palsy. *BMC Neurology*, 14(1), 203. https://doi.org/10.1186/s12883-014-0203-2

Novak, I., Morgan, C., Adde, L., Blackman, J., Boyd, R.N., Brunstrom-Hernandez, J., Cioni, G., Damiano, D., Darrah, J., Eliasson, A.C., de Vries, L.S., Einspieler, C., Fahey, M., Fehlings, D., Ferriero, D.M., Fetters, L., Fiori, S., Forssberg, H., Gordon, A.M., . . . Badawi, N. (2017). Early, accurate diagnosis and early intervention in cerebral palsy: Advances in diagnosis and treatment. *JAMA Pediatrics*, 171(9), 897–907. https://doi.org/10.1001/jamapediatrics.2017.1689

Novak, I., Morgan, C., Fahey, M., Finch-Edmondson, M., Galea, C., Hines, A., Langdon, K., Namara, M.M., Paton, M.C., Popat, H., Shore, B., Khamis, A., Stanton, E., Finemore, O.P., Tricks, A., te Velde, A., Dark, L., Morton, N., and Badawi, N. (2020). State of the evidence traffic lights 2019: Systematic review of interventions for preventing and treating children with cerebral palsy. *Current Neurology and Neuroscience Reports*, 20(2), 3. https://doi.org/10.1007/s11910-020-1022-z

Palisano, R., Rosenbaum, P., Walter, S., Russell, S., Wood, E., and Galuppi, B. (1997). Development and reliability of a system to classify gross motor function in children with cerebral palsy. *Developmental Medicine & Child Neurology*, 39, 214–23. https://doi.org/10.1111/j.1469-8749.1997.tb07414.x

Persson-Bunke, M., Hägglund, G., Lauge-Pedersen, H., Ma, P.W., and Westbom, L. (2012). Scoliosis in a total population of children with cerebral palsy. *Spine*, 37(12), E708–E713. https://doi.org/10.1097/BRS.0b013e318246a962

Rosenbaum, P., and Gorter, J.W. (2012). The "F-words" in childhood disability: I swear this is how we should think. *Child: Care, Health and Development*, 38(4), 457–63. https://doi.org/10.1111/j.1365-2214.2011.01338.x

Rosenbaum, P.L., Palisano, R.J., Bartlett, D.J., Galuppi, B.E., and Russell, D.J. (2008). Development of the Gross Motor Function Classification System for cerebral palsy. *Developmental Medicine & Child Neurology*, 50(4), 249–53. https://doi.org/10.1111/j.1469-8749.2008.02045.x

Rosenbaum, P.L., Walter, S.D., Hanna, S.E., Palisano, R.J., Russell, D.J., Raina, P., Wood, E., Bartlett, D.J., and Galuppi, B.E. (2002). Prognosis for gross motor function in cerebral palsy creation of motor development curves. *JAMA*, 288(11), 1357–63. https://doi.org/10.1001/jama.288.11.1357

Rosenbaum, P., Paneth, N., Leviton, A., Goldstein, M., and Bax, M. (2007). A report: The definition and classification of cerebral palsy April 2006. *Developmental Medicine & Child Neurology*, 49, 8–14. https://doi.org/10.1111/j.1469-8749.2007.tb12610.x

Sterling, C., Taub, E., Davis, D., Rickards, T., Gauthier, L., Griffin, A., and Uswatte, G. (2013). Structural neuroplastic change after constraint-induced movement therapy in children with cerebral palsy. *Pediatrics*, 131(5), e1664–e1669. https://doi.org/10.1542/peds.2012-2051

Sutcliffe, T.L., Gaetz, W.C., Logan, W.J., Cheyne, D.O., and Fehlings, D.L. (2007). Cortical reorganization after modified constraint-induced movement therapy in pediatric hemiplegic cerebral palsy. *Journal of Child Neurology*, 22(11), 1281–87. https://doi.org/10.1177/0883073807307084

Taub, E., Ramey, S.L., DeLuca, S., and Echols, K. (2004). Efficacy of constraint-induced movement therapy for children with cerebral palsy with asymmetric motor impairment. *Pediatrics*, 113(2), 305–12. https://doi.org/10.1542/peds.113.2.305

9

Motor Behavior and Neurodegenerative Disorders Associated with Aging

Nadja Schott

■ ■ ■

OVERVIEW

With the change in the population's age structure in industrialized countries, there is also an increasing incidence of neurodegenerative diseases, including movement disorders. In 2017, 3.8 billion people worldwide suffered from at least one neurologic disease, representing nearly 51 percent of the aging population. The prevalence is 104 million people experiencing stroke, forty-five million people experiencing Alzheimer's disease (AD), 8.5 million experiencing Parkinson's disease (PD), 1.8 million experiencing multiple sclerosis, and 450,000 experiencing amyotrophic lateral sclerosis (Lou Gehrig's disease) or Huntington's disease (Deuschl et al., 2020). Because neurodegenerative diseases occur primarily in mid- to late life, the incidence is expected to increase as the population ages. If the development continues unchecked, the number of people suffering from dementia and PD will almost double by 2050. Neurodegenerative diseases progress irreversibly and are associated with high socioeconomic costs and personal sacrifice.

In general, neurodegenerative diseases are sporadic and rare, hereditary disorders of the central nervous system in which there is a slowly progressive loss of function and failure of specific neuron populations and their connections for mostly unexplained reasons. Movement disorders represent a group of disorders characterized by impaired motor function, usually with a paucity or excess of involuntary and voluntary movements unrelated to weakness or spasticity (so-called hypo- and hyperkinetic movement disorders) or faulty movement control.

Neurodegenerative diseases can be subdivided according to different criteria. Possible criteria include etiology, an affinity for specific neurons, or common pathohistologic features (clinicopathologic and molecular biological classifications; see Table 9.1). Molecular biologic classifications include prion diseases (e.g., Creutzfeldt-Jakob), synucleinopathies (e.g., PD; Lewy body disorders; cerebellar ataxia), tauopathies (e.g., AD), polyglutamine diseases (e.g., Huntington's disease), motor neuron diseases (e.g., amyotrophic lateral sclerosis), and neuroaxonal dystrophies. A weakness of the existing classifications is that the etiologic background of

Table 9.1 Overview of Selected Neurodegenerative Diseases

	Alzheimer's disease	Dementia with Lewy bodies	Parkinson's disease	Amyotrophic lateral sclerosis	Huntington's disease
Main motor features	Bradykinesia, rigidity, postural or resting tremor, altered speech, and facial expression	Tremor, rigidity, bradykinesia, postural instability	Tremor, rigidity, bradykinesia, postural instability	Hyperreflexia, spasticity, slowing of movements; weakness, muscle atrophy, fasciculations	Chorea, dystonia, parkinsonism
Main cognitive features	Impairment in learning and recall of recently learned information; prominence of language or visuospatial or executive dysfunctions	Fluctuations of attention and consciousness. Visual hallucinations, delusions; disproportionate attentional, executive function, and visual processing deficits relative to memory and naming	Impairment in executive, memory, learning, visuospatial domains	Impairment in executive functions, emotion processing, and social cognition	Early impairment in emotion recognition, processing speed, learning, and working memory
Typical disease onset	>65 years (juvenile forms <5% of cases)	>65 years	>50 years, but early forms and juvenile forms	>45 years, but early forms and juvenile forms are also described	Variable and depending on the CAG repeat length, 35–44 years (juvenile forms <10% of cases)
Neuro-anatomical prediction	Cortex, hippocampus	Basal ganglia, brain stem	Substantia nigra	Motor cortex and anterior horns of the spinal cord, motor neurons	Striatum, basal ganglia
Main protein accumulation	Amyloid-β; three-repeat-Tau protein	Alpha-synuclein	Alpha-synuclein	TDP-43	Huntingtin
Lifetime risk without family burden	1:10 (men) 1:5 (women)	1:10 (men) 1:5 (women)	1:16 (men) 1:18 (women)	1:300 (men) 1:400 (women)	De novo mutations in described in individual cases (with familial predisposition (autosomal dominant) 50%)
Prevalence	700:100,000	500–1,600:100,000	106:100,000	10–12:100,000	10.6–13.7:100,000

Sources: Deuschl et al., 2020; Scheltens et al., 2021; Masrori and Van Damme, 2020; McColgan and Tabrizi, 2018; Simon et al., 2020.

many neurodegenerative diseases is not yet clear. In addition, for some pathohistologic changes (e.g., aggregation of tau proteins), it is unclear whether it is an underlying cause or the consequence of another fundamental disorder. These diseases have a chronic course with a relatively long (sometimes decades), clinically asymptomatic lead time, an age of onset usually between fifty and seventy years of age, and are usually associated with increasing brain deficits. If these deficits reach an extent that makes it impossible for the affected person to lead an independent life, the disease is dementia. Aging is the main risk factor for most neurodegenerative diseases.

UNDER THE MAGNIFYING GLASS: GAIT AS AN IMPORTANT PREDICTOR FOR MOTOR-COGNITIVE PERFORMANCE IN ALZHEIMER'S AND PARKINSON'S DISEASE

Walking is one of the most frequently accessed everyday sensorimotor performances requiring complex interactions between motor and sensory control, and cognitive functions and has been proposed as the sixth vital sign (Fritz and Lusardi, 2009). Slow gait speed has been shown to predict the occurrence of neurodegenerative changes in the elderly (Buckley et al., 2019).

In patients with *PD*, a change in the complete gait pattern can be observed due to increasing bradykinesia. The typical shuffling gait pattern of a patient with PD with the upper body bent forward is slower and characterized by smaller steps than healthy individuals. Steps become asymmetrical, step length and speed decrease (hypokinesia; see Figure 9.1), and initiation of walking becomes more difficult (akinesia). In addition, compared with healthy individuals, there is a proportionally smaller step length and a higher cadence (steps per minute) regardless of the given step speed (Khera and Khumar, 2022). In recent studies, arm movements have also been shown to be a promising opportunity for early detection as prodromal markers that indicate preclinical changes at an early stage. For example, arm movements differ between patients with PD and healthy controls in temporal and spatial dimensions (arm swing asymmetry, arm rotation extent) and the dimension of arm swing symmetry (Baron et al., 2018). As PD progresses, many patients often experience difficulty initiating or stopping gait movement and rotation around their axis, called festination or freezing of gait (Zhang et al., 2021). The gait pattern becomes increasingly stereotyped, but the ability to adapt to new environments or tasks decreases. Thus, affected patients with PD can usually walk unrestrictedly and quickly in familiar surroundings or open spaces. However, in unfamiliar or busy environments, the typical shuffling, small-step, slow walking, and freezing occur because the many sensory stimuli and the simultaneous learning of motor skills cannot be reconciled. Unexpected changes in floor conditions, such as sudden slopes or changes from hard to soft surfaces, pose a significant challenge, especially for older patients with advanced PD. Changing from, for example, slow walking to a faster sequence of steps, avoiding an obstacle, or adding a secondary cognitive task is also more difficult (Orcioli-Silva et al., 2020; Simieli et al., 2017). As a result of these gait impairments, many affected persons experience an increased risk of falling with the risk of injury, a loss of independence, and a reduced quality of life (Grimbergen et al., 2013; Klotzbier et al., 2022). A primary goal in treating PD is to improve gait control.

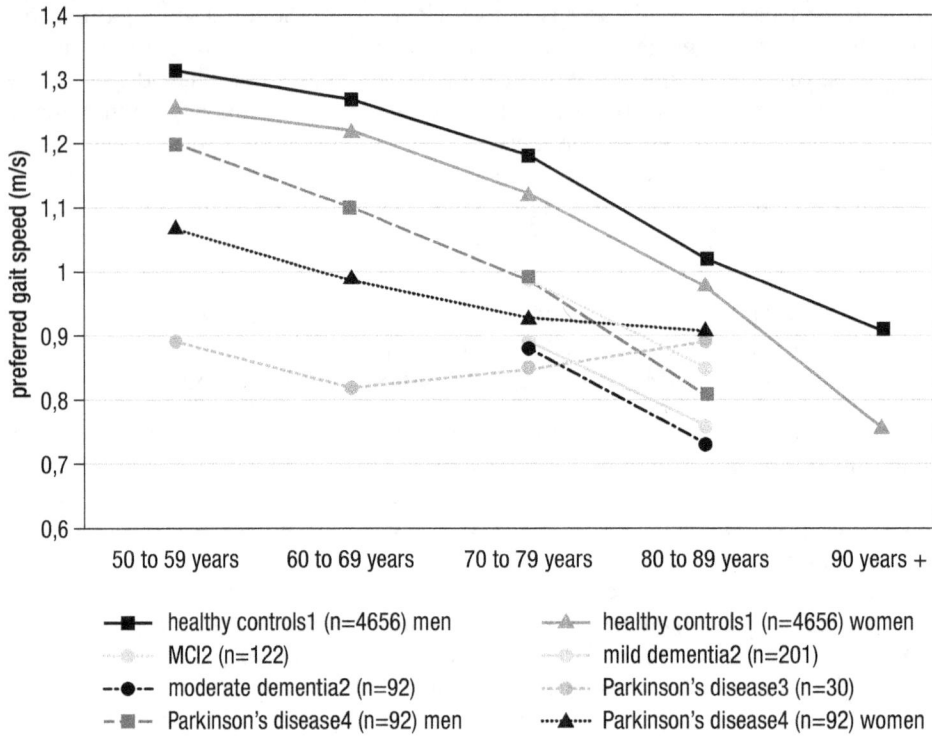

Figure 9.1 Self-selected preferred gait speed (m/s) in patients with Alzheimer's and Parkinson's disease and healthy controls

Source: Data from 1 Dommershuijsen et al., 2022; 2 de Cock et al., 2017; 3 Muñoz Ospina et al., 2019; 4 Khera and Khumar, 2022

Gait and balance disorders also occur in *dementia-related syndromes* and may already manifest at the early stages of AD (Nyul-Toth et al., 2021). Visser (1983) described early changes in quantitative gait parameters compared to healthy controls (shortened stride length, slower walking speed, lower cadence, longer double stance phase, and increased stride length variability; "cautious gait") and interpreted these findings to mean that transcortical connections involved in the integration and maintenance of a physiological gait pattern are damaged in AD. In a larger case-control study, this coincidence was determined for different types of dementia using the Tinetti test (Allan et al., 2005). Their results showed that clinically significant gait and balance disturbances are highly clustered in the non-Alzheimer dementia group (vascular dementia, Parkinson's dementia, and Lewy body dementia), even in the early stages. A longitudinal study examining the predictive value of neurologic gait disturbances concerning the development of vascular dementia showed that a neurologic gait disturbance is associated with a 3.5-fold increased risk of a later onset of vascular dementia, especially when a frontal or hemiparetic gait disturbance is present. Gait variability was recently confirmed as a predictor of mild cognitive impairment (MCI) in a longitudinal study over four years (Byun et al., 2018). Hoogendijk and colleagues (2020) found similar results in a secondary analysis of three longitudinal studies (H70: Sweden, InCHIANTI: Italy, and LASA: Netherlands) in individuals followed for nine to twenty-five years. They demonstrated decreased walking speed during the transition from the MCI stage to the severe cognitive impairment stage. In contrast, patients with AD do not show clinically manifest gait and balance disturbances (increase in track width, small-step shuffling gait pattern, and inability to accelerate to gait apraxia) until the stage of moderate to severe dementia (see also de Cock et al., 2017; Figure 9.1). Later studies evaluated the influence of executive functions on gait performance in individuals with MCI or AD and found significantly lower walking speeds under dual-task conditions (simultaneous walking and processing of a cognitive task) compared to a control group (Oh et al., 2021; Klotzbier and Schott, 2017). Increased gait variability, executive dysfunction, and fall risk may be closely related to AD (Bahureksa et al., 2017).

Despite widespread research efforts, few effective treatments for age-related neurodegenerative diseases are currently available. However, in recent years, a growing number of publications have shown that exercise benefits neurodegenerative diseases and their motor and cognitive symptoms that do not respond to pharmacologic ones, such as gait, posture, and balance. For example, several randomized controlled intervention trials suggest that physical training can still improve cognitive performance in older persons, even with mild cognitive deficit or dementia, or at least slow further cognitive decline (Huang et al., 2021). Furthermore, endurance exercise has been shown to improve brain regions' functional and structural plasticity responsible for planning, executing, and controlling movements, thus counteracting the decline of motor and cognitive functions in PD (Johansson et al., 2021). However, a critical component of rehabilitation efforts to counteract chronic progressive impairments is that people with neurodegenerative diseases can relearn, maintain, or regain motor skills or make sensorimotor adaptations.

MOTOR LEARNING IN ALZHEIMER'S AND PARKINSON'S DISEASE

The competence to move purposefully and in a coordinated manner is closely interrelated with an independent life and a central component of motor performance. While some motor skills develop as genetically determined behavioral patterns or as part of maturation, many motor skills are characterized by the fact that they require a certain amount of practice or experience before they are adequately mastered (Schott and Klotzbier, 2018). Accordingly, learning and adapting motor skills is elementary to all aspects of life. *Motor learning* is a process in which changes occur within central nervous motor control structures due to practice or experience (Magill and Anderson, 2021). The learning-related changes can occur at all levels of the motor process (i.e., from stimulus identification to movement execution). This mainly involves adaptations in goal selection, action selection, and action execution depending on the motor skill.

Neuroplastic processes accompany all learning processes: altered brain activation with repeated execution of a newly learned movement, improved functional connectivity in motor regions, and structural (anatomic) adaptations in the brain (Doyon et al. 2009). In this context, memory content is not stored in specialized regions, and learning also does not occur in specific regions but rather in a network of those areas that are also involved in the reception and processing of the respective information. In older (healthy) adults, degeneration processes can be found in the brain in the cerebral cortex, cerebellum, hippocampus, basal ganglia, and spinal cord (Grajauskas et al., 2019). Consequences of these age-related changes include greater and more widespread brain activation during the performance of the same motor task by older than younger adults (Berghuis et al., 2019) and decreases in the speed and accuracy of movements (Seidler et al., 2010). However, whether and how age with and without neurodegenerative diseases affects the acquisition and retention of new motor skills is still controversial (Bootsma et al., 2021).

Alzheimer's Disease

A typical morphologic correlate of AD is the atrophy of the hippocampus and the medial temporal lobe, which can occur very early in the disease (Tondelli et al., 2012). Other typical atrophy patterns also frequently affect the lateral and basal temporal lobes and the medial parietal cortex. In contrast, brain areas important for procedural memory, such as the basal ganglia and the cerebellum, remain intact until the more severe stages (Whitwell, 2010). Accordingly, declarative learning and memory decreases are considered characteristic criteria of AD, whereas procedural learning is thought to remain intact until disease progression (de Wit et al., 2021).

Although structural and functional brain changes may limit the ability of motor learning in individuals with dementia-related changes, some studies have demonstrated motor learning even in individuals with dementia (Rösler et al., 2002; van Tilborg et al., 2011; Werner et al., 2017; Yan and Dick, 2006). However, these results are based on experimental motor tasks with low complexity (e.g., serial reaction time tests; Yan and Dick, 2006) or complex gross motor tasks with low everyday relevance (dance; Rösler et al., 2002). Complex key motor skills, such as transfer performance, have not yet been considered in studies of motor learning in people with dementia. Moreover, previous studies have focused exclusively on the initial acquisition of motor skills after learning sessions with few training units and usually do not investigate long-term effects. A recent meta-analysis shows that overall procedural learning performance in individuals with MCI or dementia is clinically and statistically trivial compared to healthy older adults, again suggesting that procedural learning remains intact during MCI and AD dementia (de Wit et al., 2021).

Parkinson's Disease

In patients with PD, motor learning ability is preserved, as many reviews have shown (Marinelli et al., 2017; Olson et al., 2019; Udupa et al., 2022). However, learning deficits can be observed and may have different manifestations and causes but are rarely so massive that learning is no longer evident. Nonetheless, patients with PD can learn motor tasks with more practice than healthy controls, using reinforced cues or perturbations (Udupa et al., 2022).

Different studies with patients or healthy individuals with functional neuronal imaging demonstrate that both the basal ganglia, whose dysfunction PD is based on, and the cerebellum have an important role in motor learning (Udupa et al., 2022). Over time, the cerebellum seems more significant in early learning phases, and the basal ganglia is more significant in late learning phases. In terms of tasks, the cerebellum seems to support mainly adaptation learning, and the basal ganglia more the learning of movement sequences, as in classical serial reaction time tasks. Imaging studies show increased activation of the prefrontal cortex (specifically the dorsolateral prefrontal cortex), areas of the parietal cortex (specifically the precuneus), the cerebellum, and the premotor cortex during motor learning in patients with PD (Aslan et al., 2021; Marinelli et al., 2017). The altered neuronal activity patterns are interpreted as a compensatory mechanism that, although indicating an existing capacity for learning-induced neuroplasticity can be ineffective in achieving maximal learning performance. In a recent narrative review, Marinelli et al. (2017) argued that the impairment in implicit sequence learning performance in PD may also be due to a disease-related lack of self-directed attentional control and reduced movement speed.

The altered dopaminergic neurotransmission caused by PD also affects the sensorimotor striatum, which, therefore, usually manifests itself in problems with the execution of automatic movements (habitual control) as well as slower motor memory formation in visuo-motor adaptation tasks in affected individuals (Marinelli et al., 2017; Olson et al., 2019). These circuits are involved in encoding (associative striatum, fronto-striatal circuits), consolidation, and automatization (sensorimotor striatum, cortico-striatal circuits) of motor skills (Petzinger et al., 2015). In this context, the deficits appear to be most pronounced during severe perturbations as well as after a consolidation phase in a retention test, with changes within fronto-striatal circuits being particularly relevant for the development of cognitive strategies during motor learning and dopamine deficiency resulting in impaired learning-induced long-term potentiation (Marinelli et al., 2017). In a recent review, Olson et al. (2019) reiterated PD's relatively skill-independent, slower motor memory formation. However, the authors point out that skills with certain characteristics are particularly affected. This includes predominantly implicit properties and skills requiring marked reactive control (feedback control) (see also Udupa et al., 2022). To compensate, motor memory formation occurs primarily through adaptation in feedforward control. However, this causes patients with PD to have difficulty automating and transferring (re)learned skills. Olson et al. (2019) conclude that balance and gait training, particularly in terms of a motor learning process, is slowed. An additional negative influence on motor memory formation appears to be disease-related cognitive dysfunction (e.g., deficits in attention, executive function, motivation, and mental rotation ability), which is usually present during early disease stages and likely due to alterations in the fronto-striatal circuitry (Marinelli et al., 2017; Olson et al., 2019). Marinelli et al. (2017) also note that sleep disturbances already present early in the disease could worsen consolidation. In addition, drug substitution using levodopa shows insufficient effects on motor memory formation (Marinelli et al., 2017; Olson et al., 2019). Consequently, strategies that can optimize motor learning are imperative. However, all of these findings proved to be highly dependent on the specific task, the time course of the exercises, the severity of the condition, details of the site of injury, and much more (Marinelli et al., 2017; Olson et al., 2019; Udupa et al., 2022).

FUTURE RESEARCH

Our understanding of the effects of neurodegenerative diseases on motor control and learning is limited by a lack of existing research. Recent findings on neuroplasticity and motor learning can guide clinical work, but they lead to a new set of research questions. Future research efforts must address numerous unanswered questions on various aspects of motor learning in neurodegenerative diseases (see Table 9.2). A detailed discussion of the individual aspects would go beyond the scope of this chapter; therefore, reference is made to the literature given.

Table 9.2 Challenges in Motor Behavior Research in Neurodegenerative Diseases

Subject matter	Open research questions
Influence of motor skills	– Identification of motor skills that particularly benefit (e.g., depending on the extremities, on the degree of complexity) – Analysis of the primary neural circuits addressed (e.g., cognitive versus motor component) – Effects of the same effectors of cardiovascular or muscular stimulus and motor skill
Influence on various processes of motor memory formation	– Analysis of the primary consolidation process addressed (synaptic versus system consolidation) – Analysis of brain regions involved during skill acquisition, consolidation, and retention – Interaction of effects with sleep – Effects during late learning phases (e.g., autonomic phase) – Effects during long-term coupling of the exercise process with cardiovascular or muscular interventions
Influence of different parameters of cardiovascular or muscular stimuli	– Analysis of optimal parameters of the cardiovascular or muscular stimulus, e.g., intensity (submaximal versus maximal), duration, protocol (e.g., continuous versus interval), and type (e.g., running versus free weight training) – Interaction of load parameters with the timing of stimulus – Interaction of load parameters with characteristics of motor skill – Interaction of exercise-induced changes in peripheral biomarkers and the brain – Analysis of the optimal impact on brain-derived neurotrophic factor level: peak brain-derived neurotrophic factor at a given time point, e.g., after completion of exercise, or total amount of circulating brain-derived neurotrophic factor over time
Influence of various individual characteristics	– Identification of moderating person characteristics (e.g., age, gender, fitness, genotype, motivation, self-efficacy, fatigue, motor, and cognitive status) and groups of people who will particularly benefit
Influence of different principles of motor learning	– Identification of optimal combinations of determinants of motor learning (number and length of pauses, adaptation of task to performance progress, combination of different tasks or task variants ["blocked versus variable practice"], type of performance feedback ["knowledge of result" versus "knowledge of performance"], focus of attention during movement execution ["external versus internal focus of attention"], and modality [visual, auditory, haptic], precision, and frequency of feedback). – Identification of optimal motor learning strategies (e.g., errorless learning, analogy learning, observational learning, trial and error learning, dual-task learning, discovery learning, mental practice)
Analysis of dopamine-induced enhancement of motor memory formation	– Comparison of effects in subjects with neurodegenerative diseases to age-matched healthy subjects. – Effects in healthy subjects taking dopamine antagonists
Influence of gamma-aminobutyric acid on the learning process	– Identification of optimal gamma-aminobutyric acid concentration at early and late stages of the learning process
Influence of assessment	– Identification of multidimensional (digital) measures of motor (and cognitive) performance (e.g., using wearable sensors)
Influence of data analysis techniques	– Identification of optimal statistical analysis methods for mapping intraindividual learning progress (e.g., mixed-effects regression, modeling trajectories; computational simulations; machine/deep learning)

Sources: Anderson et al., 2019; Lövdén et al., 2020; Taubert et al., 2012; Wanner, 2021

PRACTICAL IMPLICATIONS

In the past, older people tended to be discouraged from physical activity to avoid overexertion; today, there is good evidence for the beneficial effects of physical activity and exercise on symptoms of PD or dementia (Emig et al., 2021; López-Ortiz et al., 2021). However, especially in individuals with neurodegenerative diseases, physical inactivity is considered an alarming problem, as physical inactivity is associated with comorbid disorders and secondary associated symptoms, such as pain, fatigue, cardiovascular symptoms, or musculoskeletal complaints (Benka Wallén et al., 2015; Block et al., 2016).

Neurodegenerative diseases are not curable so far—but while they used to be only clinically diagnosable and partly treated symptomatically, therapies are now developing that target the underlying causes and disease mechanisms. However, studies suggest that exercise is only effective up to a certain point in the neurodegenerative process; thus, some findings suggest that exercise is most beneficial as a treatment when used early in the diagnosis (Feys et al., 2019). In the last decade, a growing number of publications have shown that exercise (e.g., aerobic exercise, treadmill training, serious games, boxing, tango dancing, and Tai Chi) has a positive effect on Parkinson's symptoms that do not respond well to either pharmacologic or surgical treatments, namely gait, posture, and balance, with an associated increased risk of falls (Emig et al., 2021). However, not all types of exercises have the same beneficial effect: to be effective, exercises should have at least moderate intensity and repetition (the best results can be achieved with daily training sessions), difficulty, complexity, and specificity (i.e., they should be designed to target individual specific skills such as gait, sit to stand, fine motor dexterity) (Mehrholz et al., 2015). In addition, the heterogeneity of the PD group should be considered (i.e., Höner and Yahr stage 1–3). While general recommendations for exercise interventions are available, there is limited evidence on how to promote a disease/symptom-specific profile (Ellis and Rochester, 2018).

Physical activity may also improve cognitive function and reduce cognitive decline in patients with AD (López-Ortiz et al., 2021). Specifically, exercise has been shown to slow the deterioration of activities of daily living in patients with AD (Forbes et al., 2015). As previously named, the earlier in the disease course and the longer the exercise intervention, the better the outcome: patients with advanced AD will not readily benefit from exercise intervention, while at-risk individuals, as well as patients with MCI, are the most appropriate candidates (Gaitán et al., 2021). For example, recent randomized controlled trials have documented that aerobic exercise and strength training are associated with reduced hippocampal atrophy and improved memory performance in early AD (for review, see Babaei and Azari, 2022). Moderate- to high-intensity aerobic exercise training for sixteen to twenty-four weeks (three times per week for thirty minutes each) also significantly improves memory performance in patients with AD (Jia et al., 2019). To improve gait (especially double stance time and gait variability) in older people with MCI or early dementia, strength, balance, and functional mobility training have been shown to be effective, especially when combined with executive function training. Cognitive content focusing on attention and executive functions should be delivered alongside physical exercises rather than separately, with consideration given to transfer to activities of daily living (Zhang et al., 2019).

CONCLUSION

The early accurate diagnosis of neurodegenerative conditions is a key target within clinical research, and some studies already underline the potential of sensor-based gait analysis to identify specific features (rhythm, speed, gait, and variability) in the gait pattern of patients with neurodegenerative diseases such as PD and dementia (Buckley et al., 2019; Zhou et al., 2022). In this way, clinical examination for monitoring disease progression or evaluating therapeutic interventions can be complemented with objective gait data, and future clinical trials can be expanded to include a potential endpoint. In particular, parameters of increased gait variability have been shown in recent studies to be sensitive biomarkers of motor function limitations in neurodegenerative diseases (Byun et al., 2018). In addition, initial longitudinal findings suggest that objective gait data may reflect neurodegenerative disease progression (Gaßner et al., 2020).

A wealth of literature addresses motor learning in healthy older adults, but few studies address people with neurodegenerative diseases. While not impossible in individuals with PD or dementia, procedural learning is slower overall, learning gains are smaller, and transfer to other skills is lower (de Wit et al., 2021; Olson et al., 2019). Current research efforts promoting the combination of fitness training (endurance, strength) with motor learning content show that exercise is a promising way to influence the burden positively and possibly the course of neurologic diseases (Taubert et al., 2015). However, this will require designing studies that consider the multisystemic symptoms of the neurodegenerative disease in question, identify the specific effects of exercise, and understand the underlying pathophysiology or mechanisms. A better understanding of these relationships would allow for a more individualized approach and likely lead to better disease outcomes.

REFERENCES

Allan, L.M., Ballard, C.G., Burn, D.J., and Kenny, R.A. (2005). Prevalence and severity of gait disorders in Alzheimer's and non-Alzheimer's dementias. *Journal of the American Geriatrics Society*, 53(10), 1681–87. https://doi.org/10.1111/j.1532-5415.2005.53552.x

Aslan, D.H., Hernandez, M.E., Frechette, M.L., Gephart, A.T., Soloveychik, I.M., and Sosnoff, J.J. (2021). The neural underpinnings of motor learning in people with neurodegenerative diseases: A scoping review. *Neuroscience and Biobehavioral Reviews*, 131, 882–98. https://doi.org/10.1016/j.neubiorev.2021.10.006

Babaei, P., and Azari, H.B. (2022). Exercise training improves memory performance in older adults: a narrative review of evidence and possible mechanisms. *Frontiers in Human Neuroscience*, 15, 771553. https://doi.org/10.3389/fnhum.2021.771553

Bahureksa, L., Najafi, B., Saleh, A., Sabbagh, M., Coon, D., Mohler, M.J., and Schwenk, M. (2017). The impact of mild cognitive impairment on gait and balance: A systematic review and meta-analysis of studies using instrumented assessment. *Gerontology*, 63(1), 67–83. https://doi.org/10.1159/000445831

Baron, E.I., Miller Koop, M., Streicher, M.C., Rosenfeldt, A.B., and Alberts, J.L. (2018). Altered kinematics of arm swing in Parkinson's disease patients indicates declines in gait under dual-task conditions. *Parkinsonism & Related Disorders*, 48, 61–67. https://doi.org/10.1016/j.parkreldis.2017.12.017

Benka Wallén, M., Franzén, E., Nero, H., and Hagströmer, M. (2015). Levels and patterns of physical activity and sedentary behavior in elderly people with mild to moderate Parkinson Disease. *Physical Therapy*, 95(8), 1135–41. https://doi.org/10.2522/ptj.20140374

Berghuis, K.M.M., Fagioli, S., Maurits, N.M., Zijdewind, I., Marsman, J.B.C., Hortobágyi, T., Koch, G., and Bozzali, M. (2019). Age-related changes in brain deactivation but not in activation after motor learning. *NeuroImage*, 186, 358–68. https://doi.org/10.1016/j.neuroimage.2018.11.010

Block, V.A.J., Pitsch, E., Tahir, P., Cree, B.A.C., Allen, D.D., and Gelfand, J.M. (2016). Remote physical activity monitoring in neurological disease: A systematic review. *PLoS One*, 11(4), e0154335. https://doi.org/10.1371/journal.pone.0154335

Bootsma, J.M., Caljouw, S.R., Veldman, M.P., Maurits, N.M, Rothwell, J.C., and Hortobágyi, T. (2021). Neural correlates of motor skill learning are dependent on both age and task difficulty. *Frontiers in Aging Neuroscience*, 13, 643132. https://doi.org/10.3389/fnagi.2021.643132

Buckley, C., Alcock, L., McArdle, R., Rehman, R.Z.U., Del Din, S., Mazzà, C., Yarnall, A.J., and Rochester, L. (2019). The role of movement analysis in diagnosing and monitoring neurodegenerative conditions: Insights from gait and postural control. *Brain Sciences*, 9(2). https://doi.org/10.3390/brainsci9020034

Byun, S., Han, J.W., Kim, T.H., Kim, K., Kim, T. H., Park, J.Y., Suh, S.W., Seo, J.Y., So, Y., Lee, K.H., Lee, J.R., Jeong, H., Jeong, H.-G., Han, K., Hong, J.W., and Kim, K.W. (2018). Gait variability can predict the risk of cognitive decline in cognitively normal older people. *Dementia and Geriatric Cognitive Disorders*, 45(5-6), 251–61. https://doi.org/10.1159/000489927

Cock, A.M. de, Fransen, E., Perkisas, S., Verhoeven, V., Beauchet, O., Remmen, R., and Vandewoude, M. (2017). Gait characteristics under different walking conditions: Association with the presence of cognitive impairment in community-dwelling older people. *PLoS One*, 12(6), e0178566. https://doi.org/10.1371/journal.pone.0178566

Deuschl, G., Beghi, E., Fazekas, F., Varga, T., Christoforidi, K.A., Sipido, E., Bassetti, C.L., Vos, T., and Feigin, V.L. (2020). The burden of neurological diseases in Europe: an analysis for the Global Burden of Disease Study 2017. *The Lancet Public Health*, 5(10), e551-e567. https://doi.org/10.1016/S2468-2667(20)30190-0

Dommershuijsen, L.J., Ragunathan, J., Ruiter, R., Groothof, D., Mattace-Raso, F.U.S., Ikram, M.A., and Polinder-Bos, H.A. (2022). Gait speed reference values in community-dwelling older adults—Cross-sectional analysis from the Rotterdam Study. *Experimental Gerontology*, 158, 111646. https://doi.org/10.1016/j.exger.2021.111646

Doyon, J., Bellec, P., Amsel, R., Penhune, V., Monchi, O., Carrier, J., Lehéricy, S., and Benali, H. (2009). Contributions of the basal ganglia and functionally related brain structures to motor learning. *Behavioural Brain Research*, 199(1), 61–75. https://doi.org/10.1016/j.bbr.2008.11.012

Ellis, T., and Rochester, L. (2018). Mobilizing Parkinson's disease: The future of exercise. *Journal of Parkinson's Disease*, 8(s1), S95-S100. https://doi.org/10.3233/JPD-181489

Emig, M., George, T., Zhang, J.K., and Soudagar-Turkey, M. (2021). The role of exercise in Parkinson's Disease. *Journal of Geriatric Psychiatry and Neurology*, 34(4), 321–30. https://doi.org/10.1177/08919887211018273

Feys, P., Moumdjian, L., van Halewyck, F., Wens, I., Eijnde, B. O., van Wijmeersch, B., Popescu, V., and van Asch, P. (2019). Effects of an individual 12-week community-located "start-to-run" program on physical capacity, walking, fatigue, cognitive function, brain volumes, and structures in persons with multiple sclerosis. *Multiple Sclerosis (Houndmills, Basingstoke, England)*, 25(1), 92–103. https://doi.org/10.1177/1352458517740211

Forbes, D., Forbes, S.C., Blake, C.M., Thiessen, E.J., and Forbes, S. (2015). Exercise programs for people with dementia. *The Cochrane Database of Systematic Reviews*, (4), CD006489. https://doi.org/10.1002/14651858.CD006489.pub4

Fritz, S., and Lusardi, M. (2009). White paper: "walking speed: The sixth vital sign." *Journal of Geriatric Physical Therapy (2001)*, 32(2), 46–49.

Gaitán, J.M., Moon, H.Y., Stremlau, M., Dubal, D.B., Cook, D.B., Okonkwo, O.C., and van Praag, H. (2021). Effects of aerobic exercise training on systemic biomarkers and cognition in late middle-aged adults at risk for Alzheimer's Disease. *Frontiers in Endocrinology, 12*, 660181. https://doi.org/10.3389/fendo.2021.660181

Gaßner, H., Jensen, D., Marxreiter, F., Kletsch, A., Bohlen, S., Schubert, R., Muratori, L.M., Eskofier, B., Klucken, J., Winkler, J., Reilmann, R., and Kohl, Z. (2020). Gait variability as digital biomarker of disease severity in Huntington's disease. *Journal of Neurology, 267*(6), 1594–601. https://doi.org/10.1007/s00415-020-09725-3

Grajauskas, L.A., Siu, W., Medvedev, G., Guo, H., D'Arcy, R.C.N., and Song, X. (2019). MRI-based evaluation of structural degeneration in the ageing brain: Pathophysiology and assessment. *Ageing Research Reviews, 49*, 67–82. https://doi.org/10.1016/j.arr.2018.11.004

Grimbergen, Y.A.M., Schrag, A., Mazibrada, G., Borm, G.F., and Bloem, B.R. (2013). Impact of falls and fear of falling on health-related quality of life in patients with Parkinson's disease. *Journal of Parkinson's Disease, 3*(3), 409–13. https://doi.org/10.3233/JPD-120113

Hoogendijk, E.O., Deeg, D.J.H., de Breij, S., Klokgieters, S.S., Kok, A.A.L., Stringa, N., Timmermans, E.J., van Schoor, N.M., van Zutphen, E.M., van der Horst, M., Poppelaars, J., Malhoe, P., and Huisman, M. (2020). The Longitudinal Aging Study Amsterdam: Cohort update 2019 and additional data collections. *European Journal of Epidemiology, 35*(1), 61–74. https://doi.org/10.1007/s10654-019-00541-2

Huang, X., Zhao, X., Li, B., Cai, Y., Zhang, S., Yu, F., and Wan, Q. (2021). Biomarkers for evaluating the effects of exercise interventions in patients with MCI or dementia: A systematic review and meta-analysis. *Experimental Gerontology, 151*, 111424. https://doi.org/10.1016/j.exger.2021.111424

Jia, R.-X., Liang, J.-H., Xu, Y., and Wang, Y.-Q. (2019). Effects of physical activity and exercise on the cognitive function of patients with Alzheimer disease: A meta-analysis. *BMC Geriatrics, 19*(1), 181. https://doi.org/10.1186/s12877-019-1175-2

Johansson, M.E., Cameron, I.G.M., van der Kolk, N.M., Vries, N.M. de, Klimars, E., Toni, I., Bloem, B.R., and Helmich, R. C. (2021). Aerobic exercise alters brain function and structure in Parkinson's disease: A randomized controlled trial. *Annals of Neurology, 91*(2), 203–16. https://doi.org/10.1002/ana.26291

Khera, P., and Kumar, N. (2022). Age-gender specific prediction model for Parkinson's severity assessment using gait biomarkers. *Engineering Science and Technology, an International Journal, 27*, 101005. https://doi.org/10.1016/j.jestch.2021.05.009

Klotzbier, T.J., and Schott, N. (2017). Cognitive-motor interference during walking in older adults with probable mild cognitive impairment. *Frontiers in Aging Neuroscience, 9*, 350. https://doi.org/10.3389/fnagi.2017.00350

Klotzbier, T. J., Schott, N., & Almeida, Q. J. (2022). Profiles of Motor-Cognitive Interference in Parkinson's Disease—The Trail-Walking-Test to discriminate between motor phenotypes. *Brain Sciences, 12*(9), 1217. MDPI AG. Retrieved from http://dx.doi.org/10.3390/brainsci12091217

López-Ortiz, S., Valenzuela, P.L., Seisdedos, M.M., Morales, J.S., Vega, T., Castillo-García, A., Nisticò, R., Mercuri, N.B., Lista, S., Lucia, A., and Santos-Lozano, A. (2021). Exercise interventions in Alzheimer's disease: A systematic review and meta-analysis of randomized controlled trials. *Ageing Research Reviews, 72*, 101479. https://doi.org/10.1016/j.arr.2021.101479

Lövdén, M., Garzón, B., and Lindenberger, U. (2020). Human skill learning: expansion, exploration, selection, and refinement. *Current Opinion in Behavioral Sciences, 36*, 163–68. https://doi.org/10.1016/j.cobeha.2020.11.002

Magill, R.A., and Anderson, D.I. (2021). *Motor learning and control: Concepts and applications* (twelfth edition). New York: McGraw-Hill.

Marinelli, L., Quartarone, A., Hallett, M., Frazzitta, G., and Ghilardi, M.F. (2017). The many facets of motor learning and their relevance for Parkinson's disease. *Clinical Neurophysiology*, *128*(7), 1127–41. https://doi.org/10.1016/j.clinph.2017.03.042

Masrori, P., and van Damme, P. (2020). Amyotrophic lateral sclerosis: A clinical review. *European Journal of Neurology*, *27*(10), 1918–29. https://doi.org/10.1111/ene.14393

McColgan, P., and Tabrizi, S.J. (2018). Huntington's disease: A clinical review. *European Journal of Neurology*, *25*(1), 24–34. https://doi.org/10.1111/ene.13413

Mehrholz, J., Kugler, J., Storch, A., Pohl, M., Hirsch, K., and Elsner, B. (2015). Treadmill training for patients with Parkinson's disease. *The Cochrane Database of Systematic Reviews*, (9), CD007830. https://doi.org/10.1002/14651858.CD007830.pub4

Muñoz Ospina, B., Valderrama Chaparro, J.A., Arango Paredes, J.D., Castaño Pino, Y.J., Navarro, A., and Orozco, J.L. (2019). Age matters: Objective gait assessment in early Parkinson's Disease using an RGB-D Camera. *Parkinson's Disease*, *2019*, 5050182. https://doi.org/10.1155/2019/5050182

Nyul-Toth, A., DelFavero, J., Mukli, P., Tarantini, A., Ungvari, A., Yabluchanskiy, A., Csiszar, A., Ungvari, Z., and Tarantini, S. (2021). Early manifestation of gait alterations in the Tg2576 mouse model of Alzheimer's disease. *GeroScience*, *43*(4), 1947–57. https://doi.org/10.1007/s11357-021-00401-6

Oh, C., Morris, R.J., LaPointe, L.L., and Stierwalt, J.A.G. (2021). Spatial-temporal parameters of gait associated with Alzheimer disease: A longitudinal analysis. *Journal of Geriatric Psychiatry and Neurology*, *34*(1), 46–59. https://doi.org/10.1177/0891988720901779

Olson, M., Lockhart, T.E., and Lieberman, A. (2019). Motor learning deficits in Parkinson's Disease (PD) and their effect on training response in gait and balance: A narrative review. *Frontiers in Neurology*, *10*, 62. https://doi.org/10.3389/fneur.2019.00062

Orcioli-Silva, D., Barbieri, F.A., Dos Santos, P.C.R., Beretta, V.S., Simieli, L., Vitorio, R., Lirani-Silva, E., and Gobbi, L.T.B. (2020). Double obstacles increase gait asymmetry during obstacle crossing in people with Parkinson's disease and healthy older adults: A pilot study. *Scientific Reports*, *10*(1), 2272. https://doi.org/10.1038/s41598-020-59266-y

Petzinger, G.M., Holschneider, D.P., Fisher, B.E., McEwen, S., Kintz, N., Halliday, M., Toy, W., Walsh, J.W., Beeler, J., and Jakowec, M.W. (2015). The effects of exercise on dopamine neurotransmission in Parkinson's disease: Targeting neuroplasticity to modulate basal ganglia circuitry. *Brain Plasticity (Amsterdam, Netherlands)*, *1*(1), 29–39. https://doi.org/10.3233/bpl-150021

Rösler, A., Seifritz, E., Kräuchi, K., Spoerl, D., Brokuslaus, I., Proserpi, S.-M., Gendre, A., Savaskan, E., and Hofmann, M. (2002). Skill learning in patients with moderate Alzheimer's disease: A prospective pilot-study of waltz-lessons. *International Journal of Geriatric Psychiatry*, *17*(12), 1155–56. https://doi.org/10.1002/gps.705

Scheltens, P., Strooper, B. de, Kivipelto, M., Holstege, H., Chételat, G., Teunissen, C.E., Cummings, J., and van der Flier, W.M. (2021). Alzheimer's disease. *The Lancet*, *397*(10284), 1577–90. https://doi.org/10.1016/S0140-6736(20)32205-4

Schott, N. & Klotzbier, T. (2018). The Motor-Cognitive Connection: Indicator of Future Developmental Success in Children and Adolescents?! In R.P. Bailey, R. Meeusen, S. Schäfer-Cerasari, & P. Tomporowski (Eds.), *Physical Activity and Educational Achievement: insights from exercise neuroscience* (pp. 111–129). London, New York: Routledge.

Seidler, R.D., Bernard, J.A., Burutolu, T.B., Fling, B.W., Gordon, M.T., Gwin, J.T., Kwak, Y., and Lipps, D.B. (2010). Motor control and aging: Links to age-related brain structural, functional, and biochemical effects. *Neuroscience and Biobehavioral Reviews*, *34*(5), 721–33. https://doi.org/10.1016/j.neubiorev.2009.10.005

Simieli, L., Gobbi, L.T.B., Orcioli-Silva, D., Beretta, V.S., Santos, P.C.R., Baptista, A.M., and Barbieri, F.A. (2017). The variability of the steps preceding obstacle avoidance (approach phase) is dependent on the height of the obstacle in people with Parkinson's disease. *PLoS One*, *12*(9), e0184134. https://doi.org/10.1371/journal.pone.0184134

Simon, D.K., Tanner, C.M., and Brundin, P. (2020). Parkinson disease epidemiology, pathology, genetics, and pathophysiology. *Clinics in Geriatric Medicine*, 36(1), 1–12. https://doi.org/10.1016/j.cger.2019.08.002

Taubert, M., Villringer, A., and Lehmann, N. (2015). Endurance exercise as an "endogenous" neuro-enhancement strategy to facilitate motor learning. *Frontiers in Human Neuroscience*, 9, 692. https://doi.org/10.3389/fnhum.2015.00692

Tondelli, M., Wilcock, G.K., Nichelli, P., Jager, C.A. de, Jenkinson, M., and Zamboni, G. (2012). Structural MRI changes detectable up to ten years before clinical Alzheimer's disease. *Neurobiology of Aging*, 33(4), 825.e25–36. https://doi.org/10.1016/j.neurobiolaging.2011.05.018

Udupa, K., Bhattacharya, A., Bhardwaj, S., Pal, P.K., and Chen, R. (2022). Parkinson's disease: Alterations of motor plasticity and motor learning. *Handbook of Clinical Neurology*, 184, 135–51. https://doi.org/10.1016/B978-0-12-819410-2.00007-2

van Tilborg, I.A.D.A., Kessels, R.P.C., and Hulstijn, W. (2011). Learning by observation and guidance in patients with Alzheimer's dementia. *NeuroRehabilitation*, 29(3), 295–304. https://doi.org/10.3233/NRE-2011-0705

Visser, H. (1983). Gait and balance in senile dementia of Alzheimer's type. *Age and Ageing*, 12(4), 296–301. https://doi.org/10.1093/ageing/12.4.296

Wanner, P., Cheng, F.H., and Steib, S. (2020). Effects of acute cardiovascular exercise on motor memory encoding and consolidation: A systematic review with meta-analysis. *Neuroscience and Biobehavioral Reviews*, 116, 365–81. https://doi.org/10.1016/j.neubiorev.2020.06.018

Werner, C., Wiloth, S., Lemke, N.C., Kronbach, F., Jansen, C.P., Oster, P., Bauer, J.M., and Hauer, K. (2017). People with dementia can learn compensatory movement maneuvers for the sit-to-stand task: A randomized controlled trial. *Journal of Alzheimer's Disease*, 60(1), 107–20. https://doi.org/10.3233/JAD-170258

Whitwell, J.L. (2010). Progression of atrophy in Alzheimer's disease and related disorders. *Neurotoxicity Research*, 18(3-4), 339–46. https://doi.org/10.1007/s12640-010-9175-1

Wit, L. de, Marsiske, M., O'Shea, D., Kessels, R.P.C., Kurasz, A.M., DeFeis, B., Schaefer, N., and Smith, G.E. (2021). Procedural learning in individuals with amnestic mild cognitive impairment and Alzheimer's dementia: A systematic review and meta-analysis. *Neuropsychology Review*, 31(1), 103–14. https://doi.org/10.1007/s11065-020-09449-1

Wu, Q., Chan, J.S.Y., and Yan, J.H. (2016). Mild cognitive impairment affects motor control and skill learning. *Reviews in the Neurosciences*, 27(2), 197–217. https://doi.org/10.1515/revneuro-2015-0020

Yan, J.H., and Dick, M.B. (2006). Practice effects on motor control in healthy seniors and patients with mild cognitive impairment and Alzheimer's disease. *Neuropsychology, Development, and Cognition. Section B, Aging, Neuropsychology and Cognition*, 13(3-4), 385–410. https://doi.org/10.1080/138255890969609

Zhang, W., Low, L.F., Gwynn, J.D., and Clemson, L. (2019). Interventions to improve gait in older adults with cognitive impairment: A systematic review. *Journal of the American Geriatrics Society*, 67(2), 381–91. https://doi.org/10.1111/jgs.15660

Zhang, W.S., Gao, C., Tan, Y.Y., and Chen, S.D. (2021). Prevalence of freezing of gait in Parkinson's disease: A systematic review and meta-analysis. *Journal of Neurology*, 268(11), 4138–50. https://doi.org/10.1007/s00415-021-10685-5

Zhou, H., Park, C., Shahbazi, M., York, M.K., Kunik, M.E., Naik, A.D., and Najafi, B. (2022). Digital biomarkers of cognitive frailty: The value of detailed gait assessment beyond gait speed. *Gerontology*, 68(2), 224–33. https://doi.org/10.1159/000515939

10

Motor Behavior and Intellectual Disabilities

Alyssa LaForme Fiss and Julia Looper

■ ■ ■

OVERVIEW

The *Diagnostic and Statistical Manual of Mental Disorders* (American Psychiatric Association, 2013) and the American Association on Intellectual and Developmental Disabilities (2022) define *intellectual disability* (ID) using three criteria: (a) significant limitations in intellectual functioning, (b) significant limitations in adaptive behavior, and (c) onset of limitations prior to the age of twenty-two years. The first criteria, *intellectual functioning*, includes a person's abilities in learning, reasoning, problem-solving, planning, abstract thinking, and judgment. Intellectual functioning is typically measured by clinical observation and standardized IQ tests with a score at least two standard deviations below the mean, a score of seventy or below, representing a deficit in intellectual functioning. The second criteria, *adaptive behavior*, is the collection of conceptual, social, and practical skills that are learned and performed by people in everyday life (American Association on Intellectual and Developmental Disabilities, 2022). Table 10.1 provides examples of each component of adaptive behavior. Effective adaptive behaviors help individuals respond to and engage with their physical and social environment. Adaptive behavior is assessed using standardized tests, such as the Vineland Adaptive Behavior Scales, third edition (Sparrow et al., 2016) or the Adaptive Behavior Assessment System, third edition (Harrison and Oakland, 2015). The *Diagnostic and Statistical Manual of Mental Disorders-5* (American Psychiatric Association, 2013) categorizes ID as mild, moderate, severe, or profound based on the level of adaptive functioning.

Table 10.1 Components of Adaptive Behavior

Components of Adaptive Behavior		
Conceptual skills	**Social skills**	**Practical skills**
• Language and literacy • Functional academics • Self-direction	• Interpersonal skills • Self-esteem • Gullibility • Following rules • Avoiding victimization	• Activities of daily living • Healthcare • Travel/transportation • Schedules/routines • Safety

Table 10.2 Potential Causes of Intellectual Disability

Potential Causes of Intellectual Disability		
Prenatally	**Perinatally**	**Postnatally**
• Genetic causes (e.g., Down syndrome, Williams syndrome, Fragile X syndrome) • Cerebral malformations or infarctions • Maternal diseases (e.g., TORCH infections) • Environmental influences (e.g., fetal alcohol syndrome)	• Cerebral infarctions (e.g., hypoxic ischemic injury, neonatal brain hemorrhage) • Neonatal encephalopathy	• Hypoxic ischemic injury • Traumatic brain injury • Infections • Demyelinating disorders • Seizure disorders (e.g., infantile spasms) • Severe and chronic social deprivation • Toxic metabolic syndromes and intoxications (e.g., lead, mercury)

The prevalence of ID is estimated to be 11.0 to 13.4 per one thousand children and adolescents in the United States (Anderson et al., 2019; McGuire et al., 2019). Males have a higher prevalence of ID than females (Maulik et al., 2011; McKenzie et al., 2016). Multiple etiologies occurring across prenatal to postnatal periods may result in ID (see Table 10.2). This results in a diverse presentation of accompanying motor development. This chapter will focus on two exemplar diagnoses that frequently present with ID—Down syndrome and Williams syndrome—to discuss motor development in individuals with ID.

Examples of Genetic Causes

Down syndrome is a genetic disorder caused by spontaneous errors in the replication of genetic material on the twenty-first chromosome. It occurs in one out of every twelve hundred children and adolescents in the United States (Presson et al., 2013), making it the most common cause of ID. In addition to ID, children with Down syndrome often present with medical complications, visual and hearing deficits, hypotonia, motor skill delays, and difficulty with expressive language.

Williams syndrome is a genetic disorder most often caused by a spontaneous mutation causing deletion of part of the seventh chromosome. Williams syndrome occurs in one in seventy-five hundred to ten thousand people (National Library of Medicine, 2022). People with Williams syndrome present with mild to moderate ID, particularly with visual-spatial tasks (National Institute of Neurological Disorders and Stroke, 2019). In addition to ID, hypermobility, developmental delays, problems with coordination, and short stature are frequently noted in this population.

RESEARCH ON MOTOR AND COGNITIVE DEVELOPMENT

Researchers have hypothesized that motor development acts as a control parameter for other developmental skills such as cognitive development (Bushnell and Boudreau, 1993), with timing of the emergence of motor milestones producing varying developmental outcomes in cognitive, socialization, and language skills as children age (Burns et al., 2004; Campos et al., 2000; Libertus and Violi, 2016; Murray et al., 2006; Ross-Sheehy, 2016). The embodied cognition perspective of development suggests that cognition and language emerge in the context of a child's interactions and experiences with the physical and social environment (Needham and Libertus, 2011; Smith and Gasser, 2005). As infants grow and develop new motor skills, new opportunities to explore their environment and learn are created. For example, as children learn to sit without support, they are able to reach and interact with objects, creating new cognitive skills (Harbourne et al., 2014).

The relationship between motor and cognitive domains is supported by neurologic and behavioral evidence. Neuroimaging studies demonstrate co-activation of brain regions responsible for motor and cognition during certain tasks (Leisman et al., 2016). Additionally, the relationships between motor and cognitive abilities noted in individuals with ID may result from variations in neurologic development or from neurologic abnormalities, such as alterations in gray and white matter volume (Baglio et al., 2014; Carducci et al., 2013). These abnormalities appear to be more prevalent in children with more severe ID (van Karnebeek et al., 2005), and may account for the greater delays in gross motor development noted for children with greater cognitive impairments (Houwen et al., 2016). For children with ID, the relationships between motor and cognitive abilities have been noted to be strong (intraclass correlation coefficient = 0.61 to 0.94) (Houwen et al., 2016), with many children with ID presenting with concurrent motor limitations and/or delayed attainment of gross motor skills as compared to peers without ID (Houwen et al., 2016; Westendorp et al., 2011; Wuang et al., 2008). Therefore, recognition and consideration of both motor and cognitive development is important for individuals with ID.

For individuals with our exemplar diagnoses, the relationship between motor and cognitive development is evident. Individuals with Down syndrome present with ID, ranging from mild to severe cognitive impairment, and with delayed onset of motor skills, which emerge, on average, at double the rate of typically developing peers (Palisano et al., 2001; Winders et al., 2019). Yamauchi and colleagues (2019) examined the relationships between developmental domains for young children with Down syndrome, noting that motor development is significantly correlated with cognitive and language development, and the strength of this correlation increases with age. Specifically, the authors noted that the emergence of independent walking has a significant positive effect on cognition and language skills. Individuals with Williams syndrome also typically present with ID and corresponding motor impairments. Mervis and Klein-Tasman (2000) noted that 75 percent of children with Williams syndrome demonstrate IQ and adaptive behavior scores representing ID, and the remaining 25 percent demonstrate learning difficulties. Additionally, Mayall et al. (2021) noted that individuals with Williams syndrome, aged twelve to fifty years, demonstrate motor abilities like children aged four to five years of age, with balance abilities being particularly affected.

MOTOR CONTROL AND MOTOR LEARNING IN INDIVIDUALS WITH INTELLECTUAL DISABILITIES

Motor development is a complex process influenced by motor control and motor learning. *Motor control* is defined as "the ability to regulate or direct the mechanisms essential to movement" (Shumway-Cook et al., 2022, p. 3). Motor control describes the process of how the body gathers sensory information from the environment related to a task to be completed, processes that information, and develops and executes an appropriate movement plan to accomplish the task. This involves the coordination of the central nervous system with the muscles throughout the body. *Motor learning* is defined as "a set of internal processes associated with practice or experience leading to a relatively permanent change in the capability for a motor skill" (Schmidt et al., 2019, p. 283). Both motor control and motor learning are important considerations for understanding the processes of motor development.

Individuals with ID frequently present with impairments in motor control and motor learning. For example, children with ID have been shown to demonstrate impaired higher-order executive functions such as planning ability, strategic decision-making, and problem-solving, which may lead to delayed motor development (Hartman et al., 2010). In addition, individuals with ID may demonstrate difficulty with the integration of perceptual information into motor actions (Carmeli et al., 2008).

Specifically, individuals with Down syndrome present with alterations in brain structure including a smaller number and depth of cerebral sulci, enlarged ventricles, and hypoplasia of the brainstem, cerebellum, frontal, and temporal lobes (Baxter et al., 2000; Edgin, 2013; Koran et al., 2014). These abnormalities lead to impairments in motor control and motor learning. Additionally, individuals with Down syndrome demonstrate impaired higher order executive functioning contributing to movements that are less efficient and less functional (Horvat et al., 2013). Beerse et al. (2019) reported that compared to children who are typically developing, children with Down syndrome demonstrate longer motor task initiation times and are less able to anticipate transitioning between tasks. Children with Williams syndrome also exhibit impaired executive functioning that impacts their sensorimotor functioning (Wuang and Tsai, 2017) and visual motor abilities (Hocking et al., 2013), leading to impaired bilateral coordination and balance (Wuang and Tsai, 2017). Difficulties with motor control likely contribute to the motor developmental delays noted with individuals with ID.

Difficulties with motor learning frequently occur in children with ID and are likely influenced by the cognitive impairments impacting attention, motivation, and cognitive processing during the learning process. For example, in children with Williams syndrome, sleep problems negatively impact learning and memory consolidation, including motor learning (Dimitriou and Halstead, 2021). Children with ID often demonstrate difficulty with selective attention to environmental cues relevant to task performance (Gligorović and Buha Đurović, 2014) and decreased mastery of locomotor or object control skills compared to children without ID (Maïano et al., 2019; Rintala and Loovis, 2013). Research suggests individuals with ID may demonstrate enhanced learning and task mastery when instructions encourage an *external focus of attention* (Chiviacowsky et al., 2013) and when intervention occurs using *error-reduced learning conditions* (Capio et al., 2013) (see Table 10.3).

Conflicting research exists regarding whether children with ID display motivational deficits that may impact the learning of new motor skills (Cuskelly and Gilmore, 2014). However, strategies to improve *motivation* for learning include opportunities to engage with stimulating activities, supportive adult attitudes and expectations, environmental structure, positive reinforcement, and child autonomy. Regaieg and colleagues (2020) noted that for individuals with Down syndrome, training motor skill within games leads to more favorable outcomes than more traditional approaches, suggesting that more motivating activities may improve learning.

Table 10.3 Definitions of Key Principles of Motor Learning

Principle	Definition
Attention	*External focus of attention:* Focus directed toward the effect of movement on the environment *Internal focus of attention:* Focus directed toward components of the body during the movement
Error-reduced learning	Practice conditions are manipulated to increase the likelihood of success
Motivation	General desire or interest in participating in a task
Massed versus distributed practice	*Massed practice:* Practice occurs in an intensive block *Distributed practice:* Practice occurs over several sessions spaced out over time
Constant versus variable practice	*Blocked practice:* Practice schedule where a single variation of the task is practiced repeatedly *Variable practice:* Practice schedule where multiple variations of the task are practiced
Feedback	*Intrinsic feedback:* Feedback from within the individual while performing the task; the physical feel of the movement *Extrinsic feedback:* Feedback provided by external sources during or after the performance of a task *Self-controlled feedback:* Feedback provided when an individual requests it

Although research with children with ID is limited, literature suggests that *distributed and variable practice* may be more beneficial to motor learning (Baker, 2002; Matsouka et al., 2010). Additionally, implementation of dual-task exercises (e.g., combining functional tasks with balance training) for individuals with ID is likely to improve efficiency of their learning (Mikolajczyk and Jankowicz-Szymanska, 2015). Consideration of feedback for individuals with ID suggests that *intrinsic feedback*, feedback from internal sources or how the body feels during movement, may be more beneficial than *extrinsic feedback*, feedback from external sources such as feedback from someone observing the movement. This is because extrinsic feedback depends more heavily on cognitive processes that may be difficult for individuals with ID (Angulo-Barroso and Todd, 2016), and suggests the use of augmented, extrinsic feedback should be minimized to reduce the cognitive demand. Additionally, emerging research suggests that self-controlled practice of tasks and *self-controlled feedback* may increase motivation and learning of motor skills (Chiviacowsky et al., 2012).

However, "individuals with ID" is not a homogeneous term. Research has noted that children with Down syndrome respond differently than children with Williams syndrome when learning motor skills by observation, suggesting that researchers and clinicians should be cautious about applying any result to all people with ID (Foti et al., 2018). Therefore, it is important to explore variations that may exist for specific populations.

FUTURE RESEARCH

For individuals with ID, exploration of the interconnectedness of motor and cognitive development is warranted to delineate various aspects of this relationship that may be amenable to change and to highlight the reciprocal effects of intervention targeting either domain. Research on the most effective strategies for improving motor control and motor learning for individuals with ID would allow practitioners to more effectively design interventions to improve motor development and motor skill acquisition. While limited, research suggests that motor learning and control in individuals with ID is diagnosis specific; therefore, additional investigation could provide clarity on how people with different forms of cognitive impairment develop motor control and learning strategies. Large-scale developmental surveillance on individuals with ID through the lifespan would offer opportunities for further normative milestone development and prognostic planning. Strong randomized controlled trials of various motor learning principles would help guide intervention decision-making to improve motor skill acquisition.

PRACTICAL IMPLICATIONS

Children with ID often display delayed motor skill development, differences in motor learning, and even atypical motor control patterns which affect how they participate in recreational, school, or therapeutic environments. Because children with ID have delayed motor skills, they may be lacking in development of fundamental motor skills required for more advanced game play. Identifying these deficits and modifying games to allow for practice and development of fundamental motor skills allows children to improve their skills while participating with peers. However, practitioners may have to teach a child specific skills before the child can participate with peers. In this case, practice should take place in an environment that is set up for success with a task that is meaningful to the child. The focus of training should be on the task itself instead of the specific body positions needed for the task. Additionally, because children with ID have cognitive processing deficits, feedback should be concise and consistent. To facilitate motor learning, practice should take place in frequent but short blocks that consist of variable task conditions. Though children with ID also display atypical motor control patterns, this may be due to their atypical neurologic system. While motor control patterns can be normalized through training, it may be more functional to allow the individual's control patterns to emerge during skill practice based on their own personal constraints and strengths (Latash and Anson, 1996).

CONCLUSION

Children with ID display delayed development of both cognitive and motor skills. Neither of these developmental processes happens in isolation; decreased movement and exploration leads to cognitive delays while decreased cognitive skill may lead to decreased exploratory drive and exploratory movement. Because children with ID have atypical neural substrates, their ability to learn motor skills is also impacted. However, each diagnosis impacts different neural substrates causing motor learning and motor control to vary by diagnosis. Professionals who work with individuals with ID to develop new motor skills should intentionally focus on principles and practice factors that facilitate motor learning.

REFERENCES

American Association on Intellectual and Developmental Disabilities. (2022). Defining criteria for intellectual disability. www.aaidd.org/intellectual-disability/definition

American Psychiatric Association. (2013). *Diagnostic and Statistical Manual of Mental Disorders*, fifth edition. https://doi.org/10.1176/appi.books.9780890425596

Anderson, L.L., Larson, S.A., Mapel-Lentz, S., and Hall-Lande, J. (2019). A systematic review of U.S. studies on the prevalence of intellectual or developmental disabilities since 2000. *Intellectual and Developmental Disabilities*, 57(5), 421–38. https://doi.org/10.1352/1934-9556-57.5.421

Angulo-Barroso, R., and Todd, T. (2016). *Advances in disability and motor behavior research*. Routledge Handbooks Online. https://doi.org/10.4324/9781315743561.ch15

Baglio, F., Cabinio, M., Ricci, C., Baglio, G., Lipari, S., Griffanti, L., Preti, M. G., Nemni, R., Clerici, M., Zanette, M., and Blasi, V. (2014). Abnormal development of sensory-motor, visual temporal and parahippocampal cortex in children with learning disabilities and borderline intellectual functioning. *Frontiers in Human Neuroscience*, 8. https://www.frontiersin.org/article/10.3389/fnhum.2014.00806

Baker, B.J. (2002). An investigation of the relative effects of blocked and random practice on the learning of ballistic motor skills in typically developing children and children with Down syndrome. (Publication No. 3072055.) Doctoral dissertation, University of Washington.

Baxter, L.L., Moran, T.H., Richtsmeier, J.T., Troncoso, J., and Reeves, R.H. (2000). Discovery and genetic localization of Down syndrome cerebellar phenotypes using the Ts65Dn mouse. *Human Molecular Genetics*, 9(2), 195–202. https://doi.org/10.1093/hmg/9.2.195

Beerse, M., Henderson, G., Liang, H., Ajisafe, T., and Wu, J. (2019). Variability of spatiotemporal gait parameters in children with and without Down syndrome during treadmill walking. *Gait & Posture*, 68, 207–12. https://doi.org/10.1016/j.gaitpost.2018.11.032

Burns, Y., O'Callaghan, M., McDonell, B., and Rogers, Y. (2004). Movement and motor development in ELBW infants at 1 year is related to cognitive and motor abilities at 4 years. *Early Human Development*, 80(1), 19–29. https://doi.org/10.1016/j.earlhumdev.2004.05.003

Bushnell, E.W., and Boudreau, J.P. (1993). Motor development and the mind: The potential role of motor abilities as a determinant of aspects of perceptual development. *Child Development*, 64(4), 1005–21. https://doi.org/10.2307/1131323

Campos, J.J., Anderson, D.I., Barbu-Roth, M.A., Hubbard, E.M., Hertenstein, M.J., and Witherington, D. (2000). Travel broadens the mind. *Infancy*, 1(2), 149–219. https://doi.org/10.1207/S15327078IN0102_1

Capio, C.M., Poolton, J.M., Sit, C.H.P., Holmstrom, M., and Masters, R.S.W. (2013). Reducing errors benefits the field-based learning of a fundamental movement skill in children. *Scandinavian Journal of Medicine & Science in Sports*, 23(2), 181–88. https://doi.org/10.1111/j.1600-0838.2011.01368.x

Carducci, F., Onorati, P., Condoluci, C., Di Gennaro, G., Quarato, P.P., Pierallini, A., Sarà, M., Miano, S., Cornia, R., and Albertini, G. (2013). Whole-brain voxel-based morphometry study of children and adolescents with Down syndrome. *Functional Neurology*, 28(1), 19–28.

Carmeli, E., Bar-Yossef, T., Ariav, C., Levy, R., and Liebermann, D. G. (2008). Perceptual-motor coordination in persons with mild intellectual disability. *Disability and Rehabilitation*, 30(5), 323–29. https://doi.org/10.1080/09638280701265398

Chiviacowsky, S., Wulf, G., and Ávila, L.T.G. (2013). An external focus of attention enhances motor learning in children with intellectual disabilities. *Journal of Intellectual Disability Research*, 57(7), 627–34. https://doi.org/10.1111/j.1365-2788.2012.01569.x

Chiviacowsky, S., Wulf, G., and Lewthwaite, R. (2012). Self-controlled learning: The importance of protecting perceptions of competence. *Frontiers in Psychology*, 3. https://www.frontiersin.org/article/10.3389/fpsyg.2012.00458

Cuskelly, M., and Gilmore, L. (2014). Motivation in children with intellectual disabilities. *Research and Practice in Intellectual and Developmental Disabilities*, 1(1), 51–59. https://doi.org/10.1080/23297018.2014.906051

Dimitriou, D., and Halstead, E.J. (2021). Sleep-related learning in Williams syndrome and Down's syndrome. In S.E. Berger, R.T. Harbourne, and A. Scher (Eds.), *Advances in child development and behavior* (pp. 261–83). Burlington: Academic Press. https://doi.org/10.1016/bs.acdb.2020.07.002

Edgin, J. O. (2013). Cognition in Down syndrome: A developmental cognitive neuroscience perspective. *WIREs Cognitive Science*, 4(3), 307–17. https://doi.org/10.1002/wcs.1221

Foti, F., Menghini, D., Alfieri, P., Costanzo, F., Mandolesi, L., Petrosini, L., and Vicari, S. (2018). Learning by observation and learning by doing in Down and Williams syndromes. *Developmental Science*, 21(5), e12642. https://doi.org/10.1111/desc.12642

Gligorović, M., and Buha Đurović, N. (2014). Inhibitory control and adaptive behaviour in children with mild intellectual disability. *Journal of Intellectual Disability Research*, 58(3), 233–42. https://doi.org/10.1111/jir.12000

Harbourne, R.T., Ryalls, B., and Stergiou, N. (2014). Sitting and looking: A comparison of stability and visual exploration in infants with typical development and infants with motor delay. *Physical & Occupational Therapy in Pediatrics*, 34(2), 197–212. https://doi.org/10.3109/01942638.2013.820252

Harrison, P.L., and Oakland, T. (2015). Adaptive Behavior Assessment System: Third edition. In J.S. Kreutzer, J. DeLuca, and B. Caplan (Eds.), *Encyclopedia of Clinical Neuropsychology* (pp. 57–60). New York: Springer International Publishing. https://doi.org/10.1007/978-3-319-57111-9_1506

Hartman, E., Houwen, S., Scherder, E., and Visscher, C. (2010). On the relationship between motor performance and executive functioning in children with intellectual disabilities. *Journal of Intellectual Disability Research*, 54(5), 468–77. https://doi.org/10.1111/j.1365-2788.2010.01284.x

Hocking, D.R., Thomas, D., Menant, J.C., Porter, M.A., Smith, S., Lord, S.R., and Cornish, K.M. (2013). The interplay between executive control and motor functioning in Williams syndrome. *Developmental Science*, 16(3), 428–42. https://doi.org/10.1111/desc.12042

Horvat, M., Croce, R., Tomporowski, P., and Barna, M.C. (2013). The influence of dual-task conditions on movement in young adults with and without Down syndrome. *Research in Developmental Disabilities*, 34(10), 3517–25. https://doi.org/10.1016/j.ridd.2013.06.038

Houwen, S., Visser, L., van der Putten, A., and Vlaskamp, C. (2016). The interrelationships between motor, cognitive, and language development in children with and without intellectual and developmental disabilities. *Research in Developmental Disabilities*, 53–54, 19–31. https://doi.org/10.1016/j.ridd.2016.01.012

Koran, M.E.I., Hohman, T.J., Edwards, C.M., Vega, J.N., Pryweller, J.R., Slosky, L.E., Crockett, G., Villa de Rey, L., Meda, S.A., Dankner, N., Avery, S.N., Blackford, J.U., Dykens, E.M., and Thornton-Wells, T.A. (2014). Differences in age-related effects on brain volume in Down syndrome as compared to Williams syndrome and typical development. *Journal of Neurodevelopmental Disorders*, 6(1), 8. https://doi.org/10.1186/1866-1955-6-8

Latash, M.L., and Anson, J.G. (1996). What are "normal movements" in atypical populations? *Behavioral and Brain Sciences*, 19(1), 55–68. https://doi.org/10.1017/S0140525X00041467

Leisman, G., Moustafa, A.A., and Shafir, T. (2016). Thinking, walking, talking: Integratory motor and cognitive brain function. *Frontiers in Public Health*, 4. https://www.frontiersin.org/article/10.3389/fpubh.2016.00094

Libertus, K., and Violi, D.A. (2016). Sit to talk: Relation between motor skills and language development in infancy. *Frontiers in Psychology*, 7. https://www.frontiersin.org/article/10.3389/fpsyg.2016.00475

Maïano, C., Hue, O., and April, J. (2019). Fundamental movement skills in children and adolescents with intellectual disabilities: A systematic review. *Journal of Applied Research in Intellectual Disabilities, 32*(5), 1018–33. https://doi.org/10.1111/jar.12606

Matsouka, O., Trigonis, J., Simakis, S., Chavenetidis, K., and Kioumourjoglou, E. (2010). Variability of practice and enhancement of acquisition, retention and transfer of learning using an outdoor throwing motor skill by children with intellectual disabilities. *Studies in Physical Culture & Tourism, 17*, 157–64.

Maulik, P.K., Mascarenhas, M.N., Mathers, C.D., Dua, T., and Saxena, S. (2011). Prevalence of intellectual disability: A meta-analysis of population-based studies. *Research in Developmental Disabilities, 32*(2), 419–36. https://doi.org/10.1016/j.ridd.2010.12.018

Mayall, L. A., D'Souza, H., Hill, E.L., Karmiloff-Smith, A., Tolmie, A., and Farran, E.K. (2021). Motor abilities and the motor profile in individuals with Williams syndrome. *Advances in Neurodevelopmental Disorders, 5*(1), 46–60. https://doi.org/10.1007/s41252-020-00173-8

McGuire, D.O., Tian, L.H., Yeargin-Allsopp, M., Dowling, N.F., and Christensen, D.L. (2019). Prevalence of cerebral palsy, intellectual disability, hearing loss, and blindness, National Health Interview Survey, 2009–2016. *Disability and Health Journal, 12*(3), 443–51. https://doi.org/10.1016/j.dhjo.2019.01.005

McKenzie, K., Milton, M., Smith, G., and Ouellette-Kuntz, H. (2016). Systematic review of the prevalence and incidence of intellectual disabilities: Current trends and issues. *Current Developmental Disorders Reports, 3*(2), 104–15. https://doi.org/10.1007/s40474-016-0085-7

Mervis, C.B., and Klein-Tasman, B.P. (2000). Williams syndrome: Cognition, personality, and adaptive behavior. *Mental Retardation and Developmental Disabilities Research Reviews, 6*(2), 148–58. https://doi.org/10.1002/1098-2779(2000)6:2<148::AID-MRD D10>3.0.CO;2-T

Mikolajczyk, E., and Jankowicz-Szymanska, A. (2015). The effect of dual-task functional exercises on postural balance in adolescents with intellectual disability—a preliminary report. *Disability and Rehabilitation, 37*(16), 1484–89. https://doi.org/10.3109/09638288.2014.967414

Murray, G.K., Veijola, J., Moilanen, K., Miettunen, J., Glahn, D.C., Cannon, T.D., Jones, P.B., and Isohanni, M. (2006). Infant motor development is associated with adult cognitive categorisation in a longitudinal birth cohort study. *Journal of Child Psychology and Psychiatry, 47*(1), 25–29. https://doi.org/10.1111/j.1469-7610.2005.01450.x

National Institute of Neurological Disorders and Stroke. (2019). Williams syndrome information page. https://www.ninds.nih.gov/Disorders/All-Disorders/Williams-Syndrome-Information-Page

National Library of Medicine. (2022). Williams syndrome. http://ghr.nlm.nih.gov/condition/williams-syndrome

Needham, A., and Libertus, K. (2011). Embodiment in early development. *WIREs Cognitive Science, 2*(1), 117–23. https://doi.org/10.1002/wcs.109

Palisano, R.J., Walter, S.D., Russell, D.J., Rosenbaum, P.L., Gémus, M., Galuppi, B.E., and Cunningham, L. (2001). Gross motor function of children with Down syndrome: Creation of motor growth curves. *Archives of Physical Medicine and Rehabilitation, 82*(4), 494–500. https://doi.org/10.1053/apmr.2001.21956

Presson, A.P., Partyka, G., Jensen, K.M., Devine, O.J., Rasmussen, S.A., McCabe, L.L., and McCabe, E.R.B. (2013). Current estimate of Down syndrome population prevalence in the United States. *The Journal of Pediatrics, 163*(4), 1163–68. https://doi.org/10.1016/j.jpeds.2013.06.013

Regaieg, G., Kermarrec, G., and Sahli, S. (2020). Designed game situations enhance fundamental movement skills in children with Down syndrome. *Journal of Intellectual Disability Research, 64*(4), 271–79. https://doi.org/10.1111/jir.12717

Rintala, P., and Loovis, E.M. (2013). Measuring motor skills in Finnish children with intellectual disabilities. *Perceptual and Motor Skills*, 116(1), 294–303. https://doi.org/10.2466/25.10.PMS.116.1.294-303

Ross-Sheehy, S., Perone, S., Vecera, S.P., and Oakes, L.M. (2016). The relationship between sitting and the use of symmetry as a cue to figure-ground assignment in 6.5-month-old infants. *Frontiers in Psychology*, 7. https://www.frontiersin.org/article/10.3389/fpsyg.2016.00759

Schmidt, R.A., Lee, T.D., Winstein, C.J., Wulf, G., and Zelaznik, H.N. (2019). *Motor control and learning: A behavioral emphasis*. Champaign, IL: Human Kinetics.

Shumway-Cook, A., Woollacott, M.H., Rachwani, J., and Santamaria, V. (2022). *Motor control: Translating research into clinical practice*. New York: LWW.

Smith, L., and Gasser, M. (2005). The development of embodied cognition: Six lessons from babies. *Artificial Life*, 11(1–2), 13–29. https://doi.org/10.1162/1064546053278973

Sparrow, S.S., Cichetti, D.V., and Saulier, C.A. (2016). *Vineland adaptive behavior scales*, third edition. New York: Pearson.

van Karnebeek, C.D.M., Jansweijer, M.C.E., Leenders, A.G.E., Offringa, M., and Hennekam, R.C.M. (2005). Diagnostic investigations in individuals with mental retardation: A systematic literature review of their usefulness. *European Journal of Human Genetics*, 13(1), 6–25. https://doi.org/10.1038/sj.ejhg.5201279

Westendorp, M., Hartman, E., Houwen, S., Smith, J., and Visscher, C. (2011). The relationship between gross motor skills and academic achievement in children with learning disabilities. *Research in Developmental Disabilities*, 32(6), 2773–79. https://doi.org/10.1016/j.ridd.2011.05.032

Winders, P., Wolter-Warmerdam, K., and Hickey, F. (2019). A schedule of gross motor development for children with Down syndrome. *Journal of Intellectual Disability Research*, 63(4), 346–56. https://doi.org/10.1111/jir.12580

Wuang, Y.P., and Tsai, H.Y. (2017). Sensorimotor and visual perceptual functioning in school-aged children with Williams syndrome. *Journal of Intellectual Disability Research*, 61(4), 348–62. https://doi.org/10.1111/jir.12346

Wuang, Y.P., Wang, C.C., Huang, M.H., and Su, C.Y. (2008). Profiles and cognitive predictors of motor functions among early school-age children with mild intellectual disabilities. *Journal of Intellectual Disability Research*, 52(12), 1048–60. https://doi.org/10.1111/j.1365-2788.2008.01096.x

Yamauchi, Y., Aoki, S., Koike, J., Hanzawa, N., and Hashimoto, K. (2019). Motor and cognitive development of children with Down syndrome: The effect of acquisition of walking skills on their cognitive and language abilities. *Brain & Development*, 41(4), 320–26. https://doi.org/10.1016/j.braindev.2018.11.008

11

Developmental Delay, Developmental Coordination Disorder, and Motor Behavior

Daphne Golden and Nancy Getchell

In this chapter, we explore developmental coordination disorder (DCD), which has a profound effect on motor behavior in childhood and often throughout the lifespan. We begin with a discussion of developmental delay (DD), which may be an early indicator that an infant or toddler has some sort of developmental disorder such as DCD, then look at the identification of DCD, key findings research in DCD motor behavior, and the future of DCD research. We finish with some practical applications of DCD research that should aid practitioners who may encounter children with either diagnosed or suspected DCD.

DEVELOPMENTAL DELAY: AN EARLY SIGN OF DEVELOPMENTAL COORDINATION DISORDER

During infancy and early childhood, the sequence of motor skill acquisition occurs in a relatively consistent order with some variability in timing. These skills, known as motor milestones, along with emergent age ranges were documented during the early and mid-twentieth century (Bayley, 1969; Shirley, 1931) and provide a foundation for the acquisition of later motor skills (Haywood and Getchell, 2018). Motor development usually occurs in a similar sequence (e.g., specific motor skills tend to emerge in a relatively consistent order) with a level of variability and clustering of skills; norm referencing based on standardized motor skills tests based on these sequences allows practitioners to establish the level of delay. In general, minor or temporary delays in the acquisition of motor skills do not indicate a larger motor issue, as the range for motor milestone acquisition is broad. However, often the first signs of multiple disorders and disabilities manifest in motor development delays of milestone acquisition, which can be identified during infancy and early childhood. DDs in the acquisition of motor milestones are important indicators of potential neurodevelopmental issues such as DCD, but also many other types of disabilities described in this volume, including but not limited to visual impairment (chapter 1), autism spectrum disorders (chapters 4 and 5), cerebral palsy (chapter 8), and intellectual disabilities (chapter 10).

The impact of motor DDs can be far reaching and lifelong; however, early intervention can significantly improve outcomes in multiple developmental domains. Motor DDs are essential to catch early due to the interdependency of motor and cognitive (Veldman et al., 2019; Piek et al., 2008), intellectual (Murray et al., 2007), communication (Valla et al., 2020), problem-solving (Molinini et al., 2021), social (Holloway, 2021), and language (Campos et al., 2000) domains. A motor DD generally is identified when assessment of children's motor skills results in scores that are –2 standard deviations from the age norms or have a motor age of 25 percent below their age equivalent (Provost et al., 2007). When a child is not developing within a normal age range in any or all developmental domains, they are commonly classified or diagnosed with a DD within the healthcare and school environments. This classification occurs in children who are not meeting their developmental milestones from birth through nine years old (Lipkin et al., 2020; Khan and Leventhal, 2021).

Diagnosis of DD generally occurs early (e.g., infancy and early childhood) by a physician or other healthcare professional through routine physical screenings, developmental checklists, and parental input (Choo et al., 2019; Lipkin et al., 2020). Once diagnosed or suspected of DD, these children are referred to early intervention and educational programs, outpatient physical therapy, or developmental pediatricians for further testing. Intervention occurs either within the home educational programs or in an outpatient clinic from birth to three years old. The educational services change from the infant and toddler programs to school-aged programs. Once a child with DD is in the school system, a school psychologist performs an evaluation and provides a classification of DD. Within the school-based system, practitioners approach DD differently, as the delay must impact children's educational process for them to receive services while in school (Lipkin and Okomoto, 2015).

The earlier children with delayed development receive intervention, the more likely they are to change their trajectory of development and lifelong success. As the motor domain is one of the first measurable and observable developmental domains, identification of relationships with later diagnosis may lead to interventions at an earlier age. Thus, recent research has focused on identifying variations in motor development of specific conditions for early diagnosis. One area of focus is measuring infants' "fidgety" movements. Fidgety movements are spontaneous small movements in all directions throughout the body that occur during early infancy. These movements are observed at a moderate speed in the head, neck, and limbs in all directions and position of the infant. These movements can be superimposed on gross movements such as swiping and kicking (Einspieler et al., 2015; Einspieler et al., 2016). A firm body of evidence exists where a pattern of reduced variation and complexity of fidgety movements is strongly associated with a later diagnosis of cerebral palsy (Bosanquet et al., 2013; Einspieler et al., 2017). Other differences in infants' fidgety movements have been associated with autism spectrum disorder, neurodevelopmental disorders, and even later cognitive function (Yuge et al., 2011; Einspieler et al., 2016; Herrero et al., 2017).

Patterns in the development of early motor skills are being studied to lead to diagnosis and intervention of DCD as well as other conditions in associated developmental domains. Some children with low tone may bottom scoot or shuffle (moving forward in a seated position using buttocks, legs, or arms), as opposed to creep on hands and knees (Robson, 1970), a manifestation seen in multiple disorders. In contrast, a family history of bottom shuffling was significantly less frequent in infants with autism spectrum disorder. Some children miss crawling altogether (Khandare et al., 2016). These differences could be a red flag or early predictor leading to earlier intervention in all areas of development.

DEVELOPMENTAL COORDINATION DISORDER

Children with DCD frequently are diagnosed with DD in various domains, but primarily fine and gross motor early in development. Because of the diagnostic criteria, typical formal diagnosis of DCD will likely not occur until at least five years old. DCD is a neurodevelopmental disorder associated with significant motor impairment in the absence of a visual or neurologic impairment or intellectual disability with a reported prevalence of 5 to 6 percent in the general population (American Psychiatric Association, 2013; Barnett et al., 2019; Blank et al., 2012). Children and adults with DCD are often described as "clumsy" and have difficulty with fine and/or gross motor skills to the extent that individuals have difficulty with activities of daily living (Biotteau et al., 2020). For example, individuals with DCD may have difficulty manipulating a fork and knife while eating or participating in activities where they must throw and catch a ball. Children with DCD frequently experience delays in the acquisition of motor developmental milestones, and these delays in motor planning, coordination, and execution often persist throughout the lifespan (Wilson et al., 2013). Interestingly, with increasing age, children's motor delays/difficulties may decrease, but often they are not able to catch up to the level of their peers without DCD (Wilmut and Byrne, 2014). Further, issues resulting from DCD may have far-reaching effects beyond the motor domain into social interactions, academic performance, sport participation, and overall quality of life (Clark et al., 2005; Sumner, 2016; Zwicker et al., 2018; Karras et al., 2019). The learning and improvement of motor skills remain a challenge for individuals with DCD throughout their lifespan.

IDENTIFICATION AND DIAGNOSIS OF DEVELOPMENTAL COORDINATION DISORDER

The *Diagnostic and Statistical Manual of Mental Disorders*, fifth edition (American Psychiatric Association, 2013) lists DCD within the broad category of neurodevelopmental conditions. To be diagnosed with DCD, children must exhibit four criteria. First, a child must demonstrate a below expected age level of learning and execution of coordinated motor skills. Second, these motor difficulties must interfere with activities of daily living and impact academic productivity, leisure, and play. Third, the onset of these motor skill difficulties occurs in early childhood. Finally, these motor skill difficulties cannot be explained by other conditions, such as intellectual delay, visual impairment, or other neurologic conditions that affect movement. While teachers, physical or occupational therapists, or psychologists may initially perform identification and evaluation of motor difficulties, diagnosis falls within the purview of medical doctors, particularly pediatricians (Caçola and Lage, 2019).

THE DEVELOPMENTAL CONUNDRUM IN DEVELOPMENTAL COORDINATION DISORDER IDENTIFICATION AND DIAGNOSIS

While early DDs are generally monitored closely by pediatricians from birth throughout early childhood, they rarely lead to a diagnosis of DCD before the age of five years, particularly in the United States. This provides for the wide age range for motor milestone acquisition, as well as an opportunity for children to "catch up" if they do not have DCD; however, it does indicate that children with DCD have also received little or no remediation and generally start school without any formal diagnosis of DCD. This leads to a developmental conundrum: while the motor impairment exhibited in DCD "significantly and persistently interferes with activities of daily living appropriate to chronological age" during early childhood, it is frequently over-looked once children begin school, unless there is a negative impact on "academic/school productivity" (American Psychiatric Association, 2013). For most school-aged children who are diagnosed with DCD, they often exhibit a co-existing academic issue that comes in conjunction with their motor impairment. The impairment itself becomes secondary, even if it has a negative impact on a child's life. Herein lies the conundrum: children may experience significant motor impairment that has an enormous impact on activities of daily living and quality of life; however, unless that impairment impacts academic performance, it is not likely to be diagnosed or treated.

MOTOR BEHAVIOR RESEARCH RELATED TO DEVELOPMENTAL COORDINATION DISORDER

While researchers have studied motor behavior in DCD for more than thirty years, the focus of this research has gradually shifted from descriptions and categorization of clumsiness to identification of underlying factors characteristic of this clumsiness. Both children and adults with DCD move awkwardly and present with unique movement patterns. But what does that mean? In general, an individual with DCD tends to move more slowly and with less accuracy (Grohs et al., 2021), which results in difficulties with activities of daily living, such as zipping a zipper, writing a note, throwing and catching a ball, and eating with silverware. Compared to individuals without DCD, individuals with DCD show higher variability; difficulty in both intra- and interlimb coordination; adaptation differences in controlling the body's degrees of freedom; differences in temporal, spatial, and postural control; and anticipatory reactions differences.

Individuals with DCD show greater inconsistency and variability in their movements in general. One of the earliest identified and most reliable characteristics related to motor behavior and DCD is the existence of increased variability (Golenia et al., 2018; Smits-Engelsman and Wilson, 2013). This lack of consistency has been identified in the performance of a wide variety of motor skills, such as fine motor (e.g., Bo et al., 2008), ball catching (e.g., Van Waelvelde et al., 2004), throwing (e.g., Schott and Getchell, 2021), and walking (e.g., Rosengren et al., 2009) among others. For example, Bo et al. (2008) compared ten children with DCD to ten age- and gender-matched children without DCD on continuous and discontinuous circle drawing tasks. They found that significant group and task differences existed, with the DCD group showing greater temporal and spatial variability than the controls. Further, individuals with DCD are less consistent in both discrete movements such as reaching and grasping (Grohs et al., 2021) and in continuous movements such as finger tapping (Biotteau et al., 2020), running (Chia et al., 2013), and multilimb coordination tasks (Volman et al., 2006; Roche et al., 2011).

More recently, researchers have started to move beyond looking for variability in general in specific motor skills; they have started examining the nature and structure of variability to better understand what deficits it represents in DCD (Golenia et al., 2018; Mackenzie et al., 2008). For example, issues with different types of coordination have been well documented in DCD. Variability exists in coordinating body parts, both within individual limbs (Wilmut et al., 2022) and across multiple limbs (Astill and Utley, 2006).

Individuals with DCD have difficulty with both temporal and spatial coupling to external stimuli. One area in which individuals with DCD show greater variability is in coupling to external stimuli (Mackenzie et al., 2008; Volman and Geuze, 1998a; Volman and Geuze, 1998b; Whitall et al., 2006). This has held true in studies of bilateral finger tapping (Roche et al., 2011) and hand/foot tapping (Volman et al., 2006), coordination of clapping and marching (Mackenzie et al., 2008), clapping and jumping (de Castro Ferracioli et al., 2014), and clapping and walking (Whitall et al., 2006). For example, in the Whitall et al. study (2006), when ten children with DCD, eight age- and gender-matched controls, and ten adults were asked to clap and march to an auditory beat at four different frequencies, the DCD group showed significantly greater variability of relative phase (the relationship between the clap or step and the metronome) than the other groups. Further, while both non-DCD groups adopted absolute coupling (a convergence of clap-step-metronome mean relative phasing) as frequencies increased, the DCD group did not and in fact decreased the percentage of trials where absolute coupling was used.

Individuals with DCD are less likely to flexibly adapt movement patterns. While initially appearing to be counterintuitive, one of the reasons that individuals with DCD show greater variability is due to a decreased ability to adapt their movement patterns to specific tasks and environmental demands. "Fixation" of joints through co-contraction (Guimarães et al., 2020) to freeze their degrees of freedom when moving may be used in individuals with DCD (Utley et al., 2007), thereby reducing the number of available movement patterns for a given task and decreasing flexibility to adapt movements to different environmental and task situations. In other words, individuals with DCD often "lock" into a movement pattern and do not change it even if that would result in better performance outcomes. For example, Astill and Utley (2006) examined two-handed catching skills in eight children with DCD and eight age-matched controls, measuring limb kinematics to determine intra- and interlimb coupling. While catching significantly fewer balls than the age-matched control group, the DCD group also demonstrated significantly greater limb coupling both between the segments of the upper arm and within joints. Similar results were also found in another study of two-handed catching (Przysucha and Maraj 2013) and one-handed catching (Asmussen et al., 2014). The authors posited that DCD results in a less adaptable movement system that reduces their ability to be successful when performing tasks in ecologically valid situations. In their study of overarm throwing accuracy in seventy-four children with and without DCD, Schott and Getchell (2021) found similar results. Not only were children with DCD less accurate when throwing at three different distances to a target, but they also demonstrated fewer movement combinations at lower developmental levels than their peers without DCD.

Individuals with DCD frequently use compensatory motor patterns. Often, individuals with DCD not only move with greater variability than their peers without DCD, but they also use different movement patterns and multiple alternative movement strategies. For example, in a study of walking when transitioning between normal to fast walking to running, they exhibited poor use of plantar flexor and compensatory hip flexor power push off (Diamond et al., 2014) and used lower extremity equilibrium strategies using a greater amount of hip flexor strategy compared to their peers without DCD who rely on ankle strategies (Verbecque et al., 2021).

Another example exists in the motor skill of catching: when catching has been suggested they use compensatory strategies of decoupling of synergies with later reaching and earlier grasping; in addition, they use joint freezing (Guimarães et al., 2020; Utleyet al., 2007; Missiuna, 1994). Children with DCD also used compensatory strategies in a study of ball catching (Derikx and Schoemaker, 2020). Derikx and Schoemaker (2020) suggested that children with DCD used several different compensation strategies, including a later initiation of the reaching phase, an earlier initiation of the grasping phase, a higher degree of coupling of the joints both intra- and inter-limb, and fixating the joints. However, despite these compensation strategies, children with DCD still caught fewer balls than typically developing children in all studies. This was especially due to a higher number of grasping errors, which indicates a problem with the timing of the grasping phase. In another study by Wilmut and colleagues (2015), adult participants with and without DCD were assessed on their ability to avoid an obstacle. While walking toward a narrow aperture where they were required to turn shoulders to pass through, the DCD adults showed a different strategy: a greater propensity to rotate shoulders. No differences were observed in sway; however, a higher level of variability existed in lateral trunk movement, and they adapted by starting the movement sooner than the typically developing group. Further, they had an earlier reduction in speed.

Individuals with DCD have difficulty modulating static and dynamic motor activity for joint stabilization. Differences are seen in postural control, agonist and antagonist balance, force production, or trajectories control, controlling speed and accuracy in individuals with DCD. Deficits in postural control a requirement of static and dynamic control of the body within the base of support and for performance of suprapostural tasks. Suprapostural tasks include activities relying on stabilization including upper extremity functioning such as putting a block through a hole (Haddad et al., 2010), which can decline with even a memory task in children with DCD (Chen et al., 2012). Impairment of background postural control during movement was defined, the "limits of stability" according to Verbecque et al. (2021), as the ability to sustain one's center of mass over a base of support. Postural sway was larger in the DCD group than peers during standing, which worsened with increased task challenges (Tsai et al., 2008). Delays in contraction of abdominal muscles (ipsilateral internal obliques and contralateral rectus abdominis) to stabilize the body during a rapid arm movement were found in up to 99 percent of eight- to ten-year-olds children with DCD compared to peers (Johnston et al., 2002). Additionally, the necessary co-contraction and agonist-antagonist balance to sustaining force and control and quality of movement was impaired. Da Roche Diz et al. (2018) found less accuracy sustaining isometric finger forces in nine- to ten-year-olds at risk for DCD, scoring at or less than fifth percentile on the Movement Assessment Battery for Children - Second Edition compared to a group of children scoring greater than the thirty-fifth percentile. Temporal coordination of antagonist-agonist muscles not only can be responsible for fixation and strength, but also can impact speed and accuracy. Individuals with DCD have shown extended time of agonist activation along with a delay in antagonist control (Piek and Skinner, 1999). Grohs and colleagues (2021) performed study of a reaching task and showed poorer accuracy related to deviation from ideal path (i.e., greater deviation from an ideal path trajectory).

FUTURE RESEARCH

Because movement variability is one of the most overarching features of DCD, understanding the source as well as structure of variability should be a priority for motor behavior researchers. Using motor control theories such as the uncontrolled manifold hypothesis—which suggests that the nervous system controls certain task-relevant variables while remaining variables are free to vary leading to multiple ways to perform motor tasks (Golenia et al., 2018; Scholz and Schöner, 1999), as well as innovative measures such as approximate entropy, which provides a measure of the predictability or sequential structure over time (King et al., 2012; Mackenzie et al., 2008)—should provide means by which motor behavior specialists can better understand the nature of variability. Additional structural and functional brain imaging studies should provide more insight into neural mechanisms responsible for DCD. Paradigms where participants perform motor tasks while measurements are taken of cortical activity via functional near-infrared spectroscopy (Caçola et al., 2018) or electroencephalography (Cheng et al., 2018) should yield important information about how the cerebral cortex functions during motor tasks in this population. One of the key areas of future research should involve the development of consistent tools to track response to intervention, which is essential for care of these individuals to impact their function, participation, and quality of life. Currently, most of the research on postural control has been on static balance. Future research should focus on measurement during more functional and dynamic postural control.

PRACTICAL IMPLICATIONS

First, renewed attention should be given to early diagnosis of children with DDs, particularly in the cases where the delay may be indicative of DCD. Early diagnosis and intervention can help young children so that they do not experience severe academic issues before remediation begins. Because DCD manifests as motor issues, practitioners such as physical educators can become the first line of defense in a variety of venues. Research has found improved motor gains in (a) individual (Au et al., 2014) and group (Caçola et al., 2016) settings; (b) school (Farhat et al., 2015) and home (Fong et al., 2013) environment; and (c) sport (Fong et al., 2013), active video gaming (Jelsma et al., 2014), and during functional activities (Fong et al., 2016; Smits-Engelson et al. 2018). There are many types of interventions found to be effective in improving motor performance in those with DCD. Task-oriented approaches have been extensively reviewed in a meta-analysis, which found moderate positive effects because of intervention (Miyahara et al., 2017). Task-oriented approaches have shown gains in a variety of skills including handwriting, motor performance, motor coordination and cardiorespiratory motor proficiency (Farhat et al., 2015). Taekwondo training improved unilateral standing balance and strength (Fong et al., 2013), and circuit training on a trampoline showed gains in motor ability, body coordination, and strength. Soccer training showed improvements in motor control (Tsai et al., 2012). The use of functional movements has also been found to be effective in improving balance and force (Fong et al., 2016): physical activity game-oriented intervention showed improved strength, endurance (Tsai et al., 2014), and static balance (Kordi et al., 2016). A systematic review concluded interventions focusing on an activity and body function showed gains in motor (Smits-Engelsman et al., 2018). Findings indicate nonspecific interventions improve motor function and ability to perform activities requiring motor skills in individuals with DCD.

CONCLUSION

DCD is a neurodevelopmental disorder associated with significant motor impairment in the absence of a visual or neurologic impairment or intellectual disability. In infancy and early childhood, children at risk for DCD often demonstrate DDs in the acquisition of motor milestones. While DCD is always preceded by DDs, DDs can result from a variety of conditions that are not associated with DCD, such as autism spectrum disorder or cerebral palsy. To be diagnosed with DCD, children must exhibit lower than age-expected motor abilities that significantly interfere with academic performance and activities of daily living. These deficits are not associated with other conditions. Often, diagnosis of DCD occurs as children enter school and begin to have issues with academics. Research related to DCD indicates that a variety of deficits are present across multiple motor domains. These can include an increase in movement and performance variability, difficulty with limb coupling and coordination, a loss of flexibility/adaptability of motor patterns, and the use of compensatory movement strategies.

REFERENCES

American Psychiatric Association. (2013). *Diagnostic and statistical manual of mental disorders: DSM-5* (volume 5). Washington, DC: American Psychiatric Association.

Asmussen, M.J., Przysucha, E.P., and Zerpa, C. (2014). Intralimb coordination in children with and without developmental coordination disorder in one-handed catching. *Journal of Motor Behavior*, 46(6), 445–53.

Astill, S., and Utley, A. (2006). Two-handed catching in children with developmental coordination disorder. *Motor Control*, 10(2), 109–24.

Au, M.K., Chan, W.M., Lee, L., Chen, T.M., Chau, R.M., and Pang, M.Y. (2014). Core stability exercise is as effective as task-oriented motor training in improving motor proficiency in children with developmental coordination disorder: A randomized controlled pilot study. *Clinical Rehabilitation*, 28(10), 992–1003.

Barnett, A L., Law, C., and Stuart, N. (2019). Developmental progression in DCD. In A. Barnett and E. Hill (Eds.). *Understanding motor behaviour in developmental coordination disorder* (pp. 28–51). London: Routledge.

Bayley N. (1969). *Bayley scales of infant development*. San Antonio, TX: The Psychological Corporation.

Biotteau, M., Albaret, J.M., and Chaix, Y. (2020). Developmental coordination disorder. In *Handbook of Clinical Neurology* (volume 174, pp. 3–20). New York: Elsevier.

Blank, R., Smits-Engelsman, B., Polatajko, H., and Wilson, P. (2012). European Academy for Childhood Disability (EACD): Recommendations on the definition, diagnosis and intervention of developmental coordination disorder (long version). *Developmental Medicine and Child Neurology*, 54(1), 54.

Bo, J., Bastian, A.J., Kagerer, F.A., Contreras-Vidal, J.L., and Clark, J.E. (2008). Temporal variability in continuous versus discontinuous drawing for children with developmental coordination disorder. *Neuroscience Letters*, 431(3), 215–20.

Bosanquet M., Copeland L., Ware R., and Boyd R. (2013). A systematic review of tests to predict cerebral palsy in young children. *Developmental Medicine and Child Neurology*, 55(5), 418–26.

Caçola, P., Getchell, N., Srinivasan, D., Alexandrakis, G., and Liu, H. (2018). Cortical activity in fine-motor tasks in children with Developmental Coordination Disorder: A preliminary fNIRS study. *International Journal of Developmental Neuroscience*, 65, 83–90.

Caçola, P., and Lage, G. (2019). Developmental coordination disorder (DCD): An overview of the condition and research evidence. *Motriz: Revista de Educação Física*, 25.

Caçola, P., Romero, M., Ibana, M., and Chuang, J. (2016). Effects of two distinct group motor skill interventions in psychological and motor skills of children with developmental coordination disorder: A pilot study. *Disability and Health Journal*, 9(1), 172–78.

Campos, J.J., Anderson, D.I., Barbu-Roth, M.A., Hubbard, E.M., Hertenstein, M.J., and Witherington, D. (2000). Travel broadens the mind. *Infancy*, 1(2), 149–219.

Chia, L.C., Licari, M.K., Guelfi, K.J., and Reid, S.L. (2013). A comparison of running kinematics and kinetics in children with and without developmental coordination disorder. *Gait & Posture*, 38(2), 264–69.

Chen, F., Tsai, C., Stoffregen, T., Chang, C., and Wade, M.G. (2012). Postural adaptations to a suprapostural memory task among children with and without developmental coordination disorder. *Developmental Medicine & Child Neurology*, 54(2), 155–59.

Cheng, Y.T., Tsang, W.W., Schooling, C.M., and Fong, S.S. (2018). Reactive balance performance and neuromuscular and cognitive responses to unpredictable balance perturbations in children with developmental coordination disorder. *Gait & Posture*, 62, 20–26.

Chia, L.C., Licari, M.K., Guelfi, K.J., and Reid, S.L. (2013). A comparison of running kinematics and kinetics in children with and without developmental coordination disorder. *Gait & Posture*, 38(2), 264–69.

Choo, Y.Y., Agarwal, P., How, C.H., and Yeleswarapu, S.P. (2019). Developmental delay: identification and management at primary care level. *Singapore Medical Journal*, 60(3), 119–23.

Chung, J.W., Chow, L.P., Ma, A.W., and Tsang, W.W. (2013). Differential effect of Taekwondo training on knee muscle strength and reactive and static balance control in children with developmental coordination disorder: A randomized controlled trial. *Research in Developmental Disabilities*, 34(5), 1446–55.

Clark, J.E., Getchell, N., Smiley-Oyen, A.L., and Whitall, Jill. (2005). Developmental coordination disorder: issues, identification, and intervention. *Journal of Physical Education, Recreation & Dance*, 76(4), 49–53.

de Castro Ferracioli, M., Hiraga, C.Y., and Pellegrini, A.M. (2014). Emergence and stability of interlimb coordination patterns in children with developmental coordination disorder. *Research in Developmental Disabilities*, 35(2), 348–56.

da Rocha Diz, M.A., de Castro Ferracioli, M., Hiraga, C.Y., de Oliveira, M.A., and Pellegrini, A.M. (2018). Effects of practice on visual finger-force control in children at risk of developmental coordination disorder. *Brazilian Journal of Physical Therapy*, 22(6), 467–73.

Derikx, D.F., and Schoemaker, M.M. (2020). The nature of coordination and control problems in children with developmental coordination disorder during ball catching: A systematic review. *Human Movement Science*, 74, 102688.

Diamond, N., Downs, J., and Morris, S. (2014). "The problem with running" comparing the propulsion strategy of children with developmental coordination disorder and typically developing children. *Gait & Posture*, 39(1), 547–52.

Einspieler, C., Yang, H., Bartl-Pokorny, K.D., Chi, X., Zang, F.F., Marschik, P.B., Guzzetta, A., Ferrari, F., Bos, A.F., and Cioni, G. (2015). Are sporadic fidgety movements as clinically relevant as is their absence? *Early Human Development*, 91(4), 247–52.

Einspieler C., Peharz R., and Marschik P.B. (2016). Fidgety movements – tiny in appearance, but huge in impact. *Journal de Pediatria*, 92(3 Suppl 1).

Einspieler, C., Bos, A.F., Krieber-Tomantschger, M., Alvarado, E., Barbosa, V.M., Bertoncelli, N., . . . and Marschik, P.B. (2019). Cerebral palsy: early markers of clinical phenotype and functional outcome. *Journal of Clinical Medicine*, 8(10), 1616.

Farhat, F., Masmoudi, K., Hsairi, I., Smits-Engelsman, B.C., McHirgui, R., Triki, C., and Moalla, W. (2015). The effects of 8 weeks of motor skill training on cardiorespiratory fitness and endurance performance in children with developmental coordination disorder. *Applied Physiology, Nutrition, and Metabolism*, 40(12), 1269–78.

Farhat, F., Hsairi, I., Baati, H., Smits-Engelsman, B.C., Masmoudi, K., Mchirgui, R., Triki, C. and Moalla, W. (2016). The effect of a motor skills training program in the improve coordination disorder (DCD). *Human Movement Science*, 46, 10–22.

Fong, S.S.M., Chung, J.W.Y., Chow, L.P.Y., Ma, A.W.W., Tsang, W.W.N., and Fong, S.S. (2013). Differential effect of Taekwondo training on knee muscle strength and reactive and static balance control in children with developmental coordination disorder: A randomized controlled trial. *Research in Developmental Disabilities*, 34(5), 1446–55.

Fong, S.S., Guo, X., Cheng, Y.T., Liu, K.P., Tsang, W.W., Yam, T.T., Chun, L.M., and Macfarlane, D.J. (2016). A novel balance training program for children with developmental coordination disorder: A randomized controlled trial. *Medicine (Baltimore)*, 95(16), e3492.

Golenia, L., Bongers, R.M., van Hoorn, J.F., Otten, E., Mouton, L.J., and Schoemaker, M.M. (2018). Variability in coordination patterns in children with developmental coordination disorder (DCD). *Human Movement Science*, 60, 202–13.

Grohs M.N., Hawe R.L., Dukelow S.P., and Dewey D. (2021). Unimanual and bimanual motor performance in children with developmental coordination disorder (DCD) provide evidence for underlying motor control deficits. *Frontiers in Behavioral Neuroscience*, 11, 5982.

Guimarães, A.N., Ugrinowitsch, H., Dascal, J.B., Porto, A.B., and Okazaki, V.H.A. (2020). Freezing degrees of freedom during motor learning: A systematic review. *Motor Control*, 24(3), 457–71.

Haddad, J.M., Ryu, J.H., Seaman, J.M., and Ponto, K.C. (2010). Time-to-contact measures capture modulations in posture based on the precision demands of a manual task. *Gait & Posture*, 32(4), 592–96.

Haywood, K.M., and Getchell, N. (2018). *Life span motor development*. Champlaing, IL: Human Kinetics.

Herrero, D., Einspieler, C., Panvequio Aizawa, C.Y., Mutlu, A., Yang, H., Nogolová, A., Pansy, J., Nielsen-Saines, K., and Marschik, P. (2017). The motor repertoire in 3- to 5-month old infants with Down syndrome. *Research in Developmental Disabilities*, 67, 1–8.

Holloway, J.M., and Long, T.M. (2019). The interdependence of motor and social skill development: Influence on participation. *Physical Therapy*, 99(6), 761–70.

Holloway, J.M., Long, T.M., and Biasini, F.J. (2021). The intersection of gross motor abilities and participation in children with autism spectrum disorder. *Infants and Young Children*, 34(3), 178.

Jelsma, D., Geuze, R.H., Mombarg, R., and Smits-Engelsman, B.C.M. (2014). The impact of Wii Fit intervention on dynamic balance control in children with probable developmental coordination disorder and balance problems. *Human Movement Science*, 33, 404–18.

Johnston, L.M., Burns, Y.R., Brauer, S.G., and Richardson, C.A. (2002). Differences in postural control and movement performance during goal directed reaching in children with developmental coordination disorder. *Human Movement Science, 21*(5-6), 583–601.

Karras, H.C., Morin, D.N., Gill, K., Izadi-Najafabadi, S., and Zwicker, J.G. (2019). Health-related quality of life of children with developmental coordination disorder. *Research in Developmental Disabilities, 84*, 85–95.

Khan, I., and Leventhal, B.L. (2021). *Developmental delay*. Treasure Island, FL: StatPearls Publishing.

Khandare, S.V., Nanandkar, S.D., and Chikhalkar, B.G. (2016). Skipping history invites trouble. *Journal of Indian Academy of Forensic Medicine, 38*(3), 378–80.

King, B.R., Clark, J.E., and Oliveira, M.A. (2012). Developmental delay of finger torque control in children with developmental coordination disorder. *Developmental Medicine & Child Neurology, 54*(10), 932–37.

Kordi, H., Sohrabi, M., Saberi Kakhki, A., and Attarzadeh Hossini, S.R. (2016). The effect of strength training based on process approach intervention on balance of children with developmental coordination disorder. *Archivos Argentinos de Pediatria, 114*(6), 526–33.

Lipkin, P., and Okamoto, J. (2015). The individuals with disabilities education act (IDEA) for children with special educational needs. *Pediatrics, 136*, 6.

Lipkin, P., Macias, M.M., Chen, B.B., Coury, D., Gottschlich, A., Hyman, S.L., Sisk, B., Wolfe, S., and Levy, S.E. (2020). Trends in pediatricians' developmental screening: 2002–2016. *Pediatrics, 145*, 4.

Mackenzie, S.J., Getchell, N., Deutsch, K., Wilms-Floet, A., Clark, J.E., and Whitall, J. (2008). Multi-limb coordination and rhythmic variability under varying sensory availability conditions in children with DCD. *Human Movement Science, 27*(2), 256–69.

Missiuna, C. (1994). Motor skill acquisition in children with developmental coordination disorder. *Adapted Physical Activity Quarterly, 11*(2), 214–35.

Molinini, R.M., Koziol, N.A., Marcinowski, E.C., Hsu, L.Y., Tripathi, T., Harbourne, R. T., McCoy, S.W., Lobo, M.A., Bovaird, J.A., and Dusing, S.C. (2021). Early motor skills predict the developmental trajectory of problem solving in young children with motor delays. *Developmental Psychobiology, 63*(6), e22123.

Miyahara, M., Hillier, S.L., Pridham, L., and Nakagawa, S. (2017). Task-oriented interventions for children with developmental coordination disorder. *Cochrane Database Systematic Reviews, 7*.

Murray, G.K., Jones, P.B., Kuh, D., and Richards, M. (2007). Infant developmental milestones and subsequent cognitive function. *Annals of Neurology, 2*, 128–36.

Okai, Y., Nakata, T., Miura, K., Ohno, A., Wakako, R., Takahash, O., Mak, Y., Tanaka M., Sakaguchi, Y., Ito, Y., Yamamoto, H., Kidokoro, H., Takahashi K., and Natsume, J. (2021). Shuffling babies and autism spectrum disorder. *Brain Development, 43*(2), 181–85.

Piek, J.P., Dawson, L., Smith, L.M., and Gasson, N. (2008). The role of early fine and gross motor development on later motor and cognitive ability. *Human Movement Science, 27*(5), 668–81.

Piek, J.P., and Skinner, R.A. (1999). Timing and force control during a sequential tapping task in children with and with-out motor coordination problems. *Journal of International Neuropsychology, 5*(4), 320–29.

Provost, B., Lopez, B.R., and Heimerl, S. (2007). A comparison of motor delays in young children: autism spectrum disorder, developmental delay, and developmental concerns. *Journal of Autism and Developmental Disorders, 37*(2), 321–28.

Przysucha, E.P., and Maraj, B.K. (2013). Nature of spatial coupling in children with and without developmental coordination disorder in ball catching. *Adapted Physical Activity Quarterly, 30*(3), 213–34.

Robson, R. (1970). Shuffling, hitching, scooting or sliding: some observations in 30 otherwise normal children. *Developmental Medicine and Child Neurology, 12*, 608–17.

Roche, R., Wilms-Floet, A.M., Clark, J.E., and Whitall, J. (2011). Auditory and visual information do not affect self-paced bilateral finger tapping in children with DCD. *Human Movement Science*, 30(3), 658–71.

Rosengren, K.S., Deconinck, F.J., DiBerardino III, L.A., Polk, J.D., Spencer-Smith, J., De Clercq, D., and Lenoir, M. (2009). Differences in gait complexity and variability between children with and without developmental coordination disorder. *Gait & Posture*, 29(2), 225–29.

Scholz, J.P., and Schöner, G. (1999). The uncontrolled manifold concept: identifying control variables for a functional task. *Experimental Brain Research*, 126(3), 289–306.

Schott, N., and Getchell, N. (2021). Qualitative and quantitative assessment of overarm throwing in children with and without developmental coordination disorder. *Journal of Motor Learning and Development*, 9(2), 266–85.

Shirley, M.M. (1931). *The first two years: A study of twenty-five babies. Vol. 1: Postural and locomotor development.* Minneapolis: University of Minnesota Press.

Smith, M.R., Hildenbrand, H., and Smith, A.C. (2009). Sensory motor and functional skills of dizygotic twins: with Smith–Magenis syndrome one and a twin control. *Physical & Occupational Therapy in Pediatrics*, 29(3), 239–57.

Smits-Engelsman, B.C., and Wilson, P.H. (2013). Noise, variability, and motor performance in developmental coordination disorder. *Developmental Medicine and Child Neurology*, 55, 69–72.

Smits-Engelsman, B., Vincon, S., Blank, R., Quadrado, V.H., Polatajko, H., and Wilson, P.H. (2018). Evaluating the evidence for motor-based interventions in developmental coordination disorder: A systematic review and meta-analysis. *Research in Developmental Disabilities*, 74, 72–102.

Sumner, E., Pratt, M.L., and Hill, E.L. (2016). Examining the cognitive profile of children with Developmental Coordination Disorder. *Research in Developmental Disabilities*, 56, 10–17.

Tsai, C.L., Wu, S.K., and Huanag, V. (2008). Static balance in children with developmental coordination disorder. *Human Movement Science*, 27(1), 142–53.

Tsai, C.-L., Wang, C.-H., and Tseng, Y.-T. (2012). Effects of exercise intervention on event-related potential and task performance indices of attention networks in children with developmental coordination disorder. *Brain and Cognition*, 79(1), 12–22.

Tsai, C.L., Chang, Y.K., Chen, F.C., Hung, T.M., Pan, C.Y., and Wang, C.H. (2014). Effects of cardiorespiratory fitness enhancement on deficits in visuospatial working memory in children with developmental coordination disorder: A cognitive electrophysiological study. *Archives of Clinical Neuropsychology*, 29(2), 173–85.

Utley, A., Steenbergen, B., and Astill, S.L. (2007). Ball catching in children with developmental coordination disorder: control of degrees of freedom. *Developmental Medicine & Child Neurology*, 49(1), 34–38.

Valla, L., Slinning, K., Kalleson, R., Wentzel-Larsen, T., and Riiser, K. (2020). Motor skills and later communication development in early childhood: Results from a population-based study. *Child: Care, Health and Development*, 46(4), 407–13.

Van Waelvelde, H., De Weerdt, W., De Cock, P., Smits-Engelsman, B.C., and Peersman, W. (2004). Ball catching performance in children with developmental coordination disorder. *Adapted Physical Activity Quarterly*, 21(4), 348–63.

Van Waelvelde, H., De Weerdt, W., De Cock, P., and Smits-Engelsman, B.C. (2004). Association between visual perceptual deficits and motor deficits in children with developmental coordination disorder. *Developmental Medicine and Child Neurology*, 46(10), 661–66.

Veldman, S.L., Santosa, R., Jones, A., Sousa-Saa, E., and Okelyac, D. (2019). Associations between gross motor skills and cognitive development in toddlers. *Early Human Development*, 132, 39–44.

Verbecque, E., Johnson, C., Rameckers, E., Thijs, A., Van der Veer, I., Meyns, P., Smits-Engelsman, B., and Klingels, K. (2021). Balance control in individuals with developmental coordination disorder: a systematic review and meta-analysis. *Gait & Posture*, 83, 268–79.

Volman, M.C.J., and Geuze, R.H. (1998a). Relative phase stability of bimanual and visuomanual rhythmic coordination patterns in children with a developmental coordination disorder. *Human Movement Science*, 17(4-5), 541–72.

Volman, M.J.M., amd Geuze, R. H. (1998b). Stability of rhythmic finger movements in children with a developmental coordination disorder. *Motor Control*, 2(1), 34–60.

Volman, M.J.M., Laroy, M.E., and Jongmans, M.J. (2006). Rhythmic coordination of hand and foot in children with developmental coordination disorder. *Child: Care, Health and Development*, 32(6), 693–702.

Whitall, J., Getchell, N., McMenamin, S., Horn, C., Wilms-Floet, A., and Clark, J.E. (2006). Perception–action coupling in children with and without DCD: frequency locking between task-relevant auditory signals and motor responses in a dual-motor task. *Child: Care, Health and Development*, 32(6), 679–92.

Wilmut, K., Du, W., and Barnett, A.L. (2016). Gait patterns in children with developmental coordination disorder. *Experimental Brain Research*, 234(6), 1747–55.

Wilmut, K., and Byrne, M. (2014). Grip selection for sequential movements in children and adults with and without developmental coordination disorder. *Hum Mov Sci*, 36, 272–84.

Wilmut, K., Du, W., and Barnett, A.L. (2015). How do I fit through that gap? Navigation through apertures in adults with and without developmental coordination disorder. *PLoS One*, 10(4), e0124695.

Wilmut, K., Wang, S., and Barnett, A.L. (2022). Inter-limb coordination in a novel pedal task: A comparison of children with and without developmental coordination disorder. *Human Movement Science*, 82, 102932.

Wilson, P.H., Ruddock, S., Smits-Engelsman, B., Polatajko, H., and Blank, R. (2013). Understanding performance deficits in developmental coordination disorder: a meta-analysis of recent research. *Developmental Medicine and Child Neurology*, 55(3), 217–28.

Yuge, M., Marschik, P. B., Nakajima, Y., Yamori, Y., Kanda, T., Hirota, H., Yoshida, N., and Einspieler, C. (2011). Movements and postures of infants aged 3 to 5 months: to what extent is their optimality related to perinatal events and to the neurological outcome? *Early Human Development*, 87(3), 231–37.

Zwicker, J.G., Suto, M., Harris, S.R., Vlasakova, N., and Missiuna, C. (2018). Developmental coordination disorder is more than a motor problem: Children describe the impact of daily struggles on their quality of life. *British Journal of Occupational Therapy*, 81(2), 65–73.

12

Motor Behavior and Traumatic Brain Injury

James Wilkes, Alexa Walter, and Sam Semyon Slobounov

■ ■ ■

OVERVIEW

Traumatic brain injury (TBI) is a major health burden as one of the major causes of death and disability, affecting all sexes, ages, races, and socioeconomic classes throughout the world. Annually, in the United States, over 2.8 million people are diagnosed with a TBI (Taylor, 2017) and over sixty thousand of these TBIs result in death (Centers for Disease Control and Prevention, 2022). Mild TBI (mTBI), often termed concussion, accounts for 80 to 90 percent of all TBIs, and these injuries still result in large societal and economic burdens. For those that survive, the resulting damage is varied and can greatly impact daily life and functioning.

Importantly, many more TBIs likely go unreported (Taylor, 2017), with estimates reporting that 33 percent of individuals experiencing mTBI do not seek medical assistance (Meehan et al., 2013; Voss et al., 2015). These high incidence rates, along with high rates of disability for individuals sustaining TBI, have led the US Centers for Disease Control and Prevention to develop different education initiatives, most notably the "HEADS UP Initiative" (Centers for Disease Control and Prevention, 2021). The proliferation of media coverage, concussion education, and resultant funding of different programs has continued to aid researchers and clinicians in gaining a better understanding of best prevention, evaluation, and treatment practices.

Although there are varying definitions throughout the literature, TBI is defined by the American Congress of Rehabilitation Medicine as "an alteration in brain function, or other evidence of brain pathology, caused by an external force" (Kay et al., 1993). It is traditionally conceptualized as a primary injury event that is caused by an initial mechanical impact. Following this is a secondary insult of molecular and cellular responses occurs in reaction to the primary injury (Sandsmark et al., 2019). Briefly, immediately following the impact, there is shearing of neuronal tissue and axons resulting in cellular energy crisis, transport and signaling dysfunction, potential cell death, and long-term impairment (Giza and Hovda, 2001; Giza and Hovda, 2014). These initial responses cause further changes in ion balance, cellular depolarization, cerebral blood flow, mitochondrial function, metabolic function, neurotransmission, inflammation, and cell death (Barkhoudarian et al., 2016; Giza and Hovda, 2014). These varied cellular and molecular responses lead to TBI being classified as a heterogenous injury, with post-injury outcomes varying across time and between individuals. The consequences of TBI can have long-lasting effects, continuing to affect brain functioning decades after injury (Corrigan and Hammond, 2013) and have been linked to multiple health outcomes (Masel and DeWitt, 2010) including increased risk of dementia (Fleminger et al., 2003; Gardner and Yaffe, 2014) which may have features of Alzheimer's disease (Fleminger et al., 2003) or other neurodegenerative pathologies (Ramos-Cejudo et al., 2018).

Since outcomes after injury are not fixed, this makes treatment of TBI challenging; there currently are no effective therapies for treating the underlying physiologic damage associated with TBI. Traditionally, upon initial injury management, TBI has been categorized using the Glasgow Coma Scale (GCS; Figure 12.1) (Mena et al., 2011; Saatman et al., 2008). However, the nuanced distinctions between severities of TBI are further elucidated by clinical and research evaluation techniques including blood biomarkers (Kawata et al., 2016), imaging modalities like computerized tomography and magnetic resonance imaging (Kim and Gean, 2011), and comprehensive neurocognitive test batteries (Soble et al., 2017).

Often, individuals with mTBI present with a normal GCS score (13–15), brief or no loss of consciousness or change in mental state, altered blood biomarkers, and clinically normal imaging findings. Individuals with moderate or severe TBI are more likely to exhibit a lower GCS score (3–12), extended loss of consciousness or change in mental state, altered blood biomarkers, and clinically abnormal imaging findings (Kawata et al., 2016; Kim and Gean, 2011; Schweitzer et al., 2019).

Similarly, symptom presentation varies depending on many factors including severity of injury, history of preexisting conditions, and sex, among many other factors. Patients with TBI may present with a variety of physical, psychological, cognitive, or emotional symptoms (McAllister and Arciniegas, 2002; Prince and Bruhns, 2017). The Centers for Disease Control and Prevention has created symptom category classifications for both mTBI and moderate and severe TBI, grouping symptoms into clusters (Table 12.1).

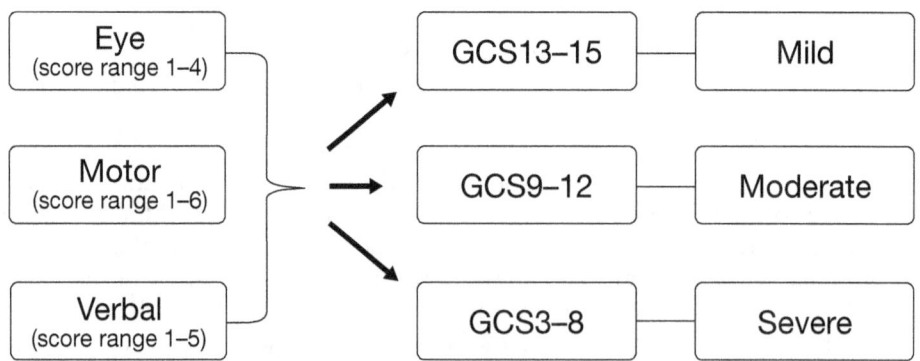

Figure 12.1 TBI severity classified by Glasgow Coma Scale (GCS) score
Note: Scores are added from the three components (eye, motor, verbal) to generate a total score.

Table 12.1 Common Symptoms of Traumatic Brain Injury as Classified by the Centers for Disease Control and Prevention

	Physical	Thinking and remembering	Social or emotional	Sleep
Mild	Bothered by light or noise	Attention or concentration problems	Anxiety or nervousness	Sleeping less than usual
	Dizziness or balance problems	Feeling slowed down	Irritability or easily angered	Sleeping more than usual
	Feeling tired, no energy	Foggy or groggy	Feeling more emotional	Trouble falling asleep
	Headaches	Problems with short- or long-term memory	Sadness	
	Nausea or vomiting	Trouble thinking clearly		
	Vision problems			
	Motor skills, hearing, and vision	*Thinking and learning*	*Emotion/mood*	*Behavior*
Moderate or severe	Weakness in arms and legs	Difficulty understanding and thinking clearly	Feeling more emotional than usual	Trouble controlling behavior
	Problems with coordination and balance	Trouble communicating and learning skills	Nervousness or anxiety	Personality changes
	Problems with hearing and vision	Problems concentrating	Feeling more angry or aggressive than usual	More impulsive than usual
	Changes in sensory perception, such as touch	Difficulty remembering information	Sadness, depression	

Source: Adapted from https://www.cdc.gov/traumaticbraininjury/.

While symptom presentation and recovery trajectory can vary greatly between individuals, even those categorized within the same level of injury severity, the focus of this chapter will be on deficits related to motor control. These symptoms in particular often appear more chronically, showing up days to weeks after injury, and therefore are often not always used in classifying and diagnosing TBI (Kozlowski et al., 2013). Motor control deficits following TBI are wide ranging and are generally affected by the severity of injury (Kozlowski et al., 2013; Krauss and Jankovic, 2002; O'Suilleabhain and Dewey, 2004). Additionally, individuals with TBI often report gait abnormalities, difficulties with balance, altered motor coordination, slower reaction times, or difficulty switching motor tasks. It is important to note that the neurologic screen and motor-based assessments are a portion of the comprehensive evaluation for TBI patients following injury, which also include assessment of neurocognition, psychological health status, symptom burden, and sleep. The scope of this chapter will review the most recent and relevant literature as it relates specifically to motor control in individuals experiencing TBI.

CLINICAL TRANSLATION OF PATHOPHYSIOLOGY TO DYSFUNCTION

In order to appropriately and adequately treat and rehabilitate TBI, clinicians are tasked with identifying the severity of TBI and the critical deficits to be treated, including subsequent neurologic motor control deficits. Currently, one of the most commonly used categorizations of TBI patients, especially during initial assessment, is the GCS (Saatman et al., 2008). Similarly, the Glasgow Outcome Score Extended is a metric by which clinicians can better gauge cognitive impairments, mental health issues, and summarize outcome pathways during the recovery period (Wilson et al., 2021). Uncharacteristic for similar scales, the Glasgow Outcome Score Extended does not rely on summing of scores for different items; instead it is more of a qualitative approach to disability and recovery that includes five levels of outcome: dead, vegetative state, severe disability, moderate disability, and good recovery. While the heterogeneous nature of the injury often requires an individualized approach (Maas et al., 2017; McMillan et al., 2016), this tool is used by most physicians for categorization of TBI and aids in creating personalized programs for caregivers (Saatman et al., 2008; Wilson et al., 2021). The varied clinical presentation of TBI symptomatology and post-injury dysfunction heightens the importance of properly identifying areas of dysfunction in order to appropriately treat and rehabilitate individuals suffering from any level of TBI.

MOTOR CONTROL DYSFUNCTION AFTER TRAUMATIC BRAIN INJURY

Generally, more severe injuries are associated with worse dysfunction and more severe movement disorders, and have greater rate of coincidence (Kozlowski et al., 2013; O'Suilleabhain and Dewey, 2004). Incorporated as a part of the post-trauma evaluation, clinicians evaluate cranial nerve function, reflexes, and perform a comprehensive motor exam. For a complete trauma neurological exam, please see the review by Clark and colleagues (2022). Abnormal findings on these exams often indicate the presence of pathology and can help clinicians determine level, location, and severity of injury. Examples of motor control issues after TBI include:

- **Bradykinesia:** Slowed or reduced frequency of movements, particularly blinking, postural adjustment, and other spontaneous actions.
- **Hypokinesia:** Decreased movement amplitude or range of motion.
- **Hyperkinesia:** Excessive or involuntary movements.
- **Tremors:** Oscillatory movements with intermittent jerking behavior that may vary in amplitude and frequency. One of the most frequent movement disorders following severe TBI (Krauss and Jankovic, 2002); likely to accompany other movement disorders.
- **Spasticity:** Excess muscle activity in response to muscle stretch reflex; likely due to upper motor neuron lesion; often seen in moderate and severe TBI.

- **Myoclonus:** Sudden single or repeated involuntary jerking movements.
- **Dystonia:** Excessive muscle contraction in response to movement initiation and excessive co-contraction of antagonist muscles in attempted corrective behavior, until the task ceases.

Each of these disorders can be seen after TBI, though Krauss and Jankovic (2002) reported only around 10 percent of patients diagnosed with mild to moderate TBI presented with a movement disorder. Of these patients, only 2.6 percent had persistent motor control dysfunction, lasting months or longer (Krauss and Jankovic, 2002). As one would expect, the presence of these dysfunctions lends to deficits and trouble with more complex movements like whole-body balance, coordination, and gait.

Balance and Gait

Balance and coordination challenges are common following TBI, with up to 30 percent of mTBI patients reporting deficit or dysfunction (Basford et al., 2003). Balance issues may be secondary to dizziness, a somatic symptom of injury, which can cause balance difficulties, falls, functional limitations, reduced quality of life, and increased psychological distress (Maskell et al., 2006). Coordination may be affected as a result of injury to the cerebellum following TBI, either direct or atrophic (Spanos et al., 2007), or from complications related to conditions described in the previous section. Currently, the gold standard for objective evaluation of postural control and balance is the Sensory Organization Test (Row et al., 2019). This test uses a balance platform to measure real-time postural changes and sway to understand sensory-motor integration under six conditions: eyes open versus eyes closed, stable surface versus unstable surface (foam pad), and fixed visual stimulus versus swaying visual stimulus (Broglio et al., 2008; Jacobson et al., 2020; Joseph et al., 2021). Recent research has used balance platforms in an attempt to understand and quantify postural sway, center of pressure, and limits of stability (Kaufman et al., 2006; Parrington et al., 2020; Row et al., 2019). Additionally, other studies have reported the use of virtual reality for both balance testing (Rausch et al., 2018; Teel and Slobounov, 2015; Wright et al., 2017) and rehabilitation (Cuthbert et al., 2014; Thornton et al., 2005; Zanier et al., 2018). The Balance Error Scoring System, Clinical Test of Sensory Organization and Balance, and the Romberg test have also been used to identify balance issues in those with varying levels of TBI, but are most often used in mTBI (Murray et al., 2014).

Gait can also be affected following TBI. Gait is a complex process involving variable temporal and spatial information, characterized and analyzed by components of stride length, width, time, and gait speed and variability (Dever et al., 2022; Stuart et al., 2020). While there is currently no consensus for gait assessment for TBI, there are several tools researchers and clinicians use to help categorize gait abnormalities for rehabilitation. For clinicians, the Dynamic Gait Index is a validated tool to measure dynamic balance in individuals with neurologic disorders which examines gait speed, variability, and adaptability (Simon and Harro, 2004). In a review of gait assessment following TBI, Dever and colleagues (2022) found most research studies used inertial measuring units to assess gait. Inertial measuring units are wearable kinematic sensors that allow for measurement of whole-body and segmental movement, including triaxial acceleration and angular velocity (Pitt et al.,

2020). Additionally, they reported that gait speed was the most distinguishing factor between TBI participants and controls, while increasing the difficulty or complexity of the task (dual-tasking) was necessary to reveal deficits (Dever et al., 2022).

With no consensus regarding the ideal evaluation for gait following TBI, categorized treatments have not been described but instead require more individualized treatment plans. Guided individualized and deficit-targeted rehabilitation programs with multidimensional functional exercises in a clinic was shown to be effective in improving balance for daily function (Ustinova et al., 2015). Additionally, Stuart and colleagues (2020) found that variability, rhythm, pace, and turning were four domains that were identified in individuals with chronic mTBI and these characteristics can be used to better implement effective interventions. Future research should aim to target gait impairment as a marker of TBI severity, and thus lead to more precise and effective gait rehabilitation techniques.

Reaction Time

Reaction time has been a commonly used test to evaluate motor function after TBI since the early 1970s. It is a combined function of processing speed and motor control, with processing speed defined as time between stimuli presentation and resultant cortical processing and motor control presented as time between motor initiation and task completion (e.g., reaching for a target) (Botwinick and Thompson, 1966). Typically, after a TBI, individuals will demonstrate worsened processing speed and reaction time, with the deficits increasing in severity as injury severity worsens (Incoccia et al., 2004; Tombaugh et al., 2007). Additionally, when the complexity of task increases (i.e., increasing number of potential choices, or adding an inhibitory component) the individual's reaction time increases (worsens) (Tombaugh et al., 2007; Wilkes et al., 2021). These findings have large real-world relevance since reaction time is critical to countless activities of daily living including walking, driving, physical activity, and avoiding objects or danger.

There is a relative paucity of research related to the targeted rehabilitation of reaction time and processing speed. Instead, it is routinely incorporated as part of a comprehensive multifactorial rehabilitation approach to target several areas of deficit or dysfunction with interdisciplinary and multimodal techniques.

Oculomotor Function

Visual impairment and visual dysfunction are extremely common following TBI. As the visual system has connections throughout all four lobes of the brain, up to 80 percent of individuals display some sort of oculomotor impairment following injury (Ciuffreda et al., 2007; Leigh and Zee, 2015). Slightly different than movement disorders, oculomotor impairment and dysfunction are likely the result of damage to the optic nerve, loss of retinal ganglion cells, and axonal injury (Sen, 2017). An important distinction is that impairment refers to blindness, reduced field of vision, or reduced visual acuity, where visual dysfunction refers to a deficit in oculomotor function, accommodation, visual spatial recognition, and/or photosensitivity (Fox et al., 2019).

In order to identify potential impairment or dysfunction, clinicians test patients in a systematic manner. The tests are performed with the patient's corrective lenses, if necessary, and assess their self-reported symptoms, near and far visual acuity, accommodation, convergence, eye alignment, binocular vision, saccades and antisaccades, smooth pursuit, visual fields, and vestibule-ocular reflex (Fox et al., 2019). Depending upon the individual's personalized deficits, clinicians have a variety of treatment techniques to aid in the rehabilitation of vision. Some techniques include the Six Eye Exercises protocol, integrated eye movements like reading and scanning, occupation-specific activities, low-light therapy, blue-light therapy, prism lenses, and oculomotor rehabilitation (Berryman et al., 2020; Fox et al., 2019).

Speech and Swallowing
Less common in mTBI, but sometimes apparent in moderate and severe TBI cases, are problems related to dysfunctional swallowing (dysphagia) and language and communication disorders. Dysphagia is often much more debilitating, requiring longer hospital stays, and some patients never recover. This condition may present as a result of the mechanical insult from the injury, inflammation creating secondary injury to surrounding structures, medication, injury to the head or neck area common in motor vehicle accidents, or extended intubation and ventilation (Howle et al., 2014). Currently, there is no specific treatment for TBI-related dysphagia; however, it is a responsibility of the clinician as part of the individual's post-injury multifactorial treatment approach to treat the condition, often through speech and language therapy, diet modification, or feeding tubes (Howle et al., 2014; Terré and Mearin, 2007).

TBI-induced language and communication disorders present different challenges and are categorized into four groups, including apraxia, aphasia, dysarthria, and cognitive communication disorder (Barman et al., 2016). According to the National Institute of Neurological Disorders and Stroke (2023), apraxia is a neurologic disorder characterized by loss of the ability to execute or carry out skilled movements and gestures, despite having the desire and physical ability to perform them; aphasia is defined as a neurologic disorder caused by damage to the portions of the brain that are responsible for language production or processing; and dysarthria is a speech disorder caused by muscle weakness that may occur in conjunction with other speech and language problems. Cognitive communication disorders, meanwhile, encompass disorders that lead to difficulty in communication as a result of disrupted cognition. These communication difficulties may be verbal or nonverbal and can affect all domains of language (phonologic, morphologic, syntactic, semantic, and pragmatic). Areas of function often affected are behavioral self-regulation, social interaction, activities of daily living, learning and academic performance, and vocational performance (Christman Buckingham and Sneed, 2018; Williams-Butler and Cantu, 2019).

Effective rehabilitation techniques for dysarthria and aphasia include constraint-induced aphasia therapy, computer-assisted therapy, melodic intonation therapy, and transcranial direct current stimulation, while gesture production exercises aided those with apraxia (Barman et al., 2016; Meinzer et al., 2005; Raymer et al., 2006; Zumbansen et al., 2014). Wenke and others (2008) reported the Lee Silverman voice treatment effectively improved loudness, intelligibility, and phonation in individuals with dysarthria following TBI. Finally, metacognitive strategy training, problem-solving training, and goal management training have shown favorable outcomes in improving self-monitoring, self-regulation, and overall executive function (Cheng and Man, 2006; Goverover et al., 2007; von Cramon et al., 1991). These may be some of the most important techniques for those with moderate to severe

TBI, as communicating and comprehending instructions is critical to any rehabilitation program, but especially more advanced tasks and interventions.

Kinesiophobia

Kinesiophobia is an irrational fear of movement stemming from psychological, biological, or a combination of both domains. Psychological causes include attitudes of self-acceptance, self-assessment of motor predispositions, state of mind, and susceptibility to social influence. Biological causes include morphology, individual need for stimulation, energetic substrates, and power of biological drives (Bränström and Fahlström, 2008; Knapik et al., 2011) Kinesiophobia is commonly reported following mTBI, with one study stating 28 percent of athletes reported kinesiophobia at return to play after injury (Reinking et al., 2022). Though still not entirely understood, Knapik and colleagues (2011) showed that this condition is not just a psychological process, and further work should be done to understand the influence of motor control to the contribution of the development of trauma-induced kinesiophobia.

FUTURE RESEARCH

While much knowledge has been gained in the last two decades illuminating the pathophysiology of TBI and resultant clinical translation into symptoms, there is still varied evidence regarding the best treatment practice. Currently, many diagnoses and treatment plans are based on self-reported symptoms and severity score, with a supplemental examination of objective tests like neuropsychological testing, balance testing, or sideline assessment tools specific to sport-related mTBI (Scorza and Cole, 2019).

Additional research after TBI focusing on motor control is greatly needed. There are still large gaps in our understanding of the physiological underpinnings of these injuries and their translation to motor deficits. Work aiming to link clinical motor control deficit findings with more physiological measures, like magnetic resonance imaging, electromyography, electroencephalography, or blood-based biomarkers, will allow for better understanding of the biological consequences of these injuries. Additionally, better understanding of physiological changes in response to targeted rehabilitation techniques using objective measures will allow for more effective, evidence-based, and individualized treatment plans targeting specific deficits post-injury.

PRACTICAL IMPLICATIONS

The concepts reviewed in this chapter have potential implications for all readers, as TBI can affect all areas of functioning. While primary causes of TBI cannot be entirely prevented, implementing educational efforts, as well as ensuring proper safety guidelines are followed (wearing a seatbelt, helmet, or other protective gear; proper drill techniques), have shown to help reduce the incidence of injury and shorten recovery following injury (Herring et al., 2021). Similarly, it is important to ensure both proper education and adequate recovery of individuals after injury. Some individuals may recover completely, whereas others may have lingering or persistent effects, as studies have shown increased risk for subsequent injury including repeat TBI (Guskiewicz et al., 2003), as well as increased risk for musculoskeletal injuries following mTBI (Buttinger et al., 2020; Nordström et al., 2014).

Motor control deficits after TBI may be less common than deficits to other domains of functioning but, regardless, they can have devastating consequences if ignored or mismanaged. Due to the potential interplay of these deficits, and their symbiotic link to other functional domains, proper evaluation, treatment, and management of these deficits after TBI is crucial. Given that these symptoms in particular often appear more chronically post-injury, continuous monitoring of domains including gait, balance and coordination, or reaction time may offer simple, but clinically useful first-step tools to assist practitioners in their decision-making process. Concerns of more serious motor control deficits will most likely require multidisciplinary teams of providers, working on the individualized patient level to correctly diagnose, with more advanced methodologies, and treat these individuals.

CONCLUSION

TBI is a complex pathophysiological process that can present with varying cognitive, emotional, psychological, or physical symptoms. A variety of motor control-related diagnoses can arise as a result of TBI, including bradykinesia, hypokinesia, hyperkinesia, tremors, spasticity, myoclonus, or dystonia. However, more commonly, individuals with TBI will report deficits relating to balance, coordination, gait, reaction time, oculomotor function, speech, or swallowing. Future research should focus on linking clinical symptoms to physiological measures like magnetic resonance imaging, electromyography, electroencephalography, or blood-based biomarkers. Additionally, TBI may have long-term effects on many areas of function, especially as injury severity worsens, that can greatly affect daily living. While TBI cannot be entirely prevented, understanding the injury process, clinical translation of pathophysiology, and optimal recovery strategies can lead to better outcomes following injury. Stakeholders should aim to improve research and guidelines surrounding clinical evaluation, classification, and treatment of TBI, along with continued efforts to increase public education and awareness for all severities of brain injury.

CONFLICT OF INTEREST

None of the authors have any conflicts of interest.

ACKNOWLEDGMENTS

We would like to acknowledge Karl Newell's effort to pursue this line of research and his vision and contribution to dynamic aspects of motor control both in normal and pathological populations.

Author AW reports funding from Grant #: T32 NS043126 Brain Injury Training Grant.

REFERENCES

Barkhoudarian, G., Hovda, D.A., and Giza, C.C. (2016). The molecular pathophysiology of concussive brain injury – an update. *Physical Medicine and Rehabilitation Clinics of North America*, 27(2), 373–93. https://doi.org/10.1016/j.pmr.2016.01.003

Barman, A., Chatterjee, A., and Bhide, R. (2016). Cognitive impairment and rehabilitation strategies after traumatic brain injury. *Indian Journal of Psychological Medicine*, 38(3), 172–81. https://doi.org/10.4103/0253-7176.183086

Basford, J.R., Chou, L.-S., Kaufman, K.R., Brey, R.H., Walker, A., Malec, J.F., Moessner, A.M., and Brown, A.W. (2003). An assessment of gait and balance deficits after traumatic brain injury. *Archives of Physical Medicine and Rehabilitation*, 84(3), 343–49. https://doi.org/10.1053/apmr.2003.50034

Berryman, A., Rasavage, K., Politzer, T., and Gerber, D. (2020). Oculomotor treatment in traumatic brain injury rehabilitation: A randomized controlled pilot trial. *The American Journal of Occupational Therapy*, 74(1), 7401185050p1–7401185050p7. https://doi.org/10.5014/ajot.2020.026880

Botwinick, J., and Thompson, L.W. (1966). Premotor and motor components of reaction time. *Journal of Experimental Psychology*, 71(1), 9. https://doi.org/10.1037/h0022634

Bränström, H., and Fahlström, M. (2008). Kinesiophobia in patients with chronic musculoskeletal pain: Differences between men and women. *Journal of Rehabilitation Medicine*, 40(5), 375–80. https://doi.org/10.2340/16501977-0186

Broglio, S.P., Ferrara, M.S., Sopiarz, K., and Kelly, M.S. (2008). Reliable change of the sensory organization test. *Clinical Journal of Sport Medicine*, 18(2), 148–54. https://doi.org/10.1097/JSM.0b013e318164f42a

Buttinger, J., Mihalik, J., Ledbetter, L., Faherty, M., and Sell, T. (2020). Concussion and lower extremity injury risk following return to activity: A systematic review. *Duke Orthopedic Journal*, 10(1), 10. https://doi.org/10.4103/DORJ.DORJ_16_20

Centers for Disease Prevention and Control. (2021, February 25). HEADS UP. https://www.cdc.gov/headsup/index.html

Centers for Disease Control and Prevention. (2022, January 6). National Center for Health Statistics, mortality data on CDC WONDER. https://wonder.cdc.gov/mcd.html

Cheng, S.K.W., and Man, D.W.K. (2006). Management of impaired self-awareness in persons with traumatic brain injury. *Brain Injury*, 20(6), 621–28. https://doi.org/10.1080/02699050600677196

Christman Buckingham, S.S., and Sneed, K.E. (2018). Cognitive-communication disorder. In J. S. Kreutzer, J. DeLuca, and B. Caplan (Eds.), *Encyclopedia of Clinical Neuropsychology* (pp. 868–75). New York: Springer International Publishing. https://doi.org/10.1007/978-3-319-57111-9_872

Ciuffreda, K., Kapoor, N., Rutner, D., Suchoff, I.B., Han, M.E., and Craig, S. (2007). Occurrence of oculomotor dysfunctions in acquired brain injury: A retrospective analysis. *Optometry* (St. Louis, Mo.), 78(4), 155–61. https://doi.org/10.1016/j.optm.2006.11.011

Clark, A., Das, J., and Mesfin, F.B. (2022). *Trauma neurological exam*. Treasure Island, FL: StatPearls Publishing. http://www.ncbi.nlm.nih.gov/books/NBK507915/

Corrigan, J.D., and Hammond, F.M. (2013). Traumatic brain injury as a chronic health condition. *Archives of Physical Medicine and Rehabilitation*, 94(6), 1199–201. https://doi.org/10.1016/j.apmr.2013.01.023

Cuthbert, J.P., Staniszewski, K., Hays, K., Gerber, D., Natale, A., and O'Dell, D. (2014). Virtual reality-based therapy for the treatment of balance deficits in patients receiving inpatient rehabilitation for traumatic brain injury. *Brain Injury*, 28(2), 181–88. https://doi.org/10.3109/02699052.2013.860475

Dever, A., Powell, D., Graham, L., Mason, R., Das, J., Marshall, S.J., Vitorio, R., Godfrey, A., and Stuart, S. (2022). Gait impairment in traumatic brain injury: A systematic review. *Sensors*, 22(4), 1480. https://doi.org/10.3390/s22041480

Fleminger, S., Oliver, D., Lovestone, S., Rabe-Hesketh, S., and Giora, A. (2003). Head injury as a risk factor for Alzheimer's disease: The evidence 10 years on; a partial replication. *Journal of Neurology, Neurosurgery, and Psychiatry*, 74(7), 857–62. https://doi.org/10.1136/jnnp.74.7.857

Fox, S.M., Koons, P., and Dang, S.H. (2019). Vision rehabilitation after traumatic brain injury. *Physical Medicine and Rehabilitation Clinics of North America, 30*(1), 171–88. https://doi.org/10.1016/j.pmr.2018.09.001

Gardner, R.C., and Yaffe, K. (2014). Traumatic brain injury may increase risk of young onset dementia. *Annals of Neurology, 75*(3), 339–41. https://doi.org/10.1002/ana.24121

Giza, C.C., and Hovda, D.A. (2001). The neurometabolic cascade of concussion. *Journal of Athletic Training, 36*(3), 228–35.

Giza, C.C., and Hovda, D.A. (2014). The new neurometabolic cascade of concussion. *Neurosurgery, 75*(0 4), S24–S33. https://doi.org/10.1227/NEU.0000000000000505

Goverover, Y., Johnston, M.V., Toglia, J., and Deluca, J. (2007). Treatment to improve self-awareness in persons with acquired brain injury. *Brain Injury, 21*(9), 913–23. https://doi.org/10.1080/02699050701553205

Guskiewicz, K.M., McCrea, M., Marshall, S.W., Cantu, R.C., Randolph, C., Barr, W., Onate, J.A., and Kelly, J.P. (2003). Cumulative effects associated with recurrent concussion in collegiate football players: The NCAA Concussion Study. *JAMA, 290*(19), 2549–55. https://doi.org/10.1001/jama.290.19.2549

Herring, S., Kibler, W.B., Putukian, M., Solomon, G.S., Boyajian-O'Neill, L., Dec, K.L., Franks, R.R., Indelicato, P.A., LaBella, C.R., Leddy, J.J., Matuszak, J., McDonough, E.B., O'Connor, F., and Sutton, K.M. (2021). Selected issues in sport-related concussion (SRC|mild traumatic brain injury) for the team physician: A consensus statement. *British Journal of Sports Medicine, 55*(22), 1251–61. https://doi.org/10.1136/bjsports-2021-104235

Howle, A.A., Baguley, I.J., and Brown, L. (2014). Management of dysphagia following traumatic brain injury. *Current Physical Medicine and Rehabilitation Reports, 2*(4), 219–30. https://doi.org/10.1007/s40141-014-0064-z

Incoccia, C., Formisano, R., Muscato, P., Reali, G., and Zoccolotti, P. (2004). Reaction and movement times in individuals with chronic traumatic brain injury with good motor recovery. *Cortex, 40*(1), 111–15. https://doi.org/10.1016/S0010-9452(08)70924-9

Jacobson, G.P., Shepard, N.T., Barin, K., Janky, K., and McCaslin, D.L. (2020). *Balance function assessment and management*, third edition. San Diego, CA: Plural Publishing.

Joseph, A.L.C., Lippa, S.M., Moore, B., Bagri, M., Row, J., Chan, L., and Zampieri, C. (2021). Relating self-reported balance problems to sensory organization and dual-tasking in chronic traumatic brain injury. *PM&R, 13*(8), 870–79. https://doi.org/10.1002/pmrj.12478

Kaufman, K.R., Brey, R.H., Chou, L.S., Rabatin, A., Brown, A.W., and Basford, J.R. (2006). Comparison of subjective and objective measurements of balance disorders following traumatic brain injury. *Medical Engineering & Physics, 28*(3), 234–39. https://doi.org/10.1016/j.medengphy.2005.05.005

Kawata, K., Liu, C.Y., Merkel, S.F., Ramirez, S.H., Tierney, R.T., and Langford, D. (2016). Blood biomarkers for brain injury: What are we measuring? *Neuroscience and Biobehavioral Reviews, 68*, 460–73. https://doi.org/10.1016/j.neubiorev.2016.05.009

Kay, T., Harrington, D., and Adams, R. (1993). Definition of mild traumatic brain injury. https://www.acrm.org/wp-content/uploads/pdf/TBIDef_English_10-10.pdf

Kim, J.J., and Gean, A.D. (2011). Imaging for the diagnosis and management of traumatic brain injury. *Neurotherapeutics, 8*(1), 39–53. https://doi.org/10.1007/s13311-010-0003-3

Knapik, A., Saulicz, E., and Gnat, R. (2011). Kinesiophobia – introducing a new diagnostic tool. *Journal of Human Kinetics, 28*, 25–31. https://doi.org/10.2478/v10078-011-0019-8

Kozlowski, D.A., Leasure, J.L., and Schallert, T. (2013). The control of movement following traumatic brain injury. In *Comprehensive physiology* (pp. 121–39). New York: John Wiley & Sons, Ltd. https://doi.org/10.1002/cphy.c110005

Krauss, J.K., and Jankovic, J. (2002). Head injury and posttraumatic movement disorders. *Neurosurgery, 50*(5), 927–40. https://doi.org/10.1097/00006123-200205000-00003

Leigh, R.J., and Zee, D.S. (2015). *The neurology of eye movements*. Cambridge: Oxford University Press.

Maas, A.I.R., Menon, D.K., Adelson, P.D., Andelic, N., Bell, M.J., Belli, A., Bragge, P., Brazinova, A., Büki, A., Chesnut, R.M., Citerio, G., Coburn, M., Cooper, D.J., Crowder, A.T., Czeiter, E., Czosnyka, M., Diaz-Arrastia, R., Dreier, J.P., Duhaime, A.C., . . . Zumbo, F. (2017). Traumatic brain injury: Integrated approaches to improve prevention, clinical care, and research. *The Lancet Neurology*, 16(12), 987–1048. https://doi.org/10.1016/S1474-4422(17)30371-X

Masel, B.E., and DeWitt, D.S. (2010). Traumatic brain injury: A disease process, not an event. *Journal of Neurotrauma*, 27(8), 1529–40. https://doi.org/10.1089/neu.2010.1358

Maskell, F., Chiarelli, P., and Isles, R. (2006). Dizziness after traumatic brain injury: Overview and measurement in the clinical setting. *Brain Injury*, 20(3), 293–305. https://doi.org/10.1080/02699050500488041

McAllister, T.W., and Arciniegas, D. (2002). Evaluation and treatment of postconcussive symptoms. *NeuroRehabilitation*, 17(4), 265–83. https://doi.org/10.3233/NRE-2002-17402

McMillan, T., Wilson, L., Ponsford, J., Levin, H., Teasdale, G., and Bond, M. (2016). The Glasgow Outcome Scale—40 years of application and refinement. *Nature Reviews Neurology*, 12(8), 477–85. https://doi.org/10.1038/nrneurol.2016.89

Meehan, W.P., Mannix, R.C., O'Brien, M.J., and Collins, M.W. (2013). The prevalence of undiagnosed concussions in athletes. *Clinical Journal of Sport Medicine : Official Journal of the Canadian Academy of Sport Medicine*, 23(5), 339–42. https://doi.org/10.1097/JSM.0b013e318291d3b3

Meinzer, M., Djundja, D., Barthel, G., Elbert, T., and Rockstroh, B. (2005). Long-term stability of improved language functions in chronic aphasia after constraint-induced aphasia therapy. *Stroke*, 36(7), 1462–66. https://doi.org/10.1161/01.STR.0000169941.29831.2a

Mena, J.H., Sanchez, A.I., Rubiano, A.M., Peitzman, A.B., Sperry, J.L., Gutierrez, M.I., and Puyana, J.C. (2011). Effect of the Modified Glasgow Coma Scale Score criteria for mild traumatic brain injury on mortality prediction: Comparing Classic and Modified Glasgow Coma Scale Score model scores of 13. *The Journal of Trauma*, 71(5), 1185–93. https://doi.org/10.1097/TA.0b013e31823321f8

Murray, N., Salvatore, A., Powell, D., and Reed-Jones, R. (2014). Reliability and validity evidence of multiple balance assessments in athletes with a concussion. *Journal of Athletic Training*, 49(4), 540–49. https://doi.org/10.4085/1062-6050-49.3.32

National Institute of Neurological Disorders and Stroke. (2023, January 31). Apraxia. https://www.ninds.nih.gov/health-information/disorders/apraxia

Nordström, A., Nordström, P., and Ekstrand, J. (2014). Sports-related concussion increases the risk of subsequent injury by about 50% in elite male football players. *British Journal of Sports Medicine*, 48(19), 1447–50. https://doi.org/10.1136/bjsports-2013-093406

O'Suilleabhain, P., and Dewey, R.B.J. (2004). Movement disorders after head injury: Diagnosis and management. *The Journal of Head Trauma Rehabilitation*, 19(4), 305–13.

Parrington, L., Popa, B., and Martini, D. (2020). Instrumented balance assessment in mild traumatic brain injury: Normative values and descriptive data for acute, sub-acute and chronic populations. *Journal of Concussion*. https://journals.sagepub.com/doi/10.1177/2059700220975605

Pitt, W., Chen, S.H., and Chou, L.S. (2020). Using IMU-based kinematic markers to monitor dual-task gait balance control recovery in acutely concussed individuals. *Clinical Biomechanics*, 80. https://doi.org/10.1016/j.clinbiomech.2020.105145

Prince, C., and Bruhns, M.E. (2017). Evaluation and treatment of mild traumatic brain injury: The role of neuropsychology. *Brain Sciences*, 7(8), 105. https://doi.org/10.3390/brainsci7080105

Ramos-Cejudo, J., Wisniewski, T., Marmar, C., Zetterberg, H., Blennow, K., de Leon, M.J., and Fossati, S. (2018). Traumatic brain injury and Alzheimer's disease: The cerebrovascular link. *EBioMedicine*, 28, 21–30. https://doi.org/10.1016/j.ebiom.2018.01.021

Rausch, M., Simon, J.E., Starkey, C., and Grooms, D.R. (2018). Smartphone virtual reality to increase clinical balance assessment responsiveness. *Physical Therapy in Sport*, 32, 207–11. https://doi.org/10.1016/j.ptsp.2018.05.017

Raymer, A.M., Kohen, F.P., and Saffell, D. (2006). Computerised training for impairments of word comprehension and retrieval in aphasia. *Aphasiology*, 20(2–4), 257–68. https://doi.org/10.1080/02687030500473312

Reinking, S., Seehusen, C.N., Walker, G.A., Wilson, J.C., and Howell, D.R. (2022). Transitory kinesiophobia after sport-related concussion and its correlation with reaction time. *Journal of Science and Medicine in Sport*, 25(1), 20–24. https://doi.org/10.1016/j.jsams.2021.07.010

Row, J., Chan, L., Damiano, D., Shenouda, C., Collins, J., and Zampieri, C. (2019). Balance assessment in traumatic brain injury: A comparison of the sensory organization and lmits of stability tests. *Journal of Neurotrauma*, 36(16), 2435–42. https://doi.org/10.1089/neu.2018.5755

Saatman, K.E., Duhaime, A.C., Bullock, R., Maas, A.I.R., Valadka, A., and Manley, G.T. (2008). Classification of traumatic brain injury for targeted therapies. *Journal of Neurotrauma*, 25(7), 719–38. https://doi.org/10.1089/neu.2008.0586

Sandsmark, D.K., Bashir, A., Wellington, C.L., and Diaz-Arrastia, R. (2019). Cerebral microvascular injury: A potentially treatable endophenotype of traumatic brain injury-induced neurodegeneration. *Neuron*, 103(3), 367–79. https://doi.org/10.1016/j.neuron.2019.06.002

Schweitzer, A.D., Niogi, S.N., Whitlow, C.T., and Tsiouris, A.J. (2019). Traumatic brain injury: Imaging patterns and complications. *RadioGraphics*, 39(6), 1571–95. https://doi.org/10.1148/rg.2019190076

Scorza, K.A., and Cole, W. (2019). Current concepts in concussion: Initial evaluation and management. *American Family Physician*, 99(7), 426–34.

Sen, N. (2017). An insight into the vision impairment following traumatic brain injury. *Neurochemistry International*, 111, 103–07. https://doi.org/10.1016/j.neuint.2017.01.019

Simon, T.A., and Harro, C.C. (2004). Reliability and validity of the dynamic gait index in individuals with brain injury. *Journal of Neurologic Physical Therapy*, 28(4), 180–81.

Soble, J.R., Critchfield, E.A., and O'Rourke, J.J.F. (2017). Neuropsychological evaluation in traumatic brain injury. *Physical Medicine and Rehabilitation Clinics of North America*, 28(2), 339–50. https://doi.org/10.1016/j.pmr.2016.12.009

Spanos, G.K., Wilde, E.A., Bigler, E.D., Cleavinger, H.B., Fearing, M.A., Levin, H.S., Li, X., and Hunter, J.V. (2007). Cerebellar atrophy after moderate-to-severe pediatric traumatic brain onjury. *American Journal of Neuroradiology*, 28(3), 537–42.

Stuart, S., Parrington, L., Morris, R., Martini, D.N., Fino, P.C., and King, L.A. (2020). Gait measurement in chronic mild traumatic brain injury: A model approach. *Human Movement Science*, 69, 102557. https://doi.org/10.1016/j.humov.2019.102557

Taylor, C.A. (2017). Traumatic brain injury–related emergency department visits, hospitalizations, and deaths—United States, 2007 and 2013. *MMWR. Surveillance Summaries*, 66. https://doi.org/10.15585/mmwr.ss6609a1

Teel, E.F., and Slobounov, S.M. (2015). Validation of a virtual reality balance module for use in clinical concussion assessment and management. *Clinical Journal of Sport Medicine: Official Journal of the Canadian Academy of Sport Medicine*, 25(2), 144–48. https://doi.org/10.1097/JSM.0000000000000109

Terré, R., and Mearin, F. (2007). Prospective evaluation of oro-pharyngeal dysphagia after severe traumatic brain injury. *Brain Injury*, 21(13–14), 1411–17. https://doi.org/10.1080/02699050701785096

Thornton, M., Marshall, S., McComas, J., Finestone, H., McCormick, A., and Sveistrup, H. (2005). Benefits of activity and virtual reality based balance exercise programmes for adults with traumatic brain injury: Perceptions of participants and their caregivers. *Brain Injury*, 19(12), 989–1000. https://doi.org/10.1080/02699050500109944

Tombaugh, T.N., Rees, L., Stormer, P., Harrison, A.G., and Smith, A. (2007). The effects of mild and severe traumatic brain injury on speed of information processing as measured by the computerized tests of information processing (CTIP). *Archives of Clinical Neuropsychology*, 22(1), 25–36. https://doi.org/10.1016/j.acn.2006.06.013

Ustinova, K.I., Chernikova, L.A., Dull, A., and Perkins, J. (2015). Physical therapy for correcting postural and coordination deficits in patients with mild-to-moderate traumatic brain injury. *Physiotherapy Theory and Practice*, 31(1), 1–7. https://doi.org/10.3109/09593985.2014.945674

von Cramon, D.Y., Cramon, G.M., and Mai, N. (1991). Problem-solving deficits in brain-injured patients: A therapeutic approach. *Neuropsychological Rehabilitation*, 1(1), 45–64. https://doi.org/10.1080/09602019108401379

Voss, J.D., Connolly, J., Schwab, K.A., and Scher, A.I. (2015). Update on the epidemiology of concussion/mild traumatic brain injury. *Current Pain and Headache Reports*, 19(7), 32. https://doi.org/10.1007/s11916-015-0506-z

Wenke, R.J., Theodoros, D., and Cornwell, P. (2008). The short- and long-term effectiveness of the LSVT for dysarthria following TBI and stroke. *Brain Injury*, 22(4), 339–52. https://doi.org/10.1080/02699050801960987

Wilkes, J.R., Kelly, J.T., Walter, A.E., and Slobounov, S.M. (2021). Reaction time task performance in concussed athletes over a 30-day period: An observational study. *Archives of Clinical Neuropsychology*, acab077. https://doi.org/10.1093/arclin/acab077

Williams-Butler, M.A., and Cantu, R.C. (2019). Concussion practice patterns among speech-language pathologists. *Health*, 11(7), 880–95. https://doi.org/10.4236/health.2019.117071

Wilson, L., Boase, K., Nelson, L.D., Temkin, N.R., Giacino, J.T., Markowitz, A.J., Maas, A., Menon, D.K., Teasdale, G., and Manley, G.T. (2021). A manual for the Glasgow Outcome Scale-extended interview. *Journal of Neurotrauma*, 38(17), 2435–46. https://doi.org/10.1089/neu.2020.7527

Wright, W.G., McDevitt, J., Tierney, R., Haran, F.J., Appiah-Kubi, K.O., and Dumont, A. (2017). Assessing subacute mild traumatic brain injury with a portable virtual reality balance device. *Disability and Rehabilitation*, 39(15), 1564–72. https://doi.org/10.1080/09638288.2016.1226432

Zanier, E.R., Zoerle, T., Di Lernia, D., and Riva, G. (2018). Virtual reality for traumatic brain injury. *Frontiers in Neurology*, 9. https://www.frontiersin.org/article/10.3389/fneur.2018.00345

Zumbansen, A., Peretz, I., and Hébert, S. (2014). Melodic intonation therapy: Back to basics for future research. *Frontiers in Neurology*, 5, 7. https://doi.org/10.3389/fneur.2014.00007

13

Motor Behavior and Rehabilitation after Spinal Cord Injury

Collin D. Bowersock and
Jessica Lynn McDonnell

■ ■ ■

OVERVIEW

The study of spinal cord injuries (SCIs) dates back to classical times, around 3000 BC (Silver, 2005). In this era, SCIs often resulted in a hasty death due to associated complications such as infections or autonomic dysreflexia. In the nineteenth century, medical professionals made large advancements in the field of SCI. Management of the secondary mechanisms of injury, which were often the cause of early death, were formally studied, helping extend an individual's lifespan after injury. Treatments of the SCI itself, such as laminectomy, a surgical technique still used today, were also much improved. By the turn of the century, dedicated medical facilities were constructed to better understand and treat individuals with SCIs. Today, the advances in the field of SCI have enabled individuals with SCIs to not only live longer but also live more functional and independent lives.

A current estimated 250,000 to half a million people suffer an SCI every year (Bickenbach et al., 2013), and less than 1 percent of those individuals will recover complete function before leaving the hospital. Affected individuals are up to five times more likely to die early in life when compared to those without an SCI (Bickenbach et al., 2013). This chapter will focus predominantly on motor impairments following traumatic SCI; however, simultaneous and comorbid impairments include cardiovascular, bowel, bladder, and sexual dysfunction, highlighting the overall disruptive nature of an SCI. Severe SCIs can lead to death if appropriate care and interventions are not implemented early and throughout the individual's life. There is an extensive body of work focused on rehabilitation after SCI, yet the ability to regain motor and sensory function after a severe SCI is still limited (Chen and Levi, 2017), leaving many individuals with some level of paralysis affecting daily life. The loss of voluntary muscular function below the level of injury can lead to a lower self-rating of life as a whole (Budh and Österåker, 2007). Thus, rehabilitation strategies to improve motor function can greatly increase the quality of life for those suffering from severe SCI.

SCIs are typically caused by direct mechanical trauma to the spinal cord or compression of the spinal cord due to vertebral fractures. The injuries often result in damage to the neural pathway tracts located within the spinal cord as part of the central nervous system. These tracts transmit efferent motor commands to the neuromuscular system and receive afferent signals from the brain as well as sensory information from the peripheral nervous system. The incurred physical trauma to the spinal cord leads to neuronal cell death at the spinal level of injury, severing the spinal tracts and imposing moderate or severe supraspinal communication disruption above and below the level of injury in the central nervous system. The loss of the supraspinal input to the region of the spinal cord below the level of injury is a predominant cause of paralysis and loss of voluntary motor functions. The higher the level of injury (an injury to the more superior part of the spinal cord), the more encompassing the injury will be on the entire motor system. An SCI at the lumbar and thoracic vertebrae levels will affect the trunk and lower extremity function, possibly leading to paralysis of the lower extremity known as paraplegia. A more superior located SCI, higher up at the cervical level of the vertebrae, will additionally affect the upper limbs and neck, leading to tetraplegia or paralysis of the lower and upper limbs. The extent of motor behavior disruption is further dependent on severity of the spinal cord lesion. Severe SCIs can cause complete paralysis below the level of injury while less severe injuries may allow for some or even substantial motor function below the level of injury.

RESEARCH OVERVIEW

The degree of disability caused by an SCI is related to the extent and level of the spinal lesion. SCIs that result in a complete transection of the spinal cord at the level of injury are known as complete SCIs; injuries that spare some neuronal tissue at the level of injury are known as incomplete SCIs (Figure 13.1). SCIs can be further categorized into subgroups based on the extent of motor and sensory paralysis using the American Spinal Injury Association impairment scale (Kirshblum et al., 2011). This scale classifies all SCIs into one of five categories—grade A to grade E—based on the clinical level of motor and sensory impairment. Grade A is used to classify injuries with complete impairment indicating no detectable motor or sensory function below the level of injury. Grade B is motor complete, sensory incomplete impairment, indicating some sensory function is preserved below the neurologic level of injury. Grade C and D are motor and sensory incomplete, but motor function is affected below the level of injury. Grade E is used to classify an injury with no sensory or motor impairment. This scale is often used throughout interventions to determine if significant recovery has occurred. The following section will highlight recent works being conducted concerning rehabilitation interventions used to treat complete and incomplete SCIs.

Incomplete SCI, graded on the American Spinal Injury Association scale as a C or D, is an injury that spares some neuronal communication across the lesion and allows for detectable voluntary motor function below the level of the spinal lesion. The residual motor function below the level of injury will be altered, with weaker and more spontaneous muscle contractions. Research has found that even clinically

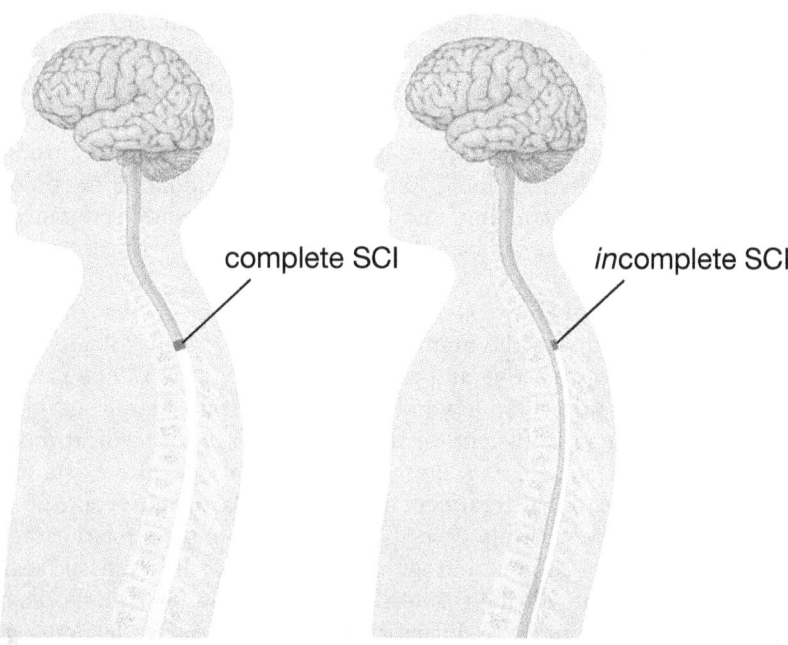

Figure 13.1 Illustration of a complete versus incomplete spinal cord injury
Note: The black spot signifies the spinal cord injury, and the gray lines represent the neurons of the spinal cord carrying afferent and efferent communications between the spinal cord and supraspinal areas (i.e., the brain). Complete spinal cord injury (SCI) results in massive neuronal cell death at the level of injury, severing the spinal tracts and leading to no clinically detectable sensory or motor function below the neurologic level of injury. Incomplete spinal cord injuries spare enough neural cells at the level of injury to allow for clinically detectable sensory and/or motor function below the level of injury.
Source: Reprinted with kind permission from Flint Rehab (Irvine, CA).

complete SCIs display some residual fibers across the level of lesion (Heald et al., 2017; Kakulas and Kaelan, 2015; Sangari et al., 2019). Although these fibers do not provide any detectable voluntary motor or sensory function, they may be an important factor in neural rehabilitation. In both complete and incomplete injury subsets, a large portion of neurons is spared below the level of injury, allowing for some spinal reflexes without input from the supraspinal areas of the brain. After appropriate treatment of care including a stay in an intensive care unit, some motor recovery will occur months to even years after injury without further intervention (Hilton et al., 2016; Raineteau and Schwab, 2001; Rasmussen and Carlsen, 2016; Rosenzweig et al., 2010). This recovery is known as spontaneous recovery, as no direct effort is necessary to see improvements in motor function. Spontaneous recovery is likely due to the overall healing of the secondary mechanisms of injury caused by the initial mechanical trauma to the spinal cord. Secondary mechanisms of injury can lead to further cell death and scarring, limiting recovery (Venkatesh et al., 2019). The healing includes the resolution of spinal shock, decreases in inflammation around the injury site, the microenvironment's return to homeostasis, and reorganization of some neural processes (i.e., ion channels and neurotransmitters) (Ahuja et al., 2017; Jeffery and Blakemore, 1999; Rank et al., 2015). The healing allows for the resumption of spinal circuity transmission of afferent and efferent signals below the injury site, therein allowing for the return of the spinal reflexes below the level of injury. In the case of an incomplete SCI, the healing will also allow signal transmission across the lesion through the remaining spinal circuity, providing more voluntary control below the level of injury. After, and even during, this acute spontaneous recovery, rehabilitation techniques can be utilized to further the recovery of the affected motor function.

Pharmacologic therapy is an avenue of treatment that has been heavily researched, especially in the animal model. These pharmacologic therapies often focus on the neuroprotective and neurogenerative effects. While promising results have been seen in animal models and some clinical trials, significant motor recovery in humans has been insufficient for the widespread use of medications (Hurlbert et al., 2015; Shah et al., 2020). Currently, no medical evidence exists for a safe and beneficial pharmacologic treatment in humans (Baroncini et al., 2021; Hurlbert et al., 2015). Tissue scarring after SCI may be responsible for this lack of success using medication. In conjunction with spontaneous recovery, tissue scarring within the spinal cord occurs during the healing process. After SCI, glial cells in the spinal cord respond to the injury by forming glial scar tissue. This response prevents any new neuronal growth across the injury site. Despite the current lack of evidence for axonal regrowth in humans, significant strides continue to be made using pharmacologic therapy. Recently, a team of researchers has been able to reprogram, in vivo, the glial cells of mice to form new neurons instead of forming into the scar tissue. The newly formed neurons directly help manage the SCI by replacing the cells lost from the physical trauma and reducing the amount of glial scarring. This type of intervention may help other pharmacologic treatments focusing on axonal growth and regeneration to become more effective. Continued research using pharmacologic treatments is vital and may result in an effective and safe treatment for individuals with SCIs.

Currently, one of the most effective and beneficial strategies for SCI rehabilitation is physical rehabilitation, specifically activity-based therapies. Activity-based therapy refers to training interventions that are used to activate the neuromuscular system below the level of the spinal lesion with the goal of retraining the nervous system to recover a specific motor task (Behrman et al., 2017). Benefits include the recovery of motor function below the level of injury as well as improvements in other biological systems (Behrman et al., 2006; Dietz et al., 2002; Sadowsky and McDonald, 2009). These types of interventions are likely successful in regaining motor function due to the central nervous system's and spinal cord's neuroplasticity. Historically, it was thought that the spinal cord was hard-wired structure and served to relay information between supraspinal structures (i.e., the brain) and the rest of the body. More recently, science has shown the spinal cord is "smart." The spinal cord can learn, adapt, and respond to different environments by processing incoming peripheral sensory information. For example, in an uninjured individual, the amount of muscle activity generated by a limb extensor muscle is positively related to the amount of load imposed on that limb. This relation can still be observed in an individual with a motor complete SCI, demonstrating the spinal cord's ability to sense changes in the environment and appropriately respond without supraspinal input (Courtine et al., 2009; Edgerton et al., 2004; Harkema et al., 1997). Therefore, a key to motor rehabilitation is to tap into this automaticity of the spinal cord through long-term intensive activity-based training to increase neurologic activity and promote the reorganization and repair of the nervous system after an SCI (Barbeau et al., 1999; Field-Fote, 2000; Harkema, 2008; Sadowsky and McDonald, 2009).

Regaining the ability to stand and walk is a focal goal for individuals after SCI (Ditunno et al., 2008), warranting the plethora of research on these motor behaviors. Activity-based therapies can focus on many different motor tasks including reaching, strength training, postural control training, and stretching with some of the most intriguing results coming from standing and locomotor training. Animal models have shown that with intensive activity-based training, animals with *complete* SCIs can recover standing and locomotor function through spinal cord activity below the level of transection without any input from supraspinal areas (Brown and Martinez, 2019; Filli and Schwab, 2015; Fouad and Tse, 2008; Moxon et al., 2014). When placed on a treadmill, the animals are able to respond to changes in the environment such as increasing step length and cadence when the speed is increased. In humans, intensive repetitive activity-based training has led to the recovery of standing in individuals with *incomplete* SCI (Harkema et al., 2012). There is no current evidence of the restoration of locomotion and standing in individuals with *complete* SCI after activity-based therapy alone. However, with the addition of spinal cord stimulation, activity-based therapy can lead to significant improvements in standing, stepping, and locomoting. Along with neurorecovery, activity-based training has other health benefits such as reduced muscle spasticity, improved bowel and bladder function, and improved body composition (Astorino et al., 2013; Dolbow et al., 2015; Hubscher et al., 2018; Jones et al., 2014).

After an SCI, the neuronal circuitry remains intact above and below the site of injury, with continued transmission of motor and sensory signals through the spinal cord. Stimulation of the spinal cord can help amplify this signal so sensory and motor commands can be delivered and acted upon across the injury site. With intensive activity-based therapy, spinal cord stimulation therapy can result in remarkable rehabilitation (Calvert et al., 2019; Hachmann et al., 2021). Typically, spinal cord stimulation is delivered epidurally using an electrode array that is implanted into the epidural space of the lumbosacral spinal cord region (Figure 13.2). The lumbosacral region has been found to be associated with the central pattern generators used for standing and stepping. Using an external controller, the electrodes deliver electrical signals to the neural networks in the spinal cord. This signal can activate the central pattern generators, or the neurocircuitry within the spinal cord (Dimitrijevic et al., 1998), to generate a motor output. The type of motor output is dependent on the stimulation parameters. Tonic, rhythmic, and complex lower limb muscular activity can be directly generated by delivering stimulation frequencies at different relative stimulation frequencies (Hofstoetter et al., 2015; Minassian et al., 2004). Low stimulation frequencies can promote lower limb extension necessary for standing, while higher stimulation frequencies promote more rhythmic lower limb activation pattern necessary for stepping and locomotion.

In the rehabilitation settings, epidural stimulation is applied tonically and the parameters are configured such that the lumbosacral spinal circuitry can use

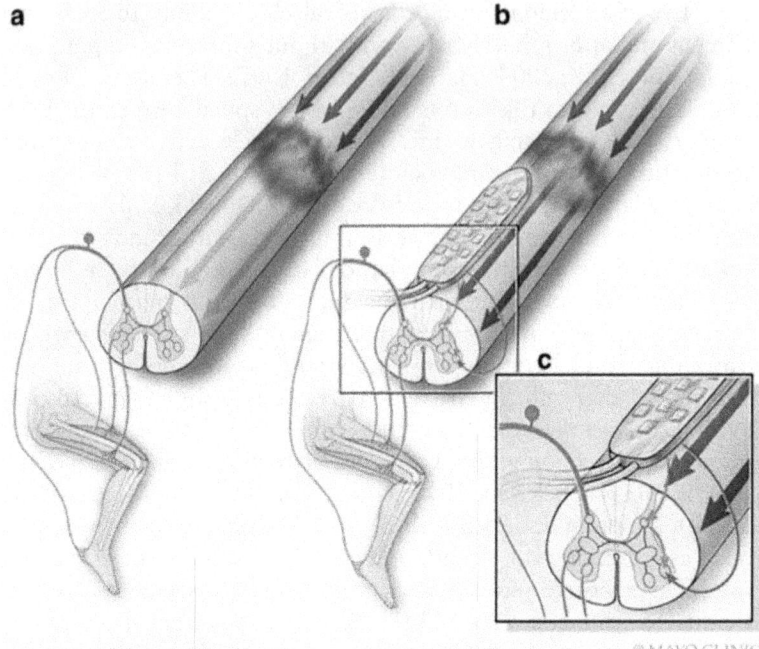

Figure 13.2 Depiction of a lumbosacral implanted epidural stimulation electrode array. In the injured spinal cord (a), the neural signals traveling down the spinal cord cannot activate the sensory and motor neurons below the level of injury, leading to the loss of sensation and motor control. With epidural stimulation (b) the neuronal activity traveling across the remaining neutral circuitry is amplified, supplemented, and carried across the level of injury enabling muscular activity through spinal reflexes and enabling some voluntary motor control. It is hypothesized that epidural stimulation acts on the dorsal root sensory nerves which synapse with motor nerves allowing for efferent signal transmission to the muscles (c). Also, epidural stimulation at higher amplitudes is thought to directly activate the motor neurons leading to tonic and rhythmic muscle activity, dependent on the stimulation frequency (c) (Calvert et al., 2019).

Source: Reprinted with kind permission: International Neuromodulation Society

peripheral sensory information and any residual supraspinal inputs as sources of motor control. The stimulation does not directly activate the muscles; rather, it enables the spinal cord to respond to the sensory information and generate appropriate musculature responses (Rejc et al., 2015) (Figure 13.3). The stimulation replaces the tonic supraspinal drive that is lost after SCI and "awakens" the remaining spinal circuitry, hijacking the reflexes of the spinal cord to generate the desired movement. When activity-based therapy and spinal cord stimulation are used together, standing and stepping can be rehabilitated as well as the voluntary control of limbs that were previously paralyzed. Remarkably, after intensive activity-based training with epidural stimulation, standing and ambulatory function can be restored in individuals with motor incomplete and complete SCIs (Gill et al., 2018; Grahn et al., 2017; Harkema et al., 2011; Herman et al., 2002; Minassian et al., 2016; Rejc and Angeli,

2019; Taccola et al., 2018). For example, four individuals with *motor complete* SCI were implanted with an epidural simulator and participated in an activity-based standing rehabilitation intervention. After completing eighty sessions of training, all four participants were able to independently maintain overground standing bearing their full body while using their hands to assist balance (Angeli et al., 2018). These results indicated that with extensive training and appropriate sensory information, the spinal cord can generate effective motor outputs to achieve standing after severe SCI. Epidural stimulation is also used to restore upper limb function (Lu et al., 2016) and improve affected autonomic functions such as blood pressure (Aslan et al., 2018; Harkema et al., 2018), respiration (DiMarco and Kowalski, 2013; Hachmann et al., 2017), and bowel, bladder, and sexual functions (Hubscher et al., 2018). The regulation of blood pressure alone has a huge impact on individuals' lives. In some cases, an individual's blood pressure will drop so suddenly that they will lose consciousness and pass out from a task as simple as sitting up from a supine position. Thus, the regulation of blood pressure is extremely important for participation in not only therapy but for the functionality of daily life.

Dynamic or targeted epidural stimulation is a different technique used to provide the spinal cord with electrical stimulation to rehabilitate motor control after SCI. Instead of tonically sending stimulation to the spinal cord, this method uses

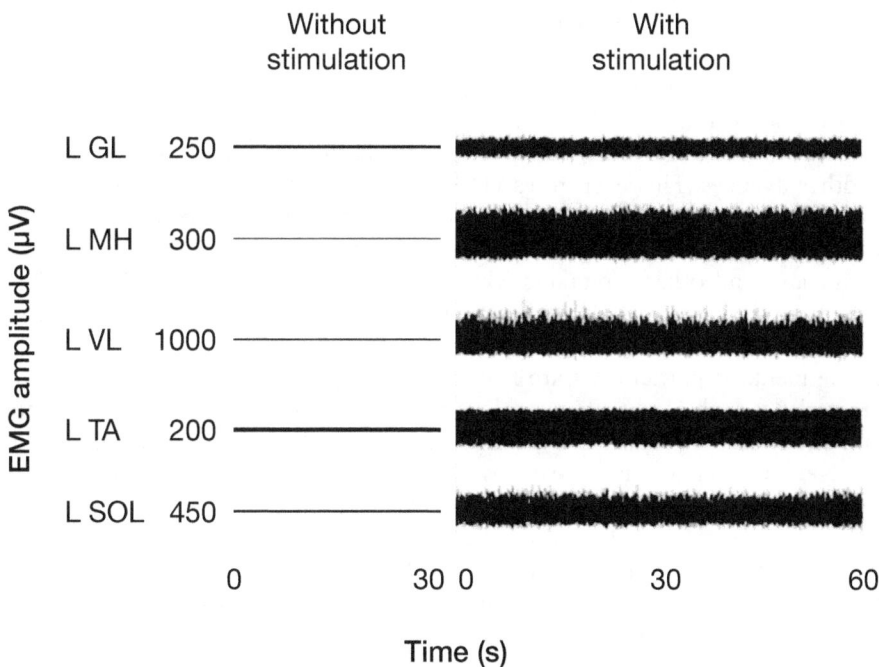

Figure 13.3 EMG activity of left (L) lower limb muscles with and without epidural spinal cord stimulation in one individual with a complete spinal cord injury while standing overground with external assistance
Note: GL = gluteus maximus; MG = medial gastrocnemius; MH = medial hamstring; SOL = soleus; TA = tibialis anterior; VL = vastus lateralis.
Source: Adapted from Rejc et al., 2015.

spatially and temporally spaced stimulation. In this way, the stimulation can be coordinated with the phase of the gait cycle or other movements. The stimulation is not only time mediated but can also target specific areas of the spinal cord instead of using the global activation method of tonic spinal cord stimulation. For example, different areas of the spinal cord associated with hip extension or knee flexion are stimulated dependent on which phase of the gait cycle the individual is in: swing, stance, or propulsion. Effective and smooth locomotion and voluntary movement of the lower extremities can be generated using this methodology (Calvert et al., 2019; Capogrosso et al., 2018; Wagner et al., 2018; Wenger et al., 2016). Spinal stimulation can also be administered less invasively using transcutaneous stimulation. This type of stimulation places electrode arrays over the skin instead of surgically implanting the electrodes under the skin. This methodology is also effective in generating locomotor patterns (Gerasimenko et al., 2015; Hofstoetter et al., 2015; Minassian et al., 2016) and can also be used to improve upper limb function (Inanici et al., 2018) for high-level SCIs. The less invasive method of spinal cord stimulation allows for more flexible application and repositioning throughout rehabilitative therapy.

FUTURE RESEARCH

Great progress in the rehabilitation of SCIs has been made, and through continued work in basic and translational science, more strategies will become available to treat and manage SCIs. Persistent work using pharmacologic therapy will likely lead to neuroregeneration within the injured spinal cord. Techniques to improve functional motor recovery through exercise training will progress, and technologies such as spinal cord stimulation will continue to advance. Life after the injury has been and will continue to be much improved for those suffering from SCI through these and other avenues. However, research with more overall heterogeneity is needed. Methodologies between studies are vastly different, including the delivery and dosage of activity-based training. It is therefore difficult to recommend best practices for clinicians and other caretakers who do not have a host of scientific minds and clinicians to develop a rehabilitation program. Understandably, human participant research of SCIs typically has a lower number of participants per study, and further, the included participants are from a broad age range and with diverse injury characteristics such as severity, time, location, and the associated sensory and motor dysfunction. Further, reported outcomes are often lacking in sensitivity. Motor function is seen to increase, but measures of success are difficult to compare between studies. Improved American Spinal Injury Association impairment scale scores or time or distance individuals can stand or walk are reported, but more standardized associated mechanistic changes need to be developed, possibly including neuroimaging pre- and post-intervention. Finally, some of these promising approaches must become available to more individuals. The vast majority of individuals living with SCI do not have the opportunity, resources, whether it be time or money, or access to technology to enroll in studies in order to get the best care or technology such as the spinal cord stimulation.

PRACTICAL IMPLICATIONS

The most overt result of SCI is the loss of voluntary motor function below the neurologic level of injury due to the discontinuity of communication between structures above and below the injury. However, this does not indicate that the motor system is completely unresponsive below the level of injury. Rehabilitation strategies that incorporate activation of these spared neural circuits see the largest improvement in motor function. Thus far, using a combination of rehabilitation approaches including task-specific training and spinal cord stimulation, whether epidurally or transcutaneous, is one of the best approaches to recover motor function in chronic SCI. However, intensive activity-based training alone can also lead to motor improvements if spinal cord stimulation treatment is not available. The main principles of motor control should be considered when using activity-based rehabilitation therapy using spinal cord stimulation for spinal cord rehabilitation. Considering training intensity and dosage, it is difficult to recommend the amount needed to produce the best outcomes as SCIs and rehabilitation techniques used to treat them are quite heterogeneous. However, evidence suggests that high-intensity training in large dosages (one to two hours) throughout an individual's life will be most effective for motor rehabilitation. The motor task likely needs to be adapted first and progressed throughout to increase the difficulty. For example, therapy focusing on locomotion will often begin by training on a treadmill using a bodyweight support system to slowly decrease the amount of support needed as the training progresses. Multiple clinical trainers should be available to initially help the individual initiate or maintain movement until the movement pattern is restored and can be independently practiced by the individual. Similarly, the amount of assistance will decrease as training progresses. It stands to reason other principles of motor learning apply; however, more research is needed to create some guidelines of best practices. Increasing the accessibility of these therapeutic interventions to all is a challenge that must be taken on in the future.

CONCLUSION

Since 3000 BC, efforts have been made to reverse the effects of SCI. Building upon the incremental progression of research as well as technological advances, current work has improved SCI prognosis. Specifically, pharmacologic research can help resolve the secondary mechanisms of injury, reducing glial scarring and allowing for more effective treatments focused on axonal growth and regeneration. Physical rehabilitation methods have improved voluntary and involuntary motor system functions. Paired with epidural stimulation, individuals with SCI who were previously unable to stand and generate locomotor patterns can now train and practice these motor functions. Also, less overt but important to recovery, these techniques have improved parasympathetic nervous system functions which leads to a more functional, engaging, and active life. SCI and recovery will continue to be an enthusiastic area of research with vast ongoing potential.

REFERENCES

Ahuja, C.S., Nori, S., Tetreault, L., Wilson, J., Kwon, B., Harrop, J., Choi, D., and Fehlings, M.G. (2017). Traumatic spinal cord injury—repair and regeneration. *Neurosurgery*, 80(3S), S9–S22.

Angeli, C.A., Boakye, M., Morton, R.A., Vogt, J., Benton, K., Chen, Y., Ferreira, C.K., and Harkema, S.J. (2018). Recovery of over-ground walking after chronic motor complete spinal cord injury. *New England Journal of Medicine*, 379(13), 1244–50.

Aslan, S.C., Legg Ditterline, B.E., Park, M.C., Angeli, C.A., Rejc, E., Chen, Y., Ovechkin, A.V., Krassioukov, A., and Harkema, S.J. (2018). Epidural spinal cord stimulation of lumbosacral networks modulates arterial blood pressure in individuals with spinal cord injury-induced cardiovascular deficits. *Frontiers in Physiology*, 9, 565.

Astorino, T.A., Harness, E.T., and Witzke, K.A. (2013). Effect of chronic activity-based therapy on bone mineral density and bone turnover in persons with spinal cord injury. *European Journal of Applied Physiology*, 113(12), 3027–37.

Barbeau, H., Ladouceur, M., Norman, K.E., Pépin, A., and Leroux, A. (1999). Walking after spinal cord injury: evaluation, treatment, and functional recovery. *Archives of Physical Medicine and Rehabilitation*, 80(2), 225–35.

Baroncini, A., Maffulli, N., Eschweiler, J., Tingart, M., and Migliorini, F. (2021). Pharmacological management of secondary spinal cord injury. *Expert Opinion on Pharmacotherapy*, 22(13), 1793–800.

Behrman, A.L., Ardolino, E.M., and Harkema, S.J. (2017). Activity-based therapy: from basic science to clinical application for recovery after spinal cord injury. *Journal of Neurologic Physical Therapy: JNPT*, 41(Suppl 3 IV STEP Spec Iss), S39.

Behrman, A.L., Bowden, M.G., and Nair, P.M. (2006). Neuroplasticity after spinal cord injury and training: an emerging paradigm shift in rehabilitation and walking recovery. *Physical Therapy*, 86(10), 1406–25.

Bickenbach, J., Officer, A., Shakespeare, T., and von Groote, P. (2013). *International perspectives on spinal cord injury*. Geneva: World Health Organization.

Brown, A.R., and Martinez, M. (2019). From cortex to cord: motor circuit plasticity after spinal cord injury. *Neural Regeneration Research*, 14(12), 2054.

Budh, C.N., and Österåker, A.L. (2007). Life satisfaction in individuals with a spinal cord injury and pain. *Clinical Rehabilitation*, 21(1), 89–96.

Calvert, J.S., Grahn, P.J., Zhao, K.D., and Lee, K.H. (2019). Emergence of epidural electrical stimulation to facilitate sensorimotor network functionality after spinal cord injury. *Neuromodulation: Technology at the Neural Interface*, 22(3), 244–52.

Capogrosso, M., Gandar, J., Greiner, N., Moraud, E. M., Wenger, N., Shkorbatova, P., Musienko, P., Minev, I., Lacour, S., and Courtine, G. (2018). Advantages of soft subdural implants for the delivery of electrochemical neuromodulation therapies to the spinal cord. *Journal of Neural Engineering*, 15(2), 026024.

Chen, S., and Levi, A.D. (2017). Restorative treatments for spinal cord injury. *Neurosurgery Clinics*, 28(1), 63–71.

Courtine, G., Gerasimenko, Y., Van Den Brand, R., Yew, A., Musienko, P., Zhong, H., Song, B., Ao, Y., Ichiyama, R.M., Lavrov, I., Roy, R.R., Sofroniew, M.V., and Edgerton, V.R. (2009). Transformation of nonfunctional spinal circuits into functional states after the loss of brain input. *Nature Neuroscience*, 12(10), 1333–42.

Dietz, V., Müller, R., and Colombo, G. (2002). Locomotor activity in spinal man: significance of afferent input from joint and load receptors. *Brain*, 125(12), 2626–34.

DiMarco, A.F., and Kowalski, K.E. (2013). Activation of inspiratory muscles via spinal cord stimulation. *Respiratory Physiology & Neurobiology*, 189(2), 438–49.

Dimitrijevic, M.R., Gerasimenko, Y., and Pinter, M.M. (1998). Evidence for a spinal central pattern generator in humans. *Annals of the New York Academy of Sciences*, 860(1), 360–76.

Ditunno, P., Patrick, M., Stineman, M., and Ditunno, J. (2008). Who wants to walk? Preferences for recovery after SCI: A longitudinal and cross-sectional study. *Spinal Cord*, 46(7), 500–06.

Dolbow, D.R., Gorgey, A.S., Recio, A.C., Stiens, S.A., Curry, A.C., Sadowsky, C.L., Gater, D.R., Martin, R., and McDonald, J.W. (2015). Activity-based restorative therapies after spinal cord injury: inter-institutional conceptions and perceptions. *Aging and Disease*, 6(4), 254.

Edgerton, V.R., Tillakaratne, N.J., Bigbee, A.J., de Leon, R.D., and Roy, R.R. (2004). Plasticity of the spinal neural circuitry after injury. *Annu. Rev. Neurosci.*, 27, 145–67.

Field-Fote, E.C. (2000). Spinal cord control of movement: implications for locomotor rehabilitation following spinal cord injury. *Physical Therapy*, 80(5), 477–84.

Filli, L., and Schwab, M.E. (2015). Structural and functional reorganization of propriospinal connections promotes functional recovery after spinal cord injury. *Neural Regeneration Research*, 10(4), 509.

Fouad, K., and Tse, A. (2008). Adaptive changes in the injured spinal cord and their role in promoting functional recovery. *Neurological Research*, 30(1), 17–27.

Gerasimenko, Y., Gorodnichev, R., Moshonkina, T., Sayenko, D., Gad, P., and Edgerton, V.R. (2015). Transcutaneous electrical spinal-cord stimulation in humans. *Annals of Physical and Rehabilitation Medicine*, 58(4), 225–31.

Gill, M.L., Grahn, P.J., Calvert, J.S., Linde, M.B., Lavrov, I.A., Strommen, J.A., Beck, L.A., Sayenko, D.G., Van Straaten, M.G., Drubach, D.I., Veith, D.D., Thoreson, A.R., Lopez, C., Gerasimenko, Y.P., Edgerton, V.R., Lee, K.H., and Zhao, K.D. (2018). Neuromodulation of lumbosacral spinal networks enables independent stepping after complete paraplegia. *Nature Medicine*, 24(11), 1677–82.

Grahn, P.J., Lavrov, I.A., Sayenko, D.G., Van Straaten, M.G., Gill, M.L., Strommen, J.A., Calvert, J.S., Drubach, D.I., Beck, L.A., Linde, M.B., Thoreson, A.R., Lopez, C., Mendez, A.A., Gad, P.N., Gerasimenko, Y.P., Edgerton, V.R., and Zhao, K.D. (2017). Enabling task-specific volitional motor functions via spinal cord neuromodulation in a human with paraplegia. Paper presented at the Mayo Clinic Proceedings.

Hachmann, J.T., Grahn, P.J., Calvert, J.S., Drubach, D.I., Lee, K.H., and Lavrov, I.A. (2017). Electrical neuromodulation of the respiratory system after spinal cord injury. Paper presented at the Mayo Clinic Proceedings.

Hachmann, J.T., Yousak, A., Wallner, J.J., Gad, P.N., Edgerton, V.R., and Gorgey, A.S. (2021). Epidural spinal cord stimulation as an intervention for motor recovery after motor complete spinal cord injury. *Journal of Neurophysiology*, 126(6), 1843–59.

Harkema, S., Gerasimenko, Y., Hodes, J., Burdick, J., Angeli, C., Chen, Y., Ferreira, C., Willhite, A., Rejc, E., Grossman, R.G., and Edgerton, V.R. (2011). Effect of epidural stimulation of the lumbosacral spinal cord on voluntary movement, standing, and assisted stepping after motor complete paraplegia: A case study. *The Lancet*, 377(9781), 1938–47.

Harkema, S.J. (2008). Plasticity of interneuronal networks of the functionally isolated human spinal cord. *Brain Research Reviews*, 57(1), 255–64.

Harkema, S.J., Hurley, S.L., Patel, U.K., Requejo, P.S., Dobkin, B.H., and Edgerton, V.R. (1997). Human lumbosacral spinal cord interprets loading during stepping. *Journal of Neurophysiology*, 77(2), 797–811.

Harkema, S.J., Schmidt-Read, M., Lorenz, D.J., Edgerton, V.R., and Behrman, A.L. (2012). Balance and ambulation improvements in individuals with chronic incomplete spinal cord injury using locomotor training–based rehabilitation. *Archives of Physical Medicine and Rehabilitation*, 93(9), 1508–17.

Harkema, S.J., Wang, S., Angeli, C.A., Chen, Y., Boakye, M., Ugiliweneza, B., and Hirsch, G.A. (2018). Normalization of blood pressure with spinal cord epidural stimulation after severe spinal cord injury. *Frontiers in Human Neuroscience*, 12, 83.

Heald, E., Hart, R., Kilgore, K., and Peckham, P.H. (2017). Characterization of volitional electromyographic signals in the lower extremity after motor complete spinal cord injury. *Neurorehabilitation and Neural Repair*, 31(6), 583–91.

Herman, R., He, J., D'luzansky, S., Willis, W., and Dilli, S. (2002). Spinal cord stimulation facilitates functional walking in a chronic, incomplete spinal cord injured. *Spinal Cord*, 40(2), 65–68.

Hilton, B.J., Anenberg, E., Harrison, T.C., Boyd, J.D., Murphy, T.H., and Tetzlaff, W. (2016). Re-establishment of cortical motor output maps and spontaneous functional recovery via spared dorsolaterally projecting corticospinal neurons after dorsal column spinal cord injury in adult mice. *Journal of Neuroscience*, 36(14), 4080–92.

Hofstoetter, U.S., Krenn, M., Danner, S.M., Hofer, C., Kern, H., McKay, W.B., Mayr, W., and Minassian, K. (2015). Augmentation of voluntary locomotor activity by transcutaneous spinal cord stimulation in motor-incomplete spinal cord-injured individuals. *Artificial Organs*, 39(10), E176–E186.

Hubscher, C.H., Herrity, A.N., Williams, C.S., Montgomery, L.R., Willhite, A.M., Angeli, C.A., and Harkema, S.J. (2018). Improvements in bladder, bowel and sexual outcomes following task-specific locomotor training in human spinal cord injury. *PLoS One*, 13(1), e0190998.

Hurlbert, R.J., Hadley, M.N., Walters, B.C., Aarabi, B., Dhall, S.S., Gelb, D.E., Rozzelle, C.J., Ryken, T.C., and Theodore, N. (2015). Pharmacological therapy for acute spinal cord injury. *Neurosurgery*, 76(suppl. 1), S71–S83.

Inanici, F., Samejima, S., Gad, P., Edgerton, V.R., Hofstetter, C.P., and Moritz, C.T. (2018). Transcutaneous electrical spinal stimulation promotes long-term recovery of upper extremity function in chronic tetraplegia. *IEEE Transactions on Neural Systems and Rehabilitation Engineering*, 26(6), 1272–78.

Jeffery, N., and Blakemore, W. (1999). Spinal cord injury in small animals 1. Mechanisms of spontaneous recovery. *Veterinary Record*, 144(15), 407–13.

Jones, M.L., Evans, N., Tefertiller, C., Backus, D., Sweatman, M., Tansey, K., and Morrison, S. (2014). Activity-based therapy for recovery of walking in individuals with chronic spinal cord injury: Results from a randomized clinical trial. *Archives of Physical Medicine and Rehabilitation*, 95(12), 2239–2246.

Kakulas, B.A., and Kaelan, C. (2015). The neuropathological foundations for the restorative neurology of spinal cord injury. *Clinical Neurology and Neurosurgery*, 129, S1–S7.

Kirshblum, S., Burns, S., Biering-Sorensen, F., Donovan, W., Graves, D., Jha, A., Johansen, M., Jones, L., Krassioukov, A., Mulcahey, M.J., Schmidt-Read, M., and Waring, W. (2011). International standards for neurological classification of spinal cord injury (revised 2011). *Journal of Spinal Cord Medicine*, 34, 535–46.

Lu, D.C., Edgerton, V.R., Modaber, M., AuYong, N., Morikawa, E., Zdunowski, S., Sarino, M.E., Sarrafzadeh, M., Nuwer, M.R., Roy, R.R., and Gerasimenko, Y. (2016). Engaging cervical spinal cord networks to reenable volitional control of hand function in tetraplegic patients. *Neurorehabilitation and Neural Repair*, 30(10), 951–62.

Minassian, K., Hofstoetter, U.S., Danner, S.M., Mayr, W., Bruce, J.A., McKay, W.B., and Tansey, K.E. (2016). Spinal rhythm generation by step-induced feedback and transcutaneous posterior root stimulation in complete spinal cord–injured individuals. *Neurorehabilitation and Neural Repair*, 30(3), 233–43.

Minassian, K., Jilge, B., Rattay, F., Pinter, M., Binder, H., Gerstenbrand, F., and Dimitrijevic, M.R. (2004). Stepping-like movements in humans with complete spinal cord injury induced by epidural stimulation of the lumbar cord: Electromyographic study of compound muscle action potentials. *Spinal Cord*, 42(7), 401–16.

Moxon, K.A., Oliviero, A., Aguilar, J., and Foffani, G. (2014). Cortical reorganization after spinal cord injury: always for good? *Neuroscience*, 283, 78–94. https://www.ncbi.nlm.nih.gov/pmc/articles/PMC4556279/pdf/nihms-611292.pdf

Raineteau, O., and Schwab, M.E. (2001). Plasticity of motor systems after incomplete spinal cord injury. *Nature Reviews Neuroscience*, 2(4), 263–73.

Rank, M., Flynn, J., Galea, M., Callister, R., and Callister, R. (2015). Electrophysiological characterization of spontaneous recovery in deep dorsal horn interneurons after incomplete spinal cord injury. *Experimental Neurology*, 271, 468–78.

Rasmussen, R., and Carlsen, E.M. (2016). Spontaneous functional recovery from incomplete spinal cord injury. *Journal of Neuroscience*, 36(33), 8535–37.

Rejc, E., Angeli, C., and Harkema, S. (2015). Effects of lumbosacral spinal cord epidural stimulation for standing after chronic complete paralysis in humans. *PLoS One*, 10(7), e0133998.

Rejc, E., and Angeli, C.A. (2019). Spinal cord epidural stimulation for lower limb motor function recovery in individuals with motor complete spinal cord injury. *Physical Medicine and Rehabilitation Clinics*, 30(2), 337–54.

Rosenzweig, E.S., Courtine, G., Jindrich, D.L., Brock, J.H., Ferguson, A.R., Strand, S.C., Nout, Y.S., Roy, R.R., Miller, D.M., Beattie, M.S., Havton, L.A., Bresnahan, J.C., Edgerton, V.R., and Tuszynski, M.H. (2010). Extensive spontaneous plasticity of corticospinal projections after primate spinal cord injury. *Nature Neuroscience*, 13(12), 1505–10.

Sadowsky, C.L., and McDonald, J.W. (2009). Activity-based restorative therapies: Concepts and applications in spinal cord injury-related neurorehabilitation. *Developmental Disabilities Research Reviews*, 15(2), 112–16.

Sangari, S., Lundell, H., Kirshblum, S., and Perez, M.A. (2019). Residual descending motor pathways influence spasticity after spinal cord injury. *Annals of Neurology*, 86(1), 28–41.

Shah, M., Peterson, C., Yilmaz, E., Halalmeh, D.R., and Moisi, M. (2020). Current advancements in the management of spinal cord injury: A comprehensive review of literature. *Surgical Neurology International*, 11.

Silver, J.R. (2005). History of the treatment of spinal injuries. *Postgraduate Medical Journal*, 81(952), 108–14.

Taccola, G., Sayenko, D., Gad, P., Gerasimenko, Y., and Edgerton, V. (2018). And yet it moves: Recovery of volitional control after spinal cord injury. *Progress in Neurobiology*, 160, 64–81.

Tai, W., Wu, W., Wang, L.L., Ni, H., Chen, C., Yang, J., Zang, T., Zou, Y., Xu, X.M., and Zhang, C.L. (2021). In vivo reprogramming of NG2 glia enables adult neurogenesis and functional recovery following spinal cord injury. *Cell Stem Cell*, 28(5), 923–37.e4.

Venkatesh, K., Ghosh, S.K., Mullick, M., Manivasagam, G., and Sen, D. (2019). Spinal cord injury: Pathophysiology, treatment strategies, associated challenges, and future implications. *Cell and Tissue Research*, 377(2), 125–51.

Wagner, F.B., Mignardot, J.B., Goff-Mignardot, L., Camille, G., Demesmaeker, R., Komi, S., . . . Caban, M. (2018). Targeted neurotechnology restores walking in humans with spinal cord injury. *Nature*, 563(7729), 65–71.

Wenger, N., Moraud, E. M., Gandar, J., Musienko, P., Capogrosso, M., Baud, L., . . . Dominici, N. (2016). Spatiotemporal neuromodulation therapies engaging muscle synergies improve motor control after spinal cord injury. *Nature Medicine*, 22(2), 138–45.

14

Motor Behavior and Profound Intellectual and Multiple Disabilities

Bethany M. Sloane, Heather A. Feldner, Lisa K. Kenyon, and Samuel W. Logan

■ ■ ■

OVERVIEW

This chapter will take a lifespan approach to motor behavior of individuals with profound intellectual and multiple disabilities (PIMD), with an emphasis on children and youth. We recognize that language is powerful and often contested and acknowledge that people with lived experience of PIMD and their families may prefer person-first or identity-first language. Our choice to use "children/adults/people with PIMD" aligns with person-first language and is based on professional conventions as well as a reflection of advocacy within the disability rights movement for person-first language by people with PIMD (American Psychological Association, 2021). We are committed to continual reflection on the language used to describe people with PIMD to prevent further oppression of this population in our ableist society. Other terms used to describe the PIMD population include profound and multiple learning disabilities, severe disability, medically complex, medically fragile, and low incidence, among others, and varies across geographical region (i.e., PIMD is used mostly in Europe; Maes et al., 2007; Nakken and Vlaskamp, 2007). This population is inconsistently defined and there is a lack of assessments to confirm a PIMD diagnosis. This causes research challenges when defining inclusion criteria and recruitment, resulting in small sample sizes (Maes et al., 2021). There is a need for development of a taxonomy to describe PIMD to decrease confusion and improve communication and research interpretation (Nakken and Vlaskamp, 2007).

PIMD consists of profound intellectual (IQ below 20–25) and motor disabilities (developmental age at or below twenty-four months; Nakken and Vlaskamp, 2007). People with PIMD often exhibit secondary characteristics or medical complications (see textbox 14.1) (Nakken and Vlaskamp, 2007). PIMD is not typically diagnosed by a physician (Maes et al., 2007). This is partly due to challenges interpreting intellectual capabilities of people with PIMD for diagnostic purposes, due to the reliance on motor or communication behaviors in most assessments combined with the lack

> **Textbox 14.1 Secondary Characteristics of Individuals with Profound Intellectual and Multiple Disabilities**
>
> - Interdependent for all activities of daily living, self-care, and mobility
> - Pre-symbolic communication skills
> - Fine motor limitations
> - Limited abilities to self-report pain or discomfort
> - Sensory impairments
> - Visual and/or hearing impairment
> - Risk of developing medical complications
> - Often require ongoing medication

of standardized assessments specifically validated for this population (Maes et al., 2021; Nakken and Vlaskamp, 2007). Rather, PIMD is a term used to describe people who require high support needs and those who experience challenges with learning, communication, mobility, and participation in social activities (Labeer et al., 2017). Example primary diagnoses that may align with PIMD include cerebral palsy (Gross Motor Function Classification Scale level IV or V) and genetic conditions such as Rett syndrome. Secondary diagnoses may include cerebral visual impairment, epilepsy, sensory processing disorder, congenital sensorineural hearing loss, and feeding disorders. These primary and secondary diagnoses are not an exhaustive list but broadly represent PIMD.

People with PIMD have historically faced adversity in meaningful inclusion in both society and in scientific research (Maes et al., 2021). This population has increased globally due to advancements in medical care and emphasis on support services for caregiving, living, and education, which has led to increased research over the past forty to fifty years (Maes et al., 2007; Nakken and Vlaskamp, 2007). People with PIMD are interdependent on caregivers (e.g., parents, legal guardians, direct support professionals) in home and educational settings for support in all areas of self-care, activities of daily living, and mobility, which means people must rely on the relative education and empowerment of others in those settings to ensure meaningful inclusion (Maes et al., 2007; Nakken and Vlaskamp, 2007). Therefore, if society does not view participation or quality of life of children with PIMD as meaningful, or underestimates their abilities to make progress, then their opportunities to engage with the world around them remains limited (Maes et al., 2007). People with PIMD can have good quality of life and show meaningful improvements in development with intervention (Maes et al., 2007). Yet most research involving this population is focused on the impairment itself, which includes the specific diagnosis, medications, or medical procedures.

There is limited evidenced-based knowledge and importance placed on motor behavior research for children with PIMD (van Alphen et al., 2019). Motor behavior includes "every kind of movement from involuntary twitches to goal-directed actions, in every part of the body from head to toe, in every physical and social context from solitary play to group interactions" (Adolph and Franchak, 2017, p. 1). This chapter will explore motor behavior research for the PIMD population utilizing the International Classification of Functioning, Disability and Health model

(ICF). We emphasize the importance of viewing people with PIMD holistically to include motor behavior research that not only focuses on impairment, body functions, and structures, but also emphasizes activity, participation, and environmental and personal factors. Our goal is to cite research where people with PIMD are clearly defined. In some cases, we cite research involving people with other diagnoses that clearly align with PIMD. This chapter will conclude with future research directions and practical implications to consider when conducting research involving the PIMD population and motor behavior.

MOTOR BEHAVIOR AND PROFOUND INTELLECTUAL AND MULTIPLE DISABILITIES POPULATION EMPIRICAL RESEARCH SUMMARY

International Classification of Functioning, Disability and Health Model

The World Health Organization (WHO) developed a conceptual framework to provide a universal language for the measurement and documentation of the health, functioning, well-being, and disability (WHO, 2022). This framework focuses on a health condition (disease or disorder) and examines the impairment through the lens of functions and structures of the body, activity, participation, and environmental and personal factors (table 14.1; WHO, 2022). This framework is dynamic with all sections interrelated. The ICF framework is based on the biopsychosocial model of disability, which combines the social and medical models of disability that emphasize care for and about the body, along with recognition and elimination of disabling barriers in the environment and in the attitudes of others (WHO, 2022). The ICF framework can be used to contextualize motor behavior research of people with PIMD.

Table 14.1 Motor Behavior Topics Included in This Chapter Mapped onto the ICF Framework

ICF domain	Motor behavior topic
Health condition	• Profound intellectual and multiple disabilities
Body functions and structures	• Motor development • Challenging behaviors • Alertness level

Activities and participation	• Motor activity
	  ◦ Motor opportunities via education (MOVE) curriculum
	  ◦ Individualized motor program
	• Physical activity
	  ◦ Power-assisted machines
	  ◦ Aquatics
	  ◦ Tandem skiing

Environmental and personal factors	• Assistive technology • Supports and relationships • Attitudes

Source: World Health Organization, 2022.
Note: ICF = International Classification of Functioning, Disability and Health model.

Body Functions and Structures

The body functions and structures domain of the ICF framework includes anatomic, physiologic functions, and any associated impairments that are involved with the health condition (WHO, 2022). This section summarizes research describing impairments related to motor development. Also, this section summarizes how the physiologic functions of challenging behaviors and alertness levels may play a role in motor behaviors of people with PIMD. Challenging behaviors and alertness are categorized under mental functions in the ICF framework.

Motor Development

People with PIMD have significant delays in motor development with their overall developmental skills being at or below twenty-four months (Nakken and Vlaskamp, 2007). Motor development includes the change in motor behavior over a person's life span (Adolph and Franchak, 2017). People with PIMD are interdependent on others to move their body and perform activities of daily living (van Alphen et al., 2019). Their motor skills typically consist of (a) small movements of arms, hands, and legs; (b) standing with assistance of a stander or taking steps with body weight support; and (c) locomotion utilizing a wheelchair. People with PIMD require equipment for upright supportive positioning and postural support (e.g., head and trunk control). They also require caregiver assistance for transfers and changes in position throughout the day. Due to restrictions in cognitive and adaptive functioning, people with PIMD have limited opportunities to engage in development and learning (Houwen et al., 2014). Development in this population depends on a structured environment that utilizes continuous personal care assistance, as well as supportive equipment and technology (Mensch et al., 2015).

Motor assessments utilized in the PIMD population are either subjective or have been adapted from assessments for a different target population, which can create issues with accuracy, consistency, and validity (Mensch et al., 2015; Wessels et al., 2021b). There are two motor assessments developed for people with PIMD: the Motor eVAluation in Kids with Intellectual and Complex disabilities and the Top Down Motor Milestone Test (Mensch et al., 2015; van der Putten et al., 2005; Waninge et al., 2013). Both assessments can be used for people with PIMD at any age. The Motor eVAluation in Kids with Intellectual and Complex disabilities is a questionnaire, and the Top Down Motor Milestone Test utilizes observation to assess the person's ability to move, maintain, or change body positions (lying, sitting, standing) independently with or without an assistive device (Mensch et al., 2016). The exploratory behavior subscale of the Behavioral Appraisal Scales is valid and reliable for people with PIMD, even though it was not designed for this population (Vlaskamp and Nakken, 1999). Other motor assessments used in research with children with PIMD, but have not been designed or validated for this population, include the motor development checklist (Gevelinger et al., 1988), Bayley Scales of Infant Development (Bayley, 1969), Kent Infant Development Scale (Katopf, 1981), The Chailey Levels of Ability (Pountney et al., 1999), Gross Motor Function Measure (Russell et al., 1989), Modified Hammersmith Functional Motor Scale (Krosschell et al., 2011), lower extremity physical functioning and mobility skills (Gorton et al., 2010), Motor Function Measure scale (Berard et al., 2005), Vulpe Assessment Battery (Jain et al., 1994), the pediatric version of the Functional Independence Measure (Braun et al., 1994), and Vineland adaptive behavior scale (Sparrow et al.,

2005). Caution is advised when using such assessments as they may lead to inaccurate measures of motor abilities and challenges connecting to therapeutic goals (Mensch et al., 2015).

Challenging Behavior
People with PIMD often have challenging behavior in greater frequency than peers without disabilities, which may include self-injury, stereotypies, aggressive behavior, or any behavior that interferes with daily activities (Balboni et al., 2020; Poppes et al., 2016). Challenging behavior can affect people with PIMD's adaptive behavior (communication, daily living skills, socialization, and motor skills) by interfering with learning and development (Poppes et al., 2016). Severity of intellectual disability, motor skill limitations, and amount of sedentary time are factors associated with increased challenging behavior in this population (Balboni et al., 2020). Challenging behavior is important to consider to form a holistic understanding of what could limit a person's ability to perform or improve motor behaviors (Balboni et al., 2020).

Alertness Level
People with PIMD may have decreased alertness levels, which are behavioral states of an individual that defines their level of ability to engage with the environment (Munde et al., 2009). Alertness in this population is summarized according to three different states: (a) active and focused on the environment; (b) awake, but inactive and only focused internally, not on the environment; and (c) asleep, not active internally or on the environment (Munde et al., 2009). Alertness is important to consider preemptively regarding motor behaviors because they have a reciprocal relationship. For example, gauging alertness is important for focusing on the presented motor behavior in a given environment; however, motor behavior itself may be a catalyst for increasing alertness and subsequent increases in motor development. The ability to detect alertness levels in the PIMD population is challenging due to their subtle signs of self-expression or communication that can go unnoticed, and also because alertness may be different for everyone (Munde et al., 2009).

Summary
Within the body functions and structures level of the ICF framework, people with PIMD may present motor behavior impairments that are further impacted by physiologic functions such as challenging behaviors and alertness levels (Nakken and Vlaskmap, 2007). Reliable and valid assessments are lacking related to motor behavior available for people with PIMD, which can cause challenges in research and clinical practice (Wessels et al., 2021b).

ACTIVITY AND PARTICIPATION

Under the ICF framework, activity refers to an "individual's ability to execute a task or action" and participation is the "involvement in a life situation and interaction with their social and physical environment" (WHO, 2022). This section summarizes research related to the abilities of a person with PIMD to execute motor behaviors (motor activity and physical activity) and participate in the ICF framework categories of mobility, self-care, and community life. The current research interventions that aid in performing motor behavior activities and promote participation are also included.

Motor Activity

Motor activity is important for everyone. People with PIMD have limitations in motor development, but they can benefit from involvement in activities that focus on the motor domain (van der Putten et al., 2017). Motor activities improve postural control, development across multiple areas (gross motor, fine motor, cognition, and communication), autonomy, engagement with others and the environment, quality of life, physical and mental health, and fitness (van Alphen et al., 2019; Maes et al., 2007; Mensch et al., 2016; van der Putten et al., 2017; Waninge et al., 2013; Wessels et al., 2021b). Common motor activities described in this population include play or manipulation of an object, changes in positions (e.g., lying down to sitting), being moved to another area, or movement using assistive technology (van der Putten et al., 2017). These activities may be performed independently or with support. However, despite benefits, motor activities are not prioritized in the daily life of people with PIMD. Research reports people with PIMD only have motor opportunities 1.5 times per day, and many interventions are passive in nature (van der Putten et al., 2017; Waninge et al., 2013).

Structured motor activity interventions in the literature for people with PIMD have been limited to two programs, the Mobility Opportunities Via Education curriculum and an individualized motor profile (van der Putten et al., 2005). These programs focused on the strengths of each person and created an individualized plan to perform motor activities with support. Both programs emphasize the need for an interdisciplinary team, goal-directed plans, and describe that a frequency of motor activities of three to five times per week is feasible and beneficial (van der Putten et al., 2005). People with PIMD who were enrolled in the Mobility Opportunities Via Education curriculum showed a statistically significant increase in motor skill performance than the control group of people with PIMD.

Physical Activity

People with PIMD have lower physical activity levels compared to their peers with and without disabilities (Waninge et al., 2013). Physical activity is defined as energy expenditure or overall movement in daily life strenuous enough to improve muscular and cardiorespiratory fitness, skeletal health, maintain healthy body weight, and reduce risk of chronic health and mental health conditions (van Alphen et al., 2021a; Waninge et al., 2013; WHO, 2020). While physical activity also includes physiologic functions described earlier, it is explicitly included in the activity section of the ICF model due to the focus on participation in exercise and fitness for this population. Children with disabilities should engage in an average of sixty minutes per day of physical activity at moderate to vigorous intensity and adults with disabilities an average of 150 to three hundred minutes at moderate intensity or seventy-five to 150 at vigorous intensity (WHO, 2020). For moderate intensity physical activity, a person should use 40 to 59 percent of their heart rate reserve and anything above 60 percent is considered vigorous exercise (Garber et al., 2011). People with PIMD most often participate in physical activity at mild to moderate intensity levels and only use 20 to 30 percent of their heart rate reserve during physical activity, but this may be due to challenges with reliability and sensitivity of measurements not validated for this population (Aherne and Coughlan, 2017; van Alphen et al., 2019; Degache et al., 2019; Waninge et al., 2013).

Research is lacking in reliable measurement of physical activity for people with PIMD (Wessels et al., 2021b). Due to movements of people with PIMD being small in range, assisted or passively performed, or challenging to interpret, measurements need to be sensitive enough to capture and differentiate between these movements (van Alphen et al., 2021a). Physical activity measurements validated for this population include a diary log (van der Putten et al., 2017), video recordings (van Delden et al., 2020), and accelerometers (van Alphen, 2021). Physiologic measures may be advantageous in this population to decrease the challenge of interpreting or validating observation measurements, which can include measuring breathing pattern, brain activity, eye blink amplitude, or skin conductance using tools such as a heart rate monitor, electroencephalography, a sensor sock, or startle reflex modulation technique (Kenyon et al., 2017; Lyons et al., 2013; Maes et al., 2021; Sterkenburg et al., 2017; Waninge et al., 2013).

Physical activity interventions described in the literature specifically for people with PIMD consist of power-assisted exercises, aquatics, and tandem skiing (Aherne and Coughlan, 2017; Bossink et al., 2017; Degache et al., 2019; Wessels et al., 2021a). Power-assisted machines facilitate a range of movements or exercises that are programmed into the machine and are passive or active-assisted depending on the person's ability level (Wessels et al., 2021a). Power-assisted machines were feasible to use for people with PIMD (Wessels et al., 2021a). However, results showed an increase in oxygen saturation measurements, but not in functional abilities, alertness, body composition, muscle tone, cardiovascular fitness, or quality of life, possibly due to a person with PIMD's challenges independent execution of exercises (Wessels et al., 2021a). Aquatics, which includes swimming lessons, exercise in the water, or recreational opportunities, has been reported as beneficial for people with PIMD as a mild to moderate physical activity intervention (Aherne and Coughlan, 2017). The buoyancy and different sensory inputs provided by the water resulted in ease of movement and participation (Aherne and Coughlan, 2017). However, barriers reported to aquatic interventions within this population include time constraints, lack of support and resources, limitations related to health, challenging behaviors, and staff hesitation (Aherne and Coughlan, 2017). The authors recommended that each person should have an individualized program to add the value and success of aquatic activity (Aherne and Coughlan, 2017). Lastly, tandem skiing provides access for children with PIMD to recreational activities. Each child rode in an adapted bucket seat with an instructor utilizing articulated skates attached to the seat (Degache et al., 2019). Tandem skiing elicited active postural control and heart rate similarly between children with PIMD and controls without disabilities (Degache et al., 2019). Tandem skiing also raised children with PIMDs' heart rate above 70 percent of the average maximal heart rate, which is within the moderate to vigorous physical activity range (Degache et al., 2019).

Within the activity and participation level of the ICF framework, there are limited evidenced-based interventions that focus on execution of motor behaviors (motor activities and physical activity) specifically for people with PIMD. This can create challenges in establishing consensus among researchers and practitioners regarding intervention effectiveness and ultimately how to approach individualized care (van Alphen et al., 2019; Wessels et al., 2021b). There is even less focus on how people with PIMD and their families are encouraged or empowered to participate in mobility, self-care, and recreational activities with many activities being relatively passive in nature. Environmental and personal factors will further play a role in motor behavior in this population.

ENVIRONMENTAL AND PERSONAL FACTORS

Within the ICF framework, environmental factors consist of physical, social, and attitudinal factors that make up an individual's life. Personal factors include the background of an individual's life that include features that are not part of the health condition such as race, ethnicity, gender, age, or socioeconomic status (WHO, 2022). This section summarizes how motor behavior by people with PIMD is influenced by environmental and personal factors such as access to assistive technology, supports and relationships, and attitudes.

Assistive Technology

Assistive technology improves participation for people with PIMD by increasing stimulation, independence, and autonomy in motor behavior within their environment (Roche et al., 2015). Assistive technology is defined as "any item, piece of equipment, or product system, whether acquired commercially off the shelf, modified, or customized, that is used to increase, maintain, or improve functional capabilities of a child with a disability" (Early Childhood Technical Assistance, 2020). Appropriate stimulation is important for people with PIMD because they often experience decreased self-initiation of movement and alertness levels (Munde et al., 2014; Nilsson and Nyberg, 2003). Examples of assistive technology utilized in this population include microswitches, power mobility, and interactive technologies.

Microswitch technology may increase participation in motor and physical activities for people with PIMD by providing preferred stimuli (Roche et al., 2015). Microswitches are a type of assistive technology that enables a person to perform adaptive behaviors or control preferred environmental stimulation via some existing motor action, such as moving a finger or arm, head turning, touching/pushing, or chin movement (Lancioni et al., 2007). Microswitches provide a preferred stimuli when an activity is completed. Examples of activities include reaching for an object (Lancioni et al., 2007), improving posture (Lancioni et al., 2005), or taking steps in a gait trainer (Lancioni et al., 2010). Preferred stimulation may include auditory, vestibular, tactile, or visual stimuli, such as music, videos, or lights (Munde et al., 2014). Microswitches are a training tool to increase activity engagement, self-initiation of movement, and enjoyment in the PIMD population (Lancioni et al., 2007). People with PIMD can activate microswitches to achieve preferred stimuli, understand cause-and-effect relationships, and can increase microswitch responses over time with training (Roche et al., 2015). Microswitches may be considered when designing interventions focused on learning a new motor behavior. The microswitch needs to be easy for the child to activate, provide a meaningful outcome, and ensure they can receive adequate support and practice to gain independence (Roche et al., 2015).

Further, power mobility may provide people with PIMD independent mobility to navigate their environment through using a motorized wheelchair or a modified ride-on car. Modified ride-on cars are battery-powered commercially available devices that are adapted to utilize an easy-to-press switch on the steering wheel and added postural supports using PVC pipe, Velcro, pool kick boards, and pool noodles (see figure 14.1). Historically, children with PIMD were excluded from power mobility research due to misconceptions regarding the necessary physical and cognitive skills to independently control the device as well as the need for extensive postural support, which was deemed a safety risk (Nilsson and Nyberg, 2006). However, power mobility provides opportunities for all people with disabilities to engage with their environment, socialize, experience independence, and have sensory and vestibular experiences that can increase alertness levels, even if they may never become independent community drivers (Nilsson and Nyberg, 2006). Young children with PIMD, including those with severe disabilities (i.e., cerebral palsy, Gross Motor Function Classification Scale level IV or V) and complex medical needs, were included in two power mobility studies, one utilizing modified ride-on cars (Logan et al., 2016) and one using alternative power mobility devices (motorized platform with control system consisting of either a joystick or switch; Kenyon et al., 2017). All participants successfully used and enjoyed the power mobility devices (Logan et al., 2016; Kenyon et al., 2017). Power mobility was shown to improve development in cognition, communication, and motor skills in this population (Kenyon et al., 2017). One assessment specific to power mobility that could be utilized for the PIMD population includes the Assessment of Learning Power mobility use, which is inclusive of all learners (Nilsson et al., 2014). The Assessment of Learning Power tool assesses a person's occupational performance in a power mobility device from novice to expert and offers facilitating strategies to help with planning interventions (Nilsson et al., 2014).

Figure 14.1 Photograph of child with a disability using a modified ride-on car
Source: Alan Calvert, College of Health, Oregon State University.

Interactive technology may also increase alertness and affective behavior for people with PIMD (van Delden et al., 2020; Embregts et al., 2020). Interactive technology involves an activity that responds to a person's movements or vocalizations and does not require assistance for participation (Embregts et al., 2020). For example, researchers have used an interactive ball that lights up, plays sounds or music, and moves in response to movement or vocalizations (Embregts et al., 2020). Engagement with the interactive ball was compared to watching television for nine adults with PIMD to understand differences in alertness or behavior between these two activities as a form of leisure (Embregts et al., 2020). Four people showed increases in alertness, three had improvements in affective behavior, and three demonstrated no differences in engagement (Embregts et al., 2020). Research with interactive technology is limited, however, and caregivers have historically reported dissatisfaction with the availability of leisure activities and supporting technologies for children with PIMD (Luijkx et al., 2016). Interactive technology is an exciting advancement with potential benefits for this population due to the person not requiring assistance from others to participate.

Supports and Relationships

Research involving motor behavior for people with PIMD is most often conducted in residential living facilities, day programs, or educational settings. However, most people with PIMD tend to live in their families' homes (Luijkx et al., 2017). Further, the only study of children with PIMD in a community-based setting was the tandem skiing study previously described (Degache et al., 2019). These disconnects demonstrate there is a need for increased motor behavior research across contexts, especially in the community and real-world settings to increase the variety of activities and participation opportunities available to people with PIMD and their families.

Caregivers are a key environmental factor in motor behavior research for people with PIMD, and they need to be acknowledged as critical partners in research (Jansen et al., 2017). However, caregivers may not feel confident in their abilities to provide motor interventions or may have significant burnout resulting from other daily care activities they must prioritize for their children (Maes et al., 2021; van der Putten et al., 2017). Further, in-depth collaboration between professionals and caregivers is needed to promote family-centered care and understand meaningful outcomes related to motor behavior (Jansen et al., 2014).

Additionally, people with PIMD have more limited social networks that tend to include only family members, healthcare professionals, and others with disabilities. This is likely because people with PIMD are reliant on others to set up and maintain social contacts (Kamstra et al., 2015). There is a lack of peer interactions involved in research related to motor behavior, which could be useful to increase participation, engagement, and stimulation of children and adults with PIMD (Nijs et al., 2016).

Attitudes

Caregivers and professionals are a potential source of attitudinal barriers to inclusion in research of people with PIMD. People with PIMD have limitations in communication, and there is a need for proxy report from caregivers or professionals to administer assessments, which may create bias (Maes et al., 2021). This is especially important to consider if the proxy underestimates the person's current abilities or ability to make progress or misinterprets their communication attempts. Further research should consider how to validate proxy reports, which could include combining assessment methods, using behavioral observations, or using physiologic measures to validate proxy reports (Maes et al., 2021). Additionally, further research should understand the impacts of attitudinal barriers, including explicit and implicit disability attitudes on assessment of people with PIMD.

Summary

Researchers should consider how environmental and personal factors may affect motor behaviors by considering use of assistive technology to improve autonomy and facilitate participation in motor behaviors. Researchers should also consider utilizing community-based research settings, validating proxy reports, utilizing peer interactions, and considering when biases may be present in motor behavior research.

FUTURE RESEARCH

Motor behavior researchers need to be more inclusive of people with PIMD as an underserved population that benefits from motor interventions (Houwen et al., 2014). Gaps in the current research include a lack of variety in settings, valid and reliable assessments, and overall motor intervention examples or protocols. Future research should focus on motor activities in the community and real-world environments. Also, assessments should either be validated for this population or researchers should facilitate the creation and validation of new assessments with robust psychometric properties. This will remain challenging, as there is little consensus on what types of motor interventions are beneficial for this population and passive interventions continue to be utilized (van Alphen et al., 2019; Waninge et al., 2013). Therefore, future research should include continued exploration of active motor interventions for this population, along with the appropriate assistive technology required to support participation in activities that encourage motor behavior and autonomy.

Limitations in current studies include small sample sizes that span large age ranges, use of low-level evidence research designs, lack of diversity in recruitment, inconsistent language, and lack of research with young children (Maes et al., 2021). Studies with larger sample sizes with diverse demographic characteristics and more narrow age ranges may improve generalizability and provide valuable information for optimization of interventions at certain ages or developmental stages. More research is needed that prioritizes early intervention (ages three and under) related to motor skills as this is considered a critical period for development (Sylva, 1997).

PRACTICAL IMPLICATIONS

Practitioners and researchers should reflect on how people with PIMD can have meaningful inclusion in motor behavior interventions over their lifespan. This begins by keeping an open mind, understanding current evidence and knowledge gaps, and self-assessing biases related to PIMD and an individual's ability to make progress, participate, and have a good quality of life (Maes et al., 2021). Practitioners and researchers should strive to be innovative, creative, and persistent when carrying out interventions or designing research studies. Some examples include collaborating with other disciplines and families, understanding a person's preferences, and routine use of assistive technology to facilitate communication, mobility, and participation.

The research presented in this chapter is focused on the motor domain. There is a gap in motor behavior research involving interdisciplinary collaboration (van der Putten et al., 2005). This may be an area where more education is needed between other disciplines on the importance of motor activities in daily life for people with PIMD (van der Putten et al., 2017). Practitioners and researchers should also take the time to learn about the person with PIMD they are working with, such as what the person likes or how they communicate (Jansen et al., 2017). Caregivers, as experts about their children, can provide this individualized information and be readily included in research, intervention, or technology development (Jansen et al., 2017). Practitioners and researchers should also prioritize use of evidenced-based interventions and validated assessments into their daily practice or research designs when working with people with PIMD (Wessels et al., 2021b).

CONCLUSION

People with PIMD have not been prioritized in motor behavior research. Most available research focuses on the impairment and body functions/structures level of the ICF model. People with PIMD can make improvements in motor behaviors, and their participation in these activities is beneficial in many ways. Researchers in the motor behavior field should be more inclusive of this population in future research.

REFERENCES

Adolph, K.E., and Franchak, J.M. (2017). The development of motor behavior. *Wiley Interdisciplinary Reviews: Cognitive Science*, 8(1–2), e1430. https://doi.org/10.1002/wcs.1430

Aherne, C., and Coughlan, B. (2017). A preliminary investigation of the suitability of aquatics for people with severe and profound intellectual disabilities. *Journal of Intellectual Disabilities*, 21(2), 118–33. https://doi.org/10.1177/1744629516646513

American Psychological Association. (2021). Inclusive language guidelines. https://www.apa.org/about/apa/equity-diversity-inclusion/language-guidelines.pdf

Balboni, G., Rebecchini, G., Elisei, S., and Tassé, M.J. (2020). Factors affecting the relationship between adaptive behavior and challenging behaviors in individuals with intellectual disability and co-occurring disorders. *Research in Developmental Disabilities*, 104, 103718. https://doi.org/10.1016/j.ridd.2020.103718

Bayley, N. (1969). *Manual for the Bayley scales of infant development*. New York: Psychological Corporation.

Berard, C., Payan, C., Hodgkinson, I., and Fermanian, J. (2005). A motor function measure for neuromuscular diseases: Construction and validation study. *Neuromuscular Disorders*, 15(7), 463–70.

Bossink, L.W., van der Putten, A.A., Waninge, A., and Vlaskamp, C. (2017). A power-assisted exercise intervention in people with profound intellectual and multiple disabilities living in a residential facility: A pilot randomised controlled trial. *Clinical Rehabilitation*, 31(9), 1168–78. https://doi.org/10.1177/0269215516687347

Braun, S.L., Msall, M.E., McCabe, M. (1994). *Guide for use of the Functional Independence Measure for Children (WeeFIM) of the uniform data system for medical rehabilitation*. Version 4.0. Buffalo, NY: Center for Functional Assessment Research, State University of New York at Buffalo.

Degache, F., Bonjour, A., Michaud, D., Mondada, L., and Newman, C.J. (2019). The effects of tandem skiing on posture and heart rate in children with profound intellectual and multiple disabilities. *Developmental Neurorehabilitation*, 22(4), 234–39. https://doi.org/10.1080/17518423.2018.1462268

Early Childhood Technical Assistance. (2020). Federal definitions of assistive technology. https://ectacenter.org/topics/atech/definitions.asp

Embregts, P.J.C.M., van Oorsouw, W.M.W.J., Wintels, S.C., van Delden, R.W., Evers, V., and Reidsma, D. (2020). Comparing a playful interactive product to watching television: An exploratory study for people with profound intellectual and multiple disabilities. *Journal of Intellectual & Developmental Disability*, 45(1), 78–88. https://doi.org/10.3109/13668250.2018.1537846

Garber, C.E., Blissmer, B., Deschenes, M.R., Franklin, B.A., Lamonte, M.J., Lee, I., Nieman, D.C., and Swain, D.P. (2011). Quantity and quality of exercise for developing and maintaining cardiorespiratory, musculoskeletal, and neuromotor fitness in apparently healthy adults. *Medicine & Science in Sports & Exercise*, 43(7), 1334–59.

Gevelinger, M., Ottenbacher, K.J., and Tiffany, T. (1988). The reliability of the Motor Development Checklist. *The American Journal of Occupational Therapy*, 42(2), 81–86. https://doi.org/10.5014/ajot.42.2.81

Gorton, G.E., Watson, K., Tucker, C.A., Tian, F., Montpetit, K., Haley, S.M., Mulcahey, M.J. (2010). Precision and content range of a parent-reported item bank assessing lower extremity and mobility skills in children with cerebral palsy. *Developmental Medicine & Child Neurology*, 52(7), 660–65.

Houwen, S., van der Putten, A., and Vlaskamp, C. (2014). A systematic review of the effects of motor interventions to improve motor, cognitive, and/or social functioning in people with severe or profound intellectual disabilities. *Research in Developmental Disabilities*, 35(9), 2093–116. https://doi.org/10.1016/j.ridd.2014.05.006

Jain, M., Turner, D., and Worrell, T. (1994). The Vulpe Assessment Battery and the Peabody Developmental Motor Scales: A preliminary study of concurrent validity between gross motor sections. *Physical & Occupational Therapy in Pediatrics*, 14(1), 23–33.

Jansen, S.L.G., van der Putten, A.A.J., Post, W.J., and Vlaskamp, C. (2014). Family-centredness of professionals who support people with profound intellectual and multiple disabilities: Validation of the Dutch "Measure of Processes of Care for Service Providers" (MPOC-SP-PIMD). *Research in Developmental Disabilities*, 35(7), 1623–30. https://doi.org/10.1016/j.ridd.2014.03.044

Jansen, S.L., van der Putten, A.A., and Vlaskamp, C. (2017). Parents' experiences of collaborating with professionals in the support of their child with profound intellectual and multiple disabilities: A multiple case study. *Journal of Intellectual Disabilities*, 21(1), 53–67. https://doi.org/10.1177/1744629516641843

Kamstra, A., van der Putten, A.A.J., and Vlaskamp, C. (2015). The structure of informal social networks of persons with profound intellectual and multiple disabilities. *Journal of Applied Research in Intellectual Disabilities*, 28(3), 249–56. https://doi.org/10.1111/jar.12134

Katopf, L., Reuter, J., and Dunn, V. (1981) *The Kent Infant Development Scale (manual)*. Kent, OH: Kent Developmental Metrics.

Kenyon, L.K., Farris, J.P., Gallagher, C., Hammond, L., Webster, L.M., and Aldrich, N.J. (2017). Power mobility training for young children with multiple, severe impairments: A case series. *Physical & Occupational Therapy in Pediatrics*, 37(1), 19–34. https://doi.org/10.3109/01942638.2015.1108380

Krosschell, K.J., Scott, C.B., Maczulski, J.A., Lewelt, A.J., Reyna, S.P., and Swoboda, K.J. (2011). Reliability of the Modified Hammersmith Functional Motor Scale in young children with spinal muscular atrophy: Project Cure SMA. *Muscle and Nerve*, 44(2), 246–51.

Lebeer, J., Nijland, M., and Grácio, L. (n.d.). *Enabling activity and participation*. 133.

Lancioni, G.E., O'Reilly, M.F., Singh, N.N., Oliva, D., Scalini, L., Vigo, C.M., and Groeneweg, J. (2005). Further evaluation of microswitch clusters to enhance hand response and head control in persons with multiple disabilities. *Perceptual and Motor Skills, 100*(3), 689–94. https://doi.org/10.2466/pms.100.3.689-694

Lancioni, G.E., Singh, N.N., O'Reilly, M.F., Sigafoos, J., Didden, R., Oliva, D., Severini, L., Smaldone, A., Tota, A., and Lamartire, M.L. (2007). Effects of microswitch-based programs on indices of happiness of students with multiple disabilities: A new research evaluation. *American Journal on Mental Retardation, 112*(3), 167. https://doi.org/10.1352/0895-8017(2007)112[167:EOMPOI]2.0.CO;2

Lancioni, G.E., Singh, N.N., O'Reilly, M.F., Sigafoos, J., Oliva, D., Smaldone, A., La Martire, M.L., Stasolla, F., Castagnaro, F., and Groeneweg, J. (2010). Promoting ambulation responses among children with multiple disabilities through walkers and microswitches with contingent stimuli. *Research in Developmental Disabilities, 31*(3), 811–16. https://doi.org/10.1016/j.ridd.2010.02.006

Lebeer, J., Nijland, M., and Grácio, L. (2017). *Enabling activity and participation. Supporting young people with complex and intense support needs*. Varna, Bulgaria: Helix Press and Enablin+ Project Group.

Logan, S.W., Feldner, H.A., Galloway, J.C., and Huang, H.H. (2016). Modified ride-on car use by children with complex medical needs. *Pediatric Physical Therapy, 28*(1), 100–07. https://doi.org/10.1097/PEP.0000000000000210

Luijkx, J., Ten Brug, A., and Vlaskamp, C. (2016). Does the severity of disability matter? The opinion of parents about professional support in residential facilities: Parental opinions about residential support. *Child: Care, Health and Development, 42*(1), 8–15. https://doi.org/10.1111/cch.12297

Luijkx, J., van der Putten, A.A.J., and Vlaskamp, C. (2017). Time use of parents raising children with severe or profound intellectual and multiple disabilities: Time use of parents raising children with PIMD. *Child: Care, Health and Development, 43*(4), 518–26. https://doi.org/10.1111/cch.12446

Lyons, G., Walla, P., and Arthur-Kelly, M. (2013). Towards improved ways of knowing children with profound multiple disabilities: Introducing startle reflex modulation. *Developmental Neurorehabilitation, 16*, 340–44. https://doi.org/10.3109/17518423.2012.737039

Maes, B., Lambrechts, G., Hostyn, I., and Petry, K. (2007) Quality-enhancing interventions for people with profound intellectual and multiple disabilities: A review of the empirical research literature. *Journal of Intellectual & Developmental Disability, 32*(3), 163–78.

Maes, B., Nijs, S., Vandesande, S., van Keer, I., Arthur-Kelly, M., Dind, J., Goldbart, J., Petitpierre, G., and van der Putten, A. (2021). Looking back, looking forward: Methodological challenges and future directions in research on persons with profound intellectual and multiple disabilities. *Journal of Applied Research in Intellectual Disabilities, 34*(1), 250–62. https://doi.org/10.1111/jar.12803

Mensch, S.M., Echteld, M.A., Evenhuis, H.M., and Ramerckers, E.A.A. (2016). Construct validity and responsiveness of Movakic: An instrument for the evaluation of motor abilities in children with severe multiple disabilities. *Research in Developmental Disabilities, 59*, 194–201. https://doi.org/10.1016/j.ridd.2016.08.012

Mensch, S.M., Ramerckers, E.A.A., Echteld, M.A., and Evenhuis, H.M. (2015). Instruments for the evaluation of motor abilities for children with severe multiple disabilities: A systematic review of the literature. *Research in Developmental Disabilities, 47*, 185–98. https://doi.org/10.1016/j.ridd.2015.09.002

Munde, V.S., Vlaskamp, C., Maes, B., and Ruijssenaars, A.J.J.M. (2014). Catch the wave! Time-window sequential analysis of alertness stimulation in individuals with profound intellectual and multiple disabilities: Catch the wave! *Child: Care, Health and Development, 40*(1), 95–105. https://doi.org/10.1111/j.1365-2214.2012.01415.x

Munde, V.S., Vlaskamp, C., Ruijssenaars, A.J.J.M., and Nakken, H. (2009). Alertness in individuals with profound intellectual and multiple disabilities: A literature review. *Research in Developmental Disabilities*, 30(3), 462–80. https://doi.org/10.1016/j.ridd.2008.07.003

Nakken, H., and Vlaskamp, C. (2007). A need for a taxonomy for profound intellectual and multiple disabilities. *Journal of Policy and Practice in Intellectual Disabilities*, 4(2), 83–87. https://doi.org/10.1111/j.1741-1130.2007.00104.x

Nijs, S., Vlaskamp, C., and Maes, B. (2016). Children with PIMD in interaction with peers with PIMD or siblings: Sibling and peer interactions in persons with PIMD. *Journal of Intellectual Disability Research*, 60(1), 28–42. https://doi.org/10.1111/jir.12231

Nilsson, L.M., and Nyberg, P.J. (2003). Driving to learn: A new concept for training children with profound cognitive disabilities in a powered wheelchair. *The American Journal of Occupational Therapy*, 57(2), 229–33. https://doi.org/10.5014/ajot.57.2.229

Nilsson, L., Durkin, J., and DipCOT. (2014). Assessment of learning powered mobility use—Applying grounded theory to occupational performance. *Journal of Rehabilitation Research and Development*, 51(6), 963–74. https://doi.org/10.1682/JRRD.2013.11.0237

Poppes, P., van der Putten, A.J.J., Post, W.J., and Vlaskamp, C. (2016). Risk factors associated with challenging behaviour in people with profound intellectual and multiple disabilities: Risk factors associated with challenging behaviour. *Journal of Intellectual Disability Research*, 60(6), 537–52. https://doi.org/10.1111/jir.12268

Pountney, T.E., Cheek, L., Green, E., Mulcahy, C., and Nelham, R. (1999). Content and criterion validation of the Chailey Levels of Ability. *Physiotherapy*, 85(8), 410416.

Roche, L., Sigafoos, J., Lancioni, G.E., O'Reilly, M.F., and Green, V.A. (2015). Microswitch technology for enabling self-determined responding in children with profound and multiple disabilities: A systematic review. *Augmentative and Alternative Communication*, 31(3), 246–58. https://doi.org/10.3109/07434618.2015.1024888

Russell, D.J., Rosenbaum, P.L., Cadman, D.T., Gowland, C., Hardy, S., and Jarvis, S. (1989). The gross motor function measure: A means to evaluate the effects of physical therapy. *Developmental Medicine & Child Neurology*, 31(3), 341–52.

Sparrow, S.S., Cicchetti, D., and Balla, D.A. (2005). *Vineland Adaptive Behavior Scales-2nd edition manual*. Minneapolis: NCS Pearson Inc.

Sterkenburg, P., Frederiks, K., Barakova, E., Chen, W.M., Peters, P., and Feijs, L. (2017). A bioresponse system for caregivers of adults with severe or profound intellectual disabilities. *Journal of Mental Health Research in Intellectual Disabilities*, 10, 121. https://doi.org/10.1080/19315864.2017.1368259

Sylva, K. (1997). Critical periods in childhood learning. *British Medical Bulletin*, 53(1), 185–97. https://doi.org/10.1093/oxfordjournals.bmb.a011599

van Alphen, H.J.M., Waninge, A., Minnaert, A.E.M.G., Post, W.J., and Putten, A.A.J. (2021a). Construct validity of the Actiwatch-2 for assessing movement in people with profound intellectual and multiple disabilities. *Journal of Applied Research in Intellectual Disabilities*, 34(1), 99–110. https://doi.org/10.1111/jar.12789

van Alphen, H.J.M., Waninge, A., Minnaert, A.E.M.G., and Putten, A.A.J. (2019). Content and quality of motor initiatives in the support of people with profound intellectual and multiple disabilities. *Journal of Policy and Practice in Intellectual Disabilities*, 16(4), 325–41. https://doi.org/10.1111/jppi.12326

van Alphen, H.J.M., Waninge, A., Minnaert, A.E.M.G., and van der Putten, A.A.J. (2021b). Development and process evaluation of a motor activity program for people with profound intellectual and multiple disabilities. *BMC Health Services Research*, 21(1), 259. https://doi.org/10.1186/s12913-021-06264-z

van Delden, R.W., Wintels, S.C., van Oorsouw, W.M.W.J., Evers, V., Embregts, P.J.C.M., Heylen, D.K.J., and Reidsma, D. (2020). Alertness, movement, and affective behaviour of people with profound intellectual and multiple disabilities (PIMD) on introduction of a playful interactive product: Can we get your attention? *Journal of Intellectual & Developmental Disability*, 45(1), 66–77. https://doi.org/10.3109/13668250.2018.1537845

van der Putten, A.A.J., Bossink, L.W.M., Frans, N., Houwen, S., and Vlaskamp, C. (2017). Motor activation in people with profound intellectual and multiple disabilities in daily practice. *Journal of Intellectual & Developmental Disability*, 42(1), 1–11. https://doi.org/10.3109/13668250.2016.1181259

van der Putten, A., Vlaskamp, C., Reynders, K., and Nakken, H. (2005). Children with profound intellectual and multiple disabilities: The effects of functional movement activities. *Clinical Rehabilitation*, 19(6), 613–20. https://doi.org/10.1191/0269215505cr899oa

Vlaskamp, C., and Nakken, H. (1999). Missing in execution, therapies and activities for individuals with profound multiple disabilities. *British Journal of Developmental Disabilities*, 45, 99–109.

Waninge, A., van der Putten, A.A.J., Stewart, R.E., Steenbergen, B., van Wijck, R., and van der Schans, C.P. (2013). Heart rate and physical activity patterns in persons with profound intellectual and multiple disabilities. *Journal of Strength and Conditioning Research*, 27(11), 3150–58. https://doi.org/10.1519/JSC.0b013e31828bf1aa

Wessels, M.D., Paap, M.C.S., and Van der Putten, A.A.J. (2021a). Validity of an instrument that assesses functional abilities in people with profound intellectual and multiple disabilities: Look what I can do! *Journal of Intellectual & Developmental Disability*, 46(3), 250–60. https://doi.org/10.3109/13668250.2020.1785851

Wessels, M.D., Putten, A.A.J., and Paap, M.C.S. (2021b). Inventory of assessment practices in people with profound intellectual and multiple disabilities in three European countries. *Journal of Applied Research in Intellectual Disabilities*, 34(6), 1521–37. https://doi.org/10.1111/jar.12896

World Health Organization. (2020 November, 26). Physical activity. https://www.who.int/news-room/fact-sheets/detail/physical-activity

World Health Organization. (2022). International Classification of Functioning, Disability and Health. https://www.who.int/standards/classifications/international-classification-of-functioning-disability-and-health?msclkid=3a41748dad3711ecbaf3989bb1b3fc32

15

Motor Competence and Health Impairments in Children

Emily Gilbert

■ ■ ■

OVERVIEW

Fifteen percent of youth with a diagnosed disability as identified by the Individuals with Disabilities Educational Act (IDEA) are classified in the category of other health impaired (OHI; e.g., heart condition, asthma, cancer, or diabetes) in the United States (US Department of Education, Office of Special Education Programs, 2021). To be classified as OHI as defined by IDEA there are two criteria: (a) "limited strength, vitality, or alertness as related to the educational environment" and (b) the diagnosed condition, disease, disorder, or injury must have a long-term (sixty days or greater) adverse effect on the student's academic performance (IDEA, 2004; Part 300, A, Section 300.8, c, 9). Children with conditions qualifying them for an OHI classification have more school absences (Echeverría et al., 2014), lower cognitive performance (Yu et al., 2010), less physical activity (Götte et al., 2014; van Brussel et al., 2005), unique social-emotional perceptions (Mühlig et al., 2016), an increased risk of other disease (Graves and Donaghue, 2019; Handakas et al., 2022; Weihrauch-Blüher et al., 2019), and a lower quality of life (Tsiros et al., 2009). Children with low levels of physical activity are often at risk for sedentary lifestyle–related diseases (e.g., obesity, type 2 diabetes) throughout childhood and into adulthood, which could result in an educational classification of OHI based on the criteria (IDEA, 2004; Robinson et al., 2015; Stodden et al., 2008). Therefore, underlying mechanisms that positively impact the potential side effects of these conditions such as physical activity and motor competence (MC) across the lifespan should be examined. OHI is a broad category, and for the purposes of this chapter motor behavior will be discussed in three populations of youth with OHIs: pediatric cancer, obesity, and diabetes.

Pediatric Cancer
In the year 2022 alone, it is estimated that approximately 10,470 children will be diagnosed with cancer in the United States (American Cancer Society, 2021). Pediatric cancer remains the second leading cause of death in children under the age of fifteen (American Cancer Society, 2021). Although the rate of cancer diagnoses in the United States is increasing annually, upwards of 85 percent of children with cancer survive five years or more (American Cancer Society, 2021). With the significant

increase in survival rates as of 2018 there were approximately 483,000 childhood cancer survivors under the age of nineteen in the United States (Howlader et al., 2021). Focus must now be shifted toward concerns for long-term quality of life for survivors and how their condition or treatment may impact their health, academics, etc. Pediatric cancer disrupts daily life, including reducing the capacity for and involvement in recreational physical activity and sports (Götte et al., 2014; van Brussel et al., 2005). This disruption is commonly associated with physical inactivity, total energy expenditure, and unhealthy weight status in comparison to peers without a previous or current cancer diagnosis (van Brussel et al., 2005; Green et al., 2013; Hartman et al., 2010b; Leone et al., 2014; Piscione et. al., 2014). Possible implications of physical inactivity and unhealthy weight put children at greater risk of entering the negative spiral of disengagement conceptualized by Stodden and colleagues (2008). It has now been supported with empirical data in the general population that MC has a positive relationship with physical activity and physical activity has a negative relationship with obesity (Barnett et al., 2021).

Obesity

Childhood obesity in the United States has long been considered an epidemic affecting upwards of 19.3 percent of youth between the ages of two and nineteen (Fryar et al., 2020). Obesity is most commonly classified based on body mass index percentiles issued by the Centers for Disease Control and Prevention: at or above the ninetieth percentile is categorized as obese and at or above the ninety-fifth percentile is classified as severely obese (Kuczmarski, 2002). Across the nation, obesity is more prevalent in different populations: 25.6 percent of Hispanic youth, 24.2 percent of Black youth, 16.1 percent of white youth, and 8.7 percent of Asian youth (Fryar et al., 2020). With such a widespread epidemic in youth of all races and ethnicities, action and resources within schools should be addressed at individual levels to provide resources and support for these children. French and colleagues (2016) clearly articulated rationale for recognizing and evaluating children who are obese under IDEA. If their weight status has limited the student's strength, vitality, or alertness and they have deficiencies in gross motor skills and/or health-related fitness, then their weight is adversely affecting their academic performance. Therefore, the child would meet the criteria for services under the category of OHI within IDEA. In addition to gross MC, obesity has been correlated with an increased risk of disease (e.g., cancer; Handakas et al., 2022; Weihrauch-Blüher et al., 2019), psychosocial-emotional impact (Mühlig et al., 2016), lower performance in the cognitive domain (Yu et al., 2010), school absences (Echeverría et al., 2014), and lower quality of life (Tsiros et al., 2009). It is also known that physical activity is one of the direct correlates with obesity, and MC has a positive relationship with physical activity (Barnett et al., 2021). Therefore, MC levels and intervention strategies are of utmost importance for the potential impact they could have on the lives of children that are obese or severely obese.

Diabetes

Diabetes is an umbrella term encompassing: (a) gestational diabetes which occurs in pregnant women without a history of diabetes, (b) type 1 diabetes which prevents the body from producing insulin, and (c) type 2 diabetes where the body doesn't effectively use insulin and struggles to keep blood sugar at normal levels (Centers for Disease Control and Prevention, 2022). In the United States, approximately 37.3 million people have diabetes, with up to 10 percent of pregnancies being affected by gestational diabetes, and 210,000 youth under the age of twenty having diabetes (Centers for Disease Control and Prevention, 2020; Centers for Disease Control and Prevention, 2022). Additionally, prediabetes impacts approximately 18 percent of adolescents in the United States between the ages of twelve to eighteen years, meaning these individuals have abnormally high blood sugar levels and are at increased risk for developing type 2 diabetes over time (Andes et al., 2019). There is a significantly higher prevalence of diabetes in youth with an obese body weight status; specifically, this occurs in 25.7 percent of youth that are obese in contrast to 16.4 percent of youth with a healthy weight status (Andes et al., 2019). Diabetes comes with many long-term health implications including increased risk of heart and kidney disease, nerve damage, vision loss, and mental health disorders (Abuelwafaa et al., 2019; Graves and Donaghue, 2019).

MOTOR COMPETENCE RESEARCH IN YOUTH WITH HEALTH IMPAIRMENTS

The importance of MC for the lives of youth with OHIs is of significance. The following section will review what is currently known in youth for three categories of OHI: pediatric cancer, obesity, and diabetes. Although this list is not and cannot be exhaustive of OHIs, hopefully this section will bring light the current knowledge in these three populations on MC and interventions to enhance MC in both gross and fine motor skills.

Pediatric Cancer

The current literature and reviews suggest that MC in youth with pediatric cancer during and after treatment is significantly delayed (Green et al., 2013; Peterson and Darling, 2018) and that their MC is not improving over time post-cessation of treatment (Hartman et al., 2006; Leone et al., 2014; Piscione et al., 2014; van Brussel et al., 2006). This delay in MC has been found in both fine and gross motor skills (Green et al., 2013). The most common subscales of low MC for children with cancer (predominately researched in acute lymphoblastic leukemia) being hand-eye coordination, balance, body coordination, ball skills, speed, and agility (Beulertz et al., 2016; Götte et al., 2015; Piscione et al., 2014; Sabel et al., 2016; Tanner et al., 2017; van Brussel et al., 2006; Wright et al., 2005). Studies have also examined the relationships of MC and other potential underlying mechanisms in youth with pediatric cancer during and after treatment. Pediatric cancer survivors' levels of physical activity, health-related quality of life, body mass index, and fitness have all been significantly correlated with their levels of MC (Götte et al., 2015; Piscione et al., 2017; Sabel et al., 2016; Wright et al., 2005).

With these children displaying significantly lower MC than peers without pediatric cancer, intervention is necessary. However, there is still limited information regarding targeted interventions to enhance and improve motor skill competence with most investigations focusing on children with acute lymphoblastic leukemia (Beulertz et al., 2016; Esbenshade et al., 2014; Gohar et al., 2011; Hartman et al., 2009; Tanner et al., 2017). Interventions that have targeted MC through varied medical treatment were not significantly correlated (Hartman et al., 2010a; Hartman et al., 2006; Wiernikowski et al., 2005). This includes the following medical interventions targeting improved MC: polymorphisms of CYP3A5, MDR-1 or the MAPT gene (Hartman et al., 2010a), cumulative does of vincristine (Hartman et al., 2006), and alendronate for steroid-induced osteopenia (Wiernikowski et al., 2005).

The most common targeted intervention to improving MC has been through the implementation of exercise programming (Beulertz et al., 2016; Esbenshade et al., 2014; Gohar et al., 2011; Hartman et al., 2009; Piscione et al., 2017; Tanner et al., 2017). Overall, these studies had a significant effect on MC with three studies finding total score improvements (Esbenshade et al., 2014; Gohar et al., 2011; Tanner et al., 2017) and two studies finding improvements in coordination (Beulertz et al., 2016; Piscione et al., 2017). Only one of the exercise interventions did not find a significant improvement in MC (Hartman et al., 2009). Of note, no study has designed a motor specific intervention to teach and practice gross and fine motor skills to our knowledge. In summary, youth with cancer have significantly lower MC that is not improving across time, and they are in need of targeted intervention such as exercise interventions that have been found to significantly increase participants' coordination and total MC scores.

Obesity

Weight status, specifically obesity and severe obesity, have consistently been found to have a negative relationship (Cattuzzo et al., 2016; Lubans et al., 2010) or bidirectional negative relationship with MC (Barnett et al., 2021; Lopes et al., 2012; Martins et al., 2010). Within MC, weight status has been significantly correlated with speed-accuracy movements (Teasdale et al., 2013), locomotor (Webster et al., 2021), and balance subscales (Teasdale et al., 2013). Researchers have also examined the relationships of MC and other potential underlying mechanisms in youth that are obese or overweight. Positive relationships have been found with physical activity and cardio-respiratory fitness (Lubans et al., 2010), while negative relationships were found between perceived MC and MC for youth that are obese and overweight (Morano et al., 2011).

Many researchers have worked on designing targeted intervention in response to the obesity epidemic in the United States. Ickes and colleagues (2014) found that less than 50 percent of school-based interventions in the United States targeting prevention and decreasing student body mass index included parents and guardians. However, 75 percent of interventions that included parents and guardians significantly aided in reduced weight statuses of students. Between 2002 and 2013, none of the studies included in the systematic review by Ickes and colleagues (2014) examined MC or focused on it in their intervention as a mechanism for targeting the obesity epidemic. Only four of twenty interventions measured and targeted MC, all of which were international (Graf et al., 2008; Hartman et al., 2010a; Sacchetti et al., 2013; Walther et al., 2009). This is a major gap knowing that MC has a strong negative bidirectional relationship with body weight status and that school-based interventions in the United States did not target MC as a potential mechanism for change in body weight status prior to 2014 (Barnett et al., 2021; Ickes et al., 2014). In summary, youth that are obese or severely obese have significantly lower MC, specifically locomotor skills, and limited interventions in the United States have targeted MC which have been found to significantly increase MC and decrease body weight status in studies conducted in Europe.

Diabetes

Youth with diabetes can develop diabetic neuropathy, which impacts the somatic and autonomic nervous systems resulting in loss of sensation, motor function, and potential numbness or pain (Graves and Donaghue, 2019). Abuelwafaa and colleagues (2019) found abnormalities in 88 percent of participants' nerve conduction including pain, numbness, tingling, reduced reflexes, and sensory motor symptoms. Motor nerve damage was twice as common in comparison to sensorimotor nerve involvement, suggesting motor nerve involvement is followed by sensorimotor and lastly sensory conduction slowing (Abuelwafaa et al., 2019). Due to damage caused by diabetic neuropathy, we expect that MC would be lower in youth with diabetes. However, there is very limited empirical data regarding youth with diabetes' actual MC; after an extensive search only two studies were found with inconsistent results (Kertzer et al., 1994; Mohammad et al., 2018). Kertzer and colleagues (1994) found MC was not impaired, while Mohammad and colleagues (2018) found significantly lower levels of MC. Specifically, girls with diabetes had significantly lower scores in all subscales (fine, manual coordination, body coordination, and agility), while boys with diabetes had significant delays in only total scores and manual coordination (Mohammad et al., 2018). The impact of gestational diabetes on the MC of the child has been an area of further research. A systematic review and meta-analysis found that gestational diabetes was associated with delayed motor development in both gross and fine motor for the child (Arabiat et al., 2021). Beyond the biological impact of gestational diabetes, another study examined the sociocultural influence parents can have on children's physical activity, naming parents "gate-keepers" (Quirk et al., 2014). Combining sociocultural data regarding parent influence and motor control impacts from diabetic neuropathy highlight the importance and need for further knowledge regarding the impact of diabetes on MC. Currently, there is limited knowledge of actual MC of youth with diabetes and no knowledge on relationships with motor for this population or intervention effectiveness in improving MC.

FUTURE RESEARCH

Significant gaps in literature remain that should be addressed in future research regarding youth with cancer, obesity, or diabetes. Descriptive research should explore the MC of youth with diabetes type 1 and 2 and MC in youth with various cancers outside lymphoblastic leukemia. Correlational research is still needed regarding the onset of cancer, diabetes, and obesity in relation to MC. Though there is growing evidence in the general population and some connecting to body weight status regarding the relationship between MC, perceived MC, and physical activity, little examination of these relationships for youth with pediatric cancer or diabetes exists. Quality interventions utilizing parent involvement designed to teach and practice gross and fine motor skills are needed for all three of these OHIs, and they should be targeted with future research. Finally, there is a need for more qualitative commentary in literature regarding facilitators and barriers to the learning, control, and development of motor skills to enhance the overall understanding of potential environmental or individual constraints impacting children's movement.

PRACTICAL IMPLICATIONS

In order to apply research to practice, the events, populations, or variables must first be examined in detail, then clearly and rationally described. For the topics described in this chapter, pediatric cancer, diabetes, and obesity are classified as OHIs based on the two sets of criteria from the IDEA. Once that determinate has been made and services are provided, students' physical educators, physical therapists, and occupational therapists can potentially play a key role in future trajectories of developing MC for this vulnerable population of youth with OHIs. Programs for students currently diagnosed with or post treatment of cancer should focus on improving the most common lower MC subscales: hand-eye coordination, balance, body coordination, ball skills, speed, and agility (Beulertz et al., 2016; Götte et al., 2015; Piscione et al., 2014; Sabel, et al., 2016; Tanner et al., 2017; van Brussel et al., 2006; Wright et al., 2005). When working with youth that are obese, there is evidence that there is a bidirectional negative relationship with MC (Barnett et al., 2021; Lopes et al., 2012; Martins et al., 2010), and two of the interventions found by targeting and improving MC body weight status may improve or result in a reduced rate of weight increase (Sacchetti et al., 2013; Walther et al., 2009). Therefore, focus should be shifted toward enhancing children's MC, with an emphasis on the lowest subscale, locomotor skills (Webster et al., 2021). Research also indicated the importance of involving parents in the process to increase the likelihood of success (Ickes et al., 2014). It is known that the motor control of youth with diabetes is impacted by diabetic neuropathy (Abuelwafaa et al., 2019) and parents can inhibit their child's involvement in physical activity (Quirk et al., 2014). Although one study does not provide enough evidence to infer, girls were delayed in fine, manual coordination,

Table 15.1 Research to Practice: Next Steps to Action

	What is known	*What to do with it*
Pediatric cancer	1. Children with pediatric cancer have significantly lower motor competence (MC). 2. MC is not improving across time without intervention. 3. Exercise interventions have been successful in improving MC.	1. Intervene with quality instruction of motor skills. 2. Design targeted exercise programs to improve coordination, balance, ball skills, speed, and agility.
Obesity	1. Obesity has a bidirectional negative relationship with MC. 2. Locomotor skills are most directly impacted by weight status. 3. Interventions are more effective when parents are targeted in the intervention.	1. Recognize that improved MC has been related to healthier weight status and that unhealthy weight status has been linked to lower MC. 2. Locomotor skills should be targeted. 3. Parent/guardian involvement is essential for increasing the likelihood of success.
Diabetes	1. Diabetic neuropathy has an impact on motor control for youth with diabetes. 2. Parents act as the "gate-keepers." 3. In one study, girls were delayed in all subscales and boys were delayed in manual coordination.	1. Recognize there may be a delay in response or sensation during movement activities. 2. Practitioners and interventionists need to communicate regularly with parents. 3. Need to focus on postural control, reaching, grasping, and object manipulation with varying speed and power. Specific emphasis for girls in subscales (fine, manual coordination, body coordination, and agility) and manual coordination for boys.

body coordination, and agility, while boys were only delayed in manual coordination (Mohammad et al., 2018) (see table 15.1).

CONCLUSION

Findings across the literature suggest that overall youth with diabetes, pediatric cancer, or obesity all have motor delays. One consistency between these populations of youth with OHIs is the importance of involvement and communication with parental figures, which should not be over-looked in practice. In populations of youth with diabetes, there is very little evidence available regarding MC; therefore, future research should examine the significant gaps in literature, particularly targeted interventions to enhance MC.

REFERENCES

Abuelwafaa, N., Ahmed, H., Omer, I., Abdullah, M., Ahmed, A., and Musa, A. (2019). Electrophysiological characterization of neuropathy complicating type 1 diabetes mellitus. *Journal of Diabetes Research, 2019*, 2435261.

American Cancer Society. (2021). *Cancer facts & figures 2022*. Atlanta: American Cancer Society.

Andes, L.J., Cheng, Y.J., Rolka, D.B., Gregg, E.W., and Imperatore, G. (2019). Prevalence of prediabetes among adolescents and young adults in the United States, 2005-2016. *JAMA Pediatrics, 174*(2), e194498.

Arabiat, D., Jabery, M.A., Kemp, V., Jenkins, M., Whitehead, L.C., and Adams, G. (2021). Motor developmental outcomes in children exposed to maternal diabetes during pregnancy: a systematic review and meta-analysis. *International Journal of Environmental Research and Public Health, 18*(4), 1699.

Barnett, L.M., Webster, E.K., Hulteen, R.M., De Meester, A., Valentini, N.C., Lenoir, M., Pesce, C., Getchell, N., Lopes, V.P., Robinson, L.E., Brian, A., and Rodrigues, L.P. (2021). Through the looking glass: A systematic review of longitudinal evidence, providing new insight for motor competence and health. *Sports Medicine, 52*(4), 875–920.

Beulertz, J., Prokop, A., Rustler, V., Bloch, W., Felsch, M., and Baumann, F.T. (2016). Effects of a 6-month, group-based, therapeutic exercise program for childhood cancer outpatients on motor performance, level of activity, and quality of life. *Pediatric Blood & Cancer, 63*(1), 127–32.

Cattuzzo, M.T., dos Santos Henrique, R., Ré, A.H.N., de Oliveira, I.S., Melo, B.M., de Sousa Moura, M., de Araújo, R.C., and Stodden, D. (2016). Motor competence and health related physical fitness in youth: A systematic review. *Journal of Science and Medicine in Sport, 19*(2), 123–29.

Centers for Disease Control and Prevention. (2020). *National diabetes statistics report 2020: Estimates of diabetes and its burden in the United States*. Atlanta, GA: Centers for Disease Control and Prevention.

Centers for Disease Control and Prevention. (2022). National Diabetes Statistics Report. https://www.cdc.gov/diabetes/data/statistics-report/index.html

Echeverría, S.E., Vélez-Valle, E., Janevic, T., and Prystowsky, A. (2014). The role of poverty status and obesity on school attendance in the United States. *Journal of Adolescent Health, 55*(3), 402–07.

Esbenshade, A.J., Friedman, D.L., Smith, W.A., Jeha, S., Pui, C.H., Robison, L.L., and Ness, K.K. (2014). Feasibility and initial effectiveness of home exercise during maintenance therapy for childhood acute lymphoblastic leukemia. *Pediatric Physical Therapy, 26*(3), 301.

French, R., Sanborn, C.B., DiMarco, N., and Stephens, T.L. (2016). Childhood obesity: Classification as an idea disability. *Palaestra, 30*(2).

Fryar, C.D., Carroll, M.D., Afful, J. (2020). Prevalence of overweight, obesity, and severe obesity among children and adolescents aged 2–19 years: United States, 1963–1965 through 2017-2018. *NCHS Health E-Stats*.

Gohar, S.F., Comito, M., Price, J., and Marchese, V. (2011). Feasibility and parent satisfaction of a physical therapy intervention program for children with acute lymphoblastic leukemia in the first 6 months of medical treatment. *Pediatric Blood & Cancer, 56*(5), 799–804.

Götte, M., Kesting, S.V., Winter, C.C., Rosenbaum, D., and Boos, J. (2015). Motor performance in children and adolescents with cancer at the end of acute treatment phase. *European Journal of Pediatrics, 174*(6), 791–99.

Götte, M., Taraks, S., and Boos, J. (2014). Sports in pediatric oncology: The role (s) of physical activity for children with cancer. *Journal of Pediatric Hematology/Oncology, 36*(2), 85–90.

Graf, C., Koch, B., Falkowski, G., Jouck, S., Christ, H., Staudenmaier, K., Tokarski, W., Gerber, A., Predel, H.G., and Dordel, S. (2008). School-based prevention: effects on obesity and physical performance after 4 years. *Journal of Sports Sciences, 26*(10), 987–94.

Graves, L.E., and Donaghue, K.C. (2019). Management of diabetes complications in youth. *Therapeutic Advances in Endocrinology and Metabolism*, 10.

Green, J.L., Knight, S.J., McCarthy, M., and De Luca, C.R. (2013). Motor functioning during and following treatment with chemotherapy for pediatric acute lymphoblastic leukemia. *Pediatric Blood & Cancer, 60*(8), 1261–66.

Handakas, E., Lau, C.H., Alfano, R., Chatzi, V.L., Plusquin, M., Vineis, P., and Robinson, O. (2022). A systematic review of metabolomic studies of childhood obesity: State of the evidence for metabolic determinants and consequences. *Obesity Reviews*, 23, e13384.

Hartman, A., Winkel, M.T., van Beek, R.D., van den Heuvel-Eibrink, M.M., Pieters, R., Keizer Schrama, S.M., and Hop, W.J. (2009). A randomized trial investigating an exercise program to prevent reduction of bone mineral density and impairment of motor performance during treatment for childhood acute lymphoblastic leukemia. *Pediatric Blood & Cancer, 53*(1), 64–71.

Hartman, A., van Schaik, R.H.N., Van Der Heiden, I.P., Broekhuis, M.J.C., Meier, M., Den Boer, M.L., and Pieters, R. (2010a). Polymorphisms in genes involved in vincristine pharmacokinetics or pharmacodynamics are not related to impaired motor performance in children with leukemia. *Leukemia Research, 34*(2), 154–59.

Hartman, A., Van den Bos, C.V., Stijnen, T., and Pieters, R. (2006). Decrease in motor performance in children with cancer is independent of the cumulative dose of vincristine. *CANCER, 106*(6), 1395–401.

Hartmann, T., Zahner, L., Pühse, U., Puder, J.J., and Kriemler, S. (2010b). Effects of a school-based physical activity program on physical and psychosocial quality of life in elementary school children: a cluster-randomized trial. *Pediatric Exercise Science, 22*(4), 511–22.

Howlader, N., Noone, A.M., Krapcho, M., Miller, D., Brest, A., Yu, M., Ruhl, J., Tatalovich, Z., Mariotto, A., Lewis, D.R., Chen, H.S., Feuer, E.J., and Cronin, K.A. (Eds.). (2021). *SEER Cancer Statistics Review, 1975–2018*. Bethesda, MD: National Cancer Institute. https://seer.cancer.gov/csr/1975_2018/

Ickes, M.J., McMullen, J., Haider, T., and Sharma, M. (2014). Global school-based childhood obesity interventions: a review. *International Journal of Environmental Research and Public Health, 11*(9), 8940–61.

Individuals with Disabilities Education Improvement Act (IDEA) of 2004. 20 U.S.C. 1400 et seq.

Kertzer, R., Croce, R., Hinkle, R., and Janson-Sand, C. (1994). Selected fitness and motor behavior parameters of children and adolescents with insulin-dependent diabetes mellitus. *Adapted Physical Activity Quarterly, 11*(3), 284–96.

Kuczmarski, R.J. (2002). *2000 CDC Growth Charts for the United States: methods and development* (No. 246). Washington, DC: Department of Health and Human Services, Centers for Disease Control and Prevention, National Center for Health Statistics.

Leone, M., Viret, P., Bui, H.T., Laverdière, C., Kalinova, É., and Comtois, A. S. (2014). Assessment of gross motor skills and phenotype profile in children 9–11 years of age in survivors of acute lymphoblastic leukemia. *Pediatric Blood & Cancer*, 61(1), 46–52.

Lopes, V.P., Stodden, D.F., Bianchi, M.M., Maia, J.A., and Rodrigues, L.P. (2012). Correlation between BMI and motor coordination in children. *Journal of Science and Medicine in Sport*, 15(1), 38–43.

Lubans, D.R., Morgan, P.J., Cliff, D.P., Barnett, L.M., and Okely, A.D. (2010). Fundamental movement skills in children and adolescents. *Sports Medicine*, 40(12), 1019–35.

Martins, D., Maia, J., Seabra, A., Garganta, R., Lopes, V., Katzmarzyk, P., and Beunen, G. (2010). Correlates of changes in BMI of children from the Azores islands. *International Journal of Obesity*, 34(10), 1487–93.

Morano, M., Colella, D., Robazza, C., Bortoli, L., and Capranica, L. (2011). Physical self-perception and motor performance in normal-weight, overweight and obese children. *Scandinavian Journal of Medicine & Science in Sports*, 21(3), 465–73.

Mohammad, J.M., Robabeh, S., Shahin, K., Saeed, T., and Maryam, A. (2018). Auditory function and motor proficiency in type 1 diabetic children: A case-control study. *International Journal of Pediatric Otorhinolaryngology*, 109, 7–12.

Mühlig, Y., Antel, J., Föcker, M., and Hebebrand, J. (2016). Are bidirectional associations of obesity and depression already apparent in childhood and adolescence as based on high-quality studies? A systematic review. *Obesity Reviews*, 17(3), 235–49.

Peterson, J.A., and Darling, T.V. (2018). Childhood cancer and treatment effects on motor performance. *International Journal of Exercise Science*, 11(3), 657–68.

Piscione, P.J., Bouffet, E., Mabbott, D.J., Shams, I., and Kulkarni, A.V. (2014). Physical functioning in pediatric survivors of childhood posterior fossa brain tumors. *Neurooncology*, 16(1), 147–55.

Piscione, P.J., Bouffet, E., Timmons, B., Courneya, K.S., Tetzlaff, D., Schneiderman, J.E., and Mabbott, D.J. (2017). Exercise training improves physical function and fitness in long term paediatric brain tumour survivors treated with cranial irradiation. *European Journal of Cancer*, (80), 63–72.

Quirk, H., Blake, H., Dee, B., and Glazebrook, C. (2014). "You can't just jump on a bike and go": A qualitative study exploring parents' perceptions of physical activity in children with type 1 diabetes. *BMC Pediatrics*, 14(1), 1–12.

Robinson, L.E., Stodden, D.F., Barnett, L.M., Lopes, V.P., Logan, S.W., Rodrigues, L.P., and D'Hondt, E. (2015). Motor competence and its effect on positive developmental trajectories of health. *Sports Medicine*, 45(9), 1273–84.

Sabel, M., Sjölund, A., Broeren, J., Arvidsson, D., Saury, J.M., Blomgren, K., and Emanuelson, I. (2016). Active video gaming improves body coordination in survivors of childhood brain tumours. *Disability and Rehabilitation*, 38(21), 2073–84.

Sacchetti, R., Ceciliani, A., Garulli, A., Dallolio, L., Beltrami, P., and Leoni, E. (2013). Effects of a 2-year school-based intervention of enhanced physical education in the primary school. *Journal of School Health*, 83(9), 639–46.

Stodden, D.F., Goodway, J.D., Langendorfer, S.J., Roberton, M.A., Rudisill, M.E., Garcia, C., and Garcia, L.E. (2008). A developmental perspective on the role of motor skill competence in physical activity: An emergent relationship. *Quest*, 60(2), 290–306.

Tanner, L., Sencer, S., and Hooke, M.C. (2017). The stoplight program: A proactive physical therapy intervention for children with acute lymphoblastic leukemia. *Journal of Pediatric Oncology Nursing*, 34(5), 347–57.

Teasdale, N., Simoneau, M., Corbeil, P., Handrigan, G., Tremblay, A., and Hue, O. (2013). Obesity alters balance and movement control. *Current Obesity Reports*, 2(3), 235–40.

Tsiros, M.D., Olds, T., Buckley, J.D., Grimshaw, P., Brennan, L., Walkley, J., Hills, A.P., Howe, P.R.C., and Coates, A.M. (2009). Health-related quality of life in obese children and adolescents. *International Journal of Obesity*, 33(4), 387–400.

US Department of Education, Office of Special Education Programs. (2021). Individuals with Disabilities Education Act (IDEA) database. *Digest of Education Statistics 2020*, table 204.30.

van Brussel, M., Takken, T., Net, J.V.D., Engelbert, R.H., Bierings, M., Schoenmakers, M.A., and Helders, P.J. (2006). Physical function and fitness in long-term survivors of childhood leukaemia. *Pediatric Rehabilitation*, 9(3), 267–74.

van Brussel, M., Takken, T., Lucia, A., van der Net, J., and Helders, P. J. (2005). Is physical fitness decreased in survivors of childhood leukemia? A systematic review. *Leukemia*, 19(1), 13–17.

Walther, C., Gaede, L., Adams, V., Gelbrich, G., Leichtle, A., Erbs, S., Sonnabend, M., Fikenzer, K., Körner, A., Kiess, W., Bruegel, M., Thiery, J., and Schuler, G. (2009). Effect of increased exercise in school children on physical fitness and endothelial progenitor cells: A prospective randomized trial. *Circulation*, 120(22), 2251–59.

Webster, E.K., Sur, I., Stevens, A., and Robinson, L.E. (2021). Associations between body composition and fundamental motor skill competency in children. *BMC Pediatrics*, 21(1), 1–8.

Weihrauch-Blüher, S., Schwarz, P., and Klusmann, J.H. (2019). Childhood obesity: increased risk for cardiometabolic disease and cancer in adulthood. *Metabolism*, 92, 147–52.

Wiernikowski, J.T., Barr, R.D., Webber, C., Guo, C.Y., Wright, M., and Atkinson, S.A. (2005). Alendronate for steroid-induced osteopenia in children with acute lymphoblastic leukaemia or non-Hodgkin's lymphoma: Results of a pilot study. *Journal of Oncology Pharmacy Practice*, 11(2), 51–56.

Wright, M.J., Galea, V., and Barr, R.D. (2005). Proficiency of balance in children and youth who have had acute lymphoblastic leukemia. *Physical Therapy*, 85(8), 782–90.

Yu, Z.B., Han, S.P., Cao, X.G., and Guo, X.R. (2010). Intelligence in relation to obesity: A systematic review and meta-analysis. *Obesity Reviews*, 11, 656–70.

Index

academics, 15, 28, 132
active start programs, 54
activities of daily living, 5
Activities-Specific Balance Confidence Scale, 18
acute lymphoblastic leukemia, 189, 191
AD. *See* Alzheimer's disease
adaptive behavior, 119
Adaptive Behavior Assessment System, 119
Adhanom Ghebreyesus, Tedros, 1
ADHD. *See* attention-deficit hyperactivity disorder
ADI-R. *See* Autism Diagnostic Interview-Revised
Affordances in the Home Environment for Motor Development (AHEMD) assessment, 17
afterschool programs, 56
aggression, 61
AHEMD assessment. *See* Affordances in the Home Environment for Motor Development assessment
Alberta Infant Motor Scale, 95
alertness level, 175, 180
allergies, to drugs, 15
Alzheimer's disease (AD), 105, *106*, *108*, 110, 113
  motor learning in, 109
amblyopia, 4
American Academy of Pediatrics, 37
American Association on Intellectual and Developmental Disabilities, 119
American Congress of Rehabilitation Medicine, 143
American Psychiatric Association (APA), 62
American Sign Language, 22–23
American Spinal Injury Association impairment scale, 158
Amyotrophic lateral sclerosis, 105, *106*
anticipatory control, 19
antisocial disorders, 62
AnxDs. *See* anxiety disorders

anxiety, 30, 62
Anxiety and Depression Association of America, 63
anxiety disorders (AnxDs), 61
  conceptual models of, 63
  definition of, 62
  motor impairments and, 63–65
  prevalence of, 63
APA. *See* American Psychiatric Association
aphasia, 149
apraxia, 149
articulation, 88–89
ASD. *See* autism spectrum disorder
Asperger, Hans, 49
asphyxia, 95
assistive reproductive technology, 93
assistive technology, 178–80, *179*, 182
asthma, 30
ataxia, *94*, 105
ataxic cerebral palsy (CP), 94. *See also* cerebral palsy
atresia choanae, 16. *See also* coloboma, heart defects, atresia choanae, restricted growth, genital hypoplasia, and ear abnormalities syndrome
attentional control theory, 63
attention deficit disorders, 28
attention-deficit hyperactivity disorder (ADHD), 30–34, 61–62
  comorbidities, 70–71
  conceptual models of, 67–68
  definition of, 66
  motor impairments and, 68–70
  prevalence of, 66–67
attention span, 22
attitudes, 180–81
atypical gait, *94*
auditory comprehension, 88
auditory stimuli, 16
auditory-visual convergence, 20
Autism Diagnostic Interview-Revised (ADI-R), 37

Autism Diagnostic Observation Schedule™, 37, 39
autism spectrum disorder (ASD), 28–34, 130
  early screening for, 37
  evidence, 42–43
  fundamental motor skill interventions for, 49–56
  future research, 43
  multisystem nature of, 43
  overview, 37–39
  practical implications, 43–44
  risk for, 37
  beyond school, 41–42
  in school-aged children, 40–41
  in young children, 39–40
autoimmune conditions, 15
autonomic dysreflexia, 157
autonomic functions, 163
autonomic nervous system, 191
autonomy, 178
avoidant behaviors, 28
Ayres, Jean, 27
Ayres Sensory Integration theory, 27

Bailey Scales of Infant Motor Development, 3
balance, 17–19, 22, 63, 84, 147–48, 151
  poor, 29
  postural control and, 5
  strategies, 5
ballistic efforts, 3
basal ganglia, 70
Bayley Scales of Infant Development, 174
Beach, Pamela, 15–23
behavior
  aggressive, 30
  challenging, 175
  intervention, 72
  management, 56
  motor, 1–8
  repetitive, 30, 37
Behavioral Appraisal Scales, 174
behavioral disinhibition model, 67
behavioral disorders, 61–72
behavioral inhibition, 67
Behavioral Teaching Rating Scale, 32
behavior analysts, 49
bilirubin, 93
binary logistic regression, 5
bioecological model, 83
biological sex, 2
bipolar disorders, 62, 66
birth
  complications, 93
  premature, 15
  weight, 30, 93
blindness, 1–2. *See also* vision

congenital, 3
deafblindness, 15–23
blood-based biomarkers, 150
blood pressure, 163
body awareness, 33
BOT-2. *See* Bruininks-Oseretsky Test of Motor Proficiency, second edition
Bowersock, Collin D., 157–65, *159*, *162*, *163*
bradykinesia, 146, 151
brain. *See also* traumatic brain injury
  development, 96
  function, 143
breech presentation, 93
Bridges, Claire, 93–102, *94*, *99*, *100*
Bronfenbrenner's ecological systems theory, 83
Bruininks-Oseretsky Test of Motor Proficiency, 3–4
Bruininks-Oseretsky Test of Motor Proficiency, second edition (BOT-2), 40

cancer, pediatric, 187–90, *192*, *193*
caregivers, 180
cataracts, 1
Cavalier, Albert R., 61–72
CD. *See* conduct disorder
Centers for Disease Control and Prevention, 143, 188
cerebellar ataxia, 105
cerebellum, 38
cerebral malformations/infarctions, *120*
cerebral palsy (CP), 28, 130, 172
  acquired, 93
  childhood interventions, 98–101, *99*, *100*
  congenital, 93
  diagnosis and classification, 95
  "do it" interventions for, *100*
  early intervention for, 96–98
  motor behavior and, 93–102, *94*, *99*, *100*
  motor symptoms of, *94*
  risk factor/possible causes of, 93–95, *94*
  symptoms, 94
  types, 94
Cerebral Palsy Research Network, 101
cerebral structures, altered, 70
cerebral systems, 2
cerebral visual impairment, 172
Chailey Levels of Ability, 174
CHARGE syndrome. *See* coloboma, heart defects, atresia choanae, restricted growth, genital hypoplasia, and ear abnormalities syndrome
Child Behavior Check List, 32
childhood obesity, 188
Child Mind Institute, 63
CI. *See* cochlear implantation

CIMT. *See* constraint-induced movement therapy
circuit training, 136
clotting disorders, 93
clumsiness, 29, 49, 64
cochlea, 15–16
cochlear dysfunction, 17–18
cochlear implantation (CI), 15, 18
cognitive abilities, 41
cognitive behavioral therapy, 72
cognitive communication disorder, 149
cognitive performance, 187
cognitive training, 72
coloboma, heart defects, atresia choanae, restricted growth, genital hypoplasia, and ear abnormalities (CHARGE) syndrome, 16–21
communication, 172
  disorders, 149
  impairments, 38
  promotion of, 51
  skills, 37
  social, 30
  supraspinal, 158
community-based intervention programs, 53
community-based recreation, 56
compensation strategies, 134
complex tasks, 53
compression, of spinal cord, 158
computerized tomography, 95
concussion, 143
conduct disorder (CD), 62, 70
conductive hearing loss, 15
congenital blindness, 3
congenital sensorineural hearing loss, 172
constraint-induced movement therapy (CIMT), 96–97, *100*, 101
coordination, 93, 147, 151, 193
corpus callosum, 70
counselors, 33
COVID-19
  lockdowns, 62
CP. *See* cerebral palsy
cranial nerve
  eighth, 16
  function, 146
Creutzfeldt-Jakob disease, 105

DCD. *See* developmental coordination disorder
DD. *See* developmental delay
deafblindness, 15–23
Deaflympics, 22
deafness, 17–19, 21–23
  acquired, 15
  congenital, 15–16
  in parents, 20

defensive behaviors, 28
dementia, 105, 144
  vascular, 108
dementia-related syndromes, 108
demyelinating disorders, *120*
depressive disorders, 62
depressive symptoms, 62
developmental coordination disorder (DCD), 28, 66, 69, 71, 83–84, 129–30
  conclusion, 136
  future research, 135
  identification and diagnosis of, 131
  motor behavior research, 132–35
  practical implications, 135–36
developmental delay (DD), 3, 132–36
  diagnosis of, 130
  as early sign of DCD, 129–31
diabetes, 189, *192*, 193
  gestational, 188, 191
  type 1, 188, 191
  type 2, 187–88, 191
diabetic neuropathy, 191
diabetic retinopathy, 1
Diagnostic and Statistical Manual of Mental Disorders-5, 30, 119, 131
diffusion tensor imaging (DTI), 30
disability, degree of, 158
disruptive conduct, 62
distractibility, 61
dizziness, 64, 147
dopamine, 70
dopaminergic neurotransmission, 111
Down syndrome (DS), 28–34, 120, *120*, 122
DTI. *See* diffusion tensor imaging
dynamic gait, 19
Dynamic Gait Index, 147
dysarthria, 149
dyskinetic cerebral palsy (CP), 94. *See also* cerebral palsy
dysphagia, 149
dyspraxia, 29
dystonia, 147, 151

ear
  abnormalities, 16 (*See also* coloboma, heart defects, atresia choanae, restricted growth, genital hypoplasia, and ear abnormalities syndrome)
  inner, 15
early intervention, 22, 54, 96–98
EBDs. *See* emotional and behavioral disorders
educators, 33
electroencephalography, 95, 135, 150
electromyography (EMG), 150, 163, *163*
elevation, poor perception of, 29
elopement, prevention of, 56

EMG. *See* electromyography
emotional and behavioral disorders (EBDs), 61, 70, 72
emotions, 61
   disturbance of, 61–62
   dysregulation of, 71
environmental stress hypothesis, 90
epidural stimulation, 161, *162*, 163, 165
epilepsy, 30, 172
error-reduced learning conditions, 122
ethnicity, 2
Everyone Can!, 41
evidence alert system, *99*
execution focus model, 63
exposure, to loud sounds, 15
external focus of attention, 122
externalizing behaviors, 62
extrinsic feedback, 123
eye disease, family history of, 2

failure, fear of, 65
family history, of eye disease, 2
fatigue, 29
fears, 61
   excessive, 62
feeding disorders, 172
Feldner, Heather A., 157–65, *159*, *162*, *163*
fetal alcohol syndrome, *120*
fidgety movements, 130
fine motor, 39–40
   in adulthood, 5
   in juvenescence, 4
   skills, 4, 38
fine musculature, 3
fitness levels, 20
Fragile X syndrome, *120*
frontal lobes, 70
functional capacity, 2
Functional Independence Measure, pediatric, 174
fundamental motor skill interventions, for children with autism spectrum disorder (ASD), 49
   future research, 54–55
   interventions, 52–54
   motor skill development, importance of, 50–51
   practical implications, 55–56

gait, 147–48, 151
   abnormalities, 145
   analysis, 114
   atypical, 38, *94*
   dynamic, 19
   slower, 18, 107
   speed, *108*
   trainer, 178

GAME. *See* Goals-Activity- Motor Enrichment intervention
GCS. *See* Glasgow Coma Scale
genital hypoplasia, 16. *See also* coloboma, heart defects, atresia choanae, restricted growth, genital hypoplasia, and ear abnormalities syndrome
geographic location, 2
gestational diabetes, 188, 191
gestures, 89
Getchell, Nancy, 129–36
Gilbert, Emily, 187–93, *192*
Glasgow Coma Scale (GCS), 144, *144*
Glasgow Outcome Score Extended, 146
glaucoma, 1
GMFCS. *See* Gross Motor Function Classification System
goal-oriented intensive motor training, 97
Goals-Activity- Motor Enrichment (GAME) intervention, 97, 102
Golden, Daphne, 129–36
gross motor, 40
   in adulthood, 4–5
   assessments, 3
   competence, 3
   deficits, 39
   delays, 50
   in juvenescence, 3
   skills, 38
Gross Motor Function Classification System (GMFCS), 95, 101–2
Gross Motor Function Measure, 174
gross musculature, 3
growth, restricted, 16. *See also* coloboma, heart defects, atresia choanae, restricted growth, genital hypoplasia, and ear abnormalities syndrome
gustatory discrimination disorder, 29
gymnastics, rhythmic, 18

hallucinations, 61
Halverson Developmental Sequences for Skipping, 41
hand-eye coordination, 29
handwriting skills, 4, 29, 38
hard of hearing, 15–23
head lag, 37
headphones, noise-reducing, 33
HEADS UP Initiative, 143
health and fitness specialists, 7
hearing aids, 15
hearing loss
   at birth, 16
   causes of, 15
   conductive, 15
   congenital, 172
   progressive, 16

sensorineural, 15–16, 18
heart defects, 16. *See also* coloboma, heart defects, atresia choanae, restricted growth, genital hypoplasia, and ear abnormalities syndrome
hemiplegia, 97
herpes viruses, 15
hip displacement, 96
hippocampus, 110
Howard-Smith, Candice, 27–34
Huntington's disease, 105, *106*
hyperactivity, 66
hyperkinesia, 146, 151
hypersensitivity, to loud noise, touch, and light, 30
hypokinesia, 146, 151
hypoplasia, genital, 16. *See also* coloboma, heart defects, atresia choanae, restricted growth, genital hypoplasia, and ear abnormalities syndrome
hypoxia, 93, 95
hypoxic ischemic injury, *120*

ICF. *See* International Classification of Functioning, Disability and Health model
ID. *See* intellectual disability
IDEA. *See* Individuals with Disabilities Education Act
identity-first language, 171
Improved American Spinal Injury Association impairment scale, 164
impulse-control disorders, 62
impulsiveness, 61–62, 66
inattention, 66. *See also* attention-deficit hyperactivity disorder
inclusion, 181
Individualized Education Program, 7, 67
Individuals with Disabilities Education Act (IDEA), 61–62, 67, 187
infections, 15
  during pregnancy, 93
infertility, 93
injury prevention, 150
inner sensory mechanism, 16
intellectual abilities, 41
intellectual disability (ID), 93, 130
  motor behavior and, *119*, 119–24, *120*, *123*
  potential causes of, *120*
intellectual functioning, 119
interactive technology, 180
internalizing behaviors, 62
International Classification of Functioning, Disability and Health model (ICF), 172–73, *173*
intrinsic feedback, 123
introversion, 64
IQ, 41, 49, 55, 84

jaundice, 93
Jebsen-Taylor Hand Function Test, 4
Journal of Speech, Language, and Hearing Research, 84

Kanner, Leo, 49
Kent Infant Development Scale, 174
Kenyon, Lisa K., 157–65, *159*, *162*, *163*
kernicterus, 93
kinder-skills, 54
kinematics, 42
kinesiophobia, 150
kinesthetic awareness, 29, 33

LaForme Fiss, Alyssa, *119*, 119–24, *120*, *123*
laminectomy, 157
language impairment, 83–90
Lewy body
  dementia, 108
  disorders, 105
Lieberman, Lauren, 15–23
limb
  coordination, 84
  coupling, 136
  praxis ability, 84–85
Lloyd, Meghann, 49–56
locomotion, 3
locomotor scores, 3
Logan, Samuel W., 157–65, *159*, *162*, *163*
Looper, Julia, *119*, 119–24, *120*, *123*
loud sounds, exposure to, 15
Lou Gehrig's disease, 105

M-ABC. *See* Movement Assessment Battery for Children
MacDonald, Megan, 37–44
macular degeneration, age-related, 1
magnetic resonance imaging, 95, 150
manual dexterity, 19, 38
MC. *See* motor competence
McDonnell, Jessica Lynn, 157–65, *159*, *162*, *163*
MCI. *See* mild cognitive impairment
meningitis, 93
mental illness, 63
microswitch technology, 178
mild cognitive impairment (MCI), 108
mild TBI (mTBI), 143, 149
Miller, Lucy, 27
Mini-BEST test, 19
mixed cerebral palsy (CP), 95. *See also* cerebral palsy
mobility, 5, 172
Modified Hammersmith Functional Motor Scale, 174
motion sickness, 64

motivation, 22
motor activity, 176
motor acts, 61
motor behavior, autism spectrum disorder (ASD) and
  evidence, 42–43
  future research, 43
  overview, 37–39
  practical implications, 43–44
  beyond school, 41–42
  in school-aged children, 40–41
  in young children, 39–40
motor behavior, cerebral palsy and
  conclusion, 102
  definitions, etiology, and diagnosis, 93–95, *94*
  empirical research, 95–101, *99*, *100*
  future research, 101
  practical implications, 101–2
motor behavior, emotional/behavioral disorders and
  anxiety disorders, 62–65
  attention-deficit hyperactivity disorder (ADHD), 66–71
  definitions of, 61–62
  future research and practical implications, 71–72
  prevalence of, 62
motor behavior, hard of hearing, deaf, or deafblind children and, 15
  balance, 17–19
  conclusion, 22–23
  motor competence, 19–22
  motor milestones, 16–17
  practical implications, 22
motor behavior, intellectual disabilities and
  conclusion, 124
  future research, 123–24
  motor control and motor learning in, 121–23, *123*
  overview, *119*, 119–20, *120*
  practical implications, 124
  research, 120–21
motor behavior, neurodegenerative disorders associated with aging and
  conclusion, 114
  future research, 111, *112*
  gait and, 107–9, *108*
  motor learning and, 109–11
  overview, 105–7, *106*
  practical implications, 113
  research challenges, *112*
motor behavior, profound intellectual/multiple disabilities and
  activity and participation, 175–78
  conclusion, 182
  empirical research, *173*, 173–75
  environmental and personal factors, 178–81, *179*
  future research, 181
  overview, 171–73, *172*
  practical implications, 181–82
motor behavior, rehabilitation after spinal cord injury and, 157–65, *159*, *162*, *163*
motor behavior, sensory processing disorder (SPD) and
  attention-deficit hyperactivity disorder (ADHD), 32
  autism spectrum disorder (ASD), 30–31
  conclusion, 34
  disabilities and, 30–32
  down syndrome (DS), 31–32
  future research, 32–33
  overview, 27
  practical implications, 33–34
  types of, 28–29
motor behavior, specific language impairment and
  conclusion, 90
  future research, 89–90
  overview, 83–84
  practical implications, 90
  research overview, 84–89
motor behavior, visual impairment and, 1–8
  background, 1–2
  conclusion, 7–8
  fine motor in adulthood, 5
  fine motor in juvenescence, 4
  frameworks and assumptions, 2–3
  future research in, 6
  gross motor in adulthood, 4–5
  gross motor in juvenescence, 3
  across the lifespan, 2
  postural control and balance, 5
  practical implications, 7
  psychological variables, 5–6
motor competence (MC), 15, 19–22
  conclusion, 193
  future research, 191
  health impairments in children and, 187–93, *192*
  overview, 187–89
  practical implications, *192*, 192–93
  research, 189–91
motor control, 2, *94*, 121
motor delays, 38
motor development, 2, 28, 174–75
  arrested, 3
  sequence, 129
Motor eVAluation in Kids with Intellectual and Complex disabilities, 174
Motor Function Measure scale, 174
motor functions, loss of, 158, 165
motor learning, 2, 109, 122

principles of, *123*
motor milestones, 16–17, 39, 50
   acquisition, 132
   delayed achievement of, *94*
motor patterns, compensatory, 134
motor planning, 38
motor proficiency, 49
   cascading effect of, 55
motor skills, 3
   interventions, 21, 52
   poor, 51
   proficient, 40–41
movement
   fear of, 150
   variability, 135
Movement Assessment Battery for Children (M-ABC), 3–4, 41, 64, 69
Movement Assessment Battery for Children - Second Edition, 135
movement disorders, 105
movement patterns, 133
movement-related outcomes, 7
mTBI. *See* mild TBI
Mullen Scales of Early Learning, 39
multiple sclerosis, 105
multisensory integration, 31
Multi-Tiered Systems of Support, 72
muscle
   stiffness, 94
   tone, 29, 93–94, *94*
myoclonus, 147, 151

National Center for Education Statistics, 62
National Institute of Neurological Disorders and Stroke, 149
National Institutes of Health, 101
nausea, 64
near-infrared spectroscopy, 135
neonatal encephalopathy, *120*
nerve damage, 191
neural substrates, 124
neuroaxonal dystrophies, 105
neurodegenerative diseases, increase in, 105
neurodegenerative disorders, associated with aging, 105–14, *106*, *108*, *110*
neurodevelopmental conditions, 93
neurodevelopmental disorder, 34, 66
neurofeedback, 72
neuromotor task training, 90
neuropathy, diabetic, 191
neurotransmitter imbalance, 70
norepinephrine, 70

obesity, 93, 190, *192*, 193
   childhood, 188
   risk, 19
Obrusnikova, Iva, 61–72

occupational therapists, 7, 27, 33, 43, 49
oculomotor function, 148–50
ODD. *See* oppositional-defiant disorder
OHI. *See* other health impaired
opportunity, lack of, 23
oppositional-defiant disorder (ODD), 62, 70
oral-motor control, *94*
other health impaired (OHI), 187
over-responsivity, 28, 34
over-sensitivity, 29

Pangelinan, Melissa, 93–102, *94*, *99*, *100*
panic disorders, 62. *See also* anxiety
paralysis, 158
parasympathetic nervous system, 165
Parent Perceptions Questionnaire, 21
parietal lobes, 70
Parkinson's disease (PD), 105, *106*, 108, *108*, 110–11, 114
   motor learning in, 109
Pediatric Balance Scale, 18
pediatric cancer, 187–90, *192*, 193
peer criticism, 65
Pennell, Adam, 1–8
perception, 29
perceptual systems, 2
peripheral vision, progressive deterioration of, 16
Perreault, Melanie, 15–23
personality disorder, 66
person-first language, 171
pervasive developmental disorder, 37
pharmacologic treatments, 72, 160
phobia-related disorders, 62
phobias, 61
physical activity, 176–78
Physical and Neurological Exam for Subtle Signs, 40
physical educators, 7
physical rehabilitation, 160
physical therapists, 7, 43
physiotherapists, 49
Piaget, 50
PIMD. *See* profound intellectual and multiple disabilities
placenta, detachment of, 93
polymorphisms, 190
posture, 64
   control, 5
   disorder, 29
power mobility research, 179
precursor patterns, 51
pregnancy, 30
premature birth, 15
preterm birth, 93
procedural deficit hypothesis, 87–90
procedural memory system, 86

processing speed, 148
prodromal markers, 107
profound intellectual and multiple
    disabilities (PIMD), 171–82, *173*, *179*
    secondary characteristics of, *172*
psychological system, 3
psychotherapy, 72
Purdue Pegboard subtests, 5

randomized controlled trials (RCTs), 96
reaction time, 148
reactive postural control, 19
reflexes, 39, 146
reflexive stage of development, 16
regulatory disorders, 28
rehabilitation, 165
    specialists, 49, 54
repetitive behaviors, 37
responsivity, 28
retinitis pigmentosa, 16
retinopathy, diabetic, 1
retractive errors, 1
retrocochlear nerve pathways, 15
Rett syndrome, 172
Roberton's developmental sequence, 42
Rosenbaum, 50

SBMD. *See* sensory-based motor disorder
school absences, 187
Schott, Nadja, 105–14, *106*, *108*, *110*
SCIs. *See* spinal cord injuries
SDD. *See* sensory discrimination disorder
Seefeldt's model, 19
seizures
    neonatal, 93
self-control, 66
self-controlled feedback, 123
self-injury, 175
semicircular canals, 17
Semyon Slobounov, Sam, 143–51, *144*, *145*
sensorimotor system, 30
sensorineural hearing loss, 15–18
sensory-based motor disorder (SBMD), 28
sensory-based programs/therapy, 31
sensory deficits, 23
sensory disabilities, 16
sensory discrimination disorder (SDD), 28
sensory function, 159
sensory hypersensitivity, 28
sensory hyposensitivity, 28
sensory information, response to, 27
sensory input, 28
sensory integration (SI), 27, 30. *See also*
    sensory processing disorder
sensory integration therapy, 31
sensory loss, 22
sensory modulation, 28

sensory modulation disorder (SMD), 28
sensory orientation, 19
sensory processing disorder (SPD), 172
    motor behavior and, 27–34
    types of, 28–29
Sensory Profile, 32
sensory receptors, 27
sensory reorganization, 20
sensory seeking, 28, 34
sensory stimuli, 28–29, 33
sequence processing, delays in, 20
sequential learning, 89
Short Sensory Profile, 31
SI. *See* sensory integration
sight. *See also* vision
    loss of, 1
sign language, 15
SLI. *See* specific language impairment
Sloane, Bethany M., 157–65, *159*, *162*, *163*
SMD. *See* sensory modulation disorder
SMs. *See* stereotyped movements
social development, 15
social impairments, 38
social interaction, 83
social skills, 28
social withdrawal, 61
socioeconomic position, 2
somatic symptoms, 62
spastic cerebral palsy (CP), 94. *See also*
    cerebral palsy
spastic diplegia/diparesis, 94
spastic hemiplegia/hemiparesis, 94
spasticity, 94, 105, 146, 151
spastic quadriplegia/quadriparesis, 94
spatial coupling, 133
SPD. *See* sensory processing disorder
Special Olympics, 53
specific language impairment (SLI), 90
    motor control-related issues in, 84–86
    motor development-related issues in,
        88–89
    motor learning-related issues in, 86–88
speech, 29, 149–50
    difficulty with, 15
    intelligible, 15
speech and language pathologists, 49
spinal cord injuries (SCIs), 157
    complete, *159*, 161
    incomplete, *159*, 161
    motor complete, 163
spinal cord injury, rehabilitation after
    conclusion, 165
    future research, 164
    overview, 157–58
    practical implications, 165
    research overview, 158–64, *159*, *162*, *163*
spinal cord stimulation, 164

spinal reflexes, 159, 162
stability skills, 19
stamina, 22
stereotyped movements (SMs), 31
Stribing, Alexandra, 1–8
substance use disorder, 62, 66
summer camps, 56
Sung, Ming-Chih, 37–44
supraspinal communication, 158
supraspinal drive, 162
swallowing, 149–50
systems- and constraints-based viewpoint, 2

tactile discrimination disorder, 29
tactile stimuli, 28–30
tauopathies, 105
TBI. *See* traumatic brain injury
temporal coupling, 133
Test for Manual Dexterity in Visually Impaired Children, 4
Test of Gross Motor Development, 3, 40, 69
Test of Gross Motor Development-2 (TGMD-2), 19–20
Test of Gross Motor Development-3 (TGMD-3), 20
Test of Infant Motor Performance, 95
textures, 28
TGMD-2. *See* Test of Gross Motor Development-2
TGMD-3. *See* Test of Gross Motor Development-3
thyroid, 93
Tinetti test, 108
toe-walking, *94*
Top Down Motor Milestone Test, 174
TORCH infections, *120*
Tourette syndrome, 66
toxoplasmosis, 15
trauma neurological exam, 146
traumatic brain injury (TBI), 93, *120*
   conclusion, 151
   consequences of, 144
   future research, 150
   motor control dysfunction after, 146–50
   overview, 143–46, *144*, *145*

pathophysiology to dysfunction, 146
practical implications, 150–51
severity of, 146
symptoms, *145*
tremor, *94*, 146, 151
type 1 diabetes, 188, 191
type 2 diabetes, 187–88, 191

ultrasound, 95
umbilical cord, 93
under-responsivity, 28, 34
Usher syndrome, 15
uterine rupture, 93

vascular dementia, 108
verbal ability, 88
vestibular discrimination, 29
vestibular dysfunction, 18
vestibular function, loss of, 16
vestibular stimuli, 16
vestibular system, 18
VI. *See* visual impairment
Vineland Adaptive Behavior Scale, 119, 174
vision
   loss, 1–2, 4, 7–8, 16
   peripheral, 16
visual cues, 34
visual discrimination, 33
visual dysfunction, 148
visual impairment (VI), 1, 148
visual impairment, motor behavior and, 1–8
visual systems, 2
visuo-motor sequence learning, 87
Vulpe Assessment Battery, 174

Wagner, Matthias O., 83–90
walking, independent, 17
Walter, Alexa, 143–51, *144*, *145*
weakness, *94*
WHO. *See* World Health Organization
Wilkes, James, 143–51, *144*, *145*
Williams syndrome, *120*, 120–21
working memory (WM), 67
   model, 68, 71
World Health Organization (WHO), 173

About the Editors

■ ■ ■

Pamela S. Beach is a professor of motor behavior in the Department of Kinesiology, Sports Studies and Physical Education. She is also a co-director of the Institute on Movement Studies for Individuals with Visual Impairments (IMSVI). Recently, IMSVI was awarded the Corrine Kirchner National Research award from the American Foundation for the Blind, and Dr. Beach has received the Hollis Fait Scholarly Award by the National Consortium for Physical Education for Individuals with Disabilities and the Nat Seaman Recognition Award by the New York State AER. Dr. Beach publishes and presents nationally and internationally on her research in motor behavior and balance in individuals across the lifespan with sensory impairments. In addition, she has published several books including *Gross Motor Development Curriculum: For Children with Visual Impairment and Physical Education & Sports for People with Visual Impairments* and *Deafblindness: Foundations of Instruction* 2e. She has also published three editions of the widely adopted undergraduate textbook *Motor Learning and Development*. Additionally, Dr. Beach produces numerous educational and training videos for parents and practitioners of youth with visual impairments and deafblindness. Dr. Beach has received accolades for her teaching including the Chancellor's Award for Excellence in Teaching and has been appointed as a SUNY Online Teaching Ambassador. She has served on the American Kinesiology Association Board and currently serves as vice president of the National Consortium for Physical Education for Individuals with Disabilities.

Ali S. Brian is the associate dean for research in the College of Education and a professor in the areas of motor behavior and adapted physical education/activity in the Department of Educational and Developmental Science at the University of South Carolina. Dr. Brian's PhD is from The Ohio State University in Kinesiology. Dr. Brian is a Certified Adapted Physical Educator and is the director of the Physical and Developmental Disabilities Research Lab at the University of South Carolina. Dr. Brian's research agenda focuses on underlying mechanisms that support positive developmental trajectories for whole-child health, including early intervention efforts, for preschoolers with and without disabilities as well as for youth with visual impairments. Dr. Brian has published three books, fourteen book chapters, ninety-one articles, seventy-three research abstracts, five keynote and thirteen invited presentations, and approximately two hundred presentations. As a result of this work, Dr. Brian has received the G. Lawrence Rarick Research Award the National Consortium for Physical Education for Individuals with Disabilities, Early Career Distinguished Scholar award from the North American Society for Psychology of Sport and Physical Activity, the David P. Beaver Adapted Physical Activity Young Scholar Award from National Consortium for Physical Education for Individuals with Disabilities, the Early Career Research Award from the College of Education at the University of South Carolina, and the Breakthrough Star Award from the Vice President of Research at the University of South Carolina. Dr. Brian was inducted as a Fellow of Research Council of SHAPE America. Dr. Brian has also served as chair of the SHAPE America Research Council and as a member of the Executive Committee of NCPEID and the International Motor Development Research Consortium. Presently, Dr. Brian is the research director for the Institute of Movement Studies for Individuals with Visual Impairments. She serves as an associate editor for *Research Quarterly for Exercise and Sport* and *Physical Education and Sport Pedagogy* journals. Dr. Brian is on the editorial board for Research Quarterly for Exercise and Sport as well as the Journal of Motor Learning and Development.

About the Contributors

Dr. Claire Bridges is currently an assistant professor of exercise science at Huntingdon College in the Department of Sport Science and Physical Education. She is the program coordinator for health promotion. Dr. Bridges received her bachelor's degree in exercise science from Huntingdon College, master's degree in exercise science from Auburn University of Montgomery, and PhD in kinesiology from Auburn University. Dr. Bridges' research interests are in health promotion, motor behavior, and nutrition.

Dr. Albert Cavalier is an associate professor in the School of Education at the University of Delaware. With over four decades of experience, his research focuses on assistive technology, self-management, and health promotion for individuals with intellectual and developmental disabilities. Throughout his distinguished career, he has been recognized with numerous awards, including the National Award for computer design and development from the National Science Foundation and The Johns Hopkins University and the Distinguished Faculty Award in the College of Education at the University of Delaware. Some of his significant publications explore the effectiveness of video modeling and activity schedule technology systems for individuals with intellectual disabilities and autism spectrum disorders.

Dr. Collin D. Bowersock is an applied human movement scientist in the Biomechatronic Lab at Northern Arizona University. His research interests include rehabilitation, performance, and the motor control of human movement. Dr. Bowersock has investigated standing posture control rehabilitation techniques for individuals with spinal cord injury while utilizing spinal cord epidural stimulation and a robotic stand trainer. Dr. Bowersock also designs and validates robotic devices for locomotor rehabilitation and aid among individuals with cerebral palsy.

Dr. Heather A. Feldner, PT, PhD is an assistant professor in the Department of Rehabilitation Medicine, adjunct assistant professor in the Department of Mechanical Engineering, core faculty in the Disability Studies Program, and an associate director of the Center for Research and Education on Accessible Technology and Experiences at the University of Washington. Her research is centered at the intersection of mobility, disability, and technology in two primary areas, including perceptions of disability and identity and how these emerge and evolve through technology use, and in the design and implementation of pediatric mobility technology, considering how attitudes and the built environment affect equity and participation. Dr. Feldner has published and presented her work nationally and internationally, and is a board-certified pediatric clinical specialist emeritus.

Dr. Nancy Getchell is a professor in the Department of Kinesiology and Applied Physiology at the University of Delaware. Her research is related to the development of motor coordination and control in individuals with and without disabilities. She also focuses on changes in the prefrontal cortex that occur as a function of learning. She is a Fellow of the National Academy of Kinesiology, the International Motor Development Research Consortium, and the Research Council of SHAPE America.

Dr. Emily Gilbert, PhD, is currently an assistant professor at the State University of New York Cortland in the Physical Education Department. As a professor, she teaches future physical educators methods courses including adapted and elementary physical education. The central focus of her research is to explore the underlying mechanisms of health-related quality of life for all children from a physical domain perspective, specifically examining the overall motor competence, perceived motor competence, physical activity, and quality of life for individuals who have been diagnosed with a visual impairment due to a previous diagnosis of cancer.

Dr. Daphne Golden, MPT, DPT, PhD is an assistant professor in the Flex Doctor of Physical Therapy Program at the University of St Augustine. She has taught movement science, patient management, evidence-based practice, and pediatrics. She has over three decades practicing as a pediatric physical therapist treating a variety of disabilities, including children with dyspraxia and the "clumsy" child after treating in the school system and encountering many children who did not qualify for services leaving them without any intervention. She went to University of Delaware where she received her doctorate in biomechanics and movement science focusing on motor control and motor learning. Her scholarly and research work is primarily in motor control, cognition, and development in children, including autism spectrum disorder. Currently, she mentors students on their doctorate of physical therapy projects.

Dr. Candice Howard-Smith is a professor and Undergraduate Teacher Education Coordinator and Coordinator for Interprofessional Health Sciences in the Department of Kinesiology and Health Promotion at Troy University in Alabama. Dr. Howard-Smith implements cognitive and perceptual-motor programs for preschool-aged children focusing on integrative, play-based interventions. Dr. Howard-Smith has been teaching for over twenty years and has presented at numerous conferences and published in journals to include *Research Quarterly in Exercise Science*.

Dr. Lisa K. Kenyon, PT, DPT, PhD, is a professor in the Department of Physical Therapy and Athletic Training at Grand Valley State University in Grand Rapids, Michigan. She heads the Grand Valley Power Mobility Project, an interprofessional project providing power mobility training and use for children who are not typically considered to be candidates for power mobility use. She currently serves on the editorial committee for the Wheelchair Skills Program and on the Pediatric Specialty

Council of the American Board of Physical Therapy Specialties. Dr. Kenyon has published numerous peer-reviewed articles and book chapters and presents nationally/internationally on topics related to power mobility and pediatric practice. She is a board-certified pediatric clinical specialist emeritus. Her work has been funded from institutions such as the National Institutes of Health and the American Academy of Cerebral Palsy, among others.

Dr. Alyssa LaForme Fiss, PT, PhD, is professor and director of the School of Physical Therapy at Texas Woman's University in Dallas, Texas. She received her bachelor's and master's degree in physical therapy from The Ohio State University and a PhD in rehabilitation science from the University of Kentucky. She is a board-certified pediatric clinical specialist from the American Board of Physical Therapy Specialties and an associate member of the CanChild Centre for Childhood Disability Research. She has published and presented widely on research related to pediatric disability and service delivery models for children with disability.

Lauren J. Lieberman, PhD, is a Distinguished Service Professor in the Kinesiology Department at The State University of New York at Brockport (SUNY), in adapted physical education. She started her career teaching at The Perkins School for the Blind in the Deafblind program. She is co-director of The Institute on Movement Studies for Individuals with Visual Impairments or Deafblindness (IMSVI) (see www.brockport.edu/IMSVI). She is the founder and director of Camp Abilities, an educational sports camp for children with visual impairments. Camp Abilities has been replicated in 20 states and eight countries (www.campabilities.org and www.campabilitiesworld.com). She has published over 200 peer-reviewed articles and 23 books on inclusion in physical education and on teaching children with sensory impairments. She has delivered keynote presentations and was an invited guest speaker all over the US and in over 20 countries. She won an Access Award from AFB for starting Camp Abilities and helping to start camps all over the world. In 2017 she won a Points of Light Award for her work with Camp Abilities from the US government. Camp Abilities has been featured on CNN, HBO Real Sports, and on NBC. In the fall of 2019, she was awarded a Global Fulbright Scholarship to promote Camp Abilities world-wide. In 2020 she won The Joy of Effort Award from SHAPE America. In 2023 she won the Julian Stein Lifetime Achievement Award from SHAPE America.

Dr. Meghann Lloyd, PhD, is associate professor at the University of Ontario Institute of Technology. Dr. Lloyd earned a bachelor of kinesiology (honours) degree from Acadia University in Wolfville, Nova Scotia, and a master of arts degree from McGill University in Montreal, Quebec. She completed her PhD at the University of Michigan in the Division of Kinesiology in Ann Arbor, Michigan. She joined Ontario Tech University in 2010 and is also a senior research associate at Grandview Children's Centre. Dr. Lloyd's research is focused on the motor development, physical activity, and health of children and youth with disabilities.

Dr. Samuel W. Logan is an associate professor in the kinesiology program within the College of Health at Oregon State University. Dr. Logan serves as the director of the Disability & Mobility Do-It-Yourself Co-Operative. His research focuses on the role of motor development on mobility, physical activity, and other developmental domains including cognition, language, and social skills. This work includes the impact of mobility technology and intervention for young children with disabilities with an emphasis on powered mobility. Dr. Logan has presented his work nationally and internationally and has received research funding from institutions such as the National Institutes of Health, National Science Foundation, and Caplan Foundation, among others.

Dr. Julia Looper, PT, PhD, is a professor in the School of Physical Therapy at the University of Puget Sound in Tacoma, Washington. She received her PhD in kinesiology from the University of Michigan and her master of physical therapy and bachelor's degree from Boston University. Her research focuses on the motor development of infants with developmental delays, particularly Down syndrome. She has published and presented nationally and internationally on physical therapy interventions that help children walk earlier and better.

Dr. Megan MacDonald is a professor of kinesiology and the IMPACT for the Life Faculty Scholar in the College of Health at Oregon State University. Dr. MacDonald is the Early Childhood Core Director at the Hallie E. Ford Center for Healthy Children and Families. In addition, Dr. MacDonald is the director of the Children and Youth with Disabilities Lab, whose vision is that every child is active and accepted and whose mission is rooted in conducting the best research, teaching, and outreach focused on youthful activity for all people. The lab aims to positively influence physical activity engagement and motor skill development for all children and, through this work, also aims to provide a gateway to positive influence in other domains of development.

Dr. Jessica Lynn McDonnell currently holds a research position at University of Louisville and teaching positions at Northern Arizona University and University of Arizona. Her research has included lower extremity biomechanics, sensorimotor integration, and the study of executive function in individuals with movement disorders. Her research agenda is rooted in finding measurable clinical outcomes to optimize performance or rehabilitation programs and aims to map neural patterns and optimization strategies across various timelines.

Dr. Iva Obrusnikova is a full professor in adapted physical activity and the director of the Health, Physical Activity, and Disability Laboratory in the University of Delaware's Department of Behavioral Health and Nutrition. With over two decades of experience, her research focuses on reducing health disparities among individuals with developmental disabilities by studying the impact of technology and specialized instruction on their physical and psychosocial outcomes. Dr. Obrusnikova has developed and validated multiple assessment scales to identify and overcome barriers in community-based physical activity environments. She has received numerous awards for her contributions to research, such as the G. Lawrence Rarick Research Award, and serves as an editorial board member for *Adapted Physical Activity Quarterly* and *Palaestra*.

Dr. Melissa Pangelinan is an associate professor of kinesiology in the School of Public Health at Indiana University Bloomington. Dr. Pangelinan is the director of the

Adapted Fitness Lab, which develops and evaluates the efficacy of adapted physical activity interventions in children, adolescents, and adults with and without intellectual and developmental disabilities. The goal of this work is to identify neurological and physiological mechanisms underlying changes in motor behavior, fitness, and health due to participation in physical activity and exercise. Dr. Pangelinan has published 37 manuscripts in high-impact journals including *Cerebral Cortex, Frontiers in Public Health, JAMA Psychiatry, Medicine & Science in Sports and Exercise,* and *NeuroImage*.

Dr. Adam Pennell is an assistant professor, certified adapted physical educator, and the director of the Motor Behavior Lab at Pepperdine University, California. Dr. Pennell's broad scope research agenda concerns the interplay between psychomotor and health-related variables in youth with and without disabilities. However, Dr. Pennell's primary line of inquiry surrounds the postural control of younger individuals with visual impairments and blindness. Dr. Pennell has published numerous peer-reviewed research articles within esteemed journals such as *Sports Medicine, Adapted Physical Activity Quarterly,* and the *Disability and Health Journal*.

Dr. Melanie Perreault is an associate professor of motor behavior and coordinator for the kinesiology program in the Department of Kinesiology, Sport Studies, and Physical Education at State University of New York Brockport as well as the communications director for the Institute of Movement Studies for Individuals with Visual Impairments or Deafblindness. Her main area of research focuses on motor development in children with sensory impairments. She has published more than thirty peer-reviewed articles, contributed to five books, and frequently presents at national and international conferences. Dr. Perreault and her research team received the Corinne Kirchner Research Award from the American Federation for the Blind and the Special Recognition Award from the CHARGE Syndrome Foundation for their contributions to the field.

Dr. Nadja Schott, full professor of psychology and movement science at University of Stuttgart, Germany, is an expert on the interactions between the cognitive and motor systems that allow us to acquire and/or maintain skilled actions across the lifespan in typically/atypically developing individuals. Her work is driven by two central questions. (a) How can we promote lifelong development and lifelong learning? More specifically, how can we help people recall optimal sensory, motor, and cognitive performance at different stages of their lives and/or in different contexts? (b) What underlying mechanisms—particularly neurobiologic processes—are responsible for lifelong learning? How can these processes be modified or improved? A variety of different research methods are used to assess cognitive-motor interactions, including standardized clinical batteries as well as neurophysiological methods (e.g., electroencephalogram, functional magnetic resonance imaging, functional near-infrared spectroscopy). Dr. Schott has published more than one hundred peer-reviewed journal articles and twenty-six book chapters and has co-edited several books.

Dr. Bethany M. Sloane, PT, DPT, is an associate professor at Oregon Health and Science University, PhD candidate at Oregon State University, a board-certified pediatric clinical specialist, co-director of the Pediatric Physical Therapy Residency Program at Oregon Health and Science University, and co-director of Go Baby Go Oregon. Her clinical expertise and research are centered around the use of powered mobility and assistive technology for young children with complex disabilities. Dr. Sloane has presented her work nationally.

Dr. Sam Semyon Slobounov, PhD, is the director of the Penn State Sport Concussion Research & Service Laboratory, a professor in the Department of Kinesiology College of Health of Human Development, and adjunct professor of orthopedics and medical rehabilitation with Penn State Milton S. Hershey Medical Center, with primary responsibilities to teach undergraduate and graduate courses in the areas of psychology of injury, neural basis of motor behavior, and psychophysiology. He has more than twenty-five years of experience in coaching and clinical work with numerous injured athletes. His research focused on the neural basis of human movements with special emphasis on rehabilitation medicine, psychology, and neurophysiology, including traumatic brain injuries. He has published more than one hundred papers in refereed journals including *Experimental Brain Research*, *Clinical Neurophysiology*, *Psychophysiology*, *Neuroscience Letters*, and other prominent peer-reviewed journals. He is an active member of Society for Psychophysiological Research and a fellow of American Academy of Kinesiology. He received his first PhD from the University of Leningrad, Department of Psychology, USSR, in 1978 and his second PhD from the University of Illinois at Urbana-Champaign, Department of Kinesiology, in 1994.

Dr. Alexandra Stribing, PhD, is an assistant professor at Kean University in Health and Physical Education. Dr. Stribing's research efforts concentrate on motor development, physical activity, and health attributes of youth populations (a) with and without disabilities and/or (b) from disadvantaged settings. Specifically, her current research focuses on perceptual influences on actual motor competence in youth with visual impairments. Dr. Stribing has published in numerous peer-reviewed journals such as *British Journal of Visual Impairment and Blindness*, *Journal of Motor Learning and Development*, and *Adapted Physical Activity Quarterly*.

Dr. Ming-Chih Sung is an assistant professor of exercise and sport science at the University of South Carolina Upstate. Dr. Sung's research focuses on enhancing motor behaviors and executive function of individuals with developmental disabilities through physical activity. Dr. Sung also has a keen interest in investigating the relationship between motor skills and executive function over child development, especially in children with autism spectrum disorders.

Dr. Matthias Wagner is full professor and head of sport psychology at the University of the Bundeswehr Munich, Germany. His research focus is on the psychological aspects of motor behavior and physical activity over the lifespan. The results of Professor Wagner's research have been published in peer-reviewed journals such as *Frontiers in Psychology*, the *Journal of Motor Learning and Development*, and *Research in Developmental Disabilities* and presented at international research conferences in Europe, Asia, and America. His early work was recognized with the Lolas E. Halverson Motor Development Young Investigator Award presented by the American Alliance for Health, Physical Education, Recreation and Dance.

Dr. Alexa Walter, PhD, is a postdoctoral fellow in the Department of Neurology, Center for Brain Injury and Repair at the University of Pennsylvania Perelman School of Medicine. She graduated from Penn State University with a BS in biology: neuroscience (2015) and a PhD in kinesiology (2020). Her work employs many different methodologies during study of traumatic brain injury, sports-related concussion, and the exposure to repetitive impacts in contact sports. Ultimately, her research goals aim to integrate both clinical and physiological research, focusing on neuroimaging and blood-based biomarkers of brain injury. Her current work is focused on these biomarkers of brain injury both within the short-term and long-term post-injury period and how they may be related to future sequelae of traumatic brain injury. Dr. Walter has published peer reviewed articles in top-tier academic journals, has contributed to textbooks, and has presented at national and international conferences.

Dr. James Wilkes, PhD, MEd, ATC, received his BS degree in kinesiology with a focus in athletic training in 2013 from Penn State University, a masters in educational leadership in 2017, and a PhD in kinesiology with a focus on concussion in 2020. Dr. Wilkes spent the last several years studying the influence of sleep on the accumulation of subconcussive impacts and resultant functional outcomes, and has numerous peer-reviewed publications investigating sleep, injury rate, concussion, biomarkers, imaging, neurocognitive testing, and others. He currently serves as a postdoctoral scholar in charge of research and education coordination for the Penn State Sport Concussion Research & Service Laboratory. Dr. Wilkes has more than ten years of experience as a certified athletic trainer assisting athletics with medical coverage as well as strengthening the relationship between the concussion lab and Penn State Athletics.